Enterprise Series Connectivity: Local Area Networks

Drew Heywood
Janos (John) Jerney
Jon Johnston
James Krochmal
Robert Lyons
Kimberly Patch
Karanjit Siyan
Eric Smalley
Chip Standifer
Elna Tynes
Roger White

New Riders Publishing, Carmel, Indiana

Enterprise Series
Connectivity: Local Area Networks

By Drew Heywood, Janos (John) Jerney, Jon Johnston, et al.

Published by:
New Riders Publishing
11711 N. College Ave., Suite 140
Carmel, IN 46032 USA

Printed in the United States of America 1 2 3 4 5 6 7 8 9 0

Library of Congress cataloging information available upon request

Publisher
David P. Ewing

Associate Publisher
Tim Huddleston

Acquisitions Editor
Brad Koch

Managing Editor
Cheri Robinson

Product Director
Drew Heywood

Developmental Editor
Nancy E. Sixsmith

Editors
Geneil Breeze
Gail Burlakoff

Technical Editors
Gary Hughes
Scott Orr
Karanjit Siyan
Michael Wirsching

Book Design and Production
William Hartman
Hartman Publishing

Proofreader
Nancy E. Sixsmith

Indexed by
Sherry Massey

About the Authors

Drew Heywood is a Product Development Specialist with New Riders Publishing. He has been involved in the computer industry since 1978 as an educator, a programmer, an author, and a network system administrator. Heywood has written books on programming for the Apple II and Macintosh, and was primary author of *NetWare on Command,* by New Riders Publishing.

Janos (John) Jerney has been in the software industry for more than five years, and he has worked at Novell, Inc. since 1990. He has extensive experience in computer networking, human-computer interaction and artificial intelligence. Jerney specializes in LAN-based electronic messaging. He has a BS in Computer Science from McGill University.

Jon Johnston is a Certified NetWare Engineer and business consultant with Creative Business Solutions, based in Minnesota's Twin Cities. He specializes in networks, telecommunications, the technology related to these subjects, and applying technology to help business productivity. Johnston has an art degree from the University of Nebraska, with minors in math and physics. He has been active in teaching and writing for the past five years.

James Krochmal has been a practicing information systems consultant in Atlanta since 1980. He specializes in designing large-scale mainframe-based information systems and distributed applications systems. A graduate of Cleveland State University, Krochmal has a degree in Computer and Information Systems.

Robert Lyons has more than 20 years of computer experience, including work with mainframe computers, minicomputers, and microcomputers. He has developed business and scientific applications for many organizations, including AT&T, the

University of Texas Health Science Center, the Resolution Trust Corporation, the U. S. Army, and Computer Science Corporation. Lyons is owner of Houston-based Professional Business Systems, which is oriented toward support of Novell and LAN Manager networks. He is a Certified NetWare Engineer and a Microsoft Certified Professional. Lyons has installed more than 400 networks and specializes in OS/2 and SQL server systems.

Kimberly Patch is a free-lance writer who lives in Boston. She grew up near Binghamton, New York and earned an English degree from SUNY at Albany. After working for United Press International, *Digital Review,* and two newspapers, Patch began free-lancing for national magazines, wire services, and book publishers.

Karanjit Siyan is president of Siyan Consulting Services, Inc., which is based in Montana. He has authored two courses for Learning Group International on Novell networks and TCP/TP networks, and he teaches advanced technology courses in the United States, Canada, and Europe. Siyan has published articles in *Dr. Dobbs' Journal, The C Users Journal,* and *Databased Advisor.* He is a CNE and has been involved with installing, configuring, and designing Novell-based networks since 1985. Before becoming an independent consultant, Siyan was a senior member of the technical staff at ROLM Corporation. He originally trained as an electronics engineer at the Indian Institute of Technology in Kharangpur, India, from which he graduated with a Bachelor of Technology degree in Electronics and Electrical Communication Engineering. Siyan later received a Master of Technology degree in computer science from the Indian Institute of Technology in Madras and a Master's degree in Engineering from the University of California at Berkeley.

Eric Smalley grew up in New London, Connecticut and graduated from Oberlin College in 1985. After holding writing and editing positions at *Digital Review* and *Network World* magazines, Smalley became a free-lance writer.

Chip Standifer has more than 13 years of experience in managing, designing, and implementing software systems. He has used his strong technical background in PCs and graphical systems to become a pioneer in the development of applications for the Microsoft Windows environment. As president of VisiSoft, Standifer leads a team of engineers that developed the VisiNet products. He also consults in areas of computer networking and Windows programming, with specific knowledge of Microsoft LAN Manager, Novell NetWare, NetBIOS, and SNMP. Standifer has been instrumental in the development of network and graphical projects at firms such as Microsoft, DCA, Racal-Milgo, and Scientific-Atlanta.

Elna Tynes has been a programmer, writer, and consultant in the computer industry for more than 25 years. She is the author of several books on personal-computer software and has been involved with computer networks and related software for a number of years. The owner of several businesses and an MBA, Tynes brings her business-applications knowledge to her writing projects.

Roger White has evolved from an MIT chemical engineering graduate into a computer industry commentator and businessperson, with an MBA from the University of Phoenix. In 1977, he opened the first Computerland retail store in Utah, and he joined Novell in 1981, when it launched the NetWare local area network system. White has developed a broad insight into the dynamics of the personal computer industry and follows companies that produce NetWare-compatible products. He has a particular interest in workstation-user interaction and in adapting personal computer technologies to Information Age challenges.

Acknowledgments

Connectivity: Local Area Networks could not have been planned or completed without the energetic efforts of many persons. New Riders Publishing expresses sincere thanks to the following individuals for their contributions.

Rick Bachoffner of IBM provided critical assistance throughout the project. In addition to contributing his knowledge of data processing, Rick was instrumental in bringing several key players into the project.

The master plan for this book reflects contributions from Chuck Brinkman and Rick Bachoffner of IBM, Prof. Robert Orr of Indiana University-Purdue University at Indianapolis, and Bill Stevens.

Numerous vendor representives assisted New Riders by providing information, products, and contacts with authors. NRP gratefully acknowledges the contributions of Marilyn B. Arnold of AMP, Inc.; Lucy Graziano and Bill Johnson of Banyan Systems, Inc.; Kerry Stanfield of Digital Communications Associates, Inc.; Dave Farmer of Digital Equipment Corporation; Dennis Drogseth of IBM; Kevin Martin of Instant Information; Christie Gersitch of Microsoft, Inc.; Rose Kearsley of Novell, Inc.; and Randy Schiff of Visisoft.

New Riders Publishing also expresses thanks to the following people for their contributions to this book:

Drew Heywood, for development of the project.

Gary Hughes, Scott Orr, Karanjit Siyan, and Michael Wirsching, for their thorough technical review of the manuscript.

Brad Koch, for assembling the authoring team and putting out many fires.

Nancy Sixsmith, for managing the project and steering the book through production.

Geneil Breeze and Gail Burlakoff, for their careful and rapid editing (and moral support).

Karen Opal, for editorial assistance wherever needed.

Bill Hartman, for speedy layout and for his accurate and creative rendering of line art.

Cheri Robinson, David Ewing, and Bill Hartman, for creating the series design.

Jerry Ellis and Dennis Sheehan of the PHCP Production Department, for working their magic with figures.

Trademark Acknowledgments

New Riders Publishing has made every attempt to supply trademark information about company names, products, and services mentioned in this book. Trademarks indicated below were derived from various sources. New Riders Publishing cannot attest to the accuracy of this information.

3Com is a registered trademark of 3Com Corporation.

Apple, AppleTalk, and Macintosh are registered trademarks, and LaserWriter, LocalTalk, System 7, are trademarks of Apple Computer, Inc.

ArcNET and Datapoint are registered trademarks of Datapoint Corporation.

AT&T is a registered trademark, and StarServer is a trademark of AT&T.

AutoCAD is a registered trademark of Autodesk, Inc.

Commodore is a registered trademark of Commodore Electronics, Limited.

COMPAQ and SYSTEM PRO are registered trademarks of COMPAQ Computer Corporation.

CompuServe Information Services is a registered trademark of CompuServe Corp. and H&R Block, Inc.

CorelDRAW! is a registered trademark of Corel Systems Corporation.

Crosstalk is a registered trademark of Digital Communications Associates, Inc.

dBASE IV is a registered trademark of Ashton-Tate Corporation.

DEC is a registered trademark of Digital Equipment Corporation.

Hayes is a registered trademark of Hayes Microcomputer Products, Inc.

HP and Hewlett-Packard are registered trademarks of Hewlett-Packard Co.

IBM, IBM PC, OS/2, PS/2, System Network Architecture (SNA), and Token Ring are registered trademarks; and NETBIOS and NetView are trademarks of International Business Machines Corporation.

Intel is a registered trademark of Intel Corporation.

Lotus and 1-2-3 are registered trademarks of Lotus Development Corporation.

Microsoft, Excel, FoxPro, MS-DOS, LAN Manager, and Windows are registered trademarks of Microsoft Corporation.

Motorola is registered trademark of Motorola, Inc.

Novell and NetWare are registered trademarks of Novell, Inc.

Warning and Disclaimer

This book is designed to provide information about the AutoCAD computer program. Every effort has been made to make this book as complete and as accurate as possible, but no warranty or fitness is implied.

The information is provided on an "as is" basis. The author and New Riders Publishing shall have neither liability nor responsibility to any person or entity with respect to any loss or damages arising from the information contained in this book or from the use of the disks or programs that may accompany it.

Contents at a Glance

Contents

Part Two LAN Technologies

Part Three: LAN NOS Local Connectivity Support

Part Four: Network Management

Connectivity: Local Area Networks

Introduction

When computer users demand a new feature on their local area network, they are not concerned with the details of running the network. They assume that the LAN administrator will have the expertise to satisfy their requirements. Most LAN administrators have tried to extend their LANs in new technological directions, and have had to hone their skills in order to meet that demand.

Today's computer users are highly sophisticated and are accustomed to having access to almost unlimited computing power. Their need for data knows few bounds. Users want to know why their PCs cannot access the data on their UNIX accounting system, why they cannot send electronic mail to the office in London, or why they need to use floppy disks to exchange files. The demand to connect computing resources has grown from a murmur to a roar. *Connectivity* is one of the hot buzzwords, and users want connectivity to happen with the same ease they enjoy when they use their favorite word processor.

Almost any sizable organization that is not starting from scratch needs to integrate several computer and network architectures. The industry term for multi-architecture computing is *enterprise computing*. When LAN administrators and data processing managers start looking for solutions to enterprise computing problems, they often find themselves overwhelmed with questions.

Connectivity: Local Area Networks can provide the solutions you need to accomplish your organization's enterprise-connectivity goals. Here you will get answers to many questions, such as the following:

- What is the most cost-effective medium for my network?
- How can I guarantee that my network will provide reliable service?
- How can I connect networks that have different topologies and protocols? (What are topologies and protocols anyway?)
- How can users on my LAN share modems, and how can outside users access resources on my network?

Some of these answers are difficult to answer. Vendors will try to sell the solutions they know. Magazine articles often do not dig deep enough. Books tend to be introductions to the subject, or they are full of engineering jargon. *Connectivity: Local Area Networks* strives for a middle ground, attempting to give you enough information to solve your problems without overwhelming you in the process.

The Problem of Connectivity

The minute you connect your personal computer or workstation to the rest of the world, technical considerations become difficult or impossible to ignore. Even the simplest case of calling an information resource through a modem brings you face-to-face with protocols, interface standards, and performance constraints that are not easily overcome. Computer connectivity remains a new frontier that becomes more rugged as you attempt to scale its mountainous terrains.

The problem is not a lack of networking standards. On the contrary, networking standards are numerous and well-defined. In contrast to the rather vague standard that defines an "IBM-compatible" personal computer, network standards are generally rigidly delimited in formal documents, by sponsoring manufacturers or by international standards organizations. These standards are usually expressed in "engineerese," which is a language that is almost indecipherable to the non-initiate. *LAN Connectivity* is an engineerese-to-English translator, telling you what you need to know without excessive detail.

Upgrading network performance is not as simple as buying a faster PC and then transferring the software to it. If an organization's Ethernet is too slow to keep up with the massive amounts of data being generated by a new document-imaging system, it is not possible to speed up the Ethernet. Instead, it may be necessary to move to an entirely new technology, such as FDDI, which can result in changes to every component in the network, from the cabling to the workstation network-interface cards.

In fact, an organization can require several types of networks to balance cost and performance. It is not uncommon to find networks that combine token ring, FDDI, and X.25 components, for example. Network planners and technicians must often understand several technologies if they are to address all of the networking needs of a complex organization.

In addition to different network requirements, various computer systems can have different network requirements. Ethernet is the traditional network standard for UNIX; token ring is the best-supported network standard when IBM mainframes are involved. What happens when you have both UNIX and IBM computers in your organization?

Even when a shop is standardized on Ethernet, the network may need to support multiple protocol standards. For example, a company's UNIX workstations that use TCP/IP protocols might be sharing the same Ethernet cable with personal computers connected to a NetWare LAN. Unless the proper interfaces are installed, however, the UNIX workstations and the PCs cannot exchange data.

You know you are involved in enterprise computing when your network must support more than one standard. Enterprise computing is complicated because it is necessary to enable communication and cooperation between computers and networks that are based on many standards. For example, DOS, Macintosh, and UNIX workstations can be networked via various combinations of Ethernet, token ring, and LocalTalk. To do this, you must understand the standards and tools for interfacing standards together.

New Riders' Enterprise Series

Connectivity: Local Area Networks is the first volume in the Enterprise Series by New Riders Publishing. This series of books will explore the many facets of enterprise computing, which is a field that is far too vast to fit into a single volume.

Practitioners of enterprise computing must concern themselves with computing at all levels. They must devise networks that enable dissimilar computers to interconnect; and they must design application environments to enable data-sharing and cooperative processing between applications running under different operating systems. Enterprise computing cuts across all levels of computing technology, and it is a considerable challenge to the ingenuity and expertise of those who must plan and implement large networks.

The Enterprise Series starts with three volumes that focus on local area networks. *Connectivity: Local Area Networks* considers enterprise computing at the lowest level. First, it examines network cabling standards, protocols, and hardware devices that are most commonly found in enterprise networks. In addition, this volume explains how the three most popular network-operating systems—Novell NetWare, Microsoft LAN Manager, and Banyan VINES—solve various network-connectivity problems. Finally, a chapter on network management explains the technologies for making enterprise networks reliable and easy to manage.

Operating Systems: Workstations and LANs, available in the fall of 1992, explores the characteristics of the most common workstation and local area network-operating systems. Included will be workstation-operating systems such as DOS, OS/2, Macintosh System 7, and UNIX. Network-operating systems will include

NetWare, LAN Manager, and VINES. Discussed will be the advantages, disadvantages, and implications of each operating system from the perspective of enterprise computing.

Applications: Local Area Networks, available in the fall of 1992, discusses advanced application topics such as electronic mail, downsizing, and the implementation of client-server applications. A variety of concerns arise when critical applications are hosted in LAN environments and when data must be shared by applications running on dissimilar computers.

Who Should Read this Book?

If you have tried to learn about enterprise computing, you know that most books fall at either the low or high ends of the information spectrum. Either they provide a basic introduction without giving you enough information to do actual planning, or else they overwhelm you with the engineering details. Topics are either addressed at the surface level in a couple of pages, or they are exposed to their bare bones in a book-length treatise.

This book was conceived to fall between those two extremes—to give you the information you need to make planning and implementation decisions without requiring that you become an electronics engineer. You will find chapters that give you the information you need to be a decision-maker in today's enterprise-computing environments. Essentially, this book is for managers and technicians who must plan and implement non-trivial networks.

How this Book is Organized

The chapters in this book roughly follow the organization of the Open Systems Interconnect (OSI) network model, which is described in Chapter 2. The OSI model describes networks, starting from the electrical interface between the network software and the network cabling (or other medium); and proceeds, in layers, through various communication considerations until it details the interface between the network and the end-user applications. Similarly, this book starts with network cabling and proceeds to examine, layer by layer, the software components that reside between the wires and the network-operating system.

Part One: A Perspective on Local Area Networks

Local area networks are increasingly prominent tools in the business data processing toolkit. No longer are they simple tools for sharing files or peripherals. Office-automation applications on LANs are commonplace. As the cost and performance characteristics of LANs have become more evident (and as powerful application environments have become available), organizations have increasingly looked toward LANs as the platforms of choice for critical business applications.

LANs are becoming more than just application environments. As more PCs are interconnected by local area network cables, planners are looking for ways to make the LAN serve as a systems integration and connectivity platform. If there is a VAX in the office, managers want to connect to the VAX by using their LAN-connected desktop PCs. If there is a PC in the branch office in Los

Angeles, there will be someone in the New York office who will want to exchange files with it.

LANs are being asked to connect to more resources, and they are being asked to do it inexpensively, reliably, and without sacrificing performance. When faced with planning such a network, you need to arm yourself with as much knowledge as possible. That is the purpose of this book.

Before you enter the rocky landscape of LAN connectivity, however, you will find it useful to scout out the territory. What is the nature of the new world of LANs and how does it differ from the old world of large multiuser computers, in which data processing has resided for so long?

Chapter 1, "Local Area Networks versus Multiuser Computer Systems," explains the characteristics that differentiate various types of networks. LANs bring a new complexion to network design and management that is best understood by comparing them to more traditional network technologies. Mainframe computers were designed with the understanding that data communication networks, usually based on telecommunications systems, would be expensive, slow, and subject to transmission errors. LANs are inexpensive, fast, and highly reliable, and make possible new computing applications, such as document imaging.

Chapter 2, "A Model of Network Communications," presents the Open Systems Interconnect network model, which is the organizational framework for this book. The OSI model is a useful tool for understanding the relationship of different network components. This chapter also introduces you to the concepts of *protocols*, which are the grammar-like rules that control network communication.

Part Two: LAN Technologies

Now that you have some background, Part Two examines a variety of topics in significant depth. As you now know, it is profitable to view network communication in terms of layers; this part examines several of those layers.

Chapter 3, "Media and Physical Topologies," describes the lowest network level, that of the cabling or other medium that is used to facilitate communication. A variety of network media are available, each of which has individual characteristics relating to cost, performance, and protocols that can be supported. In this chapter, you will examine network cabling types, including several varieties of copper wire and optical fiber. You will also encounter wireless technologies that utilize light and radio frequencies. After reading this chapter, you will understand the media options that best fit your network requirements.

Chapter 4, "Local Area Network Standards," explores some of the most prominent protocols that are used to interface the network software with the network medium. You will encounter formal standards, such as the IEEE token ring and Ethernet, which constitute the majority of the LANs in operation. You will also examine common industry standards, such as LocalTalk and ARCnet. Any enterprise network is likely to encompass two or more of these standards, and it is often necessary to exchange data between different types of networks. A variety of networking issues emerge when networks grow past a certain size or incorporate multiple standards.

Chapter 5, "Communication Protocols," explains the most important protocols that are used to facilitate LAN communication. Enterprise networks need to support several protocols, such as

IPX, AppleTalk, and TCP/IP. A protocol consists of a precise set of rules that manages communication on the network; practitioners of enterprise computing need to know the inner workings of the protocols running on their networks.

As with network standards, it is often necessary to interconnect devices that are based on different protocols. Until recently, few solutions for spanning the gaps between protocols existed. Today, however, a network vendor must give serious attention to support for the major network protocols. Specific vendor approaches will be set out in Part Three. You will encounter the protocols that are most likely to be part of your network environment.

Chapter 6, "Network Communication Services," discusses methods of connecting LANs to outside resources by using asynchronous modems. Planners increasingly view LANs as communication-integration platforms, and there is much interest in communicating through inexpensive, asynchronous modems. Various software and hardware options are available that enable network users to share modems for dialing into, and out from, the network. Asynchronous communication is an economical way of extending the range of a LAN in light-duty situations without getting into the complications of wide area network technologies.

Chapter 7, "Interconnecting Local Area Networks," examines the devices that are used to connect LANs together. These *internetworking devices*—bridges, routers, and gateways—break large networks into smaller pieces to improve performance, or they connect dissimilar networks together so that they can exchange data. Unlike the asynchronous-connectivity devices described in Chapter 6, these devices are intended for constant duty and must provide LAN-like performance. The requirement for understanding multiple LAN standards and protocols makes internetworking an extremely complex field. Bridges, routers, and gateways are among the most sophisticated devices on the network.

Part Three: LAN NOS Local Connectivity Support

Part Three describes the connectivity options supported by the three most prominent local area network-operating systems (NOSs): Novell NetWare, Microsoft LAN Manager, and Banyan VINES. To be competitive in today's demanding enterprise-computing environments, vendors of network-operating systems are scrambling to support as many standards and protocols as possible. The result is a battleground, with each vendor devising ways to support networks that range in size from a few nodes to thousands of nodes.

Chapter 8, "Novell NetWare," examines the local-connectivity options of this most popular network-operating system. Although NetWare has long focused on its native IPX protocols, options for connectivity to Macintosh and TCP/IP networks have become increasingly prominent. The recently introduced Open Data Link Interface enables multiple protocols to be supported via the same LAN adapters. NetWare also supports a suite of asynchronous-communication systems for dial-in and dial-out network support.

Chapter 9, "Microsoft LAN Manager," presents a LAN operating system that is markedly different from Novell NetWare in several respects. LAN Manager operates as an application running on an OS/2 workstation. OS/2 is especially strong as a foundation for client-server computing, and a server can support an SQL database server and the LAN Manager NOS. LAN Manager also provides peer-to-peer services, enabling workstations and servers to share their resources with the network.

Chapter 10, "Banyan VINES," introduces you to the network-operating system that is currently the most versatile NOS for implementing very large, enterprise LANs. Although Banyan has begun to make inroads into smaller networks, VINES networks are, on average, among the largest in the industry. This chapter describes the features of VINES that make it especially well-suited for enterprise networking.

Part Four: Network Management

An enterprise network is an expensive entity. It represents a large capital investment, and it controls the productivity of large numbers of workers. Failure to manage this valuable resource can be extremely costly.

Chapter 11, "Introduction to Network Management," has a broad scope. Network management consists of configuring, monitoring, controlling, and analyzing the resources available in the network; optimizing the use of those resources; and preventing or solving users' problems as they occur. Because of the disastrous effects of network downtime in networks, network management is currently focused on detecting potential faults and problems before they become critical. True network management performs a broader role in helping network administrators with their day-to-day management tasks—such as adding new users, manipulating printer queues, and scheduling backups.

Finally, two appendixes are included. Appendix A lists significant manufacturers of network products. Appendix B contains a glossary of enterprise networking terms to assist you in reading this book and in your enterprise networking reasearch in general.

Other Network Titles from New Riders Publishing

New Riders Publishing offers an expanding line of books about Novell NetWare. These books are addressed at various levels of user requirements and experience. As this volume goes to press, the following titles appear in the New Riders catalog:

Novell NetWare on Command is both an introduction to NetWare and a task-oriented guide to managing a NetWare network. New administrators will find that this book enables them to set up a NetWare server properly. Experienced administrators will find that its task-oriented approach makes it an effective reference guide to NetWare management procedures.

Inside Novell NetWare is New Riders' general-purpose tutorial and reference for Novell NetWare. It is an excellent first book for new systems administrators, but it also covers the subject in such depth that it is sure to find a permanent place among your NetWare documents.

NetWare: The Professional Reference is a detailed reference for the most prominent LAN operating system. If your NetWare LAN has grown and your other NetWare books cannot keep up, or if you find yourself looking for comprehensive information presented clearly, this book is what you need to get your network back under control.

New Riders is committed to expanding this line of network books, and several more titles are planned:

Maximizing Novell NetWare will be a tutorial and reference for intermediate and advanced managers of NetWare LANs. This comprehensive volume will introduce you to the inner workings of NetWare, including NetWare protocols, support for Macintosh and UNIX workstations, and local and wide area networking. *Maximizing Novell NetWare* will contain advanced techniques for managing NetWare servers and LANs. It will be available during the fall of 1992.

Downsizing to NetWare will be a manual of the tools and techniques for downsizing large applications for local area networks. Many corporations are reducing computing costs through downsizing, and this book will tell you what you need to know to plan and implement a downsizing strategy. *Downsizing to NetWare* will become available during the fall of 1992.

Operating Systems: Workstations and LANs, the next book in the New Riders Enterprise Series, will explore the most prominent workstation and local area network-operating systems. Enterprise networks must frequently integrate a variety of operating systems, and this volume will give you the information you need to plan a well-integrated network. This volume will be published during the fall of 1992.

Conventions Used in this Book

You will find tips throughout the text that appear with a special margin icon. These bits of text contain "extra" information that can help boost your system's productivity or provide additional details about connectivity features. The following is an example of a tip:

The right cables and cabling configurations enable your computers to operate efficiently and may save you money. A network that efficiently serves the needs of the people by using the computers can save even more money.

Part One: A Perspective on Local Area Networks

Local Area Networks versus Multiuser Computer Systems

A Model of Network Communcations

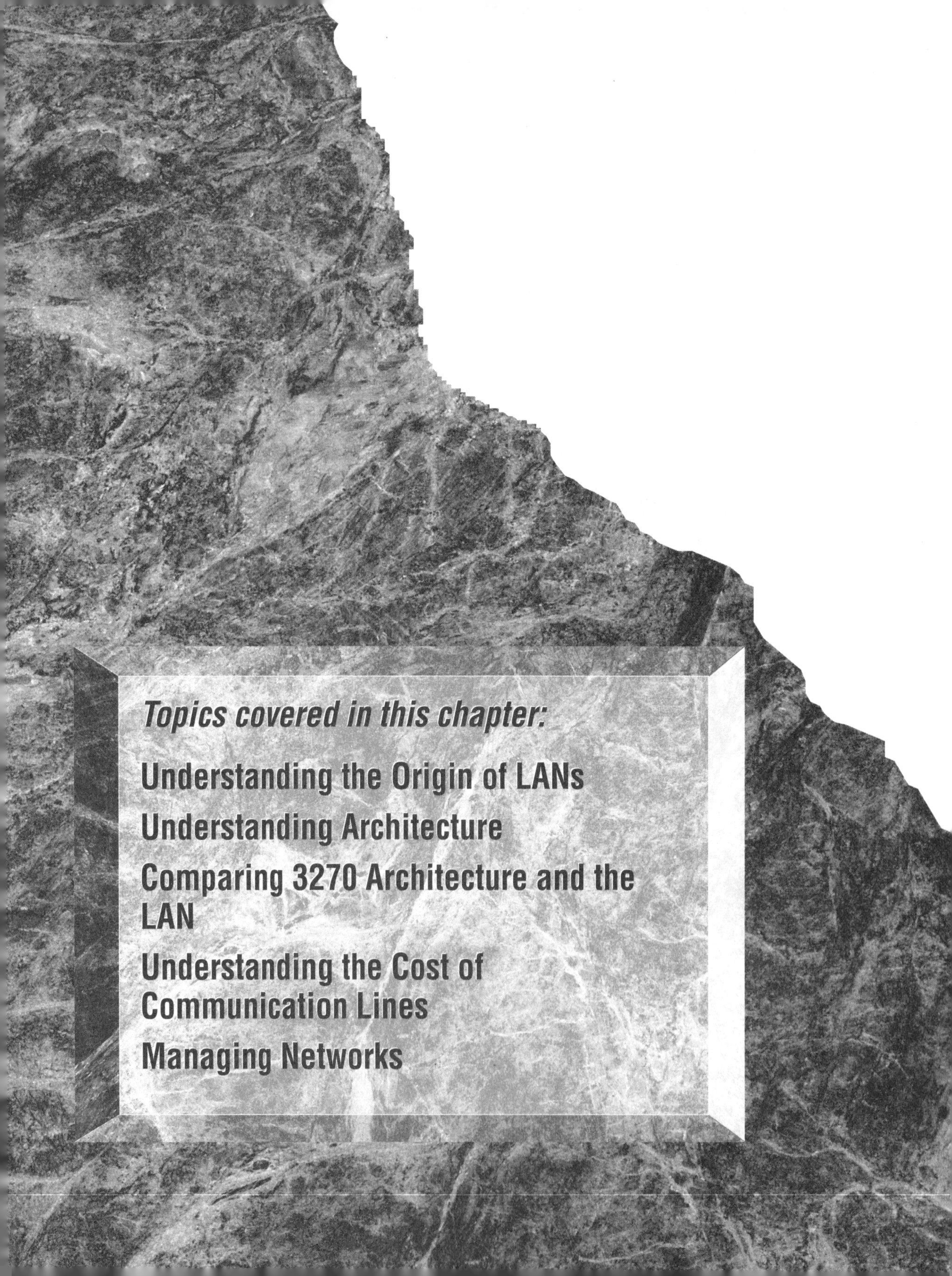
Topics covered in this chapter:
Understanding the Origin of LANs
Understanding Architecture
Comparing 3270 Architecture and the LAN
Understanding the Cost of Communication Lines
Managing Networks

Chapter 1

Local Area Networks versus Multiuser Systems

The PC-based local area network (LAN) is a different entity from the minicomputer or mainframe network. It came from different roots—it originated at a different time in the evolution of data processing, and it does not address the needs of the same kinds of users that minicomputers and mainframe computers do. For these reasons, LANs were designed to work differently from minicomputers and mainframes. Even though they are different, LANs, minicomputers, and mainframe networks must meet many of the same challenges.

They are all *networks*—they connect many people to the same system of computing power, and they must ensure that the computing power they provide is usable, reliable, and secure. This chapter explores the similarities and differences between LANs and mini/mainframe computer networks.

Understanding the Origin of LANs

Personal computers existed for five years before the first personal computer-based LANs started appearing in 1980. From their inception, these LANs worked differently than the networks that were developed for the mainframe world. The following sections discuss the origins of personal computer LANs to see where these differences came from.

The Computer World of the Early 1980s

When integrated circuits (ICs) appeared in the seventies, there were two philosophies on ways to use them. One school of thought was: "Let's use them to do what we've done before—only now we'll do it smaller, faster, and cheaper." This was the path taken by the established computer companies, and it produced new generations of mainframes and minicomputers.

The other school of thought was the following: "Smaller, faster, and cheaper can produce qualitative differences, as well as quantitative differences. We should be trying new things with this technology." This thinking produced the personal computer.

By 1980, both schools proved they were right. The mainframe and minicomputer companies were using ICs to make faster, less-expensive systems with more feature-filled peripherals, and the personal computer companies, such as Apple and Commodore, were making computers by the thousands and profits in the millions.

The Stand-Alone Computer Anomaly

The personal computer is qualitatively different from other kinds of computers. This difference stems from its "one person, one computer" origins. When the premise that only one person at a time is going to be working on a computer is taken seriously, it enables a simplicity of design that is unthinkable in a shared-computer world. For instance, the security issue vanishes entirely. So does all the overhead associated with time-sharing and file-locking; and accounting becomes an optional application feature instead of an integral operating-system feature. This simplicity allowed development projects for personal computers to be one- or few-person projects, rather than big team affairs.

Developers for personal computers took advantage of this simplicity to spend many hours on building easy-to-use utilities and user-friendly front ends for their applications. The concepts of "design committee", "security considerations." and "something for everyone" were anachronisms in early personal-computer development. By 1980, VisiCalc (Lotus 1-2-3's predecessor) was two years old and personal computer developers were showing the whole computer industry what "user friendly" really meant.

Personal computer users fell in love with this simplicity and user friendliness. They also enjoyed sharing programs, which powered a demand for standard platforms that the minicomputer and mainframe worlds had never seen. This desire for a standard showed its strength when customers drove the "non-compatible" and "sort of compatible" competitors from the personal computer marketplace in the mid-1980s. The applications developers encouraged this trend because it was another element that made personal computers simpler.

These factors converged to make personal computers something quite different from the "minicomputer writ small" that mainframe and minicomputer designers thought personal computers would become. The developers of local area networks for personal computers recognized this distinctiveness as part of the environment in which they had to work.

Linking Personal Computers

The first goal of personal computer LANs was to share expensive peripherals (hard disks and daisy-wheel printers). These peripherals had to be shared, but doing so could not change the feel of the "one computer, one user" environment that personal computer users were used to. To accomplish this, the hard disks were partitioned between the various users, and the operating system was modified slightly so that it "saw" these LAN disks as simply another disk drive.

The shared printer was also reached by adding a driver to the operating system. When the LAN developers restricted themselves to tweaking the operating system, they kept these networked systems compatible with single-user applications. The single-user environment remained intact, and users were happy.

Sharing Files

Disk service is a simple solution to the task of enabling many users to share a hard disk, but only as long as each of those users is content to remain separated from the work of other users. Disk service does not make it easy for users to share the same disk space at the same time.

There are several basic challenges to making any multiuser computer system happen, and disk service is not well-suited to dealing with all of them. The first problem is putting the CPU, RAM, and storage into a known state before handing off control to another program. The second problem is how to avoid "race condition," and the third is a problem called "deadly embrace".

The first problem can be called the *house-in-order* problem. With *time sharing*, one computer CPU splits its resources between many jobs. Regardless of the way this is implemented, the RAM, registers and other internals of the CPU must be put back into a specific state when it is time to transfer between tasks.

Putting the house in order can be accomplished in three ways: a supervisor program can be running that keeps track of these processes, the programs that are sharing can be responsible for putting things back in order as they finish a task, or the task can be moved away from the CPU entirely.

The supervisor program is the solution most often used for mini- and mainframe computers. The second option is the choice of NetWare 3.x, and moving the problem off the CPU entirely is what LANs are all about—making workstations run the applications and leaving the central unit to be a file server solves most of the timesharing problem.

The second problem, the *race condition*, deals with sharing data on files.

Suppose, for example, User A and User B are both updating the widget inventory on the computer system. User A, the order entry clerk, reads in the current widget inventory (100 widgets) and waits while the customer decides how many to order. At the same time User B, the receiving clerk, also orders up the widget inventory, and also finds that 100 widgets is the current inventory. User B then adds 100 to the total because 100 widgets just came across the dock, and moves on to update the framitz entry. User B's computer sends back for storage an updated total: 200 widgets. Meanwhile, User A's customer decides to order one widget. User A makes the entry, and one widget is subtracted from the total. Now User A's computer sends back to the computer file the updated total—there are now 99 widgets in the inventory! User A's work overwrites User B's work, and what is on the computer is no longer correct (the race condition). To understand *race condition,* suppose that User A and User B are "racing" to put information back on the disk, and the winner loses.

The solution to the race-condition problem is to allow only one user at a time to write data to a particular area. This process is called *locking* the data; many locking schemes have been invented because there are tradeoffs to be made in the way it is conducted. For instance, a simple way to do locking is to lock the entire data file (*file locking*). File locking is easy to program, but if many people want access to many different parts of the file, it is cumbersome for users, who prefer being locked out of only a small part of the data file at a time. A process that is easier on users, but harder on programmers, is *record locking*, which locks users out of only a single record at a time.

A locking system solves the race condition, but it creates a new potential hazard: *deadly embrace*. For example, suppose User A and User B have updated their software to a new version that includes locking (never again will User B win a race condition and lose his information). This new system consists of two data files: one to keep track of inventory quantities and the other to keep names and addresses. To make an entry, this new application locks both files, updates the files, then unlocks both files.

Once again, User A and User B hit their keyboards with fingers flying. User A's application gets a lock on the name and address file and User B's application gets a lock on the inventory file. User A's application then tries to lock the inventory file and User B's program tries to lock the name and address file. Neither can lock because the other's application already has the lock. Both wait patiently for the lock on the other file to go away— and they wait forever. This is deadly embrace.

There are many ways to solve the deadly embrace problem, but they all involve tradeoffs and lots of operating system complexity to do referee work.

This complexity makes it hard for a simple disk server-based operating system to meet the needs of users who want to share information, as well as disk space and peripherals. Meeting the needs of users who wanted to do more became the goal of LAN developers.

LAN Issues of the 1980s

The instantaneous and universal acceptance of the IBM PC as the standard personal computer in the mid-1980s was a watershed event for LAN makers and personal computer developers—it produced a standard platform to design for.

Prior to this acceptance, LAN designers produced their own personal computers and file servers or they designed LANs for the Apple II. After the "PC-compatibility crisis", LAN designers concentrated on developing PC-compatible connecting hardware and MS DOS-compatible operating systems. It was in response to this opportunity that Microsoft developed MS-Net, Novell developed NetWare, 3Com developed thin cable Ethernet, and Data

General started licensing ARCNet to PC-compatible board makers.

During this time, LAN leaders also saw the advantages of LANs doing more than just sharing peripherals. The designers and management at Novell recognized that to achieve more, a higher-performance operating system was needed—one that would do file service, rather than just disk service.

File service meant that the software in the file server took over the function of deciding where to store things on the disk, rather than leaving that task to the workstation operating system. To make file service happen, the server hardware had to be "smarter" and more powerful, and the workstation operating system had to be modified more extensively.

File service is not simpler than disk service, but it offers more flexibility when it is time to share data and programs among many users. Switching to file service was the first step moving toward the high-performance LAN operating systems of today.

The second step for PC-based LAN evolution was hardware independence: enabling a LAN operating system to work with many kinds of boards, rather than with a single kind. Taking this step was another legacy of LAN's personal-computer roots—only in the personal computer world was it expected that peripherals and software should be interchangeable between different brands of computers. Even so, the decision to support many boards with a single operating system was not an easy one. It was only after the choice had been made and marketed that the magnitude of the benefits became clear.

As these two goals, file service and hardware independence, were achieved, LANs became practical ways to network dozens of personal computers, and it was time to lay the foundations for even larger networks.

Adding Connectivity and Security

A LAN that can network dozens of computers equals a minicomputer in computing power; a LAN that can network hundreds of personal computers equals a respectable mainframe computer in computing power. Computing power alone does not make a useful computer system, however.

Two goals faced LAN designers in the mid-1980s: designing LANs that could match mini- and mainframe computers in security and reliability, and creating ways to interconnect with minis and mainframes. LANs could equal the computing power of the installed base of minicomputers and mainframes, but that installed base still held the data. Until the LANs could reach that existing data easily, they were on the outside.

By the mid-1980s, the mini- and mainframe computer companies were connecting to personal computers, but their interest came from a different agenda: they wanted to extend their mini/mainframe architecture down to the personal computer level. They were designing ways to transform personal computers into terminal emulators—not to make the mini- or mainframe computer "back end" the existing personal computer environment. As a result, the efforts of the mainframe and minicomputer makers to participate in the LAN marketplace remained specialized in their appeal.

These efforts made it clear to the PC-based LAN makers, such as Novell, that the mini- and mainframe computer people were not going to produce a connectivity infrastructure that enabled personal computers working as personal computers to "talk" with mini- and mainframe computers.

This represented an opportunity. The PC-based LAN makers were the "new kids on the block." They had access to the new technology and they did not have an installed base that expected "minicomputer writ small" results, so they could make connectivity happen as an extension of the personal computer environment.

Connectivity as an extension of the PC environment became a major goal of LAN makers in the mid-1980s, which was the period in which the first LAN bridges were developed. Incorporating TCP/IP, 3270, NFS (Network File Service--developed by SUN for the UNIX environment), and other communications protocols became LAN company strategies for increasing market share. The concepts of gateways and specialty servers were also taking shape, and continuing efforts to improve system reliability by supporting system fault-tolerant features were going on.

Adding Network Maintenance and Making the Client-Server Work

In the early 1990s, LANs achieved enough reliability and versatility to make *downsizing* a part of the data-processing lexicon. As hundred-unit LANs became common, and as LANs were turning into the glue that connected many different data-processing environments, network maintenance became the hot topic. Now that the connections could be made, the connection fixers said, "OK, if you're really going to do this, you need to give us the tools that will let us find problems quickly."

In the 1990s, specialty servers also became more common: print servers, communications servers, database engines, and graphics-processing engines, for example. These servers showed just how versatile the LAN platform could be.

Named service also became an issue. LANs were getting so complex that finding things on the network was no longer easy to do by scanning directories. There was a need to automate the finding of applications and data scattered among many servers so that it all could be easily organized.

LAN architecture has evolved rapidly from the simple task of sharing expensive peripherals to the complex task of becoming the glue that connects many kinds of personal computers to many kinds of mainframe systems and supports many kinds of specialty servers.

This section was a discussion of that evolution from an historical perspective. The next sections show the ways LANs compare to mini- and mainframe computers from an architectural perspective.

Understanding Architecture

Each computer architecture started as a solution to a specific problem. This solution was developed within the constraints of the technology available at its inception, and it has evolved from that inception into today's architecture.

Central versus Distributed

Mainframe and minicomputers started at a time in which processing power and communications lines were expensive. The high cost of processing dictated that the network be hierarchical in nature; the high cost of communications lines meant that the goal of any decentralization was to minimize the cost of communications lines.

The benefits of centralization are high security, easy maintenance, and the simplicity of having most of the action take place on a single platform.

The ancestors of the modern network were computers that ran in batch mode and were programmed from punch cards or tape. As processing power grew, the designers of these computers started looking for other ways to put programs and data into the job queue. The first decentralization of computer power consisted of using a time-sharing operating system and stringing terminals off the CPU. The decentralization that followed consisted of putting more and more intelligence in a hierarchical collection of hubs and terminals that connected to the host processor, and improving the reliability and security of the networking process.

The goal of adding intelligence to the peripheral parts of the network was reducing the traffic that flowed through the communications lines and increasing the robustness of the network. These early computer systems were expensive, so they were used only when data-communications volume was high and the users could pay a hefty premium for speedy, reliable response. Leased lines became a standard form of communication line because they were more reliable than were dial-up lines. NASA, for instance, was one of the early users of IBM's 3270 communications systems.

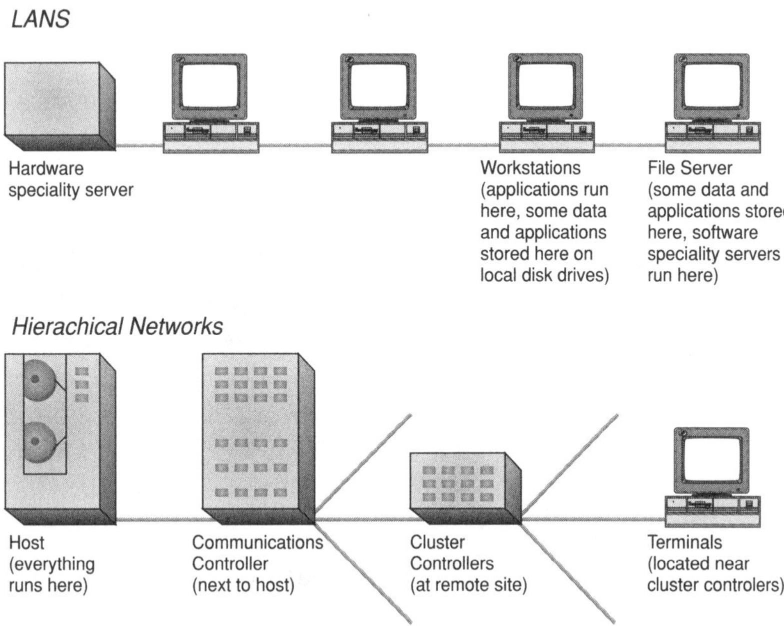

Figure 1.1:
LANs and hierarchical networks.

Defining the "Standard User"

Minicomputers and mainframes were built for different kinds of users than personal computers were. The mini/mainframe architecture centered around the data entry clerk. The goal of the system was to enable the user to enter data efficiently and to enable the user's manager and other organization managers to receive comprehensive reports. For such a system, it was important to keep the data entry people from inadvertently making errors, so applications control was kept in the hands of the computer operators. Users used the system, but they did not control it.

Operators controlled the system, but they rarely used it. This division of labor was a good way to discourage both embezzling and tinkering, but flexibility and user-friendliness have never been high-priority items in a hierarchical networked system.

The importance of control and reliability in early computer use synergized with the fact that early computers were centralized processors—big machines that sat in single rooms. Applications were executed in the central room, and decisions about which users could reach particular applications was controlled from the central room. This also synergized nicely with the kind of tasks for which computers were first used: large accounting jobs.

From the days when the Department of Defense was the largest computer user up to the arrival of the personal computer, the average user was a data-entry clerk feeding these accounting tasks. The middle managers that interpreted the results of all this data entry and processing did not use the computer, they read hard copy reports that the computer operators created for them, and used those reports to manually create charts and graphs that they could show to top management. Top management could tell when they were getting computerized reports because the data presented by middle management was so much more voluminous than that which any manual system created, but the closest they came to operating the computer was standing in front of the computer during company pictures and tours. The computer buyers could not figure out how anyone but clerks could sit down in front of a keyboard and gain any advantage.

All through the 1950s, 1960s, and 1970s, minicomputer and mainframe designers concentrated on making the hierarchical network organization work better by distributing enough intelligence to reduce communications costs (but not enough to change where applications were run). The emphasis on accounting and the split between creators of data and consumers of data encouraged system designers to continue creating paternalistic, centralized systems until personal computers demonstrated that there were other ways computers could be used.

The most enduring part of the stand-alone personal computer revolution has been to show users that there is a different way to present computer power to users. The concept that the user and operator could be the same person turned out to be an important one. For instance, deciding how to use a computer and how much computer to buy was "short-circuited" into one person—the same person who bought the computer, used it. There was no planning committee or buyer who would modify the final decision to "take advantage of a deal" or "make the system last a little longer by meeting X's needs too." There was no "I can't ask him/her to do that" excuse for not trying new things, and for not fine-tuning the computer power to exactly meet the user's needs.

This advantage was so seductive that many early personal computers were snuck into offices—they were either bought and owned personally by the users or purchased as "office equipment" so they would not have to pass through the data processing decision cycle.

One thing every personal computer user got was the capability to launch his own applications. Every personal computer had a directory-search function and a way to launch any application that the search turned up.

Because the personal computer became the professional's tool rather than the clerk's tool, it has been difficult to integrate it into clerk-oriented, mini/mainframe networks. This "war of the environments" is a continuing challenge to the easy integration of enterprise-wide, heterogeneous networks.

Comparing 3270 Architecture and the LAN

This section is an overview of the way 3270 architecture, which is a classic hierarchical architecture, compares to a NetWare network, which is a mainstream LAN architecture.

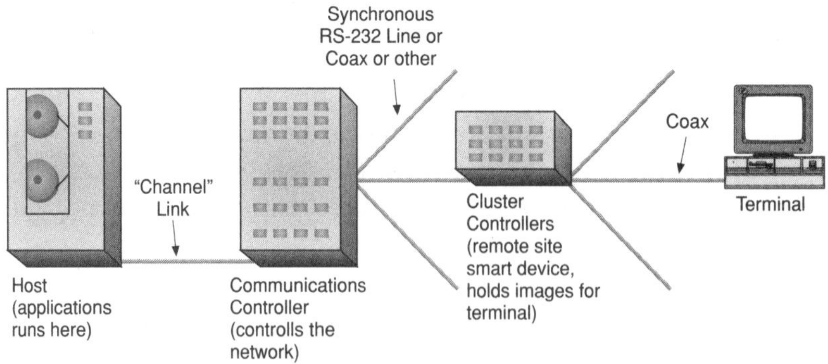

Figure 1.2:
The 3270 world.

3270 Outlined

The 3270, in its common configurations, is the typical hierarchical networking system. The heart of the system is the main CPU, which runs an operating system, a database, and various application programs. Talking with users, however, is the job of its "sidekick" in the computer room, the communications controller.

The *communications controller* is a separate computer that concerns itself with controlling the network of printers and terminals that use the host CPU. This computer has an operating system and set of commands that are entirely different from that run on the host CPU. The only thing they have in common is that they originated so long ago that both operating systems are still maintained by modifying assembly language source code.

These two computers are connected by a high-speed, short-length communications line called a *channel*. It is from the communications controller that all the lines to terminals and printers spring, but these lines do not connect directly to terminals and printers. Instead, they connect to cluster controllers, and cluster controllers attach to terminals and printers.

Cluster Controllers

An intermediate step, located between the communications controller and the terminals, reduces communications-line costs, adds flexibility, and simplifies terminal and printer design. The cluster controller becomes the "smart" device that can be reconfigured to work with the many different kinds of communications lines between the host CPU and a remote site. The cluster controller can handle a local coax connection, an RS-232 connection to a synchronous modem attached to a leased line, or anything else the customer wants. The cluster controller deals with the variability of remote communications lines. The terminals and printers that attach to the cluster controller use a standardized, high-speed, coax connection—they are insulated from the variety.

Terminals and Printers

The terminals attached to 3270 cluster controllers are the "airheads" of the computer world. They look good, but thanks to the high-speed coax connection they have with the cluster controller, they do not have to be smart. The cluster controller actually builds entire screens for the terminals, and then ships the image over the coax connection--all the terminals do is to display what the cluster controller sends them. The cluster controller also does formatting for printer data.

Applications

A major goal in the development of 3270 architecture was to avoid getting the system botched up by something a user or operator did. This system was designed from the ground up to be used by hundreds of clerks with little or no understanding of computers and to be operated by skilled, well-trained technicians.

These constraints have lead to some interesting differences between the way personal computers operate and the way a 3270 system operates. In the 3270 world, a session is dedicated to an application at one end and a terminal at the other. Operators, not users, determine which terminals are eligible to attach to a particular session. The control and robustness the 3270 system offers is outstanding; its flexibility is feeble.

Adding Capability To The Network

One area in which flexibility is lacking is in the expansion of the network. To add a new cluster controller to the communications controller's list, for instance, requires shutting down the system and reassembling parts of the communications controller's operating system. When the customer outgrows the host CPU's capacity to service the network, and the CPU must be replaced, it can be traumatic. An extreme case is when a customer decides to move from a System 36 to a System 370, which entails replacing the entire network—hardware, communications lines, and software.

In fact, it was the hope of alleviating this "transition trauma" that lead early LAN designers to explore the LAN concept.

SAA, LU6.2, PU2.1, Token Ring

The 3270 communications system of the 1970s and 1980s was a purely hierarchical design. As the PC-based LANs demonstrated the usefulness of LAN concepts, however, the 3270 and other minicomputer and mainframe architectures evolved to incorporate peer-to-peer features.

In the 3270 system, the peer-to-peer concept has been added as part of the Systems Application Architecture (SAA) concept (specifically, the LU6.2 and PU2.1 additions to the 3270 network concept, and the addition of token ring to the physical kinds of hardware that can be attached to the system). When LU6.2 is used, personal computers can talk directly with other personal computers without having to set up a session in the mainframe.

IBM and the makers of other mini- and mainframe-based networks have improved the networks, but the results have not converged easily with the personal computer environment. The improvements presume that hundreds of people are going to be using the system, and those people want a secure, reliable and backwards-compatible system more than anything else.

Minis and mainframes were designed when hierarchy was the only form of architecture that made sense. The popularity of personal computers laid the foundation for an alternative. The following is an overview of the architecture of NetWare and a discussion of one of those alternatives.

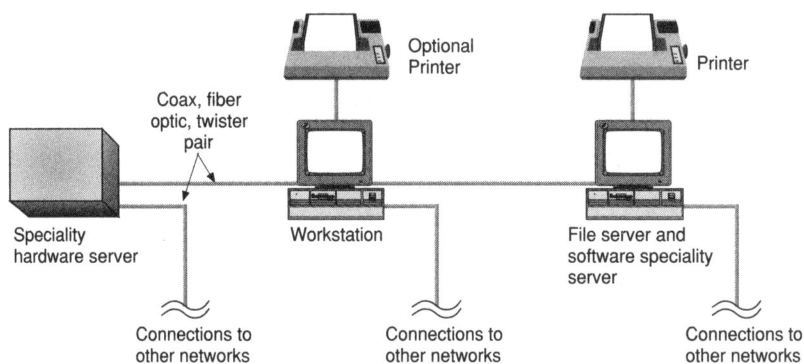

Figure 1.3:
The LAN world.

NetWare Outlined

The premise behind the NetWare LAN idea was *distributed processing*. It was the idea that adding workstations to the LAN would increase the processing power of the LAN system in the same proportion that users were added.

> Thus, no user would see degradation in system performance when other users were added to the system. The "transition trauma" experienced by mini- and mainframe-style hierarchical systems would be eliminated entirely

Not only was transition trauma eliminated, the LAN designers got more than they anticipated: they got the world of personal computer applications too. Access to these applications proved to be so valuable to LAN customers that no PC-based LAN has ever gained widespread acceptance if it does not offer compatibility with single-user operating systems such as DOS. NetWare designers recognized this early and designed the original NetWare to work with both CP/M and DOS machines. In both cases, the network looked like additional disk drives to the operating system and to any application that made calls to the operating system.

Workstations

The workstation part of NetWare slides in behind the operating system and "watches" as it makes calls for disk access. When the call is to a local drive, it is passed on, unchanged, to the disk controller. When the call is to a network drive, it is intercepted and passed the LAN card instead (see fig. 1.4).

Early single-user application software did not see a difference; single-user software could be run with the workstation setup being either stand-alone or networked. This offered a robustness different from that offered by the hierarchical networks: if the central unit on the LAN, the file server, went down, the workstations could keep operating on stand-alone projects.

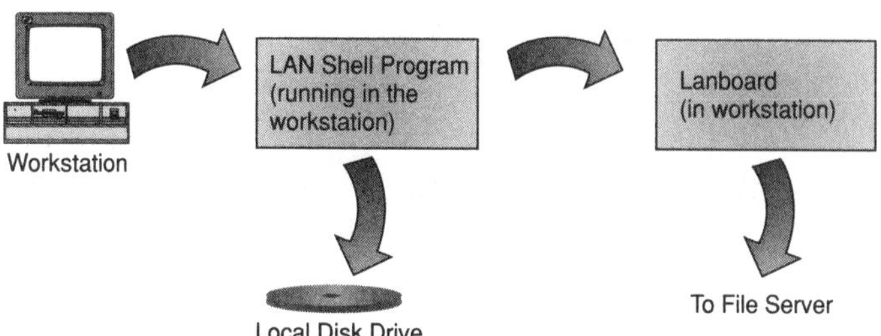

Figure 1.4:
The workstation shell.

File Servers

One of the big differences between LANs and mini/mainframes is the role of the central computer. In mini/mainframe networks, this computer runs the applications programs. In LANs, this computer is a dedicated file librarian. It doesn't run applications, it passes information back and forth with an application running on a workstation.

Because the file server's job is so specialized, it can become very good at passing information. PC-based LAN file servers typically retrieve and store data faster than a minicomputer or mainframe trying to act like a file server.

Early LAN file servers were proprietary designs, specifically dedicated to being a file server. After the PCAT was introduced, the most common kind of file server became a 286-based or 386-based personal computer used as a file server. There are still proprietary file-server designs available, but the average LAN does not need the higher performance capability.

Other Servers

File service is one example of a larger class of activities called *client-server activities*. Once the decision is made to run applications in workstations, workstations become clients, and many kinds of servers can be developed: file servers, database servers and communications servers, to name a few. In each case, the server can be a dedicated machine or it can hitch a ride in another machine (often the file server). One server can service an entire community of workstations.

Easy Bridging

The most successful players in the personal computer industry have always cultivated third-party participation. LAN developers soon discovered that the benefits of doing this applied to them as well. By 1985, hardware companies were no longer producing operating systems (and vice versa). Instead, they would OEM the parts they did not specialize in.

The result was a hodge-podge of boards, cabling systems and topologies being offered to the public. Table 1.1 shows a sample of what was being offered in 1987.

Interconnecting different media LANS was not simple. It grated against the personal computer legacy of simplicity in which LANs had been created. The solution was to create LAN operating systems that could glue all these combinations into a network that looked "seamless" to the user. Interconnecting was accomplished by *bridging*: connecting two or more networks together by putting a LAN card from each network into a file server or workstation and running a special bridge program that enabled packets from one network to move to the other network.

Table 1.1
Common LAN Technologies in 1987

Company	*Cable type*	*Protocol*	*Topology*
SMS	RG 64 Coax	Token Bus	Linear star
3Com	RG 58 Coax	CSMA/CD	Linear
Synoptics	Unshielded Twisted Pair	CSMA/CD	Linear
IBM	Shielded Twisted Pair	Token Ring	Ring

Bridging made it easy to join dissimilar networks. It also made it easy to upgrade existing networks that had different technologies. A user could start with an ARCNET network, for instance, and support six users on it. Later, that user could decide that the next ten users should be wired up with Ethernet. All he would have to do was add an Ethernet board to the file sever, add bridge software, and string Ethernet cable to the added users. This is simplicity of the sort personal computer users expect, and it is this kind of simplicity that has promoted LANs' explosive growth.

Applications

Many LAN applications are simply single-user applications that are loaded onto a file server instead of a local hard disk. But LAN-compatible applications can also be a lot more complex. The more complex applications take advantage of the distributed-processing environment to enable many users to work with the application at the same time. This multiuser capability, combined with the client-server concept for ways to accomplish data processing tasks, is the basis for such diverse LAN-oriented applications as job shop inventory control systems, groupware, and Computer Aided Drafting (CAD). LAN operating systems, such as NetWare, offer a wide range of commands that handle file- and record-locking so that race condition and deadly embrace can be avoided in a distributed-processing environment.

Adding Capability to the Network

LANs are expanded in two ways: workstations are added and servers are added. Each workstation brings its own suite of applications, and each server brings support of a specialized task. Thus, LANs are well-adapted to environments in which users engage in a wide variety of tasks.

Workstations

Workstations on LANs are personal computers with LAN cards added. Because there is a lot of variety in personal computers, there are many options for what can be attached to a LAN. LAN workstations can come with or without local disk drives. They can be PC-compatible, Macintosh-compatible, or anything else for which a LAN card and operating system drivers have been developed.

Workstations commonly run some mix of DOS, Windows, OS/2, and UNIX. Although minicomputers and mainframes usually have a common purpose and a common theme for the entire network, LANs are made for variety.

LANs can be as standardized as a minicomputer or mainframe. For instance, if the network is designed from the ground up for an inventory-control system, and the only things attached to it are diskless workstations and bar-code readers, it will act as standardized as one of the hierarchical networks (but supporting variety is what makes LANs distinctive).

Specialty Servers

LAN applications can also take advantage of specialty servers. NetWare, for instance, has a database engine, Btrieve, which is included with the operating system. If an application uses a database, it can call upon the Btrieve database engine to do the crunching. An application that has E-mail features can be designed to call upon the Message Handling System (MHS) to move messages. Servers can be software or hardware plus software. Btrieve and MHS are pure software servers. Print servers, modem servers, and FAX servers are usually composed of hardware plus software.

Understanding the Cost of Communications Lines

Suppose you are a network designer in the 1960's. You find that a long-distance line costs $10.00/hour and that you can squeeze 10,000 bits/second through that line (a 9600-bps modem). The "bit-per-buck" rate you are working with is 1000 bits/buck-second.

Now, suppose it is the 1980s and you are a LAN designer. You find that a LAN cable costs $1080 and can be amortized over three years ($360/year, or $1/day, or $.125/hour for an eight hour day). If you squeeze 10,000,000 bits through that line in one second (an Ethernet cable), the bit-per-buck rate is 80,000,000 bits/buck-second.

The LAN designers of the 1980s dealt with communications systems that were thousands of times less expensive and hundreds of thousand of times faster than those the hierarchy designers used in the 1960s. Faster and cheaper means that qualitative differences can appear. On an Ethernet line, for example, it is not really important that each packet get through. If a packet does not make it, you can try again a thousand times before a single second passes. It is not important that the quantity of the data flow be kept to a minimum—if you want to move a picture, you have the bandwidth to move it.

On the other hand, thanks to the increase in computing power available in the 1980s, you have a lot of intelligence at both ends of the communications line. Thus, it is easy to get smart about what you move and put a lot of security and compression at both ends of the system. Today's PC-based LANs are thus the best of both worlds

Managing Networks

A survey conducted in 1986 revealed that the average number of workstations attached to a NetWare LAN was six. When only seven devices make up a whole network, there is not much demand for sophisticated LAN-management tools.

Since then, the average number of workstations on a LAN has climbed steadily, and network-management tools are high-growth spin-offs of the LAN industry.

The demand for network management in LANs is new enough that few books, training, and tools exist to support it. One goal of this book is to help rectify that situation.

Network management consists of the following: hardware diagnosis, hardware inventory, maintaining applications, and security. It is different from mini/mainframe maintenance for the same reasons that personal computers are different from hierarchical networks. The flexibility and variety that make LANs so attractive to users make them difficult to maintain.

Hardware Diagnosis and Inventory

Personal computers are a standard platform, but once they are personalized, they are no longer standard. Through the years, the number of accessories available to personal computer users has grown. When the IBM PC first came out, it could be equipped with only a monochrome or CGA monitor. Today, the monitor can be mono, Hercules monographics, CGA, EGA, VGA, super VGA, or Windows-enhanced. A well-equipped personal computer is likely to have some mix of the following hardware:

- One or several floppy disk drives
- One or several hard disk drives
- A mouse, mounted from a serial port or from a bus card
- Dozens of combinations of serial and parallel ports

- An internal or external modem
- A tape drive
- A CD-ROM reader
- A joystick, a sound board or a scanner
- A LAN board (or two, if this workstation is being used as a bridge)

This variety generates two kinds of maintenance headaches: inventory and support. The support challenge is to make applications work over a family of machines that are a lot alike, but far from identical. The inventory challenge is to keep track of all of this equipment for security and accounting purposes.

Maintaining Applications

Applications on LANs can come from anywhere and can be run from local drives or network drives. The data that the applications work with and store can also come from network drives or local drives. If there are many servers connected to the LAN, the applications and data can be scattered between more than one server.

There are three major issues: providing support for applications when they are not working right, keeping unwanted applications off the network, and updating applications when new releases come out.

These issues are fertile ground for the new network-maintenance products that are introduced, and they tie into the topic discussed next: security.

Security

LANs evolved from a personal computer environment that had few security concerns. As a result, LAN security started without an installed base. The goal was to equal minicomputer security without drastically altering the personal computer environment. The result is that LAN security begins when a user logs into a file server.

One way to gain terminal-like control is to install workstations that have no local disks: *diskless workstations*. These devices have a special ROM in the LAN card that tells them to get their booting information from the file server, rather than from a local disk. This solves the control problem, but it removes a lot of user flexibility; the applications that require a local disk to work do not run on a diskless workstation. The solution has limited appeal.

Once a file server is logged into, LANs offer a variety of security features that match the rich world of personal computers they must support. LAN security systems can distinguish users by their names, by the workstations they have logged into, whether the workstation is local or remote, and by the time of day. These systems can keep track of what resources a user uses, and they can produce an accounting of that use for costing or charge-back activities.

A user can be granted access to various parts of the LAN by being added to a group. He can also be denied access to various parts of the LAN, based on the time of day or the station from which he logged in. The control system is rich because LAN users expect to do a lot of different kinds of things on the LAN and because a LAN is rarely a static system. Users and tasks change continuously.

LANs, minicomputers, and mainframes are designed to reach different people and to accomplish different kinds of tasks. They all have data processing in common, and they have human users in common, but they have different "roots"—these differences show up in the way the architecture is organized. This goal of interconnectivity is the subject of Chapter Two: the OSI model.

Summary

The primary reason why local area networks act differently than mainframe computers do is because LANs service different users. Whereas LANs service personal computers, and personal computers service professional users; minicomputers and mainframes service terminals, and terminals service clerical users.

LANs developed when computing power and communications lines were thousands of times less costly than when minicomputers and mainframes were created. LAN technology ushered in the cheap, fast communications that enabled a qualitative change in the way computing power was used.

Those users who were most excited about this new computing power were the professionals who wanted to use the power for word processing, spreadsheets, and graphics. Because these users also did not want to give up their library of personal computer applications when they were networked, the LAN technology evolved into today's networking systems.

There are still growing numbers of clerical users, as well as professional users, so there are markets for the following systems: centralized, decentralized, hierarchical, distributed, extra reliable and secure, and extra flexible. These systems support a wide variety of uses. For example, an automated teller network never needs to support users that perform the variety of applications that a university campus network users do.

These kinds of networks will be with us for a long time, so the challenge of the 1990s is to make communications between the clerical and professional use of networks an easier one. The challenge of enterprise connectivity is to develop effective ways to take advantage of many kinds of networking.

Topics covered in this chapter:
Looking at the Seven Layers
Exploring the Extra Layer
Comparing Connectionless versus Connection-Oriented Protocols
Fitting the OSI Model to the LAN Environment
Understanding Hardware and the OSI Model
Learning New Definitions for Old Concepts

Chapter 2

A Model of Network Communications

To enable data processing devices to communicate over different communications links is a complex task. In this book, you frequently encounter the term *protocol*. Aside from its use in computer technology, protocol is perhaps most familiar in diplomatic settings, in which a protocol is an agreement between parties that specifies precise rules of behavior.

Humans adhere to protocols every day in the use of language. The grammar of a particular language defines a precise set of rules that governs interpersonal communication. If two people converse in the same dialect of English, they are likely to exchange information smoothly and without error. If a French and a Chinese diplomat must engage in an error-free discussion, however, they employ translators who understand the protocols of French and Chinese and can perform the necessary translations.

The world of data communication is much like the United Nations: translation between communication protocols is an ongoing process. In both cases, many protocols must be comprehended and carefully translated if information is to be exchanged smoothly and without error.

To make the task of conceptualizing and organizing network-communication protocols more manageable, the early designers of networking systems divided the task into discrete parts. IBM, DEC, and the International Organization for Standardization (ISO) all chose to model this communications task in a structured way, as a series of layers.

IBM's interpretation of the task became Systems Network Architecture (SNA); DEC's became DECNET; and the ISO's became the Open Systems Interconnect (OSI) model. The OSI model is different from SNA and DECNET because it is not set up for a specific series of products produced by a single company. Its goal is to provide a model that many companies—the European computer community—can use. The fact that the OSI model does not define company-specific structures has increased its versatility as a descriptive tool. Many companies that deal with data-communications issues frame theirs so that they fit within the OSI model. Amazingly, the model has even proved useful in the upside-down world of PC-based LANs, in which applications run at the terminal ends of the network instead of at the center (something the OSI originally was not designed to model). Figure 2.1 illustrates the OSI stack.

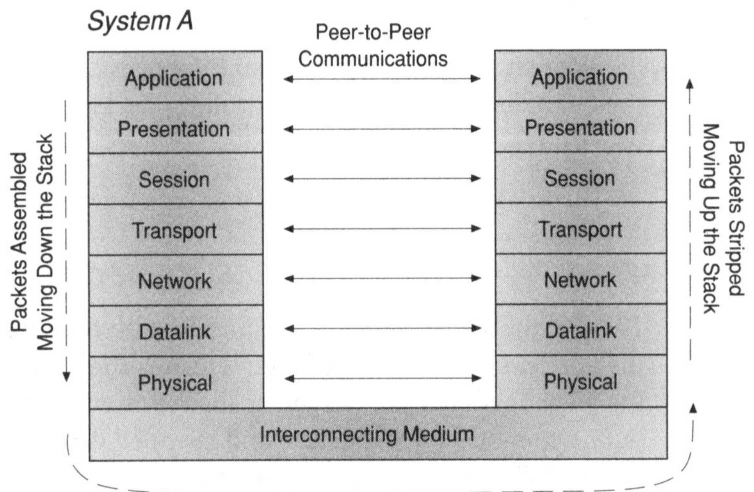

Figure 2.1:
The OSI stack.

Looking at the Seven Layers

The OSI model breaks up the job of moving data from one point to another into seven different tasks. These tasks are arranged sequentially in *layers*, and each layer contributes to the assembly of a *packet*.

Data moves through a data-communications network in discrete bundles of bits called packets. A *packet* is divided into the following four distinct parts:

- The *starting characters* that alert receiving boards that a packet is on the way

- A *packet header* that explains where the packet is going, where it came from, and what kind of packet it is (either a data or a network controlling packet)
- The data the packet is carrying
- The final error-checking bits and the end-of-packet characters

The OSI model is concerned primarily with the contents of the header section of the packet, which is the part that tells the packet where to go. In the header section, the layers are built up on outbound packets and stripped off on inbound packets. The layers are arranged in a hierarchical fashion; each layer sends information only to the layers immediately above and below it. Figure 2.2 shows the building of a packet.

Each layer sends packets to the layers above and below it, but each layer only understands and works with information that comes from the same layer on another stack. For example, the network layer (layer three) sends an inbound packet to layer four only after it strips off any layer three information. This same layer three sends an outbound packet to layer two only after it adds layer three information to the packet. On inbound packets, it examines the layer three information to see if it needs to take any action. For instance, if the layer three information says that this packet is bound for address 01 and the receiving board is address 02, it discards the packet and does not pass it on to layer four.

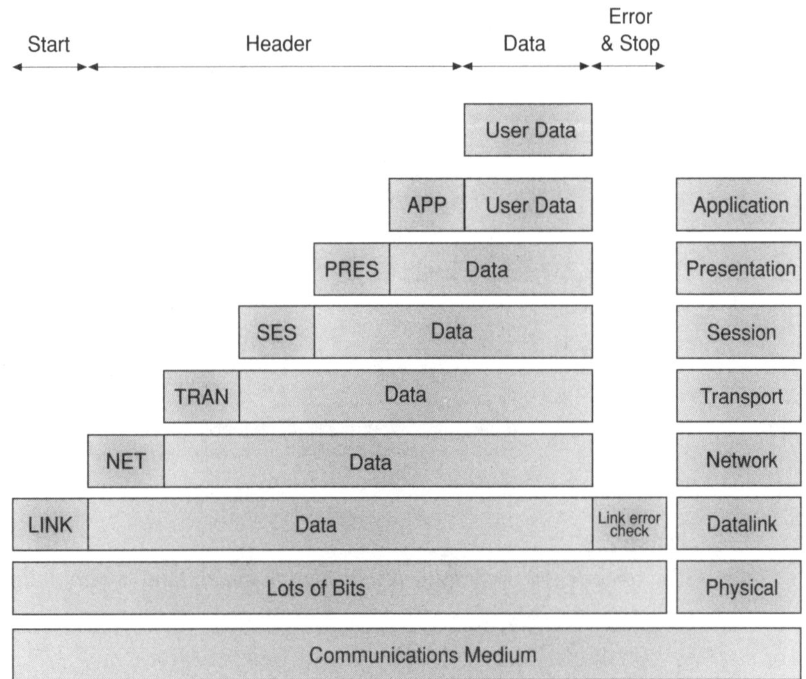

Figure 2.2:
Building a packet.

On outbound packets, layer three adds the source and destination addresses to the packet, and passes this enlarged packet to layer two for further processing. Layer three on the receiving board responds only to what layer three on the sending board adds to the packet. Each layer on the stack "talks" with the same layer on another stack and pays no attention to what other layers do. The next section takes a closer look at what each layer of the stack does. The following figure shows the way data is passed.

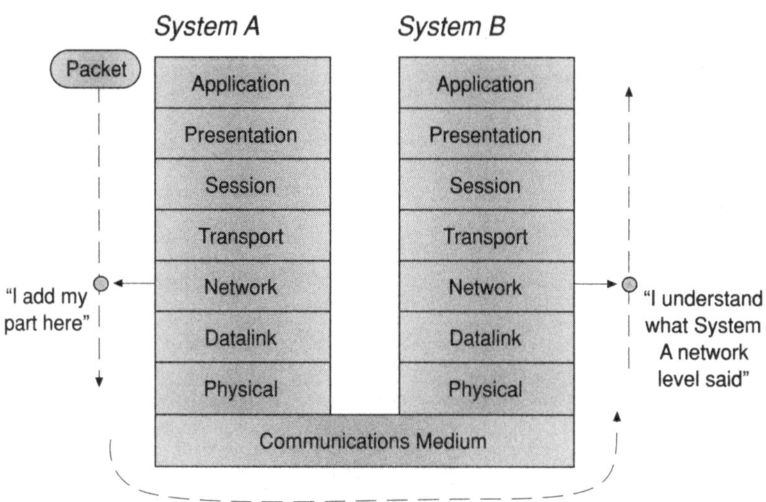

Figure 2.3:
The stack passes data vertically; the levels understand horizontally.

The Physical Layer

The physical layer generates the physical pulses—electrical currents and optical pulses—involved in moving data from the LAN card to the communications system. RS-232 is an example of a physical-layer standard. This layer does not include the communications system, but it does include the connection to it, and it handles rise times and pulse durations. The physical layer does not manage the details of connectors and cabling—these details are sometimes nicknamed the "level 0" layer of the model.

The Data-Link Layer

The data-link level is the first level that handles packets as packets. This level does the final assembly on leaving packets and the first inspection on arriving packets; it adds error correction to leaving packets and checks the checksum on arriving packets. If the packet is not intact, it is discarded. If the link layer can determine where the defective packet came from, it returns an error packet. SDLC and HDLC are examples of protocols operating at this level.

The Network Layer

The network layer routes packets through multiple devices. If the route a packet must travel (between the user and the host in a hierarchical system, or the user and the server in a peer-to-peer system) goes through routers, gateways, or bridges, the network layer is involved. This level maintains routing tables and determines which route is the fastest when alternative routes are available. This is the first layer at which a device begins filtering out packets that are not going from one network to another, so that overall network traffic is reduced. *Internet protocol*, the IP of TCP/IP, operates at this level, as does NetWare's Internetwork Packet Exchange (IPX). This network layer is the level at which "connectionless" or "datagram" services operate (these terms are defined later).

The Transport Layer

Transmission control protocol, the TCP of TCP/IP, operates at the transport layer. This is a transition level--the last of the levels that manages routing packets and error recovery. In some ways, it is a fall-back level: it makes up for any deficiencies that cannot be covered at the network level. If packets are received reliably at the network level, this level is a very simple one. If the communications system cannot provide reliable packet transmission, this level compensates by becoming more complex.

The Session Layer

The session layer is the level that maintains "connection-oriented" transmissions. The process of making and breaking a connection at this level is one of "binding" and "unbinding". At this level, packets are presumed to be reliable—error-checking is not part of this level's function. IBM's NetBIOS and NetWare's SPX operate at this level.

The Presentation Layer

This level is not yet fully defined or widely used. Processing at this level performs any conversion that may be required to render the data usable by the application layer. Data compression/decompression and data encryption/decryption processes can be implemented at the presentation level. Data encryption and compression, however, can be performed by user applications that run above the OSI application layer.

Translations of data formats also can be performed at this layer. An example is the translation between the ASCII and EBCDIC encoding schemes. This function, however, is most frequently performed by the end-user's application.

The presentation layer is frequently misunderstood as presenting data to the user. The presentation layer is a network-communication layer; it does not interface directly with end-user display devices. Production of screen displays is the responsibility of the application program executing on the user's workstation.

The Application Layer

The application layer is also in the process of being defined, so the specifics of its scope are under discussion. This layer deals with security issues and the availability of resources. The application layer is likely to deal specifically with file transfer, job transfer, and virtual terminal protocols.

Exploring the Extra Layers

The OSI model was developed when hierarchy was the norm and before the common LAN protocols—ARCnet, Ethernet, and token ring—were widely used. Since its inception, its layer definitions have evolved to make it fit in a world filled with LANs, as well as with minicomputers and mainframes. One of the adaptations is the informal addition of new layers and sublayers to the original seven layers. An example is the informal addition of level 0 to cover hardware details such as cable connectors and fiber optics.

Another change is the addition of sublayers to the data-link layer (level 2) to cover software needed so that LAN boards can support different protocol stacks simultaneously.

Comparing Connectionless versus Connection-Oriented Protocols

In some networking environments, you must insulate the application and the user from the fact that data is moving through the network in packets. In these environments, an application or user makes a *connection* with another application. This method of linking an application to a user acts like a phone call: a connection is made, the connection is used for a while, and then deliberate steps are taken to break the connection. The "binding" step for starting an SNA application is the connection-making step in SNA. Connection-oriented environments are common in hierarchical networks because they offer reliability and security.

The alternative is to have an application pump data into packet-building software and let that software send the packets. This is the *connectionless* environment, in which each packet stands alone. The packet receiving software that is part of the OSI stack sees that the packets received are complete, but the application must put them in the proper order and request the retransmission of missing packets.

The connectionless environment can process packets faster, is simpler to design, and is well-suited when the packets are mostly chunks of disk sectors. For these reasons, most PC-based LAN environments are connectionless.

Fitting the OSI Model to the LAN Environment

LAN architecture does not fit easily into the OSI model (see fig. 2.4). The concept of running applications at the workstation instead of the CPU means that the workstation runs the higher levels of the OSI stack. All the workstation needs is a route (level 3) to a file server. The workstation and the server do not need to set up a session (level 5)—dashing off packets back and forth is fine. The format (level 6) is simply that of a virtual disk sector, and security is provided (level 7) when the user logs into the network in the first place.

LAN architecture by itself is too simple for the OSI stack, but the necessity of communicating with other networks drives LAN designers to pay homage to the OSI reference model. Because LAN designers want to be the glue that connects many kinds of systems, they take the reference model seriously. They also fully support the idea that networks should intercommunicate.

Hierichical Network

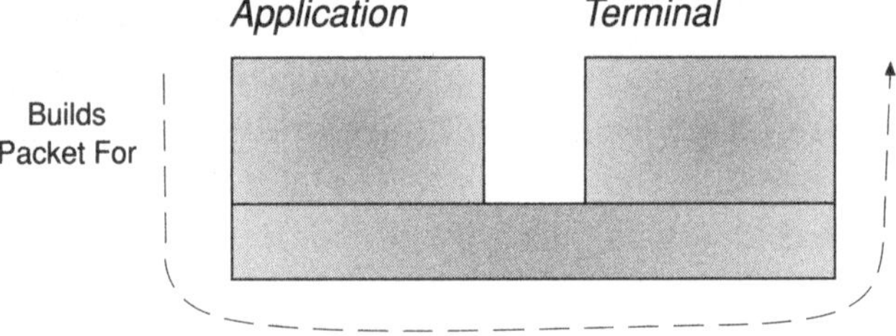

LAN Network

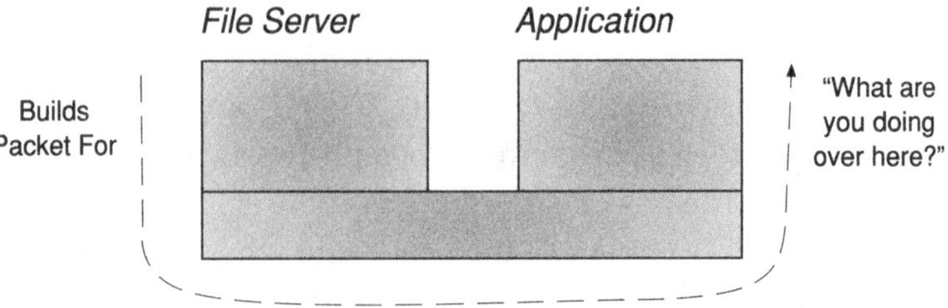

Figure 2.4:
The topsy-turvy LAN world.

Understanding Hardware and the OSI Model

Some hardware devices are designed to manipulate packets up to specific levels of the OSI stack. Repeaters, bridges, and routers manipulate packets at different levels (see figure 2.5).

Repeaters are level 1 (physical level) devices that amplify any packet that passes through them.

Bridges are designed to enable packets to move back and forth between two networks running the same protocols. The network level of the packet shows where the packet is addressed. If the packet is addressed to a local node, it is not passed through the bridge. Bridges operate at level 2 (the data-link level) of the OSI stack. Bridges can be used to reduce network traffic by splitting an existing network and putting a bridge between the two parts. Bridges are not "named" parts of a network, so they are invisible to devices that work with the higher levels of the network.

Routers, on the other hand, have names. Routers operate at level 3 (the network level) of the OSI stack. They can connect networks that do not use the same protocols. A bridge is used to connect an Ethernet network and an ARCnet network that are both running NetWare. A router is used to connect the networks when users are using a mix of NetWare, TCP/IP, and Appletalk (the Macintosh's communications protocol) on the networks. A bridge merely passes or does not pass packets along. A router has the capability to choose the best route when many choices of routes are available.

At the highest level, covering levels four through seven, are gateways. *Gateways* convert the data flow from one network environment into data flow that is suitable for another environment.

Repeater

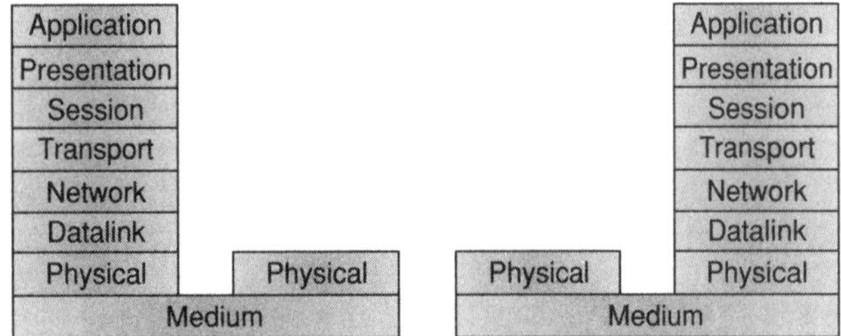

Bridge

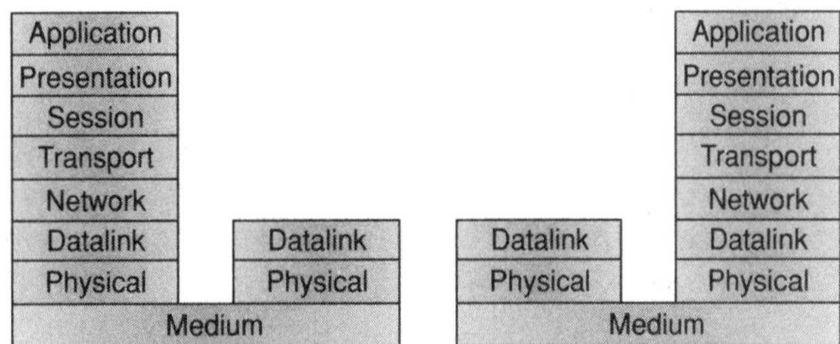

Router

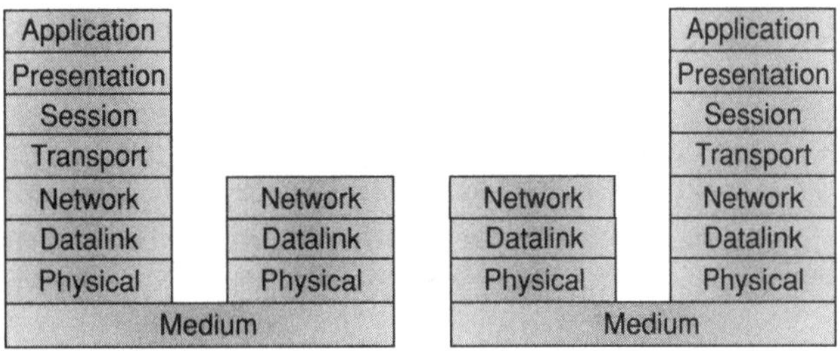

Figure 2.5:
Repeaters, bridges, routers, and the stack.

A gateway connects the NetWare LAN environment with the SNA network environment. Gateways are rarely separate hardware devices; they are more often software added to existing devices, such as workstations or file servers.

Learning New Definitions for Old Concepts

Terms such as bridges, routers, and gateways were imported into the LAN environment within the last five years, and the definitions for these terms come from different sources. As a result, the usage of these terms is not standardized. Things that act like bridges are sometimes called routers and vice versa. In addition, new terms are being invented to cover devices which do not seem to fit into either category. For instance, *brouters* are devices that act like bridges when bridge functionality is needed and routers when router functionality is required. The business of interconnecting networks is new; it is not stable or well-defined. You can expect changes in terminology to continue as the technology evolves. And you can expect old concepts, such as the OSI model, to continue to adapt to meet the needs of new networking systems such as LANs.

The OSI model is still being developed, and the ISO group is working on many more pragmatic concepts as well. OSI also is setting standards for mail transfer—the X.400 and X.500 standard—and network management (SMAPs and SMAEs). The goal of these standards is to make interconnection between various systems easier, which is the same as the LAN connectivity goal. Even though LAN architecture itself fits only modestly well into past OSI work, the OSI standards defining process is of great interest to the LAN community.

Summary

The OSI model does not specify a protocol. Rather, it is a model that can be followed by designers of many different protocols. The goal is to give protocol designers a structured framework with which to work, so the various OSI-compliant protocols can communicate more easily.

The model breaks down the task of sending data from one node on a network to another into seven sequential steps (*layers*), but many of these layers are merged together in popular existing protocols. Although users do not interact directly with OSI models, designers do. LAN designers pay attention to the OSI protocol because they want to be the "glue" that can join together many kinds of networks. This joining task is easier when the OSI model is widely supported.

In those areas in which the OSI model is complete, great strides have been made toward interconnecting different protocols. It is now possible for a single LAN board to recognize packets that are generated by different protocol stacks, and then to route those packets to different protocol handlers. For example, a single Ethernet board in a NetWare file server can handle both AppleTalk and NetWare NCP packets. This convenience would be difficult to achieve if the designers of the different protocols were not paying attention to the OSI model.

The OSI is not yet finished. Design started with the lowest layers—those closest to the hardware. As more of the model is refined, more interconnectivity will occur in the highest layers—those closest to users and applications.

Part Two
LAN Technologies

Media and Physical Topologies

Local Area Network Standards

Communication Protocols

Network Communication Services

Interconnecting LANs

Topics covered in this chapter:
Exploring Copper and Optical Fiber Data Communications Media
Using Wireless Network Media
Understanding Physical Topologies
Accessing Vendors

Chapter 3

Media and Physical Topologies

As explained in Chapter 2, the OSI physical layer does not include the underlying medium. The physical layer consists of the software protocols that control the activity on the medium.

Nevertheless, the physical layer of the network has as its foundation a medium that is sometimes called the "layer 0" of the network model. This medium can be a physical substance (such as copper cable or optical fiber) or it can be a broadcast medium (such as radio or light beams). Either way, the medium is the lowest level factor for enabling devices to exchange data on a network. In addition to the medium, various devices may be required to implement the physical layer: network interface cards, repeaters, connectors, and transceivers are all examples of these devices.

Figuring out how to network a given set of computers has become increasingly complicated. There are dozens of possible combinations of computers to connect, different types of media that can be used to connect the machines, and several networking topologies from which to choose.

This chapter details the different media and media topologies, which are part of the first, or physical, layer of the Open Systems Interconnect (OSI) seven-layer reference model. The chapter discusses the four types of copper cable, two types of optical fiber cable, and three types of wireless connections; and it illustrates the different ways these media can be configured.

To decide what kind of media to use, you must first decide what you need in terms of network speed, number of nodes, and distances between the nodes. This is analogous to basing your choice of a computer on the types of applications you want to run.

To realize the full potential of your computer equipment, you should match it with a network that can provide sufficient throughput. Conversely, a speedy network may be a waste of resources if the computers connected to it are an information bottleneck. Traveling down a dirt road, for instance, a Porsche is not necessarily going to get you somewhere faster than a pickup truck can. On the other hand, if all you want are pickup trucks, the expense of a faster road is unnecessary.

Supercomputers or fast workstations that regularly exchange bandwidth-heavy information like audio or graphical data are at the high end of the networking scale. These machines probably need the 100 million bits-per-second (Mbps) bandwidth potential of optical fiber cabling. LANs made up of PCs that exchange moderate amounts of mail and text files, however, may never need more speed than inexpensive coaxial cable can provide.

As you pick your way among the different types of media and media topologies, projecting possible future networking needs is important.

Keep in mind that the cost of implementing a network, or "pulling" wire, includes media and labor. Wiring a building is expensive. Generally, you should choose a wiring plan that will suit your needs five years from now.

The chapter addresses the following topics:

- Copper and fiber media
- Copper and fiber media installation considerations
- Wireless LANs
- Physical topologies

The four basic types of copper wire commonly used for networking computers are *thick* and *thin coaxial*, *unshielded twisted pair*, and *shielded twisted pair*. Although all four types of copper wire are relatively inexpensive, they are quickly reaching speed boundaries. The more expensive optical fiber picks up where the speed of copper wire stops. The two types of optical fiber are glass, which is more expensive and more common; and plastic, which is harder to work with but is less expensive.

The three types of wireless LANs are *radio frequency (RF)*, *infrared*, and *microwave*. These generally are used as supplements to a network for situations in which more common cabling is difficult or impossible.

There are three basic types of wiring topologies: *bus*, *star*, and *ring*. Two other topologies—*point-to-point* and *multi-point*—have limited applications. In addition, structured-wiring schemes, or *hubs*, are becoming increasingly useful for making complicated networks simpler to set up and maintain. Hubs use physical star topologies, but they also provide combinations of logical star, bus, and ring topologies.

When you are setting up a network, paying attention to LAN protocol requirements is important also. The protocols reside on the various layers of the OSI model; from the standpoint of this chapter, the most important protocols reside in the physical layer, which directly interfaces with network media. The protocols usually are implemented as firmware on LAN chips or cards.

The three basic LAN physical layer protocols are Ethernet, token ring, and ARCnet, each of which runs over a variety of media. FDDI, a 100Mbps protocol, is primarily a wide-area network technology but is utilized for LANs that require very high-performance levels. FDDI was originally designed for optical media, but standards are being developed that will enable it to run over some types of twisted-pair wiring. In addition, Digital Equipment Corporation (DEC) offers FDDI over thin coaxial cable.

Each of the standards has a default topology. A *network topology* defines both the network's physical layout and the paths that electrical signals travel between networked devices. These two types of topologies are the network physical and logical topologies.

A network's physical topology describes the method of routing the communications medium. The *physical topology* is the part of the network that you can see and touch.

A network's *logical topology* describes the network's signal paths. Although you cannot see or touch it, the logical topology defines the way the network manages communication between devices. The logical topologies of the various network standards are discussed in Chapter 4.

Exploring Copper and Optical Fiber Data Communications Media

The significant differences between the different types of copper wire are cost, capability to withstand electrical interference, and bandwidth, which determines the number of nodes a network segment can support and the maximum distances between nodes.

Optical media are considerably more expensive than copper wire and more difficult to work with, but they have no electrical interference problems because the transport medium is light and can support much higher bandwidths.

Many networks use a mix of cabling: a higher bandwidth cabling for the network backbone; cheaper, less dense cabling to connect computers and other devices to the network.

The right cables and cabling configurations enable your computers to operate efficiently and may save you money. A network that efficiently serves the needs of the people by using the computers may save even more money.

Comparing Physical Media

Physical media can be compared in different ways, including their cost factors and physical characteristics.

Cost Comparisons of Physical Media

As mentioned earlier, four types of copper wire and two types of fiber optic cabling are used in computer networks today. Copper wire has been around a long time. It is inexpensive, well-established, and is already installed at many sites.

Fiber optic cables are considerably more expensive than copper wires. Today's fiber networks are almost exclusively glass. Plastic fiber optic cabling exists but is not widely used. Fiber connectors and other accessories are also more expensive than their older copper counterparts. Although considerable strides have been made toward simplifying the installation of optical fiber, fiber remains more difficult to install than copper. Fiber has strengths, however, that often justify the initial implementation costs.

A rough estimate of prices for the various common types of network-grade cables appears in table 3.1. Of course, prices vary widely depending on such factors as the number of conductors that are bound into the cable.

Table 3.1
Comparative Costs of Media Types

Media Type	*Price Range*
Unshielded Twisted Pair	$ .10—$ .25
Shielded Twisted Pair	$ .60—$ .80
Thin coaxial	$ .30—$ .55
Thick coaxial	$1.00—$2.00
Glass Fiber	$1.00—$1.80

Characteristics of Copper and Optical Fiber Media

Copper wire transmits bits of data via currents along the wire. As a by-product of the current, copper wire tends to leak radio waves into the air. These waves can cause interference with nearby electrical devices. On the other hand, electrical devices such as elevators can generate electrical interference that may affect the data running down the wire.

Fiber optic cabling, by contrast, transmits information via pulses of light. The light does not create, nor is it affected by, electrical interference. In addition, fiber optic cables have a much higher potential bandwidth than does copper wire.

Bandwidth is a measure of the range of signal frequencies that can be transmitted through a medium. A common telephone can transmit sound frequencies between 400Hz and 4000Hz; it therefore has a bandwidth of 3600Hz. Networks can have very high bandwidth requirements—bandwiths of 10-100Mbps are quite common. When greater capacity is required, bandwidth can be increased, either by transmitting multiple simultaneous signals through the medium or by increasing the frequency of the signals. As bandwidth and signal rates increase, the requirements of the signalling medium become more and more stringent.

Light travels down an optical cable, bouncing off the sides, at the same speed that an electrical signal travels down copper wire. However, light has a much higher frequency than an electrical signal, which enables optical fiber to support very high signal bandwidths. Although new technologies continue to push upward the signalling rate of copper media, the theoretical limits of optical fiber are considerably higher than the limits for copper, and optical fiber will remain the medium of choice for the highest bandwith at any given state of network technological development.

As users need more and more bandwidth, burgeoning bundles of copper wires can take up much more space than the slim optical fibers that carry a great deal more data. One advantage of optical fiber, therefore, is that the same cable path can support much more signaling potential with optical fiber than it can with copper. In many situations, copper cables are replaced with optical fiber to make better use of crowded cable raceways and conduits.

Because optical fibers are immune to electrical interference, they are more secure. It is much more difficult for a clandestine operation to capture data from lines that carry light because the light leaks out only at the ends of the fiber. Reading electrical output of copper wire is possible without tapping into the wire; physically tapping into a copper wire is easier than tapping into a fiber optical wire. By the same token, creating legitimate taps in optical fiber is more difficult than in copper wire.

Also, in areas where lightning strikes are a danger, a strike does not affect optical fiber, but it may send a great deal of current down a copper wire.

Optical fiber is required when connecting networks that reside in different buildings. Because the buildings often have different electrical ground potentials, spurious electrical currents may be produced if the locations are joined by copper cable; these currents, called *ground loops*, can cause havoc with electrical equipment. Optical fiber electrically isolates the different network segments and prevents the formation of ground loops.

The flip side of the coin is that fiber is expensive, and it is seldom pre-installed in many sites. Many protocols, such as Ethernet, at 10Mbps per second, do not go beyond the bandwidth capacity of copper wire. It is a common misconception that optical fiber inherently carries more data than copper cable. Actual performance is limited by the protocols employed, however, and Ethernet operates at 10Mbps, whether it is running on copper or optical fiber.

Descriptions of Physical Media Types

The following sections describe the different physical media types.

Unshielded Twisted Pair (UTP)

Unshielded twisted pair (UTP), has the lowest cost of copper wiring types. UTP consists of two copper wires twisted together and covered with a thin coating of plastic (see fig. 3.1).

This type of wire is commonly used for telephone wiring, which is an advantage. Many buildings are wired with four-wire UTP for telephone services, which take only two of the four wires, leaving two wires free for special telephone services or for data.

That extra twisted pair is less helpful than it might seem, however. The most common network standards, Ethernet and token ring, require two twisted pairs, one to transmit and one to receive. Therefore, it is not certain that a building prewired with telephone UTP will have sufficient wiring already in place to support a network.

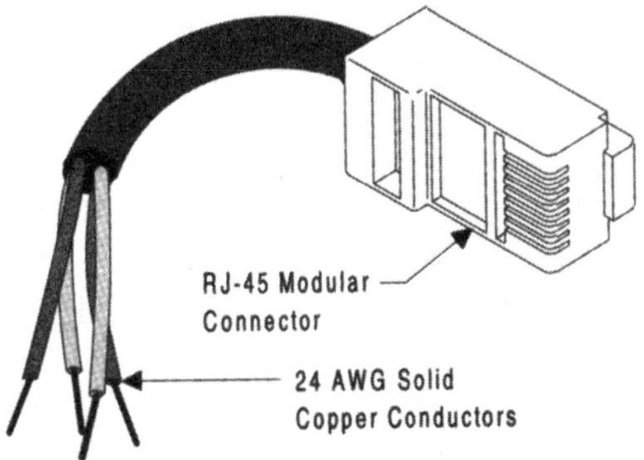

Figure 3.1:
Unshielded twisted pair (UTP) cable.

With the exception of coax, the conductors in a data cable must be twisted together. The twists in the wires act to cancel out each other's electrical emissions, help protect against outside electrical interference, and reduce radiation of radio frequencies. The twists do not completely isolate the wires from interference, however, as anyone who has strained to hear a voice on a crackling telephone can attest. The crackling you hear over phone lines may be caused by bad connectors or other devices on the line, as well as by electrical interference. Electrical interference can become a serious problem in buildings in which UTP is running close to electrical devices such as elevators.

Data cables never utilize untwisted cables. Without the twists, the cable has no capability to cancel outside interference. In fact, two parallel wires constitute an antenna, and radiated and received interference are critical problems. Uninformed installers of UTP networks frequently forget this and use conventional, untwisted, "flat satin" telephone cords to connect computers into the network (with mixed results).

Besides being sensitive to external interference, UTP has another potential risk. When wires carry an electrical current, they radiate electromagnetic fields. When the frequencies of these fields are high enough, the resulting radio frequency interference (RFI) can affect nearby electronic devices. The twists in UTP go only so far in cancelling out this interference, and a large amount of the engineering of high data-rate UTP networks has gone into controlling RFI emissions.

Another form of electrical interference can occur when multiple twisted-pair wires are bundled together. Signals from one wire pair may radiate and cause currents in nearby pairs. This phenomenon can occasionally be observed in telephone systems, when sound from one conversation interferes with another. The resulting crosstalk between the wire pairs becomes more troublesome at higher frequencies and places a limit on the maximum bandwidth of bundled UTP wires.

The three grades of UTP are categories one, two, and three. Category three has the best quality and the most common rating.

The low cost of UTP has made it attractive to many network installers, and considerable engineering expertise has been expended in extending the performance of UTP networks. Early in the development of token ring, it was thought that UTP could not support a data rate in excess of 4Mbps without interference and radiation problems. Vendors have extended the performance of UTP token ring, however, to support 16Mbps data rates. Even FDDI can be run at 100Mbps on UTP for short distances.

Although UTP has outperformed predictions of a few years ago, the potential bandwidth of UTP is now nearing a dead end. UTP has limited potential with FDDI and there will almost certainly be no future for UTP wiring beyond

FDDI. A recently proposed standard for FDDI on copper media requires shielded twisted pair. A 16Mbps token ring with short 100Mbps FDDI runs may be more than enough for many users, however, and UTP remains an attractive cabling alternatives for many networks.

The advantages of UTP are as follows:

- Relatively inexpensive
- Accessories are relatively inexpensive
- Easy to work with
- Well-established technology
- Many buildings are already wired with UTP

The disadvantages to UTP are as follows:

- Limited bandwidth
- Susceptibility to magnetic interference and crosstalk

Shielded Twisted Pair (STP)

Unlike UTP, the twisted pairs of copper wires in shielded twisted pair (STP) are individually shielded with aluminum foil or wire braid. The shield is grounded and prevents interference and signal radiation. Because each pair in a multi-pair cable has its own shield, crosstalk is not a problem with STP.

Some cabling standards call for STP to have thicker conductors than is common for UTP. Increasing conductor sizes in UTP result in only a marginal improvement in distance potential because other factors, such as interference and RFI, also contribute to limiting the range of UTP.

STP cabling standards usually enable STP cable runs to be longer than UTP. For example, the maximum distance between a station and a wiring hub on a token ring is 300 meters for STP, but it is only 100 meters for UTP.

Token rings represent the majority of STP networks. The IEEE 802.5 token-ring standards currently sanction UTP for a 4Mbps data rate only, although newly proposed standards will raise that limit to 16Mbps. See Chapter 4 for more information about token-ring cable requirements and data rates.

The advantages of STP are as follows:

- ❖ Support for longer cable runs than UTP
- ❖ Greater resistance to crosstalk and other interference than UTP

The disadvantages of STP cabling are as follows:

- ❖ More expensive than UTP and some varieties of coax
- ❖ Cable is bulkier than UTP and most types of coax; can quickly fill up cabling channels
- ❖ UTP is usually adequate in all but the most stringent environments

Coaxial Cable

Coaxial cable (*coax*) consists of a central conductor that is surrounded by a shield. The electrical nature of coax makes it highly resistant to interference and able to support wide bandwidths. Coax is frequently used in high bandwidth "backbone" networks that connect local networks. Because the backbone must support the traffic levels of all of the smaller networks, it requires greater bandwidth.

Coaxial cable is identified by its *impedance*, specified in ohms, which summarizes the cable's electrical characteristics. Common impedances are 50 ohms for Ethernet cables and 62 ohms for cables used with ARCnet. One characteristic of coax is that each end of the cable must end with a resistance that matches the impedances rating of the cable. A *terminator* is a connector that incorporates a proper resistor and can be connected to the cable end. This resistance balances the electrical characteristics of the cable and absorbs signals at the cable ends so that they cannot reflect back into the cable and cause interference.

Ethernets are among the common networks that commonly employ coax cables. Two forms of Ethernet cables exist: the heavy-gauge thick coax, known as standard Ethernet or thick Ethernet, and the smaller thin Ethernet. Both cable types are shown in figure 3.2.

Generally, thicker coax cables can carry signals farther and have greater bandwidth. Thick Ethernet network segments can service as many as 100 nodes over a total distances of up to 500 meters.

Thin coax cable is easier to work with and less expensive than thick coax cable. The tradeoff is that each thin coax network segment has a maximum cable run length of about 185 meters and supports a maximum of about 30 nodes. For many sites, this is enough.

Many businesses converting to local area networks already have large amounts of coaxial cable installed. IBM terminals, for example, are frequently connected via 62-ohm coax. Because ARCnet uses this same cable, it may be cost-effective to set up an ARCnet LAN. For new installations, however, UTP, STP, or optical fiber may be preferable choices.

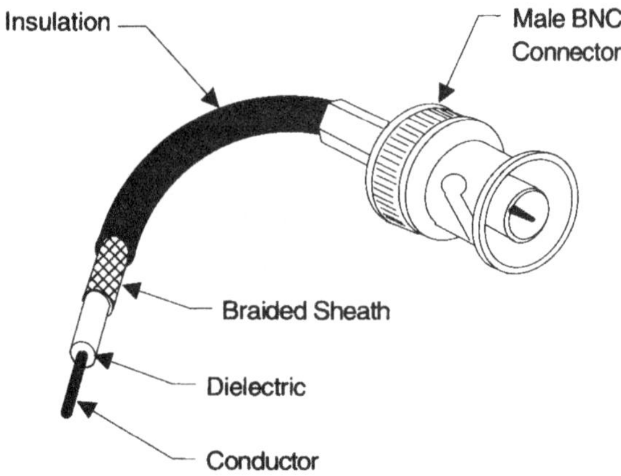

Figure 3.2:
Thick and thin coax are constructed the same way, but differ in the size of the conductors and cable diameter.

The advantages of coaxial cable are as follows:

- ❖ Easy to work with
- ❖ Resistant to interference
- ❖ High bandwidth
- ❖ Well-established technology
- ❖ Some buildings are already wired with coax cable

The disadvantages of coaxial cable are as follows:

- ❖ More expensive than twisted pair
- ❖ Not supported for some network standards, such as token ring

Optical Fiber

Optical fiber is the wave of the future, but is often a more costly choice than other cabling alternatives. Although considerably more expensive than copper wire, optical fiber outperforms copper in every respect: it has the potential to transmit more data faster and at greater distances, and it is insensitive to electrical interference.

Optical-fiber cabling uses pulses of light, rather than pulses of electricity, to transmit data. The light shoots down a thin glass tube at an angle that forces light waves to reflect back into the tube instead of leaking out.

Glass-fiber cabling is widely used. Plastic-fiber cabling has recently been introduced, and promises to reduce the cost of optical fiber cabling. Although plastic fiber is less expensive to manufacture than glass, it is less transparent, and plastic fiber cables cannot be run as far as glass. Because plastic fiber is used less often than glass, it may actually cost more than glass fiber, despite the lower manufacturing costs.

Optic fiber cable consists of a small fiber core—usually made of highly purified silicon—encased in a thin, light-absorbent plastic or glass jacket referred to as the *cladding*. The cladding is enclosed by a thicker plastic or Teflon jacket. The construction of a single fiber cable is shown in figure 3.3.

A light source at one end of the cable introduces coded light pulses into the fiber. The light source may be a laser diode or simply a light-emitting diode (LED). An LED is less expensive, but the laser diode is more efficient and can realize higher data rates. The light pulses are transmitted through the fiber to a photodiode at the other end, which receives the light pulses and converts them to electrical signals.

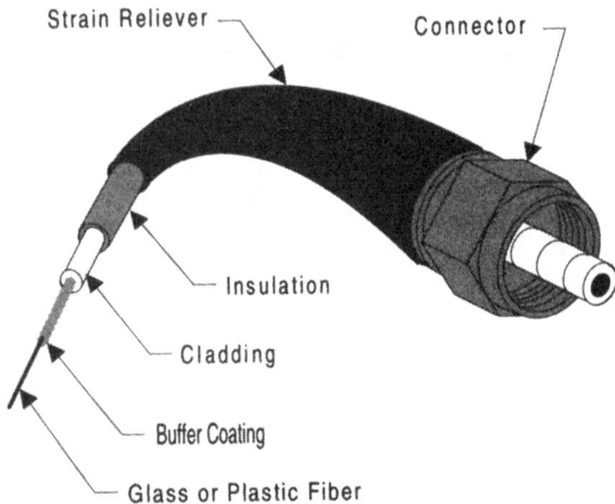

Figure 3.3:
Construction of an optical fiber cable.

One reason for turning to fiber is to achieve greater bandwidth. Fiber's bandwidth is a function of distance and type of fiber. Theoretically, if a one-kilometer length of fiber can transmit at about 100Mbps, a half-kilometer length of the same fiber can transmit twice as fast, at 200Mbps. The bandwidth of optical fiber is specified in terms of megahertz per kilometer (MHz/km).

Actual transmission rates are limited by the type of network, however. Ethernet is a 10Mbps network. There are 4Mbps and 16Mbps versions of token ring. FDDI has a theoretical limit of 100Mbps-per-second. It is possible to combine multiple network signals onto a fiber by using a technique known as *multiplexing*. A single fiber can, through multiplexing, carry the signals for ten separate Ethernets between two widely separated buildings in a campus setting. Each individual Ethernet continues to operate at an effective rate of 10Mbps, however.

Optical fiber transmission modes

As with most technologies, higher performance requires greater sophistication and comes at an elevated price. Fiber cables have three general performance levels, defined by the index and mode of the cable. The three types of cable are illustrated in figure 3.4.

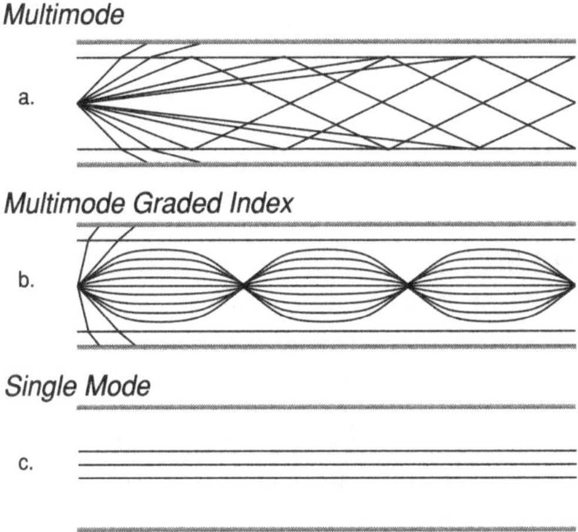

Figure 3.4:
Modes of operation for multimode, multimode graded index, and single mode optical fiber cables.

Multimode fiber is also known as *step-index multimode fiber.* Light introduced to a multimode fiber enters at a variety of angles. At some angles, the light escapes the fiber and is absorbed by the cladding. At other angles, the light is continuously reflected down the length of the fiber. The reflections in step-index fibers are slightly imperfect; spurious reflections limit the bandwidth the fiber can support. Multimode fiber has the lowest bandwidth of the three types of optical fiber and supports bandwidths up to 200 MHz/km.

Multimode graded-index fiber uses a glass fiber in which the index of refraction of the fiber is varied. Instead of reflecting signals, multimode fibers gradually bend the signals as they approach the cladding. The light remains more coherent, and bandwidth is increased. Multimode graded-index fibers are probably the most commonly used fiber types in local area networks. Multimode graded-index optical fiber supports bandwidths that range between the other two cable types, and is generally employed to support bandwidths of 100Mhz/km to 3GHz/km (giga or billion hertz).

Because light signals can follow different paths through multimode cables, the signals can take slightly different times to reach the receiving end of the cable. This characteristic limits the bandwidth that multimode cables can accommodate.

Single mode fiber has the greatest bandwidth. In this cable type, the diameter of the glass fiber is reduced so that only one coherent light signal will be transmitted. This eliminates the reflections and bendings of multimode cables, and dramatically increases bandwidth. Single mode fiber has the highest bandwidth of the three fiber types, and can provide bandwidths up to 50GHz/km.

The diameters of optical fiber cores are specified in terms of microns (millionths of a meter). This measurement is also known as the *aperture* because it represents the angle at which the cable can accept light. Common diameters are 50, 62.5, and 100 microns. 62.5-micron fiber is the most common type; it is the standard for FDDI, for example.

These extremely small diameters point to one of the major difficulties of installing fiber cable systems: in order to connect two fibers, the fiber ends must be very carefully aligned. The connectors, tools, and installation skills required to achieve this precision are all more expensive to obtain than what is required for installing copper cable. This is often the deciding factor cited by an organization selecting between optical fiber and copper; organizations usually have ready access to the tools and expertise required to install copper cabling systems.

Greater skill and care are also required for pulling optical fiber. Each cable has a minimum bend radius; bending the cable too sharply will break the glass fiber and make the cable useless. The difficulty of installing optical fiber is somewhat exaggerated, however. The technology for installing connectors has advanced considerably, and training for installation techniques is readily available.

A fiber test kit is also required. Improperly installed or damaged fiber can introduce losses that affect network operation. Cable testers should be considered mandatory tools for the support of any large network, whether it uses copper or optical fiber. A suitable instrument is available for as little as $400.

The initial expense of installing optical fiber must be measured against the potential of fiber to support data transmission rates required by busy networks. A network consisting of optical fiber may be the last network an organization needs to install.

Optical Fiber Cable Constructions

When you buy optical fiber, you are also buying the materials that surround it. The three basic optical-fiber cable constructions are *breakout*, *distribution*, and *loose tube* cable constructions. In each construction, cladding immediately surrounds the glass fiber and some kind of jacket surrounds the cladding.

The breakout and distribution constructions are commonly used indoors. The more rugged loose tube construction is most often used for outdoor cable runs.

A breakout cable has several fibers (often four), each with its own cladding and its own jacket. These subunits are bound together with a larger jacket.

A distribution cable is a breakout cable without the larger jacket.

In a loose tube cable, from one to 12 fibers float inside a loose tube filled with gel. Several of these tubes can be bound together to form thick cables. The more fibers per tube, the lower the cost per fiber. Loose tube construction is extremely rugged; the drawback is that the gel filling makes them messy to work with.

Fiber Networks

One type of network—*Fiber Distributed Data Interface* (*FDDI*)—was designed for optical fiber cabling. Fiber can be used with the other types of networks—Ethernet, token ring, and ARCnet—to extend the range of the network.

Optical fibers carry signals on one direction only, and a complete connection uses two strands of fiber, one for signals traveling in each direction.

The advantages of optical fiber are as follows:

- ❖ High bandwidth
- ❖ Technology has a long potential life
- ❖ Smaller and lighter than copper

Disadvantages of optical fiber are as follows:

- High initial expense
- More difficult and time-consuming to install than copper wire (although recent advances have closed the gap considerably)

Cabling Components

Besides the cable, there are four basic types of accessories for cable networks: connectors and taps, cross connects, repeaters, and wall plates.

Each cable type has a characteristic set of *connectors*, which are used to connect cable segments together or to interface devices with the cable. Connectors can include RJ-11 telephone-type connectors, exotic devices known as vampire *taps*, and precision connectors that are required to join segments of optical fiber. When a neat installation is required, wall plates provide unobtrusive connection points between a computer and the wiring in the walls of a building.

Because networks are seldom static, it is useful to have tools for reconfiguring from a central location. Two kinds of *cross connects*—punch-down blocks and patch panels—act like old-fashioned telephone-switchboard systems, enabling the connections between a device and the network to be easily altered. With cross connects it is easy, for example, to relocate a department in another building without changing the user's network connections.

Repeaters enable longer cabling runs by picking up, amplifying, cleaning up, and sending along electrical or optical signals. Repeaters are used when a network must exceed the maximum physical size allowed by the engineering standards.

Connectors

The most common type of connector on coax networks is the BNC connector. Connectors for coax must retain the relationship between the center conductor and the shield, and all have a pin in the center that is connected to the conductor. The BNC is a bayonet connector that twists into place; it is used for thin Ethernet, ARCnet, and a variety of other networks. The connector in figure 3.5 is a BNC. With the proper tools, these connectors are easy to install; the most important tool is a stripper designed for the specific cable and for the requirements of the specific brand of connector that will be used.

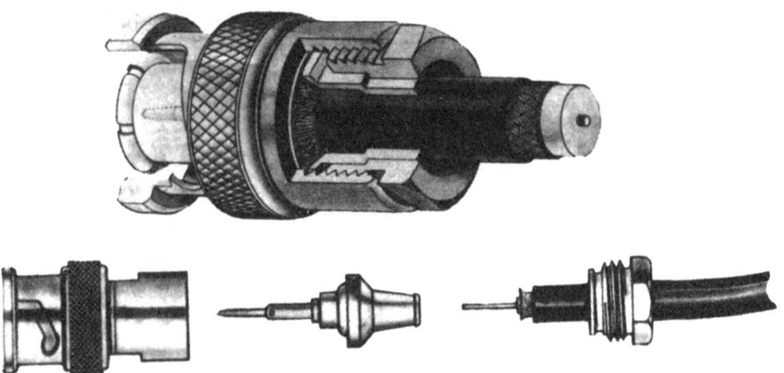

Figure 3.5:
A BNC connector.

Another common connector is the N connector used for thick Ethernet.

When coax segments must be connected, a barrel connector is employed, which enables the connectors on the end of two cables to be joined in line.

Devices usually connect to thin Ethernet coax by using a T connector (see fig. 3.6). To install a T connector, the main coax must be cut and connected to the crossbar of the T with BNC connectors. The device to be connected attaches directly to the base of the T. Connectors are generally the weakest spots in a network, and the T connector has many opportunities to fail. The many connectors and cables introduce a great deal of mechanical stress. It is recommended that top-quality cables and connectors be used to reduce the potential for failure.

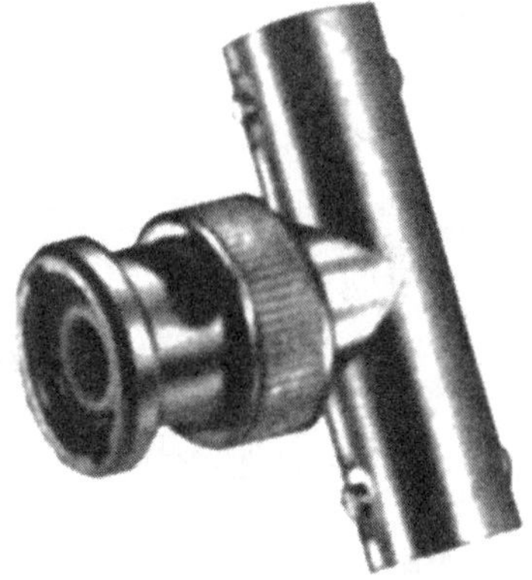

Figure 3.6:
A BNC-type T connector. (Courtesy of AMP, Harrisburg, PA.)

Alternatively, an innovative system of Ethernet connectors from AMP, Inc. can eliminate the vulnerable T connectors. The AMP LAN-LINE Thinnet Tap System consists of wall plates, cables, and drop boxes that make Ethernet cabling systems easier to reconfigure and less likely to fail. Some of the components in this system are shown in figure 3.7.

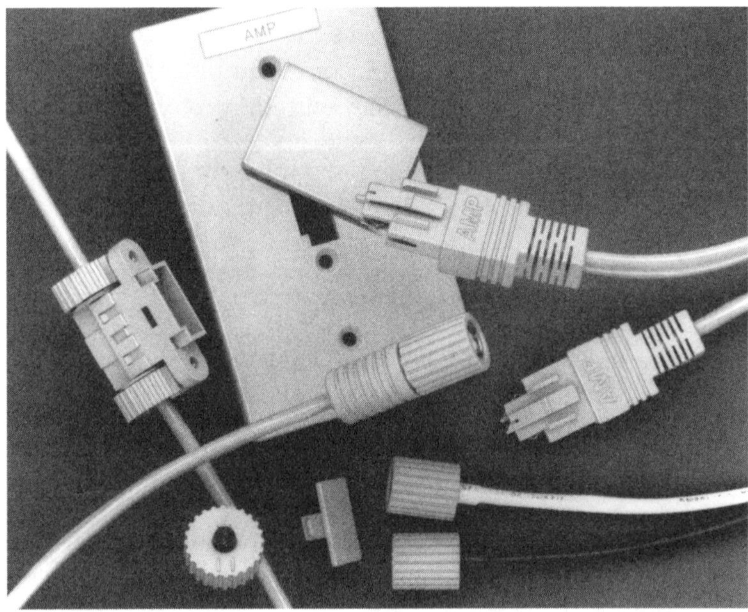

Figure 3.7:
Components in the AMP LAN-LINE Thinnet Tap System. (Courtesy of AMP, Harrisburg, PA.)

Devices are connected to a thick Ethernet by means of a *transceiver,* which is an active electronic device. A transceiver is an optional method of connecting devices to a thin Ethernet. The transceiver may be configured like a T tap, with two connectors for the main coax cable. The transceiver also has a D connector that is used to connect the network device through a transceiver cable.

Installing T connectors requires considerable work and forces installers to cut the main cable. An alternative connection method is the *vampire tap*. With this method, a hole is drilled in the connector to expose the central conductor. A tap is then clamped to the cable, so that its probes make proper contact with the shield and the conductor of the coax. Vampire taps are more commonly used with thick coax than with thin coax.

Connectors for twisted pair cables are made in bewildering variety. Common types include the following:

- D connectors, which consist of pins or sockets housed inside a D-shaped shell
- The IBM data connector, used most commonly in token rings
- Telephone-type snap connectors, such as the six-pin RJ-11 and the eight-pin RJ-45

The last option represents a highly desirable step toward standardization. Most network standards based on UTP cables utilize telephone connectors. These connectors are easy to attach to cables with the proper tools. They are inexpensive and available pre-made in a wide variety of lengths. Perhaps the only drawback of telephone connectors is that they cannot be used with shielded cables.

Repeaters

Although repeaters are not true connectors, they act like connectors. Repeaters are placed at key intervals in very long wire runs. They receive signals, amplify them, and then send them on, enabling longer cable runs.

Terminators

Terminators must be installed on the ends of most types of coax cables. A *terminator* is a connector that includes a resistor that balances the electrical characteristics of the cable. A BNC terminator is presented in figure 3.8.

Terminators are normally required only for bus physical topologies, of which Ethernet is an example. Cables in other physical topologies generally connect directly between two devices and are terminated by the devices themselves. This is the case for token ring and usually for ARCnet. Physical topologies are discussed later in this chapter.

Figure 3.8:
A BNC terminator. (Courtesy of Trompeter Electronics, Inc.)

Wall Plates

As the name implies, a *wall plate* is a plastic plate similar to those used in electrical outlets or telephone jacks. Instead of plugging an electrical device into a source of electricity, however, this type of wall plate enables you to plug a computer cable into a network.

It is seldom a good idea to string cables along the floor or to have them stick out of walls. Cables and connectors are the weakest links in a network, and any steps taken to reduce their vulnerability to damage will be repaid in greater reliability. AMP has been mentioned as one innovative manufacturer of wall plates and other cabling system accessories.

Cross Connects

Cross connects are devices that simplify the process of connecting devices to other devices. The two common types are punch-down blocks and patch panels.

Punch-down blocks are the classic cross-connect devices used for wiring in-house telephone systems. Usually used with UTP wiring, punch-down blocks consist of rows of split pins, installed in a box that is screwed to a wall. A punch-down tool is used to press the strands of wire into the split pins, which automatically cut through the insulation and make electrical contact. In the hands of an expert, the process of installing UTP on punch-down blocks is speedy and results in reliable connections. This is the system that keeps your telephone system running.

Punch-down blocks are somewhat difficult to reconfigure, however. Unless the LAN installation is carefully planned out in advance, network cabling tends to get chaotic: some parts of a department are connected to one punch-down block; some parts are connected to another. When it is time to move or reconfigure the department, it can be difficult to isolate all of the connections that are affected.

The ideal solution to this confusion is a *patch panel*, which is simply an array of connectors. Generally, the rear of the patch panel is connected directly to each network device. One device can then be connected to another by using a short patch cord to join the connectors on the front of the patch panel. This is a versatile system, and, because patch panels can be clearly labeled, an easy one to document and modify.

A potential drawback to patch-panel systems is that they require each device to be cabled to a central location, which can result in large concentrations of cables that may jam cabling paths. This problem is especially acute when heavy cables are used. UTP cables and fiber reduce the congestion.

Figure 3.9 illustrates a simple patch panel intended for installation in a standard 19-inch rack. Figure 3.10 shows other types of patch panels.

Figure 3.9:
A typical patch panel. (Courtesy of Trompeter Electronics, Inc.)

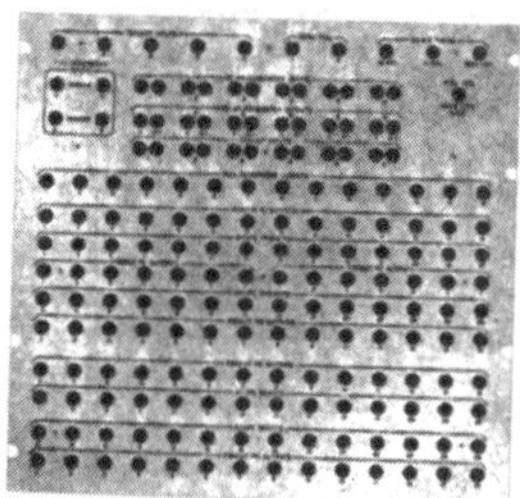

Figure 3.10:
Typical patch panels.

Copper and Fiber Installation Considerations

"Installing a network" can mean many different things. Setting up a five-node wireless LAN can take minutes or hours. Networking 25 machines that reside on four floors of a building is more demanding. Putting together a network that spans several buildings, or several states, is a whole order of magnitude more difficult.

When you are planning a LAN, the main considerations should be cost, reliability, ease of installation, and future plans. The overriding cost of installing a network is labor, not materials. It is unwise, therefore, to decide on a cabling system based only on the cost of the materials.

And then there are logistics. Where do you put the server? Where do you put the concentrator? A repeater? The wiring hub? Although the only limitations are limitations in allowable wire length, a good idea is to plan a network so that adding and removing nodes from the network is easy. The average network resident tends to move once a year.

Installing Copper Wire

Installing copper networks involves running the wire in the configuration on which you have decided, connecting computers to the network, and terminating any loose ends.

Network connectors have traditionally required at least some soldering for installation. However, the technology has now evolved to the point that most connector types are available in versions that can be installed using only crimping tools and screws. Crimping is an attractive method, but the proper tools are an absolute must. The tools can be expensive, but do not be tempted to shave costs. A good crimp is the only thing clamping the connector to the cable. Without a strong physical joint, the cable is certain to eventually fail.

UTP cable is frequently connected by using telephone connectors. These connectors are designed for speedy installation. Again, the proper tools are absolutely essential.

The two rules for connecting copper cable are to use the best connectors and to obtain the proper tools. Saving a few cents on a connector or a few dollars on a tool practically guarantees that your network will experience media failures.

Just because copper cable is familiar, it should not be taken for granted. Proper test equipment should be considered mandatory for any network, especially when any of the wiring is concealed. A cable tester is the only way to verify a cable that goes through a wall because a substitute cable cannot be put in its place.

It is also possible for a cable to be marginal when it is installed (because of a poorly installed connector, for example). By testing each cable at installation, you can identify such marginal links before they deteriorate and cause network failures.

The low-tech extreme of cable testing is to test the wires for continuity, which can be done with a voltmeter or an inexpensive battery-powered tester. However, the requirements of data cables are far more complicated than those for conducting an electrical current. At the signal frequencies employed by LANs, data cables are extremely complex electronic devices that can be made inoperable for a wide variety of reasons.

More sophisticated cable testers are available that test the wires under network conditions. Expect to pay between $1000 and $5000 for such equipment. Although the cost of a proper cable tester appears daunting, such a device can pay for itself the first time it enables you to restore proper function to a network within minutes instead of hours or days.

One advanced cable technique is time domain reflectometry. A *time domain reflectometer (TDR)* can examine a cable from one end and can, for example, estimate the distance from the end at which a cable failure might have occurred.

Installing Fiber

As a rule, installing copper wire is less difficult and less time-consuming than installing fiber cables, although recent improvements in fiber-installing technology have closed the gap considerably.

Because optical fiber is made of glass, it is a little trickier to install than copper wire. Fiber installations traditionally require epoxy to literally glue fiber pieces together. The glue then needs to dry overnight or under a heat gun. To successfully dry, or "cure," a connection takes about 30 minutes. Recently, a second system of splicing optical fiber (which is much more like that used to splice copper and does not require heat) has come onto the market.

The end of a fiber optic cable, like that of copper wire, must be prepared for a plug by stripping back the jacket materials.

Beneath the jacket material (in the case of fiber) another kind of material surrounds each glass strand. This is *kevlar*, a filament used in bulletproof vests and tires, which looks like string and is often yellow. This kevlar coating is the cladding. It cannot be removed from the glass core.

As with copper wire, the glass fiber is put into the connector and must be flush with the tip of the connector. The end of the glass fiber must then be polished, to make sure that it is even with the connector and to provide a clear, unscratched surface for the light transmission.

If you are using epoxy, you apply it as you place the fiber in the connector. Then you put the fiber end and connector into the *curing oven*, which is a little box about the size of a toaster that contains a heating element.

The curing process takes approximately 30 minutes when the connection is placed in a curing oven; it takes 24 hours when the connection must cure at room temperature.

A second method of connecting fiber is similar and takes about as long as the crimping method. A toolkit for installing connectors on fiber optic cables is available at a cost of about $1,200; this kit, manufactured by AMP and available from Black Box Corporation and other sources, uses new methods of installing connectors by crimping, which eliminates the need for heat-cured epoxy.

Some users still swear by the original epoxy, claiming that the epoxy makes for a better connection. Many consultants who have worked with both types of connections say that both are good ways to connect fiber.

Even with the new system, fiber is more difficult to work with than copper. Tools are more expensive and special training is sometimes necessary (few cable installers have experience with optical fiber).

As with copper cable, do not forget the test equipment. Earlier it was mentioned that an inexpensive tester is available for under $400. Optical time domain reflectometers also exist, but they are far more difficult to use than their copper cousins, in addition to being more expensive.

Using Wireless Network Media

There are two kinds of wireless local area networks: radio-frequency and infrared. In addition, wireless microwave technology can be used to connect LANs together.

Generally, wireless LANs are more expensive to implement than are cabled LANs. Like hubs, wireless LANs that contain a server become less expensive per node as you add nodes. In general, however, adding a node to a wireless network costs about $500, compared to about half that (or less) for the adapter card, cabling, and labor involved in attaching a new node to a conventional cabled network.

The big advantage of wireless media is network flexibility—moving a wireless node is easy. Moving a cabled node leaves cabling behind, usually requires new cable, and involves a substantial chunk of labor. A wireless move generally requires just the actual move of the equipment, and, in some cases, the realignment of wireless components. The costs for shifting a frequently moved node on a cable network go up much faster than do costs for a frequently moved wireless node. Because wireless LANs can be set up quickly, a wireless LAN may be a good choice for a portable network of laptop computers.

Wireless network connections are wonderful ways of networking portable computers in an office. Shared computers on mobile desks can be relocated at will. Laptops can be set up anywhere there is a free surface.

Wireless LANs may be a good alternative to cable in older stone buildings or in other locations in which running wire is difficult or impossible. Not all wireless networks can penetrate walls, however, including low-power radio frequency LANs and infrared LANs.

Wireless networks can also be used in combination with cabled LANs. It might be fiscally wise to use a wireless link for a workgroup slated for frequent moves in a building, for example, or for network nodes residing in a difficult-to-wire location.

There are drawbacks, however, to each of the three wireless technologies. Although the radio-frequency medium does not require line-of-sight operation, it is subject to FCC regulation of the airwaves. Microwave is subject to health regulations. In addition, direct-frequency, radio-frequency, and microwave LANs can be tapped easily by intercepting the airwaves. An infrared LAN requires line-of-sight between connections, but this makes it fairly secure—it is immediately apparent when an infrared LAN is being tapped.

Radio-frequency and infrared technologies are fairly new. According to InfoCorp, a market research firm in Acton, Massachusetts, wireless LAN use will increase substantially in the next few years to capture about six percent of the market by 1996. This should drive prices down in comparison to cabling technologies.

Radio-Frequency Wireless LANs (RF)

Radio-frequency wireless LANs rely on a variety of technologies. The most popular products are based on a technology called *spread-spectrum* or on a system similar to that used by cellular telephones.

Spread-spectrum, a technology used by most RF suppliers, uses a switching algorithm to flit between several frequencies (making the LAN much more difficult to tap). Most spread-spectrum LANs operate in a frequency range of 902-928MHz. This frequency range has been allocated by the FCC (much like citizen's band radio) as a range that can be utilized for various purposes without the requirement of a license. Any LAN designed to operate in this frequency range must be able to cope with interference from other devices that also operate on those frequencies, such as burglar alarms and amateur radios. These frequencies are also subject to electrical interference.

Unlicensed equipment using 900MHz frequencies are strictly limited to a maximum transmitting power of one watt. Nevertheless, many designs have sufficient power to transmit through masonry walls. The maximum effective distance is determined by the types of obstructions through which the signal is transmitted.

A premier spread-spectrum network system is WaveLAN, manufactured by NCR Corporation. This is a 2Mbps network system that utilizes a proprietary protocol. WaveLAN uses a robust error-checking protocol that can detect and correct most transmission errors. A data-encryption option makes the network highly resistant to electronic eavesdropping. Figure 3.11 illustrates how each station on a WaveLAN broadcasts signals to every other station. By monitoring the airwaves, the stations can suspend transmitting until the network is silent. Notice that WaveLAN can transmit through some types of wall construction.

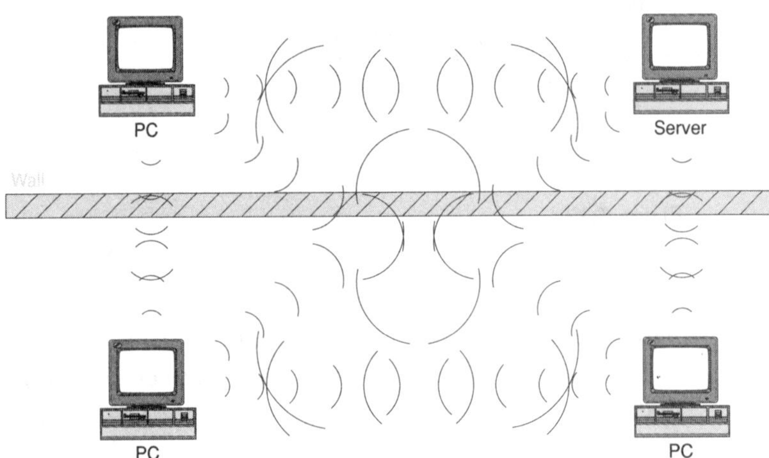

Figure 3.11:
Operation of an NCR WaveLAN network.

Today's RF LANs generally have a top bandwith of about 2Mbps and a distance range of several hundred feet. One notable exception is the Altair Plus wireless Ethernet system from Motorola. Altair Plus is a secure, cost-effective network that operates at Ethernet speeds and integrates smoothly with the Ethernet environment. Figure 3.12 is a photograph of some of the Altair network components.

Figure 3.12:
Components of an Altair Plus network. (Courtesy of Motorola, Inc.)

Altair Plus utilizes an approach that is similar to that used for cellular telephones, a technology with which Motorola is intimately familiar. Cellular telephones divide the communication geography into cells, each of which is serviced by a communication hub. Both telephones and the hubs use low-power transmissions so that they will not interfere with nearby cells; this enables nearby cells to reuse frequencies without interfering with each other.

Altair Plus likewise uses low-power radio communication, operating at a frequency of 18GHz (giga or billion Hertz) at a power level of only .0025 watts (25 milliwatts). Use of this frequency requires an FCC license. Allocation of frequencies in the assigned range is managed by Motorola in conjunction with the FCC.

Altair Plus networks center around a *microcell,* which consists of a Control Module that maintains radio contact with User Modules. Workstations are connected to the User Modules through coax or 10BASE-T Ethernet connections. A given Control Module can support up to 50 workstations, and a microcell can cover an area between 5,000 and 50,000 square feet, depending on building construction.

Because of low operating power, Altair Plus signals cannot penetrate most masonry walls. Conventional Ethernet segments can be used to build large Altair Plus LANs or to extend the network past radio obstructions. As an alternative to Ethernet cabling, Motorola has introduced the Altair VistaPoint product for bridging microcells across distances up to 500 feet.

Compatibility with Ethernet is one of the great advantages of Altair Plus, enabling conventional Ethernet segments and radio-frequency segments to be easily integrated. Figure 3.13 shows how the components in an Altair Plus network interact.

Another significant feature of Altair Plus is its capability to act as a network-management agent using SNMP standards.

Advantages of radio-frequency wireless LANs are as follows:

- Easy moves, adds, and changes to the LAN
- Connections do not require line of sight

The following are disadvantages:

- Direct-frequency RF LANs are easy to tap
- Direct-frequency RF LANs require licensing

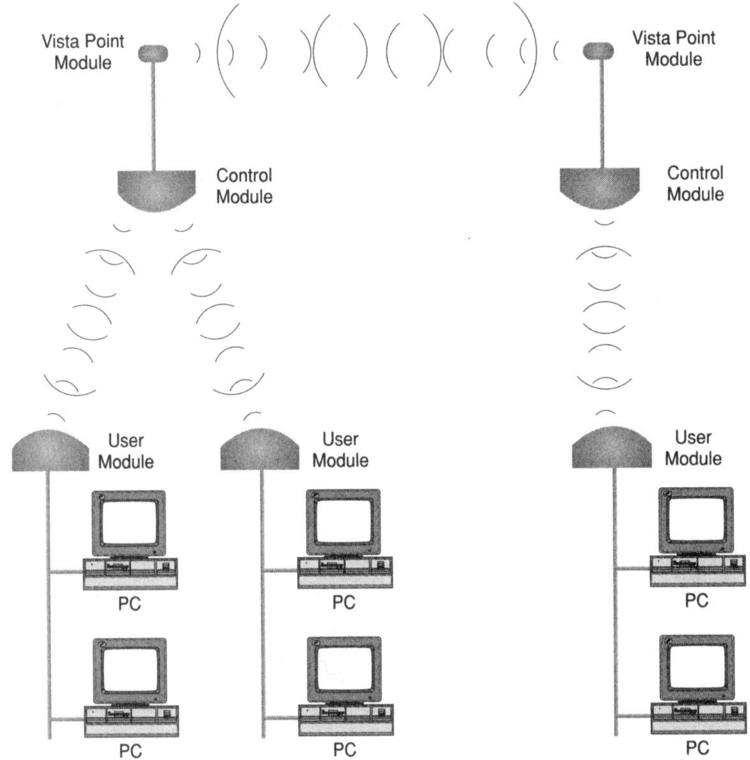

Figure 3.13:
Interaction of components in an Altair network.

- May be prone to interference in some areas
- Twice the cost of traditional cable-based LANs
- Many systems have low bandwidth

Infrared LANs

Infrared LANs use *infrared signals* (the wavelengths beyond visible light) to transmit data, using the same basic technology as the infrared remote control on a television. Infrared signals are extremely safe and are not subject to any government regulations.

The two types of infrared LANs are *sun-and-moon* and *point-to-point*. Both types use a line-of-sight signal, but sun-and-moon LANs use diffused infrared at a low-power frequency, whereas direct or point-to-point infrared uses a stronger, more precisely aimed signal. See figure 3.14 for comparisons of the two network configurations.

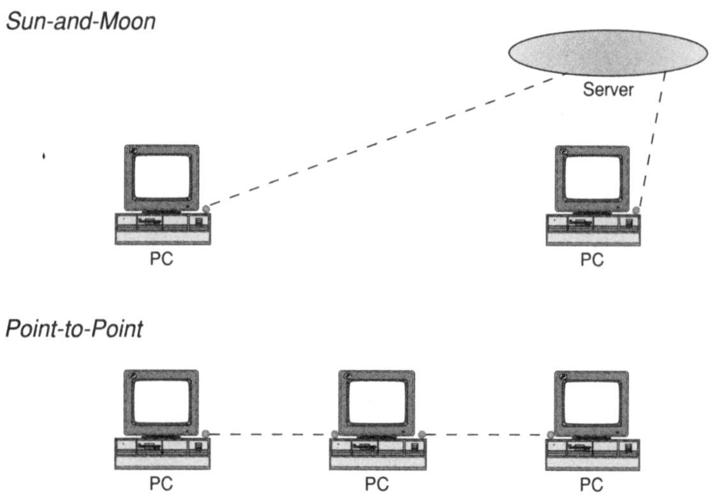

Figure 3.14:
Alternative configurations of infrared networks.

The drawback to the sun-and-moon system is that the distance between nodes and server is limited to 20 feet and bandwidth is limited to 250K per second. These systems are very easy to set up, however. Because the signals are diffused, much like those used in TV remote controls, they do not need to be precisely aimed. Consequently, they are more portable than point-to-point or cable-based LANs.

The BICC Communications InfraLAN is a point-to-point infrared LAN that supports token-ring protocols. (The token-ring architecture is described in detail in Chapter 4.) In token ring, workstations connect to devices called *multistation access units (MAUs)*. A MAU can generally support eight stations and can be connected together to support additional stations.

InfraLAN MAUs support six workstations, to which they connect via standard copper cables. The wireless network technology comes in when the MAUs must be interconnected. This is done by means of infrared receivers and transmitters. MAUs can be placed up to 80 feet apart. InfraLAN supports token-ring protocols at speeds up to 4Mbps. Figure 3.15 shows some of the InfraLAN network components from BICC Communications.

Some brands of point-to-point infrared LANs use mirrors and lenses to extend the distance between nodes to as much as 80 feet and increase bandwith to as much as 16Mbps. One drawback of point-to-point infrared LANs is that they must be aimed precisely.

A variation of the point-to-point LAN uses a laser to establish a connection over an extended distance. This technology can be used as an alternative to microwaves when networks can be connected via line of sight. Unlike microwaves, however, laser beams are subject to easy interruption and are not resistant to rain or physical obstructions.

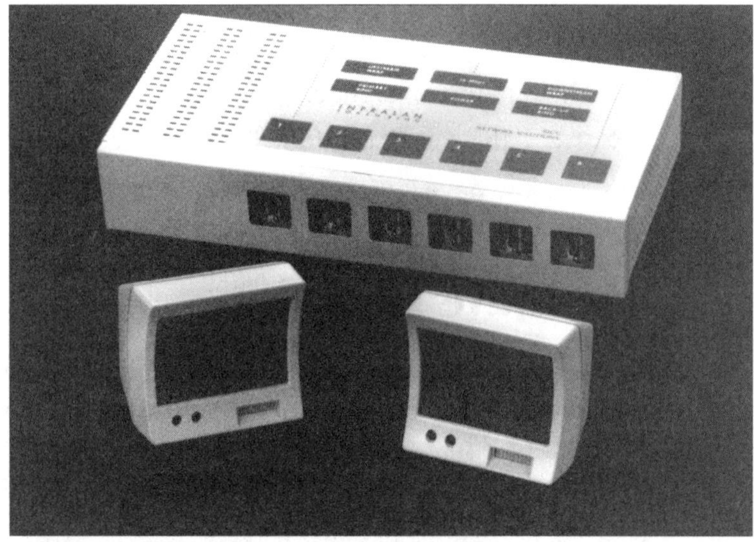

Figure 3.15:
Base unit and nodes of InfraLAN infrared wireless LAN. (Courtesy of BICC Communications.)

Infrared LANs are fairly secure. Because they can be tapped only by directly co-opting the light signal, you must be very close to the LAN to listen in. In addition, point-to-point infrared LANs can be tapped only by intercepting the light signal, which brings down the LAN.

The advantages of infrared LANS are the following:

- Ease of adding and moving equipment on the LAN
- Easy installation because cabling is not required

The disadvantages are as follows:

- ❖ Require line-of-sight configuration
- ❖ Twice the cost of traditional cable-based LANs
- ❖ Usually have low bandwiths

Microwave Technology

Microwave technology is not really a LAN technology. Rather, it is an interconnect technology used to bridge LANs between buildings or across town. Signals are carried on microwaves, which are high frequency, short-wavelength radio waves.

A microwave connection requires microwave dishes on both ends of the link. The dishes must be in a line-of-sight configuration to transmit and collect the microwave signals.

Microwave bridging is used as a bypass technology. In cities, it is a way to avoid using the telephone company to do wiring when you want to connect LANs between buildings. In the long run, a microwave link usually is cheaper than leasing a dedicated line from a telephone company. In addition, you are not subject to the telephone company's rate fluctuations.

As more and more companies use microwave and satellite dishes, there have been complaints about the looks of the large dishes. In some cities, zoning laws control the kinds of objects companies can place on buildings.

According to microwave manufacturers, weather problems are largely a myth, but those who sell alternative technologies insist that heavy rain interrupts microwave transmission. Generally, rain is not a big problem for microwave transmission. This is, after all, the technology used by telecommunications providers for many line-of-site communication links.

Advantages of microwave transmission are:

- Private and under control of the owner
- Often less costly than a leased line

Microwave transmission has the following disadvantages:

- Involves a large initial investment
- Can be an eyesore
- Problems with city zoning laws

Understanding Physical Topologies

A *physical topology* is literally the way the wiring is strung between network nodes. Figure 3.16 illustrates five basic network physical topologies, which span a wide range of complexity. Each of these network types is described in greater detail in this section.

Of the five illustrated types of networks, point-to-point and multi-point networks can be quickly dismissed as special-purpose approaches.

A *point-to-point* connection is a dedicated connection between two devices. Such connections are generally used when performance is the overriding concern. It might be used to implement a high-speed connection between two network servers or multiuser hosts, for example. Point-to-point connections are seldom utilized for normal traffic levels or to service workstations.

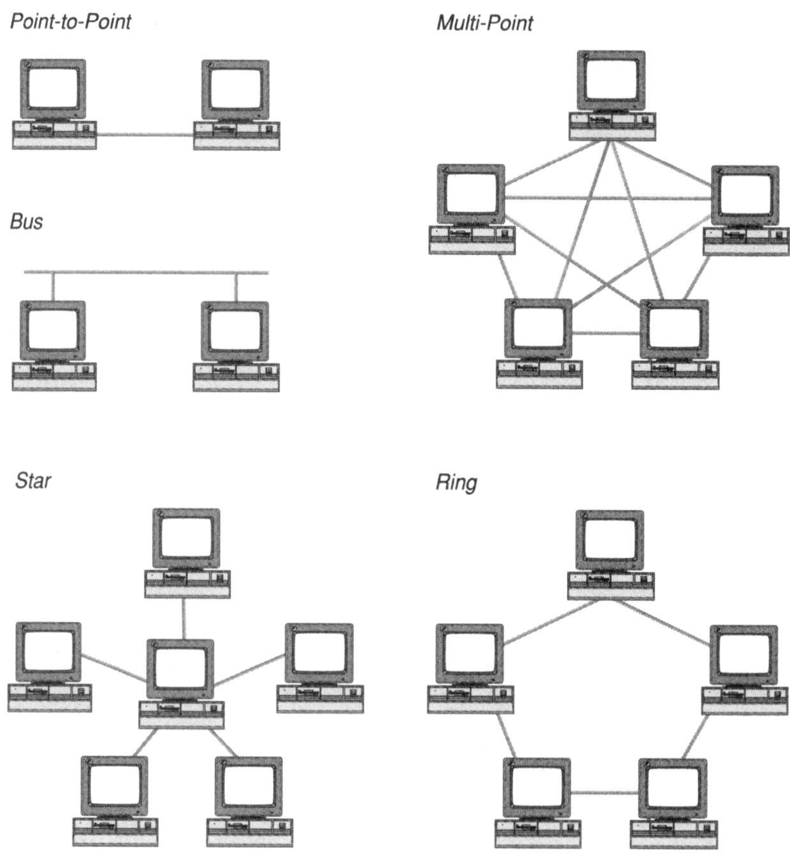

Figure 3.16:
Network physical topologies.

Multi-point connections implement a point-to-point connection between each pair of stations that needs to communicate. Cost of such a network escalates astronomically when more than a few stations are involved. This inflexible approach has little applicability to enterprise networks.

The main idea behind a local area network is that logical point-to-point connections can be established between any two stations on the network while sharing a common, inexpensive medium. A logical connection enables nodes to exchange data as if they were directly connected. The nodes, however, are sharing a common network on which various node-to-node messages are carefully routed and efficiently controlled. By combining a high-performance cabling system, as described in this chapter, with efficient protocols, stations can behave as though they are directly connected to each other even though they are "time-sharing" a common network.

The following section discusses the three LAN physical topologies that support efficient use of network resources: the star, ring, and bus topologies. Keep in mind that a network also has a logical topology that defines the way the network functions beneath the surface. A network often has a logical topology that is different from its physical topology. (Logical topologies are described in Chapter 4.)

Bus Topology

A *bus* is the simplest form of multinode network. In a bus topology, all network nodes connect directly to the same piece of cable. A bus network operates like the accessory bus in a PC. An *accessory bus* consists of a series of parallel wires that connect to every card that is plugged into an accessory slot. Although each card can potentially connect to each wire, individual cards can be selected through various schemes, such as addressing or hardware interrupts.

A segment of a network that uses a bus topology is a length of wire, usually coax, capped at each end with a terminator (see fig. 3.17); it does not connect back on itself. When a station on the network transmits a message, the electrical signal travels in both directions from the origination point until it reaches the end of the cable, where it is absorbed by the terminators. As the signals propagate down the cable, each station on the cable can examine the data. By adhering to the rules of a network protocol, each station actually retrieves only those messages that are intended for it.

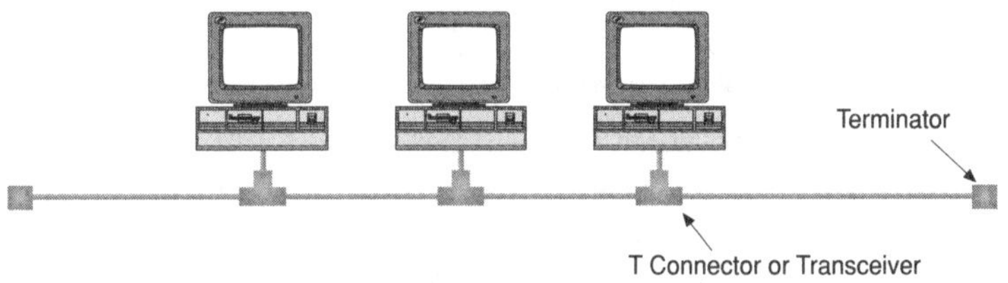

Figure 3.17:
Sample bus topology setup.

Ordinarily, servers, PCs, and workstations connect to the cable by means of transceiver lines that connect to the cable segment through T taps or vampire taps (refer to this chapter's "Cable Accessories" section).

The chief attraction of the bus topology is its extreme simplicity. Stations in close proximity can be networked simply by stringing a cable from station to station and tapping the station into the cable. A bus is also efficient to install.

The thin and thick Ethernet networking protocols runs over a bus topology, but not all buses run Ethernet. ARCnet can also be configured for a bus physical topology.

Due to the electrical characteristics of a bus, every component on a bus network is capable of affecting the entire network. If a cable is broken at some point, the problem will be more severe than simply losing contact with stations on opposite sides of the break. The break which actually causes each section of the cable to lose its termination, and signals can reflect back from the break, causes interference on the entire cable. Similarly, one bad station sending out noise can bring down the entire bus. Under such circumstances, it can be difficult to isolate the cause of the problem—where the cable break is or which station is causing the interference.

Bus topologies are limited in the number of nodes that can occupy a segment. As each new node is added to the cable, it absorbs a part of the signal on the cable; at a certain level, the signal strength falls to a point so low that it can no longer be relied on. An Ethernet segment can only support 30 nodes, for example. Beyond that, limit repeaters must be added to create new network segments that can support additional workstations.

Advantages of a bus topology are as follows:

- ❖ Uses a minimal amount of wire
- ❖ Requires only inexpensive network hardware

Disadvantages include the following:

- ❖ A single cable break or malfunctioning node can bring down the whole LAN

Star Topology

In a star cabling topology, a central system—which can be a server or a wiring hub—connects PCs or workstations. A wire runs from the central system to each node on the network, as shown in figure 3.18.

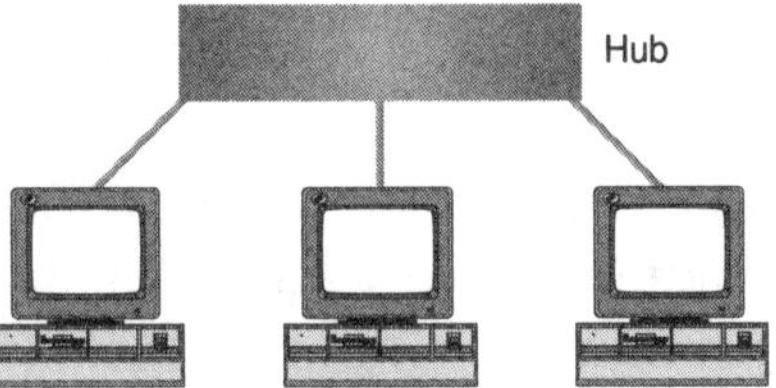

Figure 3.18:
Sample star topology setup.

Because each computer on a network requires its own wire to connect to a server or network hub, the star topology tends to use more cable than either bus or ring topologies; wiring channels may overflow with the many cables required to implement a star topology. The central wiring concentrators also represent a cost that is not required for a bus network. In general, star networks represent the highest-cost physical topologies.

Despite this high cost, however, most network designs are tending toward star topologies. Because each machine in a star network is individually wired, a cable break affects only one machine. Concentrators are also excellent places to house network diagnostic devices. Because all signals are routed through the concentrator, they can be monitored from a central place. The higher cost of a star network is usually justified by the greater reliability that it provides.

Star topologies are employed for ARCnet, token ring (despite the name, a token ring is wired in a star), and a recently introduced version of Ethernet called 10BASE-T.

The advantages of a star topology include:

- ❖ Greater node autonomy: a cable break affects only the machine connected by that cable
- ❖ Centralized locations for network diagnostic equipment

The primary disadvantages are as follows:

- ❖ Requires a great deal of cable
- ❖ Requires central concentrator components, which add to network cost

Ring Topology

The foundation of a ring network is a loop of cable. Unlike a bus, in which a signal is broadcast throughout the network cable, ring networks operate by passing signals from node-to-node around the ring. Terminal servers, PCs, and workstations connect to the ring, as shown in figure 3.19. Each node receives a message that is passed to it and, if the message is intended for another node, repeats the signal to the next node. Because this repeating action amplifies and reconditions each message in order to pass it on, ring networks are less sensitive—increasing quantities of nodes on the network.

Local area networks are seldom implemented with ring physical topologies. Chapter 4 shows that token ring, despite the "ring" in its name, is actually wired as a star because the star configuration offers advantages in terms of centralization and troubleshooting.

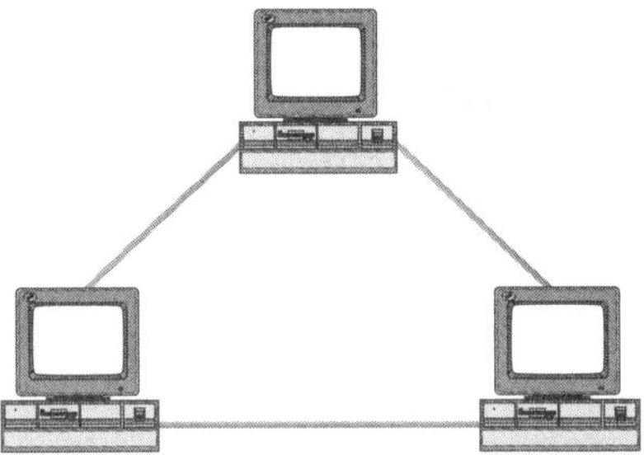

Figure 3.19:
Sample ring topology setup.

Ring topologies are seldom used in LANs because they do not offer a central point for network management. More commonly, rings are implemented over large geographic areas in which a star would be inefficient. A ring can be run to connect several sites within a city or even several cities across a multistate area. Rings are also implemented for fault-tolerant backbone technologies.

Most ring networks provide fault tolerance by implementing a backup signal path. If a break affects one of the ring segments, the signal can often be routed back through the ring's backup path. When a cable break failure occurs in a ring network, it causes the network to reroute the messages through the backup path, which usually runs in the direction opposite to the main path. This doubles the ring distance (slowing down the network), but it keeps the network running. Network-management software can monitor the network and notify operators that the backup path has been switched in.

Many networks are actually hybrids of rings and stars. Individual star concentrators are connected together to form a ring. This is the approach chosen for token ring.

Advantages of a ring topology are as follows:

- Redundant media paths can reroute messages when a cable break occurs
- Uses cables efficiently when covering a large geographic area

Disadvantages include the following:

- There is no central place to monitor the network

Structured Wiring Topology

Structured wiring is being used increasingly as networks get more complicated. Structured wiring systems consist of concentrators that accept plug-in modules. Some of these modules are wiring hubs, which support network connections between stations and the concentrator. Most hub modules support between eight and 12 connections. Many concentrator types can service several types of logical networks, as well as bridges, routers, repeaters, and terminal servers. Concentrators can also contain component spares or redundant components to make networks fault-resistant or fault-tolerant.

A network hub is illustrated in figure 3.20. This hub from Hewlett-Packard supports twelve workstations using the 10BASE-T Ethernet standard.

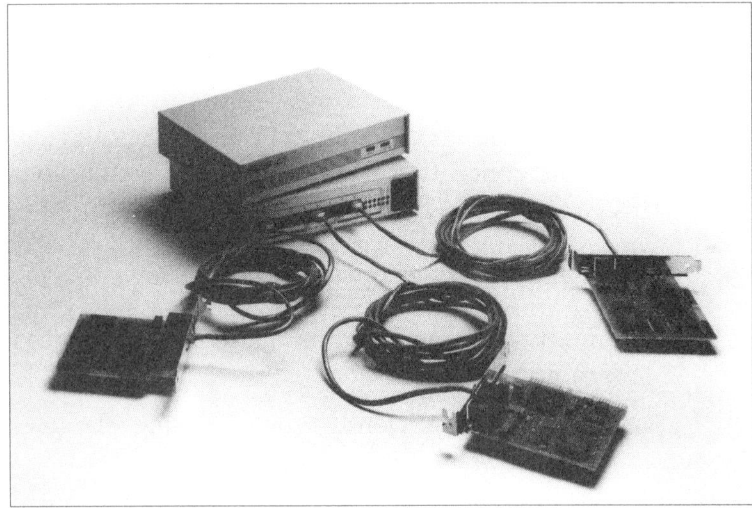

Figure 3.20:
A stand-alone Ethernet hub connected to network cards. (Courtesy of Hewlett-Packard Co.)

Several models of Cabletron concentrators are illustrated in figure 3.21. These concentrators can house a wide variety of modules.

Structured wiring is considerably easier to manage than the nonstructured types of daisy-chained or star topologies.

Structured wiring distinguishes between a network's physical and logical topologies. All hubs use physical star topologies, but the logical topology can be ring, bus, or star. Also, several different networks with the same or different logical topologies can exist at once in a single hub. The concentrator conserves cabling by putting the cable backbones in a box.

Figure 3.21:
Three models of Cabletron's large Multi Media Access Center (MMAC) smart network hubs. (Courtesy of Cabletron Systems, Inc.)

Some structured cabling systems support stand-alone hubs, which can operate outside of a concentrator. *Stand-alone hubs* are small units that cannot be expanded. Because each hub is the center of a star topology, the connections from node to hub are star connections. The connections between hubs are a distributed network, however, and can be another hub or a bus, ring, or star. Hub and concentrator architectures are highly modular. Hundreds of nodes can all be connected to one physical star topology.

Hubs can contain bridges, routers, and terminal servers as well as various logical networks. Hubs may also contain network-management cards and support Simple Network-Management Protocol (SNMP).

Many hubs are sold as segmented products. You can buy a base product with one LAN module that supports 12 nodes on an Ethernet, for example, and then buy add-in modules when you want to add more nodes, such as a token-ring LAN, router, terminal server, or bridge (such as the slide-in bridge module shown in fig. 3.22).

As a general rule, the bigger the network, the lower the hub cost per node. Hubs are more costly than simple networks but offer several savings. The hub's high-performance backplanes allow for better throughput than other networking schemes. In addition, hubs allow for more flexibility than traditional networks.

Because a hub's logical setup is different from the physical network, moves, adds, and changes can be done without changing cables.

Because a hub uses a physical star topology, locating cable faults, which account for most LAN problems, is easier because only one node is affected by a fault. Because only one node is affected, you know immediately where the cable fault is.

Although hubs are extremely flexible and can grow with a network, they often mean a heftier initial investment than that needed for more traditional wiring schemes. But the concentration of network components and the separation of physical and logical topologies makes hub-network management simpler and less expensive than other methods. Generally, the per-port price for hubs decreases as the network grows.

Figure 3.22:
A slide-in bridge module for Cabletron's line of smart hubs. (Courtesy of Cabletron Systems, Inc.)

Advantages of structured wiring systems include:

- ❖ Isolation of cabling for each node makes it easy to locate cable faults
- ❖ Plug-in modules make it efficient to move, add nodes, and change the network configuration
- ❖ Availability of integral network-management support

Disadvantages include the following:

- ❖ High start-up costs
- ❖ Higher per-node costs due to the high use of active components

Accessing Vendors

The following vendors supply these networking equipment mentioned in this chapter:

AMP Incorporated
P.O. Box 3608
Harrisburg, PA 17105-3608
(800)522-6752

BICC Communications
103 Millbury Street
Auburn, MA 01501
(508)832-8650

Black Box Corporation
P.O. Box 12800
Pittsburgh, PA 15241
(800)552-6816

Cabletron Systems, Inc.
35 Industrial Way
P.O. Box 5005
Rochester, NH 03867-0505
(603)332-9400

Motorola, Inc.
Altair Products Operations
3209 N. Wilke Road
Arlington Heights, IL 60004
(708)632-4723

NCR Corporation
1700 S. Patterson Blvd.
Dayton, Ohio 45479
(800)225-5627

Summary

Cabling, connectors, and wiring topologies may not be as interesting as the hot new superfast RISC machine on your desk, but choosing the right wire, accessories, and configuration for your current and future needs is as important as your choice of a computer. A network should be able to handle the traffic you need as you grow and it should be one you feel comfortable supporting.

The general trends in cabling are moving toward unshielded twisted pair wiring, fiber optic wiring, and wireless networks (away from thick and thin coax and shielded twisted pair wiring).

Unshielded twisted pair is and will remain the cheapest way to network computers. It is inexpensive, easy to work with and install, and already exists in many buildings. UTP has performance limitations, however, that prevent it from becoming the foundation for the next generations of copper network systems, such as FDDI on twisted pair. In the short term, shielded twisted pair remains attractive as a low-cost alternative to optical fiber.

Fiber optic cabling, with its low bulk, high bandwidth, and immunity to electrical interference, is becoming the cabling of choice for new network backbones. Fiber connections to the desktop will become more common as costs come down, as performance requirements go up, and as the technology becomes more familiar.

Wireless LANs are likely to be used mostly for niche applications, especially in situations in which wiring is physically difficult and a more portable LAN is needed.

According to InfoCorp, a market research firm located in Acton, Massachusetts, LAN use will continue to increase by more than 10 percent each year through 1996. During that time, UTP, optical fiber, and wireless LANs will increase considerably; thick and thin coax and STP use will decline (see table 3.2).

The big change in network topologies in the next few years will be the increased use of structured wiring. Because of their flexibility, wiring hubs will be increasingly popular, especially as networks grow larger.

These are the trends, but you should not follow them just because they are trends. In choosing networking media and means, the factors to weigh are the kind of cabling and cabling schemes you already have in place, your current needs, your future needs, and what is comfortable to maintain.

Table 3.2

Estimates of LAN Installations Worldwide

Media Type	*1992*	*1993*	*1994*	*1995*	*1996*
Coax-Broadband	4.2%	4.0%	3.8%	3.5%	3.0%
Coax-Thick	21.5%	20.1%	18.6%	17.1%	15.5%
Coax-Thin	13.3%	12.8%	12.1%	10.5%	8.7%
Fiber	5.9%	6.2%	6.6%	7.1%	7.6%
STP	28.7%	26.5%	23.6%	21.1%	18.0%
UTP	23.7%	28.8%	32.4%	36.5%	41.1%
Wireless	0.7%	1.6%	2.9%	4.2%	6.1%

Topics covered in this chapter:
Understanding the IEEE Local Area Network Standards
Understanding Vendor LAN Standards
Understanding Structured-Wiring Systems

Chapter 4

Local Area Network Standards

A variety of standards define the methods of implementing the local area network physical layer. This chapter discusses some of the standards most commonly associated with enterprise LANs. The two most popular standards are defined by the IEEE (International Electrical and Electronic Engineers), an international standard-setting body. Other standards have been set by vendors and have become prominent through acceptance in the vendor community.

This chapter will consider some of the most prominent physical layer standards. First to be discussed are two IEEE standards: 802.3, which describes the standard based on Ethernet, and 802.5, which describes the standard derived from IBM's token-ring technology.

Two vendor standards are also mentioned. LocalTalk is commonly found, simply because it is built into every Macintosh computer. ARCnet has been a common LAN physical layer standard because of its early availability and vendor support. Although neither technology has found widespread use in large networks, implementation of enterprise networks often requires that LocalTalk and ARCnet be integrated with networks, based on the 802.3 and 802.5 standards.

The standards mentioned in this chapter describe baseband networks. In a *baseband network*, only one signal can exist on the network at any given time. Baseband is usually adequate in LANs, which are designed to support a moderate number of stations in a limited geographic area and must do so at a reasonable cost-per-station.

When networks grow to campus size, 10-20Mbps of performance may be inadequate to connect large numbers of workstations in multiple departments or buildings. A common strategy is to interconnect local baseband networks via broadband networks—frequently designated as *backbones*—which can simultaneously transport multiple signals.

A broadband network has a very high data rate. Signals share the network by sharing time or by subdividing the frequency spectrum on the network. Broadband networks require expensive hardware to combine and break out the signals for the various local networks.

Understanding the IEEE Local Area Network Standards

The IEEE undertook Project 802 in February of 1980 to identify and formalize LAN standards for data rates not exceeding 20 megabits-per-second (Mbps). Standardization efforts resulted in the IEEE 802 LAN standards. The number 802 was chosen to mark the date when IEEE undertook the LAN standardization efforts (80 for 1980, 2 for February).

The IEEE standards divide the OSI data-link layer into two sublayers: the Media Access Control (MAC) layer and the Logical Link Control (LLC) layer. The MAC layer deals with media-access techniques to access shared physical medium. Token ring and Ethernet have different implementations of the MAC layer because their methods of sharing the physical media are different. The relationship of the IEEE 802 standards to the OSI model is illustrated in figure 4.1.

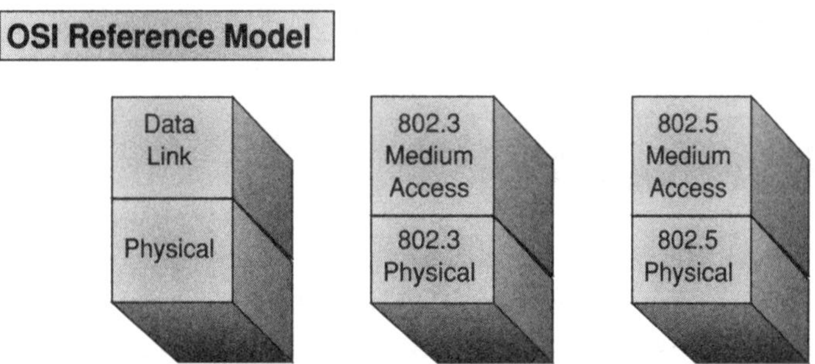

Figure 4.1:
The relationship of the IEEE 802 standards to the OSI reference model.

All IEEE LANs have the same LLC layer, as defined by standard 802.2. The advantage of a common sublayer, such as the LLC, is that upper layer mechanisms can be the same, regardless of the kind of networking hardware you use.

The 802.3 and 802.5 standards define both the physical and MAC components of Ethernet and token ring. Each standard is discussed in detail later in this chapter.

You have probably heard arguments regarding the superiority of Ethernet or token ring networks. In reality, however, the standards perform in a similar way, and either network can be a suitable choice for a corporate network. Major network vendors, including IBM, recognize that Ethernet and token ring will coexist for the foreseeable future, and all are rushing to market tools for integrating the standards. Network planners are now free to match the cabling system to the application, secure in the knowledge that future network-integration issues can be successfully dealt with.

Ethernet LANS

Robert Metcalfe, David Boggs, and others who worked for Xerox Corporation developed a LAN based on carrier-sensing mechanisms. This LAN spanned a distance of one kilometer, supported 100 personal stations, and achieved data rates of 2.94 Mbps. This system was called *Ethernet* (in honor of that elusive substance, called ether, through which electromagnetic radiation was once thought to propagate).

Ethernet was proposed as a standard by Digital Equipment Corporation (DEC), Intel, and Xerox. The first Ethernet standard was published in September, 1981, and was called the DIX 1.0. *DIX* stood for *D*igital, *I*ntel, and *X*erox. DIX 1.0 was followed by DIX 2.0 (published in November, 1982).

Meanwhile, Project 802 from IEEE had undertaken LAN standardization efforts. Not surprisingly, Digital, Intel, and Xerox proposed the adoption of Ethernet as a standard. IBM proposed the token ring as a standard, based on prototypes built at IBM's Zurich Lab. The Ethernet proposal became known as the IEEE 802.3 and the token ring proposal became the IEEE 802.5.

Not surprisingly, the Ethernet standard evolved as it was molded to meet the diverse requirements of the 802.3 committee members, and there are important differences between 802.3 and Ethernet networks. Although 802.3 and Ethernet are incompatible standards, the term *Ethernet* is almost always used to designate 802.3-compliant networks. This book bows to common usage and applies the term Ethernet for both standards, making distinctions as required when a specific standard is discussed.

Ethernet Operation

Before an Ethernet station transmits, it listens for activity on the transmission channel. Ethernet frequently is described as a "listen before talking" protocol. *Activity* is any transmission caused by other Ethernet stations. The presence of a transmission is called a *carrier.* The station electronics can sense the presence of a carrier.

If an Ethernet station detects a busy channel, it refrains from transmitting. After the last bit of the passing frame, the Ethernet data-link layer continues to wait for a minimum of 9.6 microseconds to provide proper interframe spacing. After that, if a data frame is waiting for transmission, the transmission is initiated. If the station has no data to transmit, it resumes the carrier sense (listening for a carrier) operation. The interframe gap provides recovery time for other Ethernet stations.

If a station tries to transmit when the channel is busy, a garbled transmission results. These garbled transmissions are called *collisions*.

If the channel is free (no carrier is detected), the station can transmit. Because multiple stations attached to the Ethernet channel use the carrier-sense mechanism, it is called *carrier sense with multiple access* (CSMA).

If two stations decide to transmit at the same time, a collision occurs. Collisions occur during the normal operation of Ethernet LANs because stations transmit based only on one fact: the presence of a carrier on the channel. They do not know whether packets are queued for transmission on other stations. Furthermore, the CSMA operation is complicated by propagation delay in LANs. In Ethernet, for example, signals propagate at 0.77 times the speed of light on standard (thick) cables and at 0.65 times the speed of light on thin Ethernet cables. A delay occurs before a transmission is heard by all stations, and a station may transmit because it has yet to hear another station's transmission.

Collisions are a fact of life in Ethernet LANs. Ethernet stations minimize the effects of collisions by detecting the collisions as they occur. (The name *CSMA/CD* describes the Ethernet media access mechanism—*CD* stands for *c*ollision *d*etection). The stations involved in the collision abort their transmissions. The first station to detect the collision sends out a special jamming pulse to alert all stations that a collision has taken place. After a collision occurs, all stations set up a random interval timer. Transmission takes place only after this interval timer expires. Introducing a delay before transmission can lessen the probability of collisions.

When successive collisions occur, the average random time-out value is doubled. This doubling takes place up to 10 consecutive collisions. Beyond that, doubling the average random time-out value does not significantly improve the performance of the network.

Under the worst-case scenario, a station may wait indefinitely for an opportunity to transmit. Because this scenario is not acceptable for real-time applications, Ethernet is not suited for real-time applications. Although this potential problem is frequently mentioned when comparing Ethernet to other LAN standards (such as token ring), problems with excessive collisions are seldom encountered on real-world Ethernets.

At moderate traffic levels, Ethernet is an extremely efficient protocol. Later in this chapter, it will be shown that token ring requires a wide variety of control mechanisms that generate network traffic. Apart from collisions, however, most of the network traffic on an Ethernet is related to network transmission. As a result, Ethernet offers very high performance at most data rates; a 10M Ethernet often provides comparable performance to a 16M token ring until high traffic levels are reached.

Ethernet Cable Options

The following three baseband Ethernet cabling standards are in common use:

- Standard Ethernet (10BASE5), based on thick coaxial cable
- Thin Ethernet (10BASE2), based on thin coaxial cable
- UTP Ethernet (10BASE-T), based on unshielded twisted pair cable

These cabling standards are described in the following sections.

Standard Ethernet Wiring Rules

Another name for *standard ethernet* is *thick wire Ethernet* (because the coaxial cable it uses is much thicker than that used for thin wire Ethernet). The IEEE version of standard Ethernet is called *10BASE5*. The 10 stands for 10 Mbps operation; the BASE stands for baseband operation; and the 5 stands for 500 meters per segment.

Stations on thick Ethernet communicate to the external network through external transceivers attached to the shared media. Transceivers are also called a *medium attachment unit (MAU)*. The shared media is called the *trunk segment cable,* or just *segment*. Because of signal attenuation, a segment cannot be longer than 500 meters.

The external transceiver and the NICX are connected by a transceiver cable. The DIX connector plug mates with the DIX connector socket on the NICX (A slide lock is used to secure this connection.) The other end of the transceiver fits into a connector on the external transceiver.

Thick Ethernet cable is a 0.4-inch diameter, 50-ohm cable, and is available in various precut lengths with an N-series connector plug attached to each end. Thick Ethernet cable can be purchased in spools or bulk quantities, which come without the N-series connector attached at the ends.

A trunk segment must be terminated with an N-series *terminator*. A terminator connector includes a resistor, which is 50 ohms for Ethernet. The terminator blocks electrical interference on the segment and cancels out any signal reflections caused by signals reaching the end of the cable. The N-series terminator is attached to the male N-series terminator on the end of the segment.

N-series terminators come with a grounding wire. One end of the cable must be connected to an electrical ground; the other end must remain ungrounded.

Thick Ethernet can be extended beyond 500M by joining two trunk segments with a repeater. A *repeater* is an active device that enables a LAN to expand beyond a single segment by linking two segments together. The repeater amplifies and regenerates the signal so that it can be transmitted over longer distances. A multiport repeater, such as a DEMPR (Digital's multiport repeater), can link a number of Ethernet segments together.

Table 4.1 describes the rules for thick Ethernet wiring. Figure 4.2 illustrates an example of a thick Ethernet network.

Table 4.1

Thick Ethernet Parameters and Wiring Rules

Thick Ethernet Parameters	*Value*
Max data rate	10 Mbps
Max repeaters without IRLs	
Max repeaters with IRLs	4
Max coax segment	500 meters
Max transceiver cable length	50 meters
Max number of link segments	2
Max combined link segment length	1000 meters
Max stations per segment	100
Max number of stations	1024
Distance between stations	Multiples of 2.5 meters

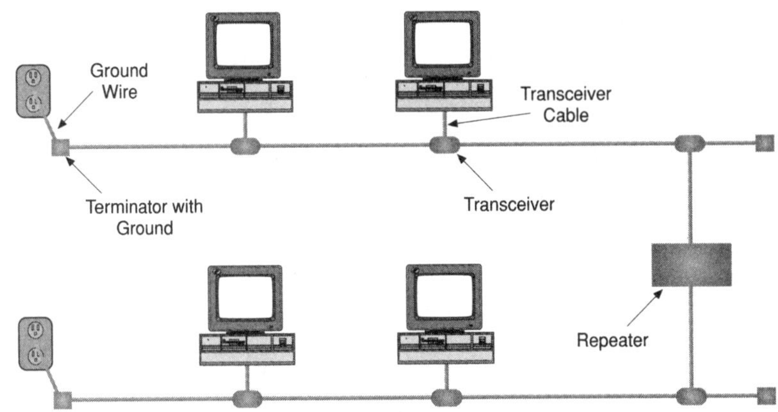

Figure 4.2:
Example of a thick Ethernet network.

When traveling from one station to another station on an Ethernet LAN that consists of coax trunk segments only, a signal cannot travel through more than two full repeaters. A *full repeater* joins two coaxial segments together directly. A coaxial segment is distinct from a link segment.

A *link segment*, made of fiber optic or twisted-pair cable, can join two coaxial segments over a longer distance. The purpose of a link segment is to extend the range of an Ethernet LAN. There can be a maximum of two link segments on an Ethernet LAN. Link segments do not have stations attached to them; they are connected to coaxial segments by repeaters. Another name for them is *inter repeater link-segment* (IRL).

A *half-repeater* joins a coaxial segment to a link segment. Another name for a half-repeater is a *remote repeater.* The trunk coaxial segment length cannot exceed 500 meters in length. The combined lengths of the two link segments cannot exceed 1000 meters. Using these wiring parameters, you can deduce the maximum length of an Ethernet LAN.

Figure 4.3 illustrates the longest possible Ethernet. T1 through T6 represent transceivers. Using this diagram, you can calculate the length of this network, as shown in Table 4.2.

Table 4.2
Calculating the Longest Possible Thick Ethernet

Entity	*Length*
Coax Segment 1 length	500 Meters
Coax Segment 2 length	500 Meters
Coax Segment 3 length	500 Meters
Combined Link Segment 1 and 2 length	1000 Meters
Total Ethernet Length	2500 Meters

Some people cheat and add the transceiver cable lengths to transceivers T1, T2, T3, T4, T5, and T6, shown in figure 4.3. Because the maximum transceiver cable length is 50 meters, this gives a combined transceiver length of 300 meters. Table 4.3 shows the method of calculating this length.

By cheating a little, the maximum Ethernet length becomes 2500 meters plus 300 meters (2800 meters).

The maximum number of stations that you can attach to a thick Ethernet segment is 100; the total number of stations in all segments cannot exceed 1024. The repeater attachment to a segment counts as one station. The minimum distance between any two stations is 2.5 meters, and it is recommended that you separate stations at distances of multiples of 2.5 meters to minimize interference.

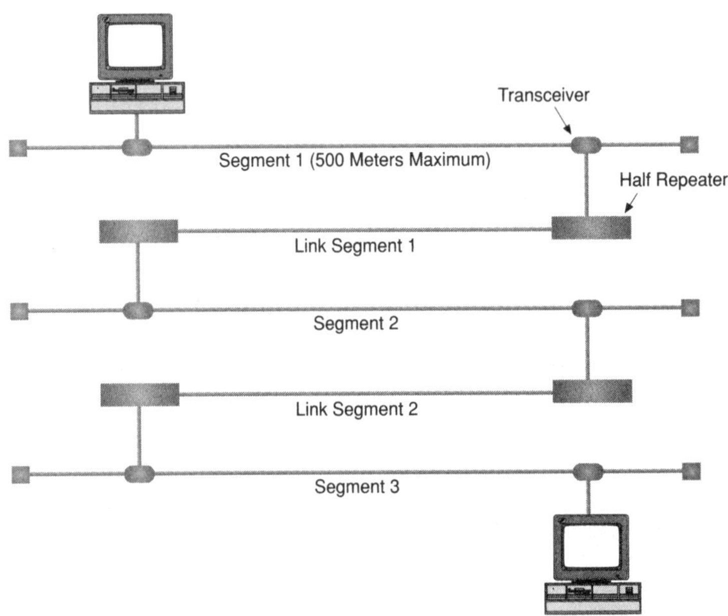

Figure 4.3:
The longest possible thick Ethernet.

Table 4.3
Including Transceiver Cables when Calculating Ethernet Length

Entity	*Length*
Transceiver cable length of transceiver T1	50 Meters
Transceiver cable length of transceiver T2	50 Meters
Transceiver cable length of transceiver T3	50 Meters
Transceiver cable length of transceiver T4	50 Meters
Transceiver cable length of transceiver T5	50 Meters
Transceiver cable length of transceiver T6	50 Meters
Combined transceiver cable length	300 Meters

Thin Wire Ethernet Wiring Design Rules

Other names for thin wire Ethernet are *thinnet* and *cheapernet* (because it is cheaper than standard Ethernet). Compared to thicknet coax, thinnet cable is much thinner, less expensive, and easier to install. The IEEE version of thin wire Ethernet is called *10BASE2*—10 stands for 10Mbps operation, BASE stands for baseband operation, and 2 stands for approximately 200 meters (actually, 185 meters) per segment.

The transceiver functions for a thin wire Ethernet are performed by the electronics on the Network Interface Card (NIC). No external transceiver connections are required. Instead, BNC T-connectors are used to connect the NIC with the cable. The two opposing jacks of the T connector are used to join two lengths of thin wire Ethernet cable, and the remaining plug is attached to the BNC connector jack on the NIC.

The shared media is called the *trunk segment cable* (or just *segment*). Due to signal attenuation, a thin wire segment cannot be longer than 185 meters. Thin Ethernet cable has a 0.2-inch diameter, has an RG-58 A/U 50-ohm cable, and is available in various pre-cut lengths with a standard BNC plug attached to each end. Thin Ethernet cable also can be purchased in spools or bulk quantities that come without the BNC connectors attached at the ends.

The BNC terminator is a connector incorporating a 50-ohm resistor that blocks electrical interference on the segment. Additionally, it cancels out any signal reflections caused by signals bouncing off the end of the cable. The BNC terminator is attached to one of the two jacks on a T connector to which no cable is attached. There is a grounded BNC terminator that has a grounding wire. One end of the cable must be grounded; the other end must remain ungrounded.

Figure 4.4 shows an example of a thin Ethernet network. In this network, there are two trunk segments that are joined together by a device called a *repeater,* which is an active device that enables an Ethernet LAN to be expanded beyond a single segment by linking two segments together. The repeater amplifies and regenerates the signal so that it can be transmitted over longer distances. A multiport repeater, such as a DEMPR (*DEC* *M*ulti*P*ort *R*epeater), can link a number of Ethernet segments together.

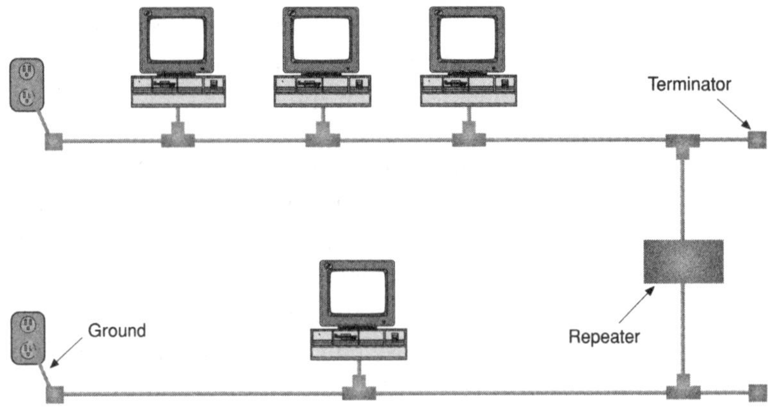

Figure 4.4:
Example of a thin Ethernet network.

There are a number of rules related to thin Ethernet wiring, which are summarized in Table 4.4. The repeater rules for thin Ethernet are the same as for thick Ethernet.

Table 4.4
Thin Ethernet Parameters and Wiring Rules

Thin Ethernet Parameters	*Value*
Max data rate	10 Mbps
Max repeaters without IRLs	2
Max repeaters with IRLs	4
Max coax segment	185 Meters
Max number of link segments	2
Max stations per segment	30
Max number of stations	1024
Min distance between stations	0.5 Meters

The trunk coaxial segment length for Thin Ethernet cannot exceed 185 meters. The maximum number of stations that can be attached to a thin Ethernet segment is 30; the total number of stations cannot exceed 1024. The repeater attachment to a segment counts as one station. The minimum distance between any two stations is 0.5 meters.

10BASE-T Wiring Design Rules

The topology of coax Ethernet is a bus, both physically and logically. The physical topology of a network is defined by the method of routing the cable between the nodes; the physical network is what you can see and touch. The logical network topology is defined by the electrical characteristics of the network; you cannot see or touch it, but the logical topology really defines the way the network functions.

All devices on a bus receive signals on the bus more or less simultaneously (electrical signals always require some time to travel down the cable). A signal on an Ethernet coax radiates in both directions from the originating station until it has reached the ends of the cables and is absorbed by the terminators. Besides desired signals, however, noise and interference can also affect the entire cable. A break in the center conductor of the cable can cause signals to be reflected back into the cable from the break, thus rendering the entire network inoperable. This characteristic can make it extremely difficult to identify which station or which part of a cable is generating the network interference.

One way to make problems easier to isolate is to configure the network in a star, with each station connected to a hub by an individual wire. The hub can thus provide some degree of electrical isolation between the nodes. These hubs are frequently implemented as parts of structured wiring systems, as discussed in Chapter 3.

The 10BASE-T standard was primarily developed to support Ethernet on unshielded twisted-pair wiring. The physical topology of 10BASE-T is a star instead of a bus, however, so that troubleshooting can be simplified.

It is important to remember that 10BASE-T remains a logical bus. Unless routers are used to segment the network, as described in Chapter 7, all signals on the network are propagated to all stations. It can, therefore, remain difficult to identify a troublesome network component without proper diagnostic equipment.

10BASE-T has become increasingly popular, due to increasing availability of lower-cost components and to growing interest in configuring networks based in unshielded twisted-pair wiring. The 10 stands for 10Mbps operation, BASE stands for baseband operation, T stands for twisted pair wiring.

A 10BASE-T NIC has a telephone-type RJ-45 port, which is officially called a *Media Dependent Interface (MDI)* port. Many NICs are also equipped with an Ethernet DIX connector. The DIX connector is used to connect, via a transceiver, to thick or thin wire Ethernet. Many NICs require a switch setting to enable either the 10BASE-T or DIX port; others, such as the SMC Elite16T card have an auto-sense mechanism.

The transceiver functions for a 10BASE-T are performed by the on-board NIC electronics.

The 10BASE-T uses a physical star topology with the 10BASE-T hub serving as the central switching element. Each concentrator accepts cables to several workstations, usually twelve. Unshielded twisted-pair wiring is used to connect a 10BASE-T concentrator to the workstation. This wiring normally consists of 0.4 to 0.6mm diameter (26 to 22 America Wire Gauge —AWG) unshielded wire in a multipair cable. The performance specifications are generally met by 100 meters of 0.5mm telephone twisted-pair wiring.

There are two twisted-pairs (four wires) between each NIC and the concentrator. One pair is used for transmitting and the other for receiving. Table 4.5 shows the pin assignments for a four pair twisted-pair wiring. Only two pairs, one for transmission and another for receiving, are used.

The pin configurations are the same at each end of a 10BASE-T cable. Therefore, a crossover function is implemented in every cable so that the transmitter at one end will be connected to the receiver at the other end. Crossover functions may be implemented in two ways: by using an external crossover UTP cable that reverses the transmit and receive pairs at the RJ-45 connector at on end of the UTP cable; or by using an internal crossover function, in which the crossover is designed as part of the internal circuitry in the 10BASE-T device. An MDI port with this function is marked with the symbol "X".

Table 4.5
Pin Assignments for the MDI (Media Dependent Interface) Connector

Contact	*MDI signal*
1	TD+
2	TD–
3	RD+
4	Not used by 10BASE-T
5	Not used
6	RD–
7	Not used
8	Not used

The 10BASE-T hub serves the role of a repeater. It performs the following functions:

- Data-packet retiming (IEEE 802.3 standard)
- Per-port Link Integrity Test ("Good Link Test")
- Per-port autopartitioning, which disconnects the port in the event of 30 consecutive collisions, an excessively long single collision, or jabber input

The proper operation of the CSMA/CD 10BASE-T network requires network size to be limited to control round-trip propagation delays (the time it takes a signal to reach the extremity of the network and return).

There are two configuration rules for more than one hub. First, a maximum of four concentrators may be in the data path between any two stations. Second, UTP segments should be no longer than 100 meters.

Mixed Media Ethernet Networks

Different Ethernet media (coax, twisted pair, fiber) may be mixed on a LAN. 10BASE-T segments may be connected to coax segments through 10BASE-T transceivers. Also, many 10BASE-T hubs and devices are equipped with an AUI connector that may be connected to a coax Ethernet through a transceiver.

Table 4.6 summarizes the maximum delays of the various media segments. This table is important for the LAN manager because Ethernet segments can be built by combining cables from different vendors, which may differ from the specifications by small amounts. Test equipment, such as Time Domain Reflectometers (TDRs), can be used to see that the delays are within the specifications.

Table 4.6

Maximum Delays for Ethernet Media

Media Segment Type	*Max MAUs per Segment (meters)*	*Max Segment Length (ns)*	*Min Propagation Velocity*	*Max Delay per segment*
Coaxial Segment				
10BASE5	100	500	0.77c	2165
10BASE2	30	185	0.65c	950
Link Segment				
FOIRL	2	1000	0.66c	5000
10BASE-T	2	100	0.59c	1000
AUI (Transceiver Cable)				
AUI	DTE/1 MAU	50	0.65c	257

c = 300,000,000 meters/sec (Velocity of light in vacuum)

FOIRL = Fiber Optic Inter Repeater Link

The following network topology constraints apply to mixed-media networks:

- Repeater sets are required for all segment inter-connections.
- The maximum transmission path between any two stations may consist of up to five segments, four repeater sets (including optional AUIs), two MAUs, or two AUIs.
- If a network path consists of five segments and four repeater sets, up to three segments may be coax trunks (the remainder must be link segments). If five segments are present and FOIRL (Fiber Optic Inter-Repeater Link) is used as the link segment, the link segment should not exceed 500 meters.
- If a network path consists of four segments and three repeater sets, the maximum allowable length of the FOIRL segments is 1000 meters each.

Combining Thin/Thick Cable in a Segment

You can combine thin and thick Ethernet cable in a single segment by using as much thin cable as possible. Thin cable is cheaper and easier to install than thick cable.

Combined thin/thick cable length ranges between 185 meters and 500 meters. The minimum length is 185 meters because coax segments shorter than 185 meters can be built exclusively with thin cable. The maximum of 500 meters is the limit for a segment made out of thick coax exclusively.

To compute the maximum amount of thin cable that may be used in one combination trunk segment, use the following formula:

thinLen = (500 - trunkLen)/3.28 meters

In this formula, trunkLen is the length of trunk segment you want to build and thinLen is the maximum length of thin length cable you can use.

To build a trunk segment of 400 meters, for example, the maximum length of thin coax cable that may be used is the following:

thinLen = (500 - 400)/3.28 = 30.48 meters

30.48 meters of thin coax can share a segment with 400 - 30.48 = 369.52 meters of thick cable. Thin and thick coax cable must be connected via an N-series to a BNC adapter.

IEEE 802.3 versus Ethernet-II (DIX 2.0)

Both Ethernet-II and IEEE 802.3 have a minimum frame size of 64 bytes and a maximum frame size of 1518 bytes. The next section examines their respective frame structures, which are compared in figure 4.5.

Ethernet-II

The Ethernet frame begins with a preamble of eight *octets* (one octet = eight bits), consisting of an alternating pattern 1010 (ending in 101011). At 10Mbps, this preamble has a 6.4-microsecond duration, which is sufficient time for the receiving station to synchronize and get ready to receive the frame.

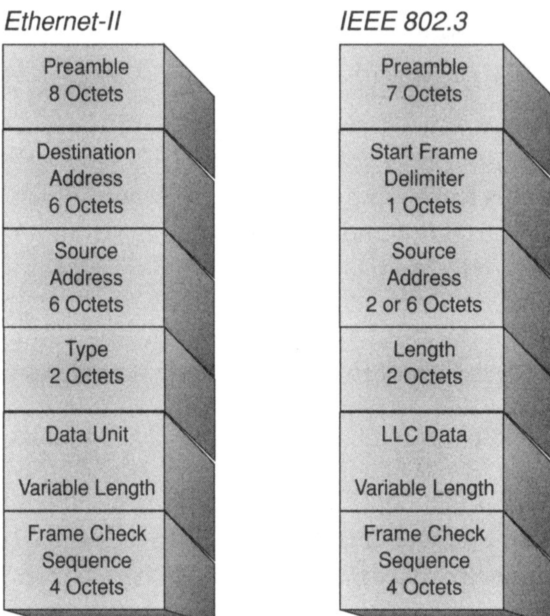

Figure 4.5
Comparison of Ethernet-II and IEEE 802.3 frame structures.

Both the *destination address (DA)* field and *source address (SA)* field follow this preamble. Each address field is six octets long. The first three octets represent a manufacturer's code; the remaining three octets are assigned by the manufacturer. This assignation is made so that any two Ethernet cards will have a unique six-octet address. This address is usually burned into a ROM chip on the Ethernet card.

The *least significant bit (LSB)* of the first octet is the Physical/ Multicast bit (it is 0 for Ethernet addresses). A value of 1 for this LSB indicates a *multicast address,* which is a message intended for more than one receiving station. For instance, a hex value of

FFFFFFFFFFFF, all 1's, for the DA field represents a broadcast. The manufacturer code was formerly assigned by Xerox; it is now assigned by IEEE.

The *type* field, also referred to as *Ethertype*, is a two-octet field used to indicate the type of data in the data field. Thus, if the Ethernet frame is used to carry NetWare data, the Ethertype value is 8137 hex. If it is used to carry DoD Internet Packet (IP) data, it has the value of 0800 hex. XNS packets used in 3COM networks have the value of 0600hex. The type field is used by network drivers or the network layer to demultiplex data packets to the appropriate protocol stack. It enables multiple-protocol stacks to run on a single Ethernet card.

The *data unit* field is a variable-length field that can range from 46 to 1500 bytes. The remaining fixed-length fields add up to 18 bytes.

The *(FCS) frame check sequence* field is generated by the Ethernet hardware at the end of the data field and is a 32-bit Cyclic Redundancy Checksum (CRC) over the address, type, and data fields. It is used to detect errors in transmission. Bad frames are retransmitted.

IEEE 802.3

The IEEE frame begins with a preamble of seven octets (one octet = eight bits), consisting of an alternating pattern: 1010. At 10Mbps, this preamble has a 5.6-microsecond duration, which is sufficient time for the receiving station to synchronize and get ready to receive the frame.

The *SFD (start frame delimiter)* field follows after the preamble and is defined by the pattern 10101011. (IEEE 802.3 preamble +

SFD = Ethernet preamble.) Note that the IEEE 802.3 preamble and the SFD field combined are identical to the eight-octet Ethernet preamble.

The destination address (DA) and the source address (SA) fields follow the SFD. Each address field can be six octets or two octets long (six-octet addressing is the most common). The first three octets represent a manufacturer's code; the remaining octets are assigned by the manufacturer.

This assignation is made so that any two Ethernet and IEEE cards have a unique six-octet address. This address is usually burned into a ROM chip on the IEEE 802.3 card. The least significant bit (LSB) of the first octet represents the individual/group field and is similar to the physical/multicast field in Ethernet. The next bit is the universe/local (U/L) field and indicates whether the addressing is global or local.

The length field follows the address fields and is two octets long. It indicates the data size of the LLC layer. A minimum of 46 octets are required in the LLC data field to make up the minimum size of 64 octets for the complete packet. The maximum value of the length field is 1500, resulting in a maximum frame size of 1518 octets.

The LLC data field is a variable-length field containing 46 to 1500 octets of LLC data.

The FCS field is generated by the IEEE 802.3 hardware at the end of the data field and is a 32-bit Cyclic Redundancy Checksum (CRC) over the address, type, and data fields. It is used to detect errors in transmission. Bad frames are retransmitted.

Differences between Ethernet-II and IEEE 802.3

There are differences between Ethernet-II and IEEE 802.3; Ethernet-II uses a two-byte type field to indicate the type of data. The type-field values were at one time assigned by Xerox; they are now assigned by IEEE. Instead of the type field, IEEE 803.3 has a two-byte length field. The length field for Ethernet packets is supplied by a higher layer, such as the network layer. In some cases, the NIC can determine the length of the frame, based on signal duration, and passes this information to upper layers. For IEEE 802.3 frames, the type information is supplied by the IEEE 802.2 (logical control layer) frame that is part of the data unit field.

For example, a hex code of E0 indicates a NetWare packet. A hex code of A0 is reserved to transmit upper-layer packets that were generated by non-IEEE LANs. This is referred to as the *SNAP (Sub Net Access Protocol)* mechanism.

Ethernet has no provision to pad the data to make a minimum Ethernet frame of 64 bytes. IEEE 802.3 frames have a length field to encode the pad information. In Ethernet, the padding has to be performed by upper layers.

Incompatibility between LattisNet UTP and 10BASE-T

Before 10BASE-T became an official standard, a number of vendors jumped the gun and announced UTP Ethernet network cards and concentrators. These older cards, which are not compliant with the 10BASE-T cards, include the popular Western Digital

8003 EtherCard PLUS series. Reasons for incompatibility include the following:

- ❖ Voltage levels for old cards is 2V peak-to-peak; the new cards have 5V peak-to-peak
- ❖ Low DC current is used in old cards to indicate link integrity; the new cards use a "good link beat" message
- ❖ Jabber detection is done at the concentrator for old cards; the new cards perform this at the concentrator and the transceiver
- ❖ Equalization of signal timing is done after packet reception in old cards; the new cards do this after packet transmission
- ❖ The noise squelch is done differently in the two cards

One way of integrating the older cards with 10BASE-T is to use the Intellicom Model 312M concentrator, which has an RS-232 management port that can be used to connect to a terminal or a PC that runs terminal-emulation software. Using the terminal, each of the 12 individual ports in the Intellicom 312M may be programmed to be compatible with the older UTP cards or 10BASE-T cards.

Ethernet Hardware

Unless the network is to be extended with repeaters or segmented with bridges or routers, coax Ethernet has extremely simple hardware requirements.

Ethernet interfaces are included as standard equipment in most engineering workstations. Network interface cards for PC compatibles are manufactured by many different vendors (too many to list here). With the exception of some older cards, the majority of modern Ethernet NICs should offer adequate performance in all but the most demanding applications. The costs of eight-bit and 16-bit Ethernet NICs differ only slightly, so you should standardize on 16-bit cards to ensure the best possible throughput.

It is a bad idea to mix brands of Ethernet cards on the same network segment. Different manufacturers may implement the collision backout algorithms differently and some stations may be serviced unequally when network traffic reaches highly competitive levels.

Thick Ethernet requires the use of MAUs to connect stations to the coax segment; MAUs are active devices and add to the expense of Thicknet.

Besides the NICs, thin Ethernet does not require much, except cables and connectors, to create a network. Thin Ethernet is probably the least expensive high-performance network to implement. If there is a downside to Ethernet, it is that this electrical simplicity can make it difficult to isolate some causes of network failures.

10BASE-T requires the use of network hubs; most hubs can accommodate 12 stations. The cost-per-connection for 10BASE-T is, therefore, highly dependent on how fully the capacities of the hubs are utilized. (The cost-per-connection on a fully-utilized hub is about $100.

The motivation behind 10BASE-T is the desire to minimize cabling costs by utilizing UTP wiring, instead of more expensive coax. The cost of 10BASE-T hubs often negates the cost advantage of UTP wiring, however, particularly in small networks. In any case, it is rarely advisable to make a strategic decision about a network based solely on the cost of the cable. Issues of performance, reliability, and expandability are far more cogent.

A more important reason for implementing 10BASE-T networks is that the hubs, being active, can provide some isolation between the stations—making it easier to isolate and disconnect malfunctioning stations. 10BASE-T hubs can also include some network problem-reporting services. They may, for example, support the Simple Network Management Protocols (SNMP), which enables them to be monitored and managed by an SNMP console, as described in Chapter 11.

In the context of enterprise networking, the most significant trend in Ethernet is toward structured-wiring systems, as described in Chapter 3. Structured-wiring systems consist of concentrators that house hubs for various network standards. Because network concentrators are becoming homes to increasing numbers of network services, they will be discussed in more detail after descriptions of the network cabling standards.

Although there are too many vendors to list, some vendors are included in the section on structured-wiring systems because they also produce products for other cabling systems.

A vendor with particular strength in Ethernet is one of original developers of the technology: Digital Equipment Corporation. Digital is as closely associated with Ethernet as IBM is associated with token ring, and Ethernet/802.3 technologies are integral components of Digital's networking strategies. The OPEN DECconnect structured cabling system supports Ethernet and other data technologies, including voice and data. Local Digital sales representatives are usually the most effective source of information about Digital services and products. You can also get information about Digital network products by contacting:

Digital Equipment Corp.
146 Main Street
Maynard, MA 01754
(508)493-5111

Other important Ethernet vendors include the following:

3Com Corporation
5400 Bayfront Plaza
Santa Clara, CA 95052-8145
(408)764-5000

Eagle Technology
1160 Ridder Park Drive
San Jose, CA 95131
(408)441-7453

3Com manufacturers a wide variety of Ethernet NICs. Because 3Com hardware is broadly distributed, software-compatibility issues are rarely a problem. Appropriate driver software is available for most LAN operating systems, as well as for UNIX platforms.

Eagle Technology is the current manufacturer of the Ethernet cards that are distributed under the Novell trademark. The NE1000, NE2000, and NE32 cards have a good reputation for high performance at reasonable cost. These cards may not be supported by all vendors, however, and some research should be done before you select one of these cards to ensure compatibility.

Token Ring LANS

Ring-based networks have been around for many years. Ring LANs are a concatenation of point-to-point links, so they are not really a broadcast LAN like Ethernet. They may be considered to be sequential broadcast LANs, with the point-to-point links forming a circle. The technology of ring LANs is digital, unlike that of Ethernet LANs, in which the carrier-sense mechanism may be analog. Another attractive feature of ring-based LANs is its deterministic-response time, even under heavy load conditions.

The token ring LAN encountered most often is the IEEE 802.5. This LAN is often referred to as the IBM token ring because IBM was the prime mover behind the IEEE 802.5 standard.

Token Ring Operation

A special group of bits, called the *token*, is used to arbitrate access to the ring. The token circulates from station to station around the ring. If a station wants to transmit a frame, it must wait and seize the token. While holding on to the token, it can transmit a frame. At the end of the transmission, it must release the token so that other stations can access the ring.

For proper operation of the ring, the token must circulate continuously, even if there is no activity on the ring. There are 24 bits (three octets) in the token, and the ring must have enough latency or delay to hold 24 bits. If the bit rate on the ring is 4Mbps, the ring must have a latency of 24/4Mbps = six microseconds. Six microseconds may seem like a very short delay, but consider a twisted pair medium in which the propagation velocity is 0.59

times the speed of light. To compute the size of the ring that will have a latency of 6 microseconds, use the following formula:

Size of Ring = Latency x Propagation speed of media
= 0.0000006 x 0.59 x 3 x 100000000 meters
= 1062 meters
= 1.062 kilometers

Thus, the minimum size of the ring is 1 kilometer! This size is enormous, considering that it may be desirable to install only a few stations in a single room. For this reason, a special station, designated as the active monitor, adds a 24-bit delay buffer to the ring. This buffer also compensates for any accumulated phase jitter on the ring. The active monitor is important for maintaining normal operation of the ring.

A token ring station operates in one of four modes:

- Transmit mode
- Listen mode
- Bypass mode
- Receive mode

Figure 4.6 shows stations operating in these modes. Station A is in the *transmit mode*. To enter this mode, it seizes a free token. The token has a token bit called the *T bit*, which has the value of one in a free token. The transmitting station changes this T bit to a 0, indicating a busy token, and transmits the data frame. Station A is sending this data frame to station D, and the destination address field holds station D's address and the source address field holds station A's address.

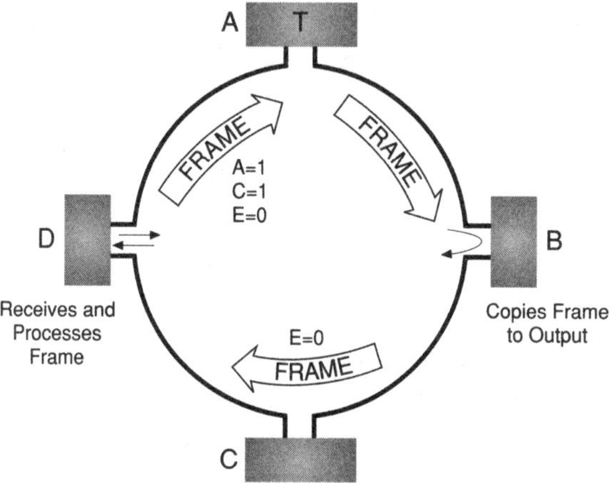

Figure 4.6:
Token ring relay-bypass mechanism.

Station B is operating in the *listen mode.* It checks the destination address field of the frame to see if it holds its address (B's address). Because the frame is addressed to station D, it enters the listen mode. In the listen mode, a station copies the incoming bits to the output link.

Station C has been powered down, so it is in the *bypass mode.* The bits flow through the bypass relay.

Station D examines the destination address field. It discovers that it is indeed the addressed station—thus, it enters the *receive mode.* In the receive mode, the data frame is copied into the station's memory and is also sent along the ring. A number of flags, called the *frame status flags,* are modified to indicate proper reception of the data frame. Station A receives the data frame that it sent and examines the frame status flags. The frame status flags serve the purpose of a hardware-based acknowledgment. The sending station can determine these flags and determine if the frame was received correctly. The frame status flags are the address-recognized (A) flag, frame-copied (C) flag and the error (E) flag. The E flag is computed and set by every station; the A and C flags are set by the destination station only. Table 4.7 defines these flags.

Table 4.7

Frame Status Flags

Frame Flags	*Value*	*Meaning*
A	1	Address recognized
A	0	Address not recognized
C	1	Frame copied successfully
C	0	Frame not copied
E	1	Bad frame (CRC error)
E	0	Good frame

The legal combinations of these flags are as follows:

- AC = 00 implies that the address was not recognized; therefore, the copy operation did not take place.
- AC = 10 implies that the station exists, but the frame was not copied. If E = 1, a bad frame was received. If the E flag is 0, then the frame was not copied for unknown reasons.
- AC = 11 implies that the station exists and the frame was copied to the station.

The only illegal combination is AC = 01, which indicates that the station was not recognized, but a user still copied the frame (in other words, some station illegally copied the data frame). As the bits that were sent by station A come back to it, it removes them from the ring.

Although all stations seem equal, some stations are more equal than others. One such station is called the *active monitor.* There is a monitor bit (M-bit) in the token that is set to 0 by the transmitting station. The active monitor examines this M-bit and changes it to a 1 if it is a 0. If the active monitor bit sees an M-bit value of 1, it concludes that this data frame has been circulating around once too often. This can happen because of a crash of the transmitting station, which failed to remove the data frame from the ring.

If the token is lost because it got mangled by noise on the ring, the active monitor times out and generates a new token. The active monitor keeps track of this *token rotation time* (TRT) and times out if it exceeds a threshold value. For small token-ring networks, a typical value of TRT is 8 microseconds. Under heavy load conditions, this value may rise slightly.

The active monitor is not a station with special networking hardware. Any station on the token ring can become an active monitor; all other stations act as standby monitors. The choice of which station becomes an active monitor is made through a ring-initialization procedure. If the active monitor fails, one of the standby monitors become the active monitor.

When no data frames are circulating around the ring, the active monitor issues an active monitor Present (AMP) MAC frame. This frame is sent at regular intervals, usually seven seconds. Other stations in the role of standby monitors send standby monitor Present (SMP) MAC frames. Standby monitors detect the AMP frame and conclude that the active monitor is doing its job. If the active monitor skips a beat; that is, it does not send out the

AMP frame when it should, one of the standby monitors takes over the role of the active monitor. The standby monitor that detects the failure of the active monitor sends its claim on the token ring in the form of Claim Token (CL_TK) MAC frames. The standby monitor stops sending these frames if one of the following conditions occur:

- Another CL_TK frame is received and the sender's address is greater than this station's address. If two or more stations send out CL_TK, the resolution as to who becomes the active monitor is made in favor of the station with the higher address.
- A Beacon (BCN) MAC frame is received. This frame is sent as a result of a major ring failure such as a ring break. The BCN frame is used to locate and isolate the fault. In this case, the ring needs to be healed before deciding the winner of this contest.
- A Purge (PRG) MAC frame is received. This frame is sent out at the end of the Claim Token procedure by the station that has become the new active monitor. This means that the race has already been won by another station—so there is no point in continuing.

In any of the preceding cases, the standby monitor backs off. If a station receives the CL_TK frame it generated, it becomes the active monitor (the new king of the hill) and issues a Purge MAC frame to inform other stations that there is a new active monitor. At this point, the new active monitor adds the 24-bit latency buffer to the ring and commences monitoring the network.

Before joining a ring, a new station sends out the Duplicate Address Test (DAT) MAC frame as part of the ring-initialization procedure. The DAT frame is sent with its own address in the destination address field. If another station responds with the AC bits set to 11, then another station has the same address. The new station returns an appropriate status code. Network-monitoring software can detect this code and process it with an appropriate error message.

Another feature of IEEE 802.5 is the priority access mechanism. The token has two fields, the priority field and the reservation field, that consist of three bits. A total of eight priorities' values can be defined (0 to 7). The reservation field is set to 0 by the transmitting station. If a station wants priority access, it can place its priority value in the reservation field. After the transmitting station receives the frame it sent, it copies the reservation field value in the priority field of the new token that it generates. The Token now has the requested priority value. Only stations with higher or equal priority can access this token.

16Mbps stations do not wait for the return of the data frame to place the token on the network; they release a free token immediately after transmission of the data frame is completed. This is called the *early token release mechanism*, and it enables up to two data frames to be transmitted on a token ring LAN at a time.

Token Ring LAN Components

Token ring LANs consist of three basic components:

- Network interface cards, which are available in 4Mbps and 16Mbps versions
- Network cabling system
- Multistation access units, which serve as hubs for the cabling system

Because the most frequently used token ring hardware is manufactured by IBM, the various network components are described here in terms of IBM products.

The *multistation access unit* is also called the *MAU* (although token ring terminology has recently shifted to using the abbreviation *MSAU*, so it will not be confused with the media attachment unit in IEEE 802.3). The MAU is a wiring center to which stations are attached. In addition to the ports for the stations, each MAU is equipped with RI (Ring In) and RO (Ring Out) ports, which are used to connect multiple MAUs together.

Workstations are connected to the MAU via adapter cables. The standard IBM token ring network adapter cable is made of eight feet of IBM Type 1 cable. Type 1 cable is STP cable that uses unstranded conductors. Type 6 cable is similar to Type 1, but it incorporates stranded conductors and is therefore more flexible; Type 6 cable can also be used to connect workstations, although its primary use is to patch cables between wiring centers. Type 6 cable has a shorter working range than Type 1 cable has. One end of this cable connects to the token ring adapter at the station and the other end is a dual-gender connector that plugs into one of the station ports in the IBM 8228 MAU.

Type 3 cabling, which refers to conventional telephone wiring (UTP) can also be used. The 802.5 standard currently sanctions STP cable for 4Mbps and 16Mbps data rates. UTP cable is sanctioned only for 4Mbps data rates. However, vendors such as Proteon have developed proprietary strategies for implementing 16Mbps token ring on UTP cables. IBM has recently announced products that support 16Mbps token ring on UTP, and has, with Synoptics, developed a standard proposal that has been submitted to the IEEE.

IEEE 802.5 Design Rules

The rules for planning a token ring can get quite involved, especially if the network is pushing the limits of the technology. Planners of token-ring installations are advised to obtain the various token ring planning guides that are available from IBM and other token ring vendors. This is particularly the case when implementing 16Mbps over UTP cable because rules differ for each manufacturer's proprietary cabling system.

Table 4.8 summarizes the rules for 4Mbps token ring wiring.

Table 4.8
Token Ring Wiring Rules

Token Ring Parameters	*Type 1, 2*	*Type 3*
Max devices per ring	260	96
Tested data rates	16 Mbps	4 Mbps
Station-to-single MAU LAN	300 Meters	100 Meters
Station-to-multiple MAU LAN	100 Meters	45 Meters
Max MAUs-per-LAN	12	2
MAU-to-MAU distance	200 Meters	120 Meters

Type 1, 2 Cabling

A maximum of 260 devices can occupy a ring wired with Type 1,2 cables; however, MAUs count as devices (as do repeaters and other network components). A more reasonable number of devices is 100. The limit on the maximum stations is due to accumulated clock jitter. For networks implemented with the IBM 8228 MAU, only 12 MAUs should appear on a ring (see Table

4.8).Therefore, the ring can have a maximum of 8 x 12 = 96 stations on the token ring.

For Type 1, 2 cables, the maximum distance between workstation to MAU is 300 meters for a single MAU LAN, but this distance drops to 100 meters for multiple MAU LANs. As a practical measure, it is better to work with the tighter constraint of 100 meters, even for a single MAU LAN, because LANs have a tendency to grow and, as stations are added, more than one MAU will probably be required.

The maximum MAU-to-MAU distance for a token ring LAN is 200 meters for Types 1 and 2 cables.

Type 3 cabling

For Type 3 cabling, the maximum distance between workstation to MAU is 100 meters for a single MAU LAN, but this distance drops to 45 meters for multiple MAU LANs. As a practical measure, it is better to work with the tighter constraint of 45 meters, even for a single MAU LAN. The reason for this is that LANs have a tendency to grow and, as you add more stations, you eventually need a multiple MAU LAN.

The maximum MAU-to-MAU distance for a token ring LAN is 120 meters for Type 3 cabling.

Guidelines for Token-Ring Cabling

General guidelines for token-ring cabling are as follows:

- ❖ Stations located within eight feet of the MAU can be connected by using an eight-foot adapter cable.

- Stations farther than eight feet from the MAU can be connected by using extension cords (or longer adapter cables can be constructed).
- To form a ring by using multiple MAUs, connect a patch cable from the RO (Ring Out) of the first MAU to the RI (Ring In) of the second MAU. Continue doing this for all the MAUs until the last MAU is encountered. Then connect the RO of the last MAU to the RI of the first MAU.
- Stations cannot be connected to the RI and the RO port. The RI and RO ports are only used for interconnecting multiple MAUs.
- Patch cables (IBM Type 6) should not be spliced.
- Patch cables (IBM Type 6) should not be used in any duct, plenum, or other space used for air handling. IBM Type 9, which is a plenum-rated cable, can be used instead.

Token-Ring Hardware

Token-ring hardware has evolved significantly since its first generation. Early token-ring interface cards were expensive compared to NICs for Ethernet and ARCnet, and were limited to a data rate of 4Mbps. The original IBM MAU was the 8228, which added a cost of about $80 per network station.

Thin Ethernet required no similar device, and the cost of building the network was limited primarily to the required coax cabling. Thin Ethernet cable runs tend to be shorter than those required for token ring. Ethernet cables can daisy chain from station to station.

Each token ring station must have an individual cable that runs to the central wiring hub, even if it is only a few feet from a neighbor station. Because early token-ring networks required expensive and bulky Type 1 or Type 2 cable, the cabling overhead was often viewed as a serious liability.

At this stage, Ethernet held both performance and cost advantages that slowed down the acceptance of token ring. Most network planners saw advantages in token ring only when higher reliability or compatibility with IBM mainframe network architectures justified the higher cost of a token-ring installation.

Even early token ring offered significant advantages in terms of reliability, fault tolerance, and diagnostics. Among these advantages were the following:

- A redundant wiring path that enabled the network to continue functioning, despite a failure of the primary path.
- A star cabling topology that made it easier to identify malfunctioning stations and remove them from the network.
- Elaborate protocol controls that automatically detected and corrected many soft network errors.
- Network-management interfaces between IBM's token ring NICs and IBM network-management tools, such as NetView and NetView PC.
- A deterministic access-control mechanism that made token ring especially suitable in real-time network applications, such as manufacturing-process control.

There were, therefore, significant incentives to raise the performance and lower the cost of token-ring networks, and both IBM and competing vendors have continued to raise the standard. A variety of industry analysts have predicted that token-ring installations will overtake or surpass Ethernet installations sometime in the 1990's. The following factors account for this growth:

- ❖ The cost of token-ring hardware has dropped, due to increased competition from vendors using the chip sets developed by Texas Instruments.
- ❖ As costs have dropped, performance has improved. 16Mbps token ring now costs little more to implement than 4Mbps token ring does.
- ❖ Vendors have increasingly developed ways of implementing token ring on UTP wiring, even at 16Mbps speeds.

IBM has seldom lead the trend toward less costly token-ring networks. In part, this is due to an extremely conservative approach to the implementation of 16Mbps token rings on UTP cable. IBM has said that UTP cable would generate too much radio-frequency interference to be acceptable, and has sanctioned 16Mbps token ring only for the fairly expensive Types 1 and 2 cable.

Competing vendors were far in advance of IBM in commercializing the 16Mbps token ring on UTP. Perhaps the most notable vendor was Proteon, which markets an extremely successful line of 16Mbps MAUs that accepted UTP cabling. Recently, IBM and Synoptics have developed a proposal for a 16Mbps UTP network standard that has been submitted to the IEEE.

The oldest MAU, the IBM 8228, is a passive device, containing a system of relays that controls the connections of the stations to the network. The 8228 is equipped with eight station ports in addition to the RI and RO ports. Because it is passive, the 8228 does not require a power supply; it is rugged and reliable. However, it does not offer any network management support. For this reason, passive MAUs are gradually falling out of favor in larger networks.

The Series 70 Wiring Centers from Proteon are intelligent MAUs that are available in models supporting UTP via RJ45 connectors, as well as STP token ring, using the traditional token ring data connector. The Series 70 MAUs are equipped with status LEDs and switches that make it easy to monitor and reconfigure the network. Proteon has long been in the forefront of token-ring performance, and Series 70 supports 16Mbps-data rates over STP and UTP cabling.

Proteon's TokenVIEW Plus and TokenVIEW Monitor are network-monitor software packages that can centrally monitor and manage Proteon's active MAUs. TokenVIEW Plus monitors the status on individual rings; TokenVIEW Manager works with multiple TokenVIEW PLUS stations to create an overall distributed-management system that brings all statistics to a centralized management console.

IBM has also moved toward active hub technologies. The IBM 8230 Controlled Access Unit (CAU) is an active, intelligent token ring wiring concentrator that enables up to 80 devices, operating at either 4Mbps or 16Mbps, to share the same hub. Many formerly manual ring error-recovery functions are now automatic. The 8230 reports a variety of performance and fault data to network-management programs such as IBM LAN Network Manager.

IBM token ring management tools become even more valuable in an environment that includes IBM mainframes; Netview running on the mainframe can receive alerts from the token rings and can unify the management of token ring and SNA networks. Netview is almost certainly the premier management facility for enterprise networks and is in a constant state of enhancement. Netview even has facilities for managing local area network servers, such as NetWare from a Netview console.

IBM has also entered the 16Mbps UTP area. IBM and Synoptics have jointly submitted to the IEEE a standards proposal for a 16Mbps UTP. Establishment of such a standard would increase the acceptance of token ring as a network cabling system. IBM is not waiting for approval of a new standard; recent enhancements to 8230 Controlled Access Unit components support 16Mbps UTP token ring networks.

Understanding Vendor LAN Standards

Although they do not figure prominently in enterprise networks, manufacturers' standards may occasionally need to be dealt with. ARCnet is a popular network standard for small networks, and it has long been promoted by Novell and other vendors. LocalTalk is a low-program network that is standard on Apple Macintoshes.

ARCnet LANS

In 1976, four engineers from Datapoint Corporation built a LAN that evolved into a widely used, but relatively unknown, LAN—*ARCnet* (*A*ttached *R*esource *C*omputer *net*work*)*. The goal of the design team was to develop network links between Datapoint's computer systems, so that customers could share resources while still retaining the benefits of stand-alone processing.

A data rate of 2.5Mbps was selected, primarily because that was the transfer rate of the disks that Datapoint was using at the time. A small frame size (a maximum of 508 bytes) was chosen because a study done by ARCnet's designers revealed that more than 90% of all messages transmitted on a network were small. The designers wanted to make the network reliable, so that failures in stations and cables had a minimum impact on the rest of the network. Another requirement was to make ARCnet work with a variety of media such as coax, twisted pair, and fiber optic cable. Today, products exist that support these media.

By 1977, the project was complete. It did not make a big splash in the industry, however, because ARCnet was not a separate product; it was embedded in Datapoint's computing machines.

ARCnet technology predates Ethernet technology, even though many people think that Ethernet technology was the first. ARCnet has not achieved widespread implementation, for several reasons. One reason is that Datapoint kept the technology proprietary. It was not until 1982 that Datapoint enabled SMC (Standard Microsystems Corporation) to market an ARCnet chip set to other OEMs. Ethernet had already become popular by this time.

Unlike Digital, Intel, and Xerox, Datapoint did not propose ARCnet as a standard to the IEEE committee, and ARCnet remains a vendor standard. Consequently, network designers have felt less secure about implementing large, critical networks by using ARCnet technology. The SMC chip set, developed in 1982, started a grass-roots movement. More than a dozen vendors have used this chip set to manufacture ARCnet network cards; far fewer, however, than the number of vendors who have implemented Ethernet hardware.

ARCnet uses the same RG/62 93-ohm coaxial cable that is used with IBM 3270 terminals. This coax cable is cheaper than the 50-ohm coax cable used in Ethernet. Additionally, many older office buildings and airport complexes are wired with this type of cabling, which makes the transition to ARCnet easy.

ARCnet uses a token passing mechanism, which makes ARCnet deterministic. There is a fixed upper bound on the amount of time a station has to wait before it can transmit. The electrical configuration of ARCnet is a bus, and signals are broadcast similarly to Ethernet.

A significant advantage of ARCnet is that it is possible to implement large networks without expensive repeaters. The maximum distance between two stations is 2,000 feet. When active hubs are included, an ARCnet can grow to a maximum of 20,000 feet between any two network stations. Active hubs are relatively inexpensive devices compared with Ethernet and token ring bridges.

ARCnet has one disadvantage: a low data rate (2.5Mbps). A number of ARCnet vendors have formed the ARCnet Trader's Association (ATA), which disseminates information to users about ARCnet technology. Membership in ATA is open to vendors, system integrators, and users. Under its auspices, a new ARCnet standard (ARCnet Plus) is being developed, which has a designed data rate of 20 Mbps.

ArcNet Trader's Association
3413 North Kennicott, Suite B
Arlington Heights, IL 6004
(312)255-3003

ARCNet Operation

Fig 4.7 shows an ARCnet LAN. Station transmission is broadcast in the same manner as for a bus LAN, but access to the bus is determined by a token (hence the name, token passing bus). The figure shows stations that have node addresses of 1, 25, 50, and 255 on a bus. At start-up time, a logical ordering is made, so that these stations form a logical ring. Each station keeps track of two pieces of information: who is its successor (S) and who is its predecessor (P). A *successor* for a station is defined as the station on the ring with the next highest address. A *predecessor* for a station is defined as the station with the next lowest address.

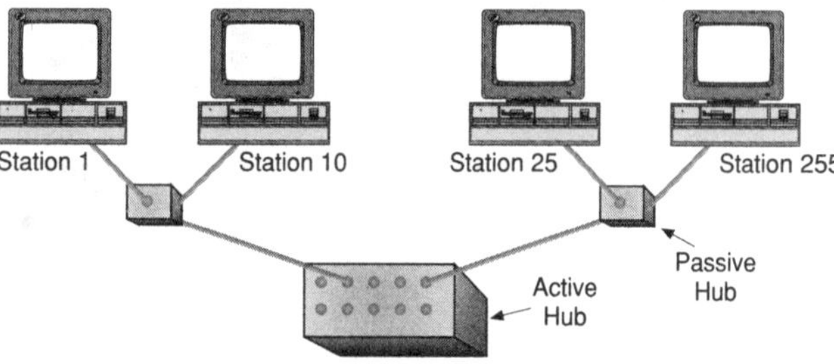

Figure 4.7:
ARCnet LAN operation.

A maximum of 255 stations are allowed in ARCnet; the lowest station address is 1. Station address 0 is used for broadcast. The successor for station 255 is 1 and the predecessor for station 1 is 255. The predecessor and successor information for the stations is summarized in table 4.9.

Table 4.9
Predecessor/Successor Rules for ARCnet

Station	*Predecessor (P)*	*Successor (S)*
1	255	10
10	1	25
25	10	255
255	25	1

A special frame, called the *token frame,* is passed from a station to its successor. The passing of this frame from station to station forms a logical ring. The token frame is called the Invitation To Transmit (ITT) frame. Its structure is the following:

ITT = _ ALERT _ EOT _ DID _ DID _

All ARCnet frames are preceded by an ALERT burst, which is similar to the preamble for Ethernet. An *ALERT burst* consists of six-bit intervals of mark (1). A *mark (1)* is represented by a dipulse pulse, which consists of a positive pulse followed by a negative pulse. A *space* (0) is represented by the absence of a pulse. The EOT is the ASCII EOT (04 hex) and is followed by two bytes. Each of the bytes contains the successor information called the DID (Destination ID) number. The DID field is repeated for reliability.

A station that has the ITT frame can transmit only one frame before passing the frame to its successor (next DID). Before a data frame is sent to a destination node, it must be queried to see if it has enough buffer space to accept the frame. A special frame called the FBE (Free Buffer Enquiry) performs this function.

FBE = _ ALERT _ ENQ _ DID _ DID _

The *ENQ (ENQUERY) is* the ASCII ENQ character (05 hex), and it is followed by two bytes. Each of the bytes contains the destination address (DID) of the station for which free buffer status is desired. The DID field is repeated for reliability.

If the destination node sends a positive response, an ACK frame, the sending node can send the data frame. A positive ACK frame consists of two bytes, as follows:

ACK = _ ALERT _ ACK _

The ACK (*Ack*nowledgment) is the ASCII ACK character (06 hex). When sent in response to a FBE frame, it indicates availability of buffer spaces at the receiver. There is no DID field because it is sent as a broadcast frame.

A NAK (*N*egative *Ack*nowledgment) is the ASCII NAK character (15 hex). It indicates non-availability of buffer space at the receiver. It is not sent to indicate improper data frame reception. There is no DID field because it is sent as a broadcast frame. A NAK frame consists of two bytes, as follows:

ACK = _ ALERT _ NAK _

Once an ACK frame is received in response to an FBE frame, a data frame can be sent. Data frames are transmitted by the PAC frame, as follows:

PAC = _ALERT_SOH_SID_DID_DID_CP_DATA_CRC_CRC

The SOH (*S*tart *o*f *H*eader) is the ASCII SOH (01 hex). The source and destination addresses are indicated by the *SID* (*S*ource *ID*) and DID (*D*estination *ID*) fields. Again, the DID field is repeated for reliability. The CP (Continuation *P*ointer) field indicates the place in its memory in which the station finds the beginning of the transmitted data. The data field DATA is of variable length between 1 and 508 bytes. A two-byte CRC, determined by the DATA field, is appended by the sender for error-checking purposes.

If a fault occurs to disrupt the proper passing of the token, the network must be reconfigured. Reconfiguration or resequencing also takes place when a station is added or removed from the token passing ring. This can happen when a station is added or removed from a ring.

If an active node fails to receive an ITT token frame after 840 milliseconds (or if it is powered up), a RECON pattern (consisting of eight mark intervals), followed by one space, is sent 765 times.

This RECON burst lasts for 2754 microseconds, which is long enough to disrupt any token-frame transmission that is under way. The result is that the token frame is lost. After seeing no activity for 78 microseconds, all stations realize that a reconfiguration is occurring. Each station then sets its successor (NID) to its own address (ID) plus one, and it sets a time-out value according to the following equation:

TIME-OUT = 146 x (255 - ID) microseconds

The node with the highest address has the first time out and issues an ITT to its successor (NID). The station with address 255 has a time-out value of 0. If no activity occurs after 74 microseconds (less than 78 microseconds), the highest address station assumes that the node with the successor address of NID does not exist. It increments the NID value and sends another ITT with the DID field set to the new NID value. This procedure is repeated until the highest address station discovers its successor. At this time, the token is transferred to the successor, and the successor repeats this process.

Once all active nodes are found, the normal token-passing operation is resumed. Reconfiguration can take between 24 and 61 milliseconds, depending on the number of active nodes and the value of their node addresses. To minimize the initial time-out value to 0 and to reduce the reconfiguration time, set at least one ARCnet node to address 255.

Deleting a node is a simpler process under ARCnet, and it does not invoke the full reconfiguration mechanism. In figure 4.7, if station 10 drops from the ring and does not respond to the ITT sent from station 1 for a period of 74 microseconds, station 1 assumes that station 10 is no longer active. Node 1 then increments its NID value (new value 11) and sends an ITT to station 11. If there is no response, the process repeats in another 74 microseconds. The next station address is 25, so within (25 - 10) x 74 microseconds = 1.1 milliseconds, station 1 figures out that its successor is station 25.

If station 10 wants to re-enter the network, it waits for a period of 840 milliseconds for the token. If it has not been invited to transmit via an ITT frame sent to it, it invokes the full reconfiguration mechanism.

ARCnet Components

An RG-62/U 93-ohm cable is used to connect the components of an ARCnet LAN. BNC twist-lock connector plugs are attached to both ends of the cable. BNC connector jacks mate with the BNC connector plugs and are located on several pieces of ARCnet hardware—active and passive hubs, network cards, and active links.

Passive hubs contain no electronic circuitry; they interconnect two or more network cables. Most passive hubs are equipped with four network connectors. Unused ports in passive hubs must be terminated. Unlike the active hubs, they do not have special isolation circuits.

ARCNet *active hubs* contain electronics that amplify and recondition network signals. They usually have eight ports, although active hubs with more ports are available. Terminating unused ports on an active hub is recommended, but not necessary, because of the isolation circuitry used in most ARCnet active hubs. Active hubs serve as network repeaters, and an ARCnet can grow to its maximum size using only passive and active hubs. Active hubs also provide some degree of isolation between the various ARCnet segments, although not to the degree provided by token ring.

Hubs in ARCnet give the network the physical topology of a star. It is important to realize, however, that the electrical (logical) topology of the network is a bus: signals transmitted by a station are broadcast to all stations on the network. ARCnet is, therefore, frequently defined as a star-wired bus.

The ARCnet star topology is illustrated in figure 4.8. All distances specified in the figure represent the maximum distances that can be used for that type of segment.

ARCnet Star Wiring Design Rules

The design rules for an ARCnet LAN using distributed star topology are summarized in table 4.10.

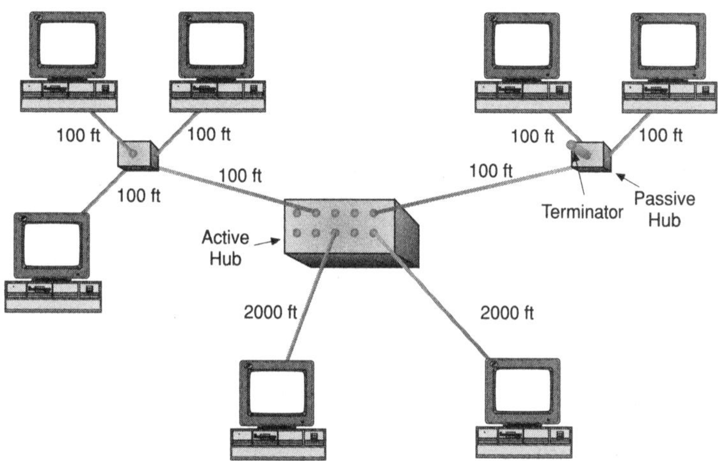

Figure 4.8:
Architecture of a typical ARCnet LAN.

Table 4.10
Cable Distance Limitations

From	*To*	*Max Distance (feet)*
One network end	The other end	20,000
Network station	Network station	2,000
Network station	Active hub	2,000
Network station	Passive hub	100
Active hub	Active hub	2,000
Active hub	Passive hub	100
Passive hub	Passive hub	Does not work

Thus, the maximum span of an ARCnet network is 20,000 feet (3.8 miles). ARCnet LANs are quite resilient to out-of-spec installations for distances between active components. They can frequently span distances of 4.5 miles, even though this is outside the ARCnet specification.

When passive hubs are employed, the distances are considerably shorter. The distance between a station and a passive hub cannot exceed 100 feet. Also, a passive hub cannot be connected in series with another passive hub—the signal attenuation is too great for this to work.

The following are general rules for ARCnet networks:

- Active hubs can connect to other hubs (active and passive) and ARCnet stations.
- Passive hubs can connect to active hubs and ARCnet stations. They cannot connect to other passive hubs directly.
- Do not create loops in an ARCnet LAN. (A *loop* is created when a cable coming from a hub goes through other hubs and then connects back into the original hub.)
- Always terminate unused ports in a passive hub.
- Keep a log of station addresses. Two stations cannot have duplicate addresses. No automatic mechanism exists to prevent this from occurring, as is the case in IEEE 802.5.
- To minimize reconfiguration time, set the most reliable station that is active most of the time to station address 255, which can be the file server.

ARCnet Coaxial Bus Design Rules

ARCnet can be used in a bus topology, in which up to eight stations can be daisy-chained with RG-62/U cables over a maximum distance of 1000 feet. In the bus topology, a T connector is used to connect the workstations; a single bus segment must be terminated with a nine-ohm impedance at both ends.

ARCnet coax bus topology can be mixed with the distributed-star topology provided by an active hub. One end of the bus can be connected to an active hub. The total number of workstations that can be connected to a single eight-port active hub in this manner is $8 \times 8 = 64$. If two active hubs are to be connected, one port in each active hub is used up for connecting the active hubs. Therefore, each active hub supports 56 stations; the two active hubs support a total of 112 stations. Table 4.11 summarizes the configuration rules for the coax bus.

Table 4.11

Configuration Rules for ARCnet Coax Bus

Parameters	*Value*
Maximum stations per bus	8
Maximum length of bus	1000 feet
Maximum stations on single eight-port active hub	64

ARCnet Twisted Pair Wiring Design Rules

Twisted-pair wiring can be used for ARCnet LANs. With ARCnet, twisted-pair bus topology is functionally and logically equivalent to the coax bus topology. Only one pair of twisted-pair wiring is needed. The twisted-pair ARCnet board has two six-pin modular jacks that can be used to daisy-chain the ARCnet board, unless the board is at the beginning or end of the daisy-chain segment. Terminators must be placed on unused plugs. A maximum of 10 stations can be used in the twisted-pair daisy-chain, whose length cannot exceed 400 feet. The minimum spacing between stations in the daisy chain is six feet.

Twisted-pair bus topologies can be mixed with the distributed-star topology provided by an active hub. One end of the bus can be connected to an active hub. Table 4.12 summarizes the configuration rules for the twisted-pair bus.

Table 4.12
Configuration Rules for ARCnet Twisted-Pair Bus

Parameters	*Value*
Maximum stations per TP bus	10
Maximum length of TP bus	400 feet
Minimum distance between nodes	6 feet
Maximum stations on single eight-port active hub	80

Large ARCnet Networks

The total number of stations in a single ARCnet LAN cannot exceed 255 and its maximum span is 20,000 feet. Within these limitations, any combination of distributed star, coax bus, and twisted pair bus can be used.

20Mbps ARCnet Plus

One of the most amazing features of the 20Mbps ARCnet Plus is that it improves the performance of ARCnet by a factor of eight; yet it retains downward compatibility with the 2.5Mbps ARCnet.

Nodes on the standard ARCnet signal a logical 1 by a single cycle of a 5Mhz sine wave, followed by a silence of equal length. A logical 0 consists of two intervals of silence. (The interval is 1/5Mhz = 200 nanosecond duration.) Two such intervals are necessary to send one bit (0 or 1) of information, which works out to a duration of 400 nanoseconds (a maximum data rate for ARCnet of 1/400 nanoseconds = 2.5 Mbps).

ARCnet sends data in integral multiples of bytes. Each byte is preceded by a three-bit calibration pattern (110), to keep the receiver in pace with the transmitter. There is an overhead of three bits for every eight bits of data. Therefore, the effective data rate for ARCnet is $8/11 \times 2.5$ Mbps = 1.82 Mbps, which is a lot of wasted bandwidth. The periods of silence are wasteful and the calibration overhead takes up 27% of the bandwidth.

ARCnet Plus uses the bandwidth more effectively. One way of achieving higher data rates is to cut out periods of silence. Another method is to send calibration patterns once every eight bytes. The most ingenious technique is to use Amplitude Modulation to squeeze four bits of information into every 200-nanosecond interval. A pulse can be either a positive or negative sine wave with eight possible amplitudes, from 0 to 12 volts. This gives a total of $2 \times 8 = 16$ combinations of pulses, enough to represent four bits of data.

Thus, total ARCnet Plus data rate = 4 bits × 5 million pulses-per-second = 20Mbps, excluding overhead. When the calibration overhead is taken into account, this yields an effective data rate of 16.84Mbps, which is faster than Ethernet and 16Mbps token ring.

During initialization, the ARCnet Plus node sends a special signal that informs others that it can operate at higher speeds. This signal is also sent when an ARCnet Plus node passes the token. An ARCnet Plus node communicates to another ARCnet Plus node at 20 Mbps, but steps down gracefully to 2.5Mbps to communicate with a 2.5Mbps ARCnet node.

The new standard enables packet lengths of up to 4096 bytes and to a maximum of 2047 nodes. IEEE 802.2 or DoD IP addressing mechanisms can be used for easier integration with Ethernet, token ring, and TCP/IP networks.

To upgrade to ARCnet Plus, follow these guidelines:

- To mix the two types of cards together, the cabling can remain the same, but the active hubs must be replaced with ARCnet Plus active hubs. If older active hubs are used, the high-speed ARCnet Plus signals are filtered out as they pass through the hubs.
- It is also possible to utilize the old ARCnet active hubs, provided that all ARCnet Plus nodes appear on the same side of the older active hub.

LocalTalk

LocalTalk is a common cabling system—every Apple Macintosh is equipped with a LocalTalk network connector. Perhaps no other computer platform networks with the ease of the Macintosh. Because of the universality of LocalTalk on Macs, many users want to connect their LocalTalk networks into larger corporate networks.

The performance of LocalTalk is disappointing: the network has a maximum data rate of roughly 230Kbps, and practical data rates of only about 90Kbps. LocalTalk is, therefore, suitable only for very small networks with few workstations, and it has little significance in the context of enterprise networks beyond being the means of connecting Macintoshes into the corporate LAN.

In most cases, Macintosh users are better served by equipping the station with an Ethernet or token ring adapter. Both are available in NuBus configurations that fit all bus-equipped Macs. Ethernet adapters are also available that can be connected to Mac SCSI ports. In general, these alternatives make considerably more sense than LocalTalk in the context of modern networks. In fact, Apple has begin to equip top-of-the-line Macintoshes with built-in Ethernet ports.

LocalTalk is a low-speed variant on the same CSMA/CD technology used by Ethernet. As such, LocalTalk networks are configured in a bus topology. It is easy to connect nearby workstations because LocalTalk cables can simply be strung from desk to desk. The ease of LocalTalk setup has been a major factor in its acceptance.

LocalTalk network segments can theoretically span 1000 feet and support 32 stations. In practice, far fewer stations are able to occupy a LocalTalk segment; the exact number depends on the type of work being done. When performance falters, LocalTalk networks are frequently subdivided by installing bridges, which increases the cost of the network cabling system.

The original cabling for LocalTalk was shielded twisted-pair cable terminated with DIN-8 miniplugs. Cables were connected to the Macs through LocalTalk connectors. A short cable from the LocalTalk connector was plugged into the Mac, and two jacks in the connector enabled the network cable to daisy-chain from one station to the other.

Besides lack of performance, the original LocalTalk cabling system had two other shortcomings. Its components were more expensive than many users thought reasonable. Also, it required the use of shielded twisted pair cable. The cable and connectors chosen by Apple were difficult to wire, and many users were forced to use pre-made cables. Dependence on STP also prevented installers from taking advantage of any telephone twisted-pair cabling that might be in place.

A variety of vendors have responded to these shortcomings by introducing UTP cabling systems for LocalTalk. These cabling systems generally cost less than Apple's LocalTalk components, and they can be easily interfaced by using telephone cables equipped with RJ-11 connectors. One innovative vendor of UTP LocalTalk products is:

> Farallon Computing, Inc.
> 2000 Powell Street, Suite 600
> Emeryville, CA 94608
> (510)596-9000

Farallon's PhoneNET network products are frequently used alternatives to standard LocalTalk components. Farallon has considerable expertise with LocalTalk networks and with interfacing LocalTalk to other network environments. They have also incorporated their PhoneNET technology into modules for use in network concentrators manufactured by Synoptics and David Systems.

Understanding Structured-Wiring Systems

The concept of structured-wiring systems was introduced in Chapter 3. These systems represent the industry trend to bring various network topologies together in concentrators in which they can be smoothly integrated and managed.

Structured-wiring systems are designed around concentrators that accept plug-in modules to support various protocols, media, and topologies. If concentrators consisted of little more than a home for the plug-in modules, however, there would be little to recommend them, other than their neatness.

Concentrators are increasingly serving as integration platforms. Recent developments include the following:

- ❖ Most vendors have introduced or are developing concentrator architectures that support at least the four cabling systems described in this chapter.
- ❖ Advanced backplane designs provide higher fault tolerance and the ability to hot-swap modules.
- ❖ Bridging and routing modules eliminate the need to employ separate bridges and routers.

- Concentrators are being interfaced to the PC bus and given the ability to execute programs. It has become possible, for example, to run NetWare server software directly in the concentrator; this enables the concentrator to provide services such as mainframe connectivity, messaging services, or routing via network-operating system routing systems.

Thus, concentrators are becoming an effective way to neatly integrate network servers with communication services.

Perhaps the chief advantage of structured-wiring concentrators, however, is that they provide the foundation for network management. Concentrators can be equipped to serve as network-management agents. This is seldom practical when each device on the network must provide its own network-management agent support. Chapter 11 contains much more information about network management, using such protocols as the Simple Network Management Protocol (SNMP), supported by most advanced network-wiring concentrators.

If there is a disadvantage to structured-wiring concentrators, it is related to initial costs. Concentrators are not inexpensive devices. If the full capacity of a concentrator is not required, some of the concentrator's value is unrealized and the cost-per-port is fairly high. The advantage of concentrators begins to become significant when reducing cable tangles in the wiring closet outweighs the cost factor.

At least one vendor, David Systems, enables users to start with stand-alone 12-port 10BASE-T modules. When the network grows large enough to justify the acquisition of a concentrator, the electronics can be removed from the stand-alone modules and installed in the concentrator chassis.

All manufacturers of wiring concentrators provide some form of network-management software. Unless the network is to consist of only one brand of hardware, however, it is important to determine that all of the components can be managed centrally. If a vendor's proprietary software does not manage other brands of equipment, network administrators should investigate independent products that can manage multivendor networks.

The competition among manufacturers of network structured-wiring systems is intense, and a variety of well-engineered systems are available. The following lists several of the most significant manufacturers:

Cabletron Systems, Inc.
35 Industrial Way
P.O. Box 5005
Rochester, NY 03867-7386
(603-332-9400)

David Systems Incorporated
701 E. Evelyn Avenue
Sunnyvale, CA 94086-3718
(408)720-8000

Hewlett-Packard Company
3000 Hanover Street
Palo Alto, CA 94304
(800)752-0900

NetWorth, Inc.
8404 Esters Road
Irving, TX 75063
(214)929-1700

Proteon
Two Technology Drive
Westborough, MA 01581
(508)898-2800

Synoptics Communications, Inc.
4401 Great America Parkway
P.O. Box 58185
Santa Clara, CA 95052-8185
(408)988-2400

The IBM 8320 Controlled Access Unit was mentioned earlier in this chapter. Although it is essentially a concentrator system for token ring, the 8320 does not provide support for other cabling standards. Rather, IBM has chosen to seek out strategic relationships with other vendors of LAN network equipment, such as Synoptics and Novell. IBM remains one of the most experienced network companies and is increasingly marketing itself as an integrator of network systems, whether or not it relies on IBM technologies and products. Because numerous IBM divisions manufacture network products, the best place to start when seeking information is to call the IBM dealer channel information number: (800)IBM-2468.

Summary

This chapter has discussed the following network cabling standards in some depth:

- Ethernet/IEEE 802.3
- Token ring/IEEE 802.5
- ARCnet
- LocalTalk

Equipment supporting any or all of these standards may be found in large organizations that seek to integrate their computing resources into enterprise networks.

Current technologies, particularly the latest developments in structured wiring systems, make it possible to smoothly integrate multistandard networks. This makes it possible to conserve investment in current technologies while positioning the organization to take advantage of new, higher performance options.

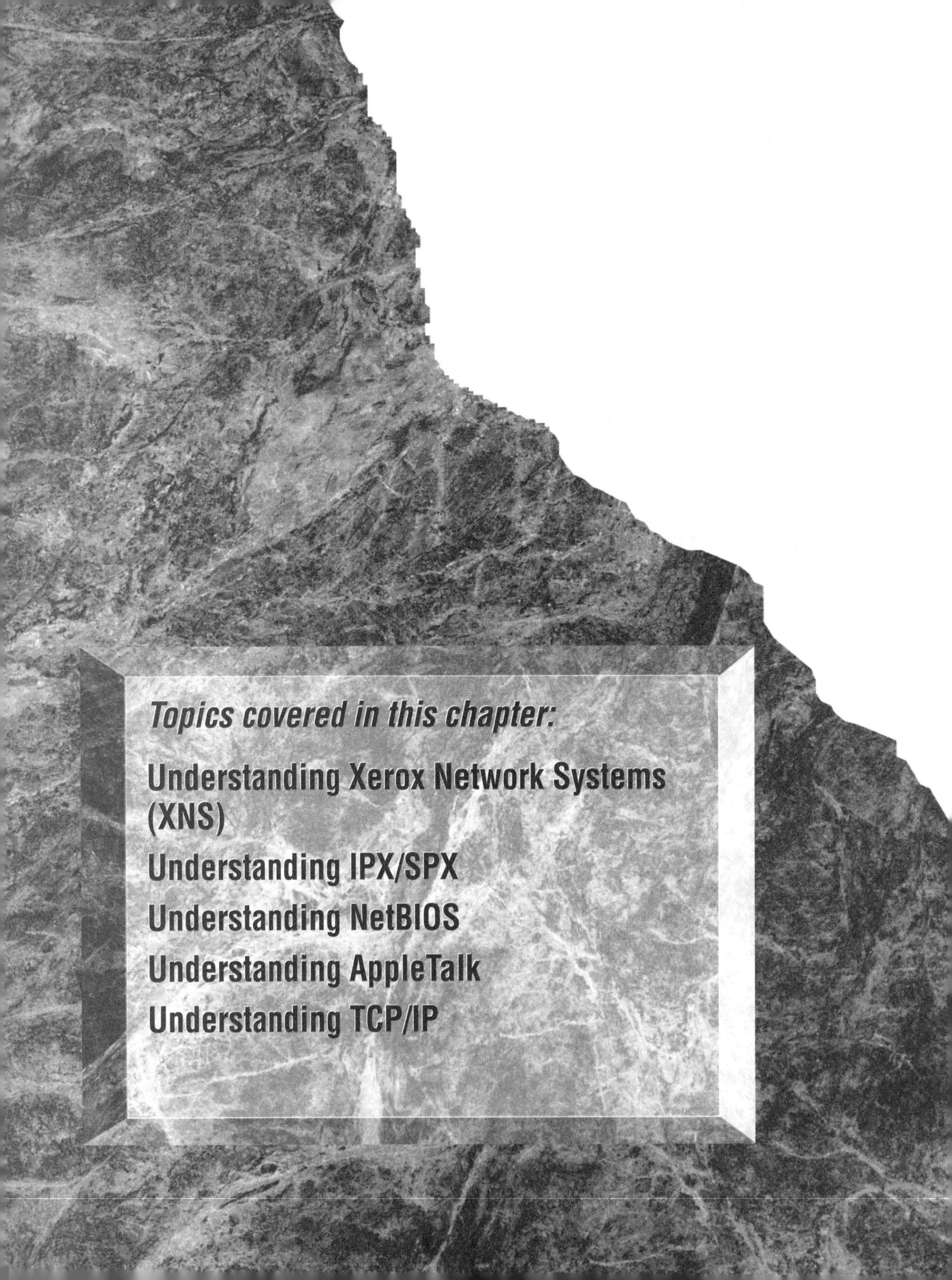
Topics covered in this chapter:
Understanding Xerox Network Systems (XNS)
Understanding IPX/SPX
Understanding NetBIOS
Understanding AppleTalk
Understanding TCP/IP

Chapter 5

Communication Protocols

Data communications protocols are used to coordinate the exchange of information between different network devices. They establish the mechanism by which each device recognizes meaningful information from another device. In the communications world today, there are a number of protocols in use, along with several basic structures that handle different aspects of data communication.

In this chapter, you look at five of the more widely implemented protocols in the context of the OSI Reference Model. You also learn about protocol structure in detail and the ways that protocols communicate over a network.

Once the domain of the small workgroup and office department, local area networks are becoming the major integration platform for enterprise-wide computing. The simple twenty-user network has now expanded to the three or five thousand-user enterprise internetwork, spanning time zones as easily as it used to span office cubicles.

To match these new demands, LAN protocols have become increasingly powerful and flexible. This chapter examines the following five major LAN protocols that support the workgroup and the enterprise model to varying degrees:

- Xerox Network Systems (XNS)
- Novell's IPX/SPX
- NetBIOS
- Apple's AppleTalk
- Internet's TCP/IP protocol suite

The following sections discuss each of these communication protocols in detail.

Understanding Xerox Network Systems (XNS)

The *Xerox Network Systems (XNS)* was developed by researchers at Xerox Corporation's Palo Alto Research Center (Xerox PARC). It evolved from the PUP internetwork, which was a research prototype developed at PARC. Initially designed to connect computers to be used in Xerox's office environment, XNS was a seminal design that became the foundation of many local area network architectures by such influential firms as Ungermann-Bass, 3Com, and Novell.

Much of the success that XNS enjoyed as a basis for multiple LAN architectures can be attributed to its clean and simple design, coupled with the relative ease of implementing its required functions.

XNS is one of the earliest layered network architectures. It predates the OSI Reference Model, and it was one of the inspirations for the seven-layer model.

The architecture for XNS was largely dictated by the environment and user community it was designed to serve. In particular, researchers at PARC were interested in creating an electronic community from the familiar office environment. They envisioned users making use of a range of services on the network: electronic mail, electronic document exchange, and remote printing of documents. This vision suggested that the *stations* (computers) would be close together in a building or campus. Because of the proximity, equipment could be designed for fast and reliable communications between the stations.

In the XNS architecture, several types of devices may be interconnected. The two most important of these devices are called *hosts* (workstations) and *routers*. Workstations are connected to each other in a local network (*subnet*, in XNS terminology). Subnets or networks are connected together to form larger entities called *internetworks* or *internets*. It is assumed that routers are located at the juncture of networks and are used to route *datagrams* (data packets) between the distinct subnets.

The XNS Layered Architecture

The XNS architecture is made up of five layers (in contrast to the seven-layer OSI Reference Model). Like the OSI model, however, the upper layers make use of services provided by the lower layers to complete any requests made of them.

The protocols provide a range of services, including datagram delivery, a request-reply packet exchange, and sequenced packet and byte streams.

The layers are numbered from 0 to 4; layer 0 is the lowest layer that interacts with the network communications media, and layer 4 contains network applications and services (see fig. 5.1).

Layer 4

Layer 4 is the highest layer in XNS and corresponds most closely to the application layer (layer 7) in the OSI model. Two protocols and services are defined in XNS for this layer:

- **Clearinghouse**. A distributed-name service that provides XNS-connected computers with a way to associate or bind names to resources and computers.
- **Gateway Access Protocol (GAP)**. Provides a gateway service that enables XNS systems to be connected to non-XNS systems.

File, print, and messaging (electronic-mail) services generally belong in layer 4.

Layer 3

Layer 3 in the XNS corresponds with the session and presentation layers (layers 5 and 6) in the OSI Reference Model. The protocol defined in XNS for this layer is called *courier.* Courier controls access to remote procedure calls on the network or internetwork. *Remote procedure calls* (*RPCs*) are network extensions of the familiar local procedure calls, and they can provide an application with access to files, printers, remote displays, and other resources on the network.

Layer 2

Layer 2 of XNS corresponds to the transport layer in OSI (layer 4). This layer contains several protocols, in addition to what is considered as a transport protocol. The following lists the protocols found in this layer:

- **Sequenced Packet Protocol (SPP)**. A full duplex-transport protocol, which provides a sequenced stream of packets between two processes on connected computers. SPP handles flow control between the two communicating processes so that a fast sender does not overrun a slower receiving station. This protocol also provides a retransmission capability for lost, damaged, or out-of-sequence packets. In effect, it provides a reliable communications stream between the two stations using the unreliable Internet Datagram Protocol (IDP) that is implemented at layer one (discussed in the next section).
- **Packet Exchange Protocol (PEP)**. A request-response protocol that retransmits the packet after a specified time if a response is not heard. PEP is well suited for transactional-type applications that require a simple, fast protocol for information exchange.
- **Routing Information Protocol (RIP).** Exchanges routing information between computers. Each router in the internet (and many stations) keeps and maintains a routing table to determine an efficient way to send packets from one station to another, even if the stations are located on distinct networks (as long as the networks are connected together).

- **Error Protocol.** An optional protocol that enables any system on the internetwork to report a packet error. When an error is discovered, an Error Protocol packet is sent to the source socket taken from the offending packet. The error packet contains an error number, an error parameter, and the first *n* bytes (the suggested number is 42—to hold the IDP and SPP headers) from the faulty packet. Each application receiving an error packet is free to act on the information in a suitable manner.
- **Echo Protocol.** A simple protocol that determines whether a packet can reach a device on the internet. The Echo Protocol requires the receiving application to return the packet to the source. An operation field in the Echo packet indicates whether the packet is a request or a reply echo. In general, an echoer should be implemented at a well-known socket on every host in the internet.

Layer 1

Layer 1 in the XNS model corresponds to the network layer (layer 3) in the OSI model. Essentially, layer 1 performs the functions of a router—it routes packets through the internet, based on the source and destination packet addresses. The protocol used to implement this service is called the Internetwork Datagram Protocol (IDP). This protocol implements an unreliable datagram service that higher-level protocols, such as SPP, can use to provide the basis for their reliable, end-to-end data-stream service.

Layer 0

Layer 0 corresponds with the physical and data-link layers (layers 1 and 2) in the OSI model. Xerox refers to the protocols at this layer as *transmission medium protocols*. As in the OSI model, layer 0 is responsible for transmitting and receiving data over a physical communications medium. Protocols that are supported at this layer include Ethernet, RS-232-C, and RS-449. For the purposes of XNS, X.25 is considered to be a transmission medium protocol.

An XNS internetwork may be comprised of several distinct connected networks. Networks are connected together by computers called routers, which are capable of routing packets of data between the attached networks. In turn, each network can have numerous computer workstations (hosts) attached, with the possibility of multiple processes (applications) running on each workstation.

To uniquely identify a communications end point, XNS uses the following three numbers for internetwork addressing:

- The *network number* is a 32-bit value that identifies a network (or a subnetwork in XNS terminology) that is part of an internet.
- The *host number* is a 48-bit address that uniquely identifies a network interface card (NIC) and the host (computer) in which it is located. This 48-bit address is a universally unique address that is associated directly with the board at the time of manufacture and cannot be configured or modified.

  This address is the Media Access Control (MAC) address, as defined by the IEEE Project 802 specification. No two network interface cards that adhere to this spec can have the same address anywhere in the world. The XNS designers envisioned that, because most systems would be connected to Ethernets, the performance of the system could be enhanced by not requiring a table-driven lookup translation between host and network addresses. The choice of a 48-bit value, however, did not compromise the generality of the address if new or different transmission media was used.

- The *socket number* is a 16-bit value that applications use to identify a communications end point. Applications on a host use a socket to send and receive data over the network. Certain applications that provide advertised services to other hosts on the network can make use of well-known socket numbers. This guarantees that everyone can have easy access to the service, if they are authorized.

Because the host number is unique across the entire internetwork, the network number may appear to be unnecessary. By relying on the network number for internetwork routing, however, routers are able to reduce the size of their routing tables and to switch packets at a quicker rate because there are usually fewer networks than hosts. Additionally, the amount of bandwidth required to update and maintain the routing tables is reduced by having smaller tables.

The Internetwork Datagram Protocol

The Internetwork Datagram Protocol (IDP) is the XNS packet protocol that provides an unreliable datagram service. Each packet is routed through the internetwork independently on a best-effort basis. No guarantee is made for the order of delivery or whether duplicate packets are to be delivered.

The general model for using the services IDP provides are as follows. The sending application may know the network, host, and socket number of the receiving application. If so, it passes it to the IDP and it is used directly. If the address is unknown, the sending application can make use of the Clearinghouse name service to determine the address. (This is essential because ISP only understands IDP addresses.) The address may be stored locally or elsewhere on the network, because the Clearinghouse service is implemented as a distibuted database. This process of determining the association of a name with an address is called *binding* or *name resolution*. Once the address is resolved, IDP can use it to route the packet to the proper network and host. The IDP packet is as follows:

Checksum	2 bytes
Length	2 bytes
Transport Control	1 byte
Packet Type	1 byte
Destination Network	4 bytes
Destination Host	6 bytes
Destination Socket	2 bytes
Source Network	4 bytes
Source Node	6 bytes
Source Socket	2 bytes
Data	up to 546 bytes

Each field is described in detail in the following sections.

- **Checksum**. An optional computational sum used to verify the integrity of the IDP packet. It is the complement add and rotate sum of all the 16-bit words of the packet, excluding the checksum field. If the checksum is not computed, the field is set to all ones. The checksum algorithm is designed to incrementally recalculate the packet if it is legitimately modified en route to the destination.
- **Length**. The length of the packet in bytes. The maximum length of an IDP is 576 bytes. Because the length of the header is 30 bytes, 546 bytes remain for the data and the control information from higher-layer protocols. The data section was conveniently designed to hold the usual disk-page size of 512 bytes.
- **Transport Control**. Controls the passage of packets through the internet. Only internet routers make use of this field. One of the uses of the field is to keep track of the number of routers that the packet passes through. If this number exceeds 16, the packet is dropped. This prevents packets from looping around the internet forever. The field should be initialized to zero at the source.
- **Packet Type**. Used by layer 2 protocols to specify the format of the data field. IDP does not interpret this field; it delivers the field to the destination and presents it to an upper layer for interpretation. Xerox has defined the following IDP packet types:

0	Unknown packet type
1	Routing Information Packet
2	Echo Packet
3	Error Packet
4	Packet Exchange Packet
5	Sequenced Packet Protocol Packet
16-31	Experimental Protocols

- **Destination and Source Networks**. The addresses of the respective networks; each network in the internetwork has a unique 32-bit identifier.
- **Destination and Source Hosts**. The addresses of the hosts on the network. Each host has a 48-bit identifier that uniquely identifies the host on the entire internet.
- **Destination and Source Sockets**. The 16-bit addresses of application processes on the sending and receiving hosts.
- **Data**. A 546-byte buffer for holding the data transmitted over the network.

The IDP also performs the packet-routing functions in the XNS network. The routing is based on the network address, which is used to determine whether the packet can be delivered directly to the destination station, or whether it needs to be sent to a router that is closer to the destination network and station. If the final destination is on a remote network, the router that the packet is handed off to is called the next *hop*. In this way, packets hop from router to router, based on their network addresses, until they reach the network of the destination host.

The process at each router is as follows. The incoming packet's destination network address is examined. If the router is directly attached to that network, the router delivers the packet directly to the desination host address, as specified in the packet. If the packet needs to be routed to a network that is not directly connected, the router searches its routing table and determines whether it is connected to a router closer to the final destination. If so, it sends the packet to the device (host) address of this router. This procedure continues until a router is reached that is attached directly to the destination network, and the packet is delivered.

The IDP is an unreliable protocol that has no acknowledgments for successfully delivered packets and no retransmissions if a packet is lost or damaged. It performs what is called a *best-effort* delivery. Higher-layer protocols, such as the SPP (examined later) take on the responsibility of performing all the steps necessary to ensure reliability. Because not all applications require the overhead of a reliable transmission mechanism, the services provided by the IDP are well suited for fast, simple, and effective routing and delivering of data packets through an internetwork.

As mentioned earlier, the maximum size of an IDP packet is 576 octets. It is especially important to have a well-defined maximum size when routers are used to move packets between networks. In these cases, the router only understands packets up to a fixed size, and it drops packets not conforming to the maximum.

Every system on the internetwork, including workstations and file servers, can perform a limited amount of packet routing. This routing is generally limited to the local host and directly attached networks. Internetwork routers can also route a packet to any location on the internet. Routers tend to be dedicated machines, but they can be configured to operate on a shared system.

Routing Information Protocol (RIP)

The Routing Information Protocol is a layer 2 protocol that uses the IDP to exchange routing information between routers. The purpose of RIP is to collect and maintain correct information about the way to route packets within the internet.

Conditions in an internetwork are constantly changing with new networks, stations, and routers being added, removed, or suffering from temporary failure. To expect a human administrator to keep up with these conditions and to update the routing tables is unrealistic. The RIP fills this requirement by providing a means for network stations and routers to automatically maintain the routing tables of the internetwork.

The routing table can be thought of as a map of the internetwork; each entry in the table contains several pieces of information. These include the following:

- ❖ The network address.
- ❖ The device (host) address of the router that gets the packet one step closer to the desired network.
- ❖ The hop count, which is the number of routers the packet has to go through until it reaches the router that is connected to the destination network.
- ❖ The port in the router on which the packet is sent to reach the next hop.
- ❖ A timer to ensure that only up-to-date information is kept in the table. The default value for this timer is three minutes. If this timer expires, the entry is marked for removal from the table.

Routers exchange information among themselves using RIP. Routers do this by enclosing information in a RIP packet and broadcasting across the entire internetwork (this happens every 30 seconds). The amount of traffic that RIP can generate to maintain network routing tables has become a problem as internetworks become larger and larger.

The routing information packet is placed in the data field of the IDP packet. It consists of the following fields:

- **Operation field.** A 16-bit field that indicates whether the packet is a request (value 1) for information or a response (value 2) to a routing request.

  Following the operation field, information concerning multiple networks can be specified.
- **Network**. A 32-bit number, identifying a network.
- **Internetwork Delay**. A 16-bit number, indicating the number of hops to the associated network.

If the operation is a request, the network number is initialized to the identifier of the network and the delay is set to 16 hops (which, for the purposes of XNS is infinity). If the packet is a reponse to a request for information, the delay is set to the number of hops to reach the network. A returned value of infinity means that the network is unreachable.

Because of near-constant change and the unpredictable nature of additions or failures on the internet, entries in the routing table have a fixed lifetime associated with them. If new information relating to the entry is not received before the time expires, the entry is automatically deleted. (Old, out-of-date information is of less value than is no information.) If a packet comes through the router that requires information that is not present, a dynamic RIP message can determine the routing information.

In addition to the routing table kept in the network routers, each station (host) on the network can also contain a smaller routing table. When the table is consulted for a packet whose destination is not on the local network, the device (host) address in the routing table will be for the router leading to the remote network. Stations can also make use of the RIP to maintain their local routing tables.

The use of the information in the routing table is not necessarily restricted to the routing protocols. Additional programs or monitors may use the information in the tables to determine and display the status of the internetwork.

Sequenced Packet Protocol (SPP)

The XNS Sequenced Packet Protocol is a connection-oriented protocol that establishes a virtual circuit between the sender and the receiver. It implements a reliable full-duplex data stream on top of XNS' unreliable IDP datagram delivery system.

SPP builds a reliable data stream between two sockets by labelling each octet of data with a unique sequence number. This enables the receiving end to determine if any of the packets have been lost, duplicated. or delivered out of order. This type of service is important because many applications require and assume that data can be moved as a reliable stream between processes or devices. In general, this is the model of data transfer when it is confined to a local computer. Providing this type of service reduces the size and complexity of all network applications that make use of SPP.

A packet can be lost by malfunctioning hardware or by being dropped by an overloaded router on the internetwork. In this case, the sender may time out waiting for an acknowledgment from the receiver and then resend the packet. If, however, the packet is received and the acknowledgment is lost, the sender still times out and resends a packet (in this case, a duplicate). Sequence numbers enable communication processes to recover from these situations. Additionally, sequence numbers in packets enable the receiver to reorder them if they are received out of order.

SPP also implements a system of flow control so that a faster sending process does not overwhelm a slower receiving process. This can cause packets to be dropped and to force retransmissions, thus reducing the throughput of the connection. SPP implements this by a system called the *sliding window protocol*—the receiver informs the sender about the number of unacknowledged packets the sender is allowed to transmit before buffers are filled and packets are dropped. The sender can also specify, in advance, the desire to get an acknowledgment immediately after reception.

To increase the throughput of the connection, SPP enables a single acknowledgment to be sent for multiple packets. Network traffic is reduced by not requiring the receiving process to acknowledge each packet received individually.

By using multiple sockets, SPP performs the function of multiplexing multiple data streams over an internetwork connection, enabling multiple processes on a single computer to communicate with processes on one or more remote computers. This functionality gives efficient use of the network by multitasking operating systems. The SPP packet is as follows:

Connection Control	1 byte
Datastream Type	1 byte
Source Connection ID	2 bytes
Destination Connection ID	2 bytes
Sequence Number	2 bytes
Acknowledgment Number	2 bytes
Allocation Number	2 bytes
Data	up to 54 bytes

Each field is described in detail in the following list.

- **Connection Control**. An eight-bit field that contains a set of flags. Bits 0 to 3 represent the System Packet, Send Acknowledgment, Attention, and End-of-Message flags, respectively. Bits 4 to 8 are unused and reserved.
- **System Packet bit**. Used if the source host needs to send a packet to the destination without the request of the client application process. The System Packet bit may also be used to implement probes from a source to determine if the destination is reachable. The bit is also set in a return acknowledgment.
- **Send Acknowledgment bit**. Requests the receiver to return an acknowledgment. If data is also being returned, the acknowledgment can be "piggybacked" on the data packet. Otherwise, a system packet containing the acknowledgment can be returned.
- **Attention bit**. Used to indicate that the packet should be brought to the attention of the receiving process as soon as the packet arrives. The receiving process may not be ready to accept data, but it is expected to make an extraordinary effort to receive the packet. Aware of this, the sending process should use this flag infrequently and include only a single byte of data.
- **End-of-Message bit**. Enables applications to use a model of communication in which messages are exchanged, instead of using the regular data stream. To accommodate this, the bit enables the sending process to delineate messages sent in the data portion of the packet. If this bit is set, the end of data in this packet is the end of a message; the next packet contains the beginning of the next message.

- **Datastream Type**. An eight-bit field that is used by higher-layer protocols to pass control information between communicating processes without having to embed this information in the data itself. (This field is not used by the Sequenced Packet Protocol.) The meaning attached to the field is defined by the high-layer protocol. It can coordinate the transfer of a data file from a server to an application on the workstation. In this case, the field would contain control information about the initiation, the transfer of data, and the end of transfer.
- **Source and Destination Connection ID**. Fields that are used to uniquely determine a connection. Although the internetwork address—consisting of the network, host, and socket number—uniquely identifies a sending or receiving process on the internet, the connection IDs identify a connection between the two end points. This is important because if stations start a new session using the same internet address (down to the socket), any packets still in transit can mistakenly seem to belong to the previous connection. By using the connection IDs, which are presumed to be created in a sufficiently random manner (based on the system clock, for example), each connection between source and destination can be unambiguously identified.
- **Sequence Number.** A 16-bit field that is incremented with each packet sent and identifies the packet for the purposes of detecting duplications, determining packet order, and specifying flow-control information. The Sequence Number is used in conjunction with the Allocation Number to inform the sending process the number of packets that the receiver can safely handle.

The Sequence Number provides the basis for implementing a reliable data stream.

- **Acknowledgment Number**. A 16-bit field used by the destination to notify the sender of the next sequence number it expects to receive. This number also informs the sender that packets with sequence numbers up to the acknowledgment number has been successfully received.
- **Allocation Number**: Informs the sender that it can safely receive packets with sequence numbers up to and including the allocation number. This is the field that is used to implement the Sequenced Packet Protocol's flow control.
- **Data**. Contains the data to transfer to the destination. The length of the data may be up to 534 bytes long. This figure is derived as follows: the 576-byte maximum packet size minus the 12-byte SPP header and the 30-byte header of the Internetwork Datagram Protocol.

In order for communication to occur between two processes, a connection needs to be established. Both ends of the connection must know the network, host, socket numbers, connection IDs of the source, and destination processes. The processes can use SPP to determine the connection IDs of the source and destination.

In order to terminate the connection, a three-way handshake is used to affect an orderly teardown, ensuring that both processes agree and no packets are lost. The first message indicates that the sender has no more data to transmit. The second message is a reply, indicating that the data has been received and the destination process is ready to terminate the connection. The third and final message in the handshake is a reply from the sender, saying that the connection has been terminated. The Datastream Type field in the SPP header described earlier can be used to carry the signals for the three-way handshake.

Packet Exchange Protocol (PEP)

The Packet Exchange Protocol (PEP) provides a connectionless protocol for simple request/response-type communications between application processes. PEP is a layer-two protocol that uses the IDP to transmit the packets across the internet.

The packet structure for the protocol is simple and efficient. It contains a 32-bit ID field, identifying the request and enabling the reply (using the same ID) to be matched up with the request. A second field, the Client Type, identifies the higher-layer client of the request. An optional Data Field can contain the response from the remote application or service.

The type of service provided by PEP is similar to IDP, except that PEP is request-response oriented. If no response is heard for a particular request before a certain time, the packet is retransmitted. For this reason, it is slightly more reliable than vanilla IDP, but less reliable than the SPP. PEP relies on the applications using the protocol to provide the extra reliability, if any is needed.

PEP is ideally suited for one-shot transactions. An example is a client application that requests the time of day from a server on the network.

Courier Protocol

Courier has also been called the Remote Procedure Call (RPC) protocol in the XNS environment. It controls the calling of remote procedures that are located and executed on remote computers.

The model for this service is the familiar client-server model. In a local-procedure call, the calling procedure is located on the same computer as the procedure it wants to call. In a remote-procedure call, the calling procedure and the procedure that is called are located on different computers. Courier takes care of packaging the procedure call and its arguments into a request packet and sending it across the network. The procedure is executed on the remote computer; the results from the call are packaged and returned to the calling function. From the caller's point of view, nothing interesting has happened. A procedure was called and a result was returned. Courier makes the calling procedure unaware and unconcerned about where the procedure was actually executed.

The client-server model is a powerful paradigm for network programming because it provides a model of application development that is very familiar to most developers. The power of the networked environment can thus be exploited with little extra effort.

Clearinghouse Name Service

Clearinghouse is a name service for the XNS. A *name service* is sometimes called a *directory service* because it provides a directory of named users, programs, network resources, and other objects, along with their associated XNS addresses.

The purpose of the Clearinghouse name service is to enable users and programs (written by programmers) to use friendly names to identify network objects instead of the generally unfriendly (to humans) network, host, and socket addresses.

The Clearinghouse database is distributed across the network. It is consulted by programs and users to determine the XNS address before a service can be requested. It can be tied in with an Authentication Service that checks to ensure that the requesting user has the proper privileges and rights to utilize the requested service.

Understanding IPX/SPX

The Novell NetWare protocol suite is based on the Xerox Network Systems (XNS) suite of protocols. Layer structure, protocol interaction, and even network addressing closely correspond to XNS.

Novell's implementation of Xerox's Internetwork Datagram Protocol and Sequenced Packet Protocol are called the Internetwork Packet Exchange (IPX) and Sequenced Packet Exchange (SPX), respectively. SPX is a reliable, connection-oriented protocol; IPX is an unreliable datagram protocol.

NetWare uses a slightly modified version of the Routing Information Protocol (RIP) to query and maintain routing-information tables on workstations and servers.

Novell adopted the internetwork-addressing structure of XNS. A complete address is given by the network number, the host number, and the socket number on the host. The network number is

32 bits long, the host number is 48 bits long, and the socket is 16 bits long.

The following sections examine the core NetWare protocols including IPX, SPX, RIP, the NetWare Core Protocols (NCP), and the Service Advertising Protocol (SAP).

Internetwork Packet Exchange (IPX)

The Internetwork Packet Exchange (IPX) is Novell's network layer protocol. IPX was derived from Xerox's Internetwork Datagram Protocol (IDP) and shares an identical packet structure.

IPX provides a connectionless, unreliable, datagram service to workstations and servers. IPX makes a best-effort attempt to deliver a packet to the destination but requests no acknowledgment to verify if the packet has indeed reached its destination. IPX relies on high-layer protocols, such as SPX or NCP to provide a reliable, sequenced datastream service.

An IPX packet consists of a header and data section. The header is 30 bytes long. Because IPX does not provide any facilities for packet fragmentation, IPX implementations must ensure that the packets they send are small enough to be transmitted on any physical networks they need to traverse. IPX requires that all physical links be able to handle IPX packets that are 576 bytes long, thus, the safest approach is to send no packet larger than 576 bytes. Many implementations refine this process slightly by detecting when they are sending packets directly to the destination over a single physical link. If this physical link can handle packets larger that 576 bytes, larger packets are used. The IPX packet stucture is as follows:

Checksum	2 bytes
Length	2 bytes
Transport Control	1 byte
Packet Type	1 byte
Destination Network	4 bytes
Destination Host	6 bytes
Destination Socket	2 bytes
Source Network	4 bytes
Source Node	6 bytes
Source Socket	2 bytes
Data	up to 546 bytes

The fields are discussed in the following sections.

- **Checksum**. Not used by IPX; this field must contain the value FFFFh.
- **Length**. Contains the number of bytes of the entire IPX datagram, header and data included. The minimum length of a packet is 30 bytes (the header); the maximum is 576 bytes (if the packet passes through internetwork routers).
- **Transport Control**. Ensures that a datagram never loops around an internet indefinitely. The field is initially set to zero and is incremented when it is handled by a router. When the value in this field is equal to 16, the datagram is discarded.
- **Packet Type**. Enables IPX to pass the packet to the proper higher-layer protocol. IPX defines the following four packet types:

0	Unknown Packet Type
4	Packet Exchange Protocol
95	Sequenced Packet Exchange
17	NetWare Core Protocol

An *internetwork address* is composed of the network address, the host (computer) address, and the socket address. The *socket address* identifies the communicating process on the computer. IPX supports up to 50 sockets per station. A network address of zero implies the local network.

Several well-known socket addresses are defined by Novell to provide important internetwork-wide services. The following lists the most important socket numbers. The h following the number signifies that the number is presented in hexadecimal.

451h	NetWare Core Protocol (NCP)
452h	Service Advertising Protocol (SAP)
453h	Routing Information Protocol (RIP)
455h	NetBIOS
456h	Diagnostics

❖ **Data**. Contains the information that is to be sent over the network. Application programs can use an API to place data in the packet and use IPX to send it to the remote computer. The packets of higher-layer protocols, such as SPX, NCP, RIP, and SAP, are placed in the data section of the IPX packet. This process of stuffing a higher-layer protocol packet in the data section is called *encapsulation*.

IPX interfaces with the data-link layer. The *data-link layer* assembles the data into a frame for transmission across the network. The destination host address that IPX supplies to the data-link layer depends on whether the host is attached to the local network or to a remote network. All stations on a network share the same network number.

If the destination station is located on the local network, the station's address is handed to the data-link layer with the IPX packet for direct delivery to the destination station. If the destination station is on a network different from the source station, some extra work must be done.

In this case, IPX sends a Route Request packet, using the Routing Information Protocol (RIP) to determine the fastest route to send the packet. A reply, containing the host address of the router capable of forwarding the packet to the destination network, is returned. With this information, the source and destination address of the local and remote computer is kept inside the IPX packet, but the host address of the router is handed to the data-link layer for delivery to this intermediary station (the router). (RIP is examined later in the chapter.).

When the router receives the packet, it determines whether the packet is attached to the destination network stored in the IPX packet. If it is, it delivers the packet directly. If not, the router consults its routing table to determine the next router to forward the packet to. It then passes the next router's address to the data-link layer while supplying its own address as the source. At all times, the IPX packet's source and destination addresses remain untouched. Under normal circumstances, the packet ultimately arrives at a router directly connected to the destination station and the packet is delivered. On the destination station, IPX delivers the packet to the proper socket.

Sequenced Packet Exchange (SPX)

The Sequenced Packet Exchange (SPX) is Novell's transport layer protocol. It was derived from Xerox's Sequenced Packet Protocol (SPP).

SPX provides a reliable, connection-oriented, virtual circuit service between network stations. SPX makes use of IPX's datagram service to provide a sequenced data stream. It does this by implementing a system that requires each packet sent to be acknowledged. It also provides flow control between the network stations and ensures that no duplicates are delivered to the remote process.

In order to decrease the congestion on the network, SPX reduces the number of times that an unneeded retransmission occurs. Retransmission should normally occur after the sending station has timed-out waiting for an acknowledgment (when a packet has been either lost or damaged—therefore, dropped). SPX uses a heuristic-enhanced timing algorithm to estimate accurate retransmission times. It also uses historic information to determine the initial time, and it then increases the time by 50% if a time-out occurs. This process continues until a maximum time-out value is reached or until acknowledgments return in time and retransmissions are no longer required. In the latter case, the time-out stabilizes at a value that is accurate for the network conditions.

SPX adds 12 bytes to the IPX packet header, mostly to carry connection control information. Added to the 30 bytes of the IPX header, this results in a combined header of 42 bytes. The maximum size of an SPX packet is also set at 576 bytes, the same as the maximum for an IPX packet. The SPX header is as follows:

Connection Control	1 byte
Datastream Type	1 byte
Source Connection ID	2 bytes
Destination Connection ID	2 bytes
Sequence Number	2 bytes
Acknowledgment Number	2 bytes
Allocation Number	2 bytes
Data	up to 534 bytes

- **Connection Control**. A set of flags that regulates the flow of data over the connection. Flags in this field can signify end-of-message signs and requests for acknowledgment.
- **Datastream Type**. Enables higher-layer protocols to assign meanings to the data in the packet. The meaning of the information in this field is dependent on the protocol using the field.
- **Source Connection IDs and Destination Connection IDs**. Uniquely identifies a connection between peer processes. By using connection IDs, a single IPX socket can multiplex multiple connections.
- **Sequence Number**. Used to implement SPX's flow control, packet sequencing, and suppression of duplicate packets.
- **Acknowledgment Number**. Used by the destination to inform the sender of the next sequence number it expects.
- **Allocation Number**. Informs the sender about the number of buffers the receiver has available for the connection. This assists SPX in implementing the flow control of the connection and prevents a fast sender from overwhelming a slower receiver.

Routing Information Protocol (RIP)

The Novell Routing Information Protocol is used to query and exchange routing information in an internetwork. Novell's RIP was derived from the Xerox Network System's RIP, with the addition of an extra field for the estimated time that it takes to reach the destination network. This extra field enables the routing information protocol to determine the fastest routes to a network when multiple routes exists.

Unlike Xerox's network architecture, in which hosts and routers serve distinct functions, each NetWare server has a full IPX router built into it, providing flexibility and responsiveness of network routing. For the purposes of this section, however, consider the router as a functionally separate unit from the server.

The main structure used in IPX internet routing is the routing table. The routing table includes entries that contain the following information:

- Destination network number
- Address of the next router toward the network
- Number of hops (routers) to the network
- Port or Network Interface Card on which to send the packet out
- Number of ticks required to deliver the packet
- Status or reliability of the network
- Age of this entry

Several of these fields need additional explanation. As mentioned earlier, a significant difference between NetWare and XNS routing is the addition of the time required to deliver the packet to its destination. The unit of measure in the NetWare routing table is called the *tick*. There are roughly 18 ticks-per-second. For the purposes of a local area network, delivery time is assumed to be one tick, but is measured and updated for wide-area links, such as X.25 and asynchronous connections.

The age of each entry is recorded in the routing table. If the age reaches three minutes, the router assumes that the route to the network is unavailable and removes the entry from the table. This change is broadcast to other routers and helps to maintain the integrity of the table by weeding out outdated and incorrect information. If the entry is updated before the age expires, the age field is reset.

If multiple routes exist to any particular network address, the routing table has the desirable property of only keeping the most efficient route (the one providing the fastest packet delivery to the destination).

The Routing Information Protocol makes use of the well-known socket number of 453h (in the IPX header) to exchange routing information. The RIP packet is put into the data area of the IPX packet. The structure of the RIP packet is as follows:

Operation	2 bytes
Network Number	4 bytes
Number of Router Hops (1)	2 bytes
Number of Ticks (1)	2 bytes
Network Number (2)	4 bytes
Number of Router Hops (2)	2 bytes
Number of Ticks (2)	2 bytes

- **Operation**. Specifies whether the packet is a request (01h) or a response (02h) for routing information. The number of router hops indicates how many routers the packet will have to travel through before it reaches its destination network. The number of ticks is the estimated time it will take to reach the network. This field is not present in the XNS specification of the Routing Information Protocol.

- **Network Number.** When the operation is a request for routing information, only the network number is significant. The values for the other fields are filled in by the responding router.

The router automatically broadcasts a list of the active network numbers in its routing table every 60 seconds to all network segments to which it is directly attached. This is not so, however, for wide-area connections such as T1, X.25, or asynchronous links, in which frequent overhead activity can cause drops in the throughput of the link or add additional costs. In these cases, routing information is propagated only when the router comes up, goes down (when the server is downed), or when changes are made to the routing table. Examples of changes to the table include new servers being added to the network or changes in the times and distances to reach remote networks as internetwork conditions change.

NetWare Core Protocol (NCP)

Novell's NetWare Core Protocol (NCP) is the interface that workstations use to make requests for network services from NetWare file servers. The NCP is a core set of generic services that extends the client workstation's operating system by providing services over networks. It is implemented as a shell that sits on top of the client operating system and redirects network requests to the server and passes other calls through to the native OS.

The NCP uses the datagram service provided by IPX, but it specifies its own session control and error detection and retransmission. It requires an acknowledgement for every IPX packet. The NCP packet is placed in the data area of the IPX packet and places the well-known NCP socket number 451h in the destination socket field of the IPX packet.

The NCP packet contains information that is used to relate to the request from the workstation or the response from the server. In addition, it has information about the connection to identify the network connection and the security rights associated with it. The structure of the NCP packet is as follows:.

Request Type
Sequence Number
Connection Number
Task Number
Reserved
Service Code
Data

Only one NCP request may be outstanding at any given time. The sequence number identifies the request and allows the workstation to associate the reponse with the proper request. The sequence number is incremented for each request. The service code in the NCP packet identifies the service requested by the workstation from the server.

Service Advertising Protocol (SAP)

The Service Advertising Protocol (SAP) enables network servers to advertise their names and the type of services that they provide. Examples of servers that make use of SAP to broadcast their services across the internetwork include file servers, print servers, and gateway servers.

Servers that use SAP broadcast information about their service every 60 seconds. A NetWare server receiving the SAP packet puts the name, type, and internetwork address of the server providing the service in its local Bindery for quick access by programs and attached workstations. The *NetWare Bindery* is a database of network objects such as users, groups, and servers. Workstations can use SAP to query the server based on name, type, and nearest provider of the service.

The Service Advertising Protocol uses IPX to move the information around the network. The SAP packet is put in the data area of the IPX packet and the well-known socket address of 452h is used to identify it as a SAP packet.

The basic server types are defined by Novell and are also used to identify objects in the NetWare Bindery. The following list illustrates several server types and their associated value:

File Server	4h
Job Server	5h
Gateway	6h
Print Server	7h
Archive Server	9h
SNA Gateway	21h
Remote Bridge Server	24h
TCP/IP Gateway	27h
NetWare Access Server	98h

The structure of the SAP packet is as follows:

Operation	2 bytes
Server Type (1)	2 bytes
Server Name (1)	48 bytes

Network Address (1)	4 bytes
Node Address	6 bytes
Socket Address (1)	2 bytes
Hops to Server (1)	2 bytes
Server Type (2)	2 bytes
Server Name (2)	48 bytes
Network Address (2)	4 bytes
Node Address (2)	6 bytes
Socket Address (2)	2 bytes
Hops to Server (2)	2 bytes
...	

Several operations are defined for the Service Advertising Protocol. These include the following:

- ❖ Getting the name and address of the nearest server of a particular type
- ❖ Getting all the servers on the internet or getting all servers of a particular type
- ❖ Responding to a "get nearest server" request
- ❖ Sending a regular broadcast of information across the network
- ❖ Sending a broadcast indicating that some SAP information has changed

The maximum number of servers that a single SAP packet can contain information about is seven. When a SAP broadcast packet is sent, all fields in the packet are used. For a request for information, only the server type and the server name need to be specified. A response to a request for information fills in all the fields.

Understanding NetBIOS

The *Net*work *B*asic *I*nput/*O*utput *S*ystem (NetBIOS) is a high-level application program interface that was designed to enable programmers to build network applications by using IBM's PC Network. It was developed by a company called Sytek, and it was originally implemented completely on an IBM PC Network Adapter card. It was introduced by IBM in 1984 and adopted by Microsoft for use with its MS-Net network product. Later, IBM provided an emulator, enabling NetBIOS to work with network interface cards used with its token-ring networks.

Today, nearly all networking companies, including IBM, Novell, Microsoft and 3Com, support the NetBIOS interface (either directly or through the use of emulators over their respective protocol stacks). In particular, IBM's LAN Server network-operating system and Microsoft's LAN Manager support NetBIOS.

For Novell, NetBIOS support is provided by using the IPX protocol stack; 3Com's implementation uses its XNS stack. Regardless of the implementation, the NetBIOS interface presented to the distributed application on the network remains consistent.

An incredible number of network applications have been written using the NetBIOS interface. Because of its ubiquitous nature, it continues to be a popular vehicle for developing distributed applications.

NetBIOS is not a really a protocol; it is an interface providing network applications with a set of commands to establish communications sessions, send and receive data, and name network objects. As seen from the perspective of the OSI Reference Model, NetBIOS provides a session-layer interface. At this level,

NetBIOS is capable of providing a reliable, connection-oriented data-transfer stream, along with a naming system for identifying stations on the network. Additionally, NetBIOS provides an unreliable connectionless datagram service. NetBIOS does not provide a routing service, however, making the construction of internetworks very difficult.

NetBIOS provides a set of commands to assign and manage the names of stations on the network. Names are 16 characters long; there can be from one to 254 names in a name table. One name, referred to as NETBIOS_NAME_NUMBER_1, is always present in the name table. This name consists of the first 10 bytes of zero followed by the six-byte (48-bit) address of the network interface card. This NetBIOS enables a connection to be established between two named objects on the network.

NetBIOS names can be either unique names or group names. The former name is unique across the entire network and cannot be duplicated. On the other hand, a group name may be used by more than one station in the network.

When the application wants to establish a connection to a remote application, it uses the name of the remote station to initiate the call and then uses the session created to exchange data between the applications.

To communicate with a remote application, the following steps are followed. The application program builds a structure called the NetWork Control Block (NCB) and fills in the data required by the particular command. The application then performs an INT 5Ch, passing the address of the NCB structure as a parameter through a register. The NCB structure is described in the following table:

Table 5.1
Network Control Block (NCB) Structure

Name	*Length (bytes)*	*Description*
NCB_COMMAND	1	Command
NCB_RETCODE	1	Return code
NCB_LSN	1	Local session number
NCB_NUM	1	Application program name's number
CB_BUFFER@	4	Address of the message buffer (segment:offset)
NCB_LENGTH	2	Length of buffer
NCB_CALLNAME	16	Local or remote NetBIOS name; CHAIN.SEND and RESET use it differently
NCB_NAME	16	Local NerBIOS session name
NCB_RTO	1	Receive time-out
NCB_STO	1	Send time-out
NCB_POST@	4	Address of routine NetBIOS should call when command is completed (segment:offset)
NCB_ADAPTR_NUM	1	Network adapter: 00h for primary adapter, 01h for secondary adapter
NCB_CMD_CMPL	1	Status of command
NCB_RESERVE	14	Reserved area

The following sections explain each of the fields in the NCB structure.

- **NCB_COMMAND** contains the NetBIOS command to be performed. The application may wish to "block" or wait for the command to complete, or it may prefer to perform the command asynchronously (or not wait until completion). This is indicated by setting the high-order bit to 0 for wait, or 1 for no-wait.

  If the application blocks, the next instruction is not executed until the NetBIOS command returns. The application should then check the NCB_RETCODE field (explained next) or the AL register to determine the outcome.

  If the application chooses no-wait, the application execution continues while the NetBIOS command is being processed. In this case, an immediate return code is placed in the AL register and the final return code from NetBIOS is placed in the NCB_RETCODE field. If the value in the AL register is 00h, the NetBIOS command will be performed. Values other than 00h indicate an error; the NetBIOS command will not be executed. After command completion, the application should check the NCB_RETCODE field or AL register as usual.

  In the no-wait situation, it is important for the application to know when the command is completed. Two ways are possible: the application can set the NCB_POST@ field to the address of a routine that NetBIOS should execute after the command is completed, or the application can set the field to 00h and poll the NCB_CMD_CPLT status field to check for completion. The NetBIOS command is completed when the value in the status field changes from FFh.

- **NCB_RETCODE** is the return code for the NetBIOS command. The value of 00h means successful completion. Other values indicate an error.
- **NCB_LSN** holds the number associated with the current communications session with another application on the network. This field is not used when the datagram service is being used. It is used by the NCB.SEND and NCB.RECEIVE command; it is only meaningful after a NCB.CALL or NCB.LISTEN command has initiated a connection successfully. Only the values 01h to FEh are valid.
- **NCB_NUM** is the number NetBIOS returns after the application calls NCB.ADD.NAME or NCB.ADD.GROUP.NAME. The number should also be placed in this field for calls using the datagram service. The values 01h to FEh are valid in this field.
- **CB_BUFFER@** is the address of the buffer area provided by the application for use by NetBIOS. The NCB.SEND command looks for the message in this buffer.
- **NCB_LENGTH** is the length of the buffer area. In the case of a NCB.SEND command, the application supplies the length of the message in the buffer. NetBIOS supplies the length of a message received in this buffer.
- **NCB_CALLNAME** is the NetBIOS name with which your application wants to communicate.
- **NCB_NAME** is the name of the local node or station. The name NETBIOS_NAME_NUMBER_1 can be used, which is simply 10 zero bytes and the six-byte address of the node. The 48-bit Media Access Control (MAC) address of a network interface card is this six-byte address.

- **NCB_RTO** is the time that a receive command should wait before it times out, measured in 500-millisecond increments. Different sessions or the two ends of the same session may use different time-outs. However, once the time-out has been set for a session, it cannot be changed. A value of 00h means no time-out.
- **NCB_STO** is the time that a send command should wait before it times out, measured in 500ms increments. As with the receive time-out, different sessions or the two ends of the same session can use different time-outs. Once the time-out has been set for a session, however, it cannot be changed. A value of 00h means no time-out. A time-out on a send command ends the session.
- **NCB_POST@** is the address of the routine NetBIOS calls after completing a no-wait command. If the value is 00h, no routine is called and the application should poll the NCB_CMD_CMPL status field to determine completion. Otherwise, the routine whose starting address is placed in this field is called when the command completes.
- **NCB_ADPTR_NUM** indicates which LAN adapter card should be used with the command. 00h specifies the primary adapter; 01h specifies the secondary adapter.
- **NCB_CMD_CMPL** contains the same value as the NCB_RETCODE field. FFh indicates that the command has not completed; 00h indicates a successful completion. All other values indicate error conditions.
- **NCB_RESERVE** is a work area reserved for NetBIOS.

NetBIOS Commands

NetBIOS commands can be neatly divided into four categories, depending on the type of service they provide to the network application. The four categories of NetBIOS are as follows:

- Connectionless datagram-oriented commands
- Connection-oriented session commands
- Name-administration commands
- General service commands

The connectionless datagram-oriented commands enable an application to send datagrams to individual stations or to broadcast them to all stations on the network. Using the datagram commands, an application can also receive datagrams.

The connection-oriented session commands enable applications to establish and release communications sessions. Using session IDs, applications can send and receive messages across the session.

The name-administration commands enable station names and group names to be assigned and managed. These names are then used in other NetBIOS commands to identify network stations.

General service commands enable the application to perform functions not directly associated with name management or data communications. For example, an application can request adapter status information, cancel a NetBIOS command, or reset a network adapter.

Each NetBIOS command is transmitted on the network in a data link frame with the frame type equal to the command. Figure 5.1 shows the NetBIOS frame header.

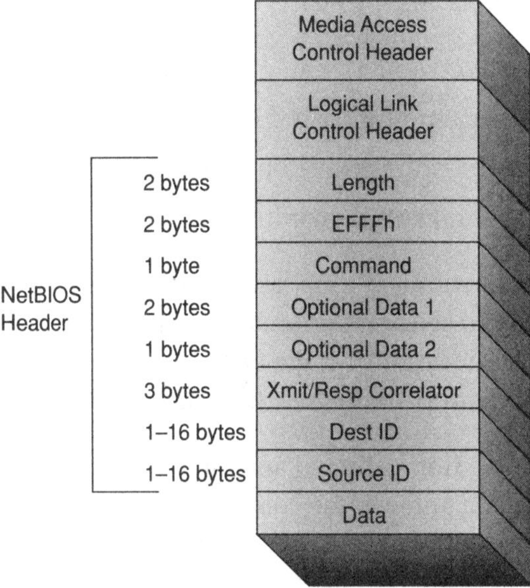

Figure 5.1:
The NetBIOS frame header.

Many of the commands can be called in wait or no-wait mode. The following sections describe the NetBIOS commands in detail.

Connectionless Datagram-Oriented Commands

- **NCB.SEND.DATAGRAM** sends a datagram to a unique or group name. The intended receipients should have a pending NCB.RECEIVE.DATAGRAM issued (or the datagram will be discarded and not delivered). Command values: wait 20h, no-wait A0h.

- **NCB.SEND.BROADCAST.DATAGRAM** sends a datagram to every network station that has a pending NCB.RECEIVE.BROADCAST.DATAGRAM. If the station does not have the broadcast receive outstanding, it will not receive the datagram. If the same station that sends the broadcast also has a broadcast receive pending, it will receive its own broadcast datagram. Command values: wait 22h, no-wait A2h.
- **NCB.RECEIVE.DATAGRAM** receives a datagram that is addressed to the local name or group name specified in the NCB_NUM field from anyone on the network that sends a datagram using the NCB.SEND.DATAGRAM. This command will not receive broadcast datagrams; a value of FFh in the NCB_NUM field, however, will receive a datagram for any of the computer's local names. Command values: wait 21h, no-wait A1h.
- **NCB.RECEIVE.BROADCAST.DATAGRAM** receives a datagram from anyone on the network that sends a datagram using the NCB.SEND.BROADCAST.DATAGRAM. If the receiving data buffer is not large enough, the excess data is lost and cannot be recovered, as it can with a session-oriented receive command. Command values: wait 23h, no-wait A3h.

Connection-Oriented Session Commands

- **NCB.CALL** opens a session to the name specified in the NCB_CALLNAME field. The NCB_NAME field contains the local name. The called name must have already issued an NCB.LISTEN command. Also, the send and receive time-out values (NCB_STO and

NCB_RTO) must be specified in the call command. More than one session may be initiated between the local and the remote name. Command values: wait 10h, no-wait 90h.

- **NCB.LISTEN** instructs NetBIOS to accept a NCB.CALL command from either the name specified in the NCB_CALLNAME field or any network station if an asterisk '*' is specified. The local name used is in the NCB.NAME field. The send and receive time-out values (NCB_STO and NCB_RTO) must be specified. Command values: wait 11h, no-wait 91h.
- **NCB.SEND** sends data using the session identified in the NCB_LSN (session number) field. The data is placed in the NCB_BUFFER@ field; data may be between 0 and 65535 bytes in length. The time-out value associated with the session when it was created is used and cannot be changed by this command. Multiple pending sends are handled in a first-in, first-out basis. Command values: wait 14h, no-wait 94.
- **NCB.SEND.NO.ACK** is a send command that does not ask for an acknowledgment to be returned when the data is received. This results in slightly quicker exchanges. The NCB.SEND.NO.ACK command sends the data in the NCB_BUFFER@ field with similar size restrictions as the NCB.SEND command. Because NetBIOS does not require acknowledgments, it is the responsibility of the application to ensure a reliable data stream. Command values: wait 71h, no-wait F1h.
- **NCB.RECEIVE** receives data that was sent across the session by any of the session-oriented send commands. Time-out values that were set when the session was initiated are used; they cannot be changed by this

command. If the value 06h is returned in the NCB_RETCODE field, the receive buffer was too small for the incoming message. In this case, additional receive commands can be issued to retrieve the message before the send command times out. Command values: wait 15h, no-wait 95h.

- **NCB.RECEIVE.ANY** receives data from any session partner that sends data by using the session-oriented send commands. The NCB.RECEIVE command has priority over the NCB.RECEIVE.ANY command, if both are outstanding. The NCB_NUM field must be used to specify the local name. If the NCB_NUM used is FFh, the command will receive data from a session with any remote name, using any local name. A value of 06h in the NCB_RETCODE field indicates too small a receive buffer; it can be handled in a similar manner as NCB.RECEIVE. Command values: wait 16h, no-wait 96h.
- **NCB.CHAIN.SEND** enables data in two buffers to be joined together and sent as a single message using the session specified in the NCB_LSN field. The first data buffer is in the NCB_BUFFER@ field; the second data buffer, with its associated length, is specified in the NCB.CALLNAME field in the following manner: the first two bytes of NCB.CALLNAME indicates the length of the buffer, and the next four bytes specifies the address of the data. This enables two messages of up to 65535 bytes (total 131070 bytes) to be transmitted. Command values: wait 17h, no-wait 97h.
- **NCB.CHAIN.SEND.NO.ACK** sends data chained together from two buffers (exactly like the NCB.CHAIN.SEND command), but it does not require

NetBIOS to return an acknowledgment. Command values: wait 72h, no-wait F2h.

- **NCB.SESSION.STATUS** collects the status of sessions for the local names. If the NCB_NAME field has an asterisk as the first byte, the status of sessions for all local names is obtained. If a name is specified in the field, the status of that name (adapter) is returned. The information is placed in the NCB_BUFFER@ field. Command values: wait 34h, no-wait B4h.
- **NCB.HANG.UP** requests NetBIOS to close the session given in the local session number (NCB.LSN) field. All pending NCB.RECEIVE operations are cancelled; pending NCB.SEND commands are given up to 20 seconds to complete their operation, however. Command values: wait 12h, no-wait 92h.
- **NCB.LAN.STATUS.ALERT** alerts the application of temporary ring errors that are over one minute in duration. The value for a no-wait command is F3h.

Name-Administration Commands

- **NCB.ADD.NAME** adds a unique name to the name table. NetBIOS queries the network; no reply to the query means that the name can be inserted into the table. The station is now associated with this name. Command values: wait 30h, no-wait B0h.
- **NCB.ADD.GROUP.NAME** adds a group name to the name table (the name must not be a unique name). When the command is called, NetBIOS queries the network to see if the name is unique. No reply to the query means that the group name can be associated

with the network station. Command values: wait 36h, no-wait B6h.

- **NCB.FIND.NAME** causes NetBIOS to query the network for the specified name. All replies from stations on the network before the time-out expires are placed in the NCB_BUFFER@ field and the NCB_LENGTH field is set. The reply also indicates if the names are unique or they are group names. Command values: wait 78h, no-wait F8h.
- **NCB.DELETE.NAME**. Deletes a name from the name table. If the name is associated with an open session, the name is marked for deletion and removed when the session is closed. Command values: wait 31h, no-wait B1h.

General Service Commands

- **NCB.STATUS** obtains the status information for either a local or remote network adapter. NCB_CALLNAME contains the NetBIOS name that the status information is requested for. If an asterisk is placed in the first byte of the field, the status information of the local adapter is returned. The information is placed in the NCB_BUFFER@ field. Command values: wait 33h, no-wait B3h.
- **NCB.CANCEL** cancels the NetBIOS command with the NCB address that is stored in the NCB_BUFFFER@ field. All except a few commands can be cancelled—cancelling a connection-oriented session command, however, will end the session. The value for a wait command is 35h.

- **NCBRESET** resets the adapter specified in the NCB_ADPTR_NUM field, which clears the NetBIOS name and session tables and aborts all current sessions. The value for a wait command is 32h.
- **NCB.TRACE** initiates or halts the tracing of all NCBs (Network Control Blocks) and some CCBs used by the NetBIOS application. The trace is initiated by placing the value FFh in the NCB_NUM field and is terminated by setting the field to 00h. Command values: wait 79h, no-wait F9h.
- **NCB.UNLINK** is provided for NetBIOS compatibility. An earlier version of the PC Network NetBIOS used the unlink command with Remote Program Load (RPL). In this case, unlink caused the session to be dropped—this operation is now treated as a NOP (no-operation), however. The value for a wait command is 70h.

Understanding AppleTalk

In late 1983 and early 1984, Apple Computer began to design a set of communication protocols called AppleTalk. The goal was to connect their new line of Macintosh personal computers—along with printers, print servers, file servers, routers, and gateways—to computer systems built by other manufacturers.

The greatest inital use of AppleTalk (and certainly one of its greatest impacts) was to connect the graphical computer to the the new Apple LaserWriter laser printer. In combination with exciting new software, this hardware, and the flexible underlying network support provided by AppleTalk, the so-called desktop publishing revolution began.

Each Macintosh and LaserWriter comes with built-in hardware support for the AppleTalk networking architecture. In addition, the system software includes comprehensive network support. This combination of built-in hardware and software helps make AppleTalk one of the most common networking solutions for personal computers in use today.

AppleTalk was designed to be more than a way to attach peripherals to the Mac. It was designed, from the ground up, to be an open, extensible network architecture to support new physical network technologies and new protocol stacks. AppleTalk was designed to connect large numbers of computers and peripherals over a potentially large geographic area by connecting local networks into internets.

Independent of the size of the network, AppleTalk is also designed to support peer-to-peer networking when there is no need for a separate name server to control the assignment and use of network names. This service is implemented in each network node and operates in a distributed fashion, which reduces the entry cost of creating a fully functional network (an important design criteria for the AppleTalk designers).

The overall design philosophy of the Macintosh computer also extended to the network design. The user's model of interaction with the network had to be as transparent as possible, so that the standard operations and metaphors are extended to the use of multiple resources spread over an internetwork. In particular, this means that users can mount volumes on their desktop and make use of the files and folders by using the standard select and click operations.

The installation of the network nodes was designed to support a "plug-and-play" model, in which the user attaches the physical link, and then most of the configuration is automatically managed by the system software.

AppleTalk Phase 2 was introduced in June 1989 as an upwardly compatible extension to the existing AppleTalk (AppleTalk Phase 1). AppleTalk Phase 2 provides support for larger, enterprise-wide networks by enabling a greater number of nodes (workstations, printers, and servers) on the network. Although AppleTalk Phase 1 supported a maximum of 254 nodes on a single network, Phase 2 enables multiple network numbers to be associated with a single network, while enabling 253 nodes per network number.

AppleTalk Phase 2 also provides support for LocalTalk, EtherTalk and TokenTalk. (As discussed later, LocalTalk is the physical and data-link specification for Apple's familiar shielded twisted pair cabling scheme; EtherTalk and TokenTalk are Apple's implementation of Ethernet and token ring, respectively). The AppleTalk Internet Router was also modified to enable the connection of up to eight AppleTalk networks in any mix of LocalTalk, EtherTalk, and TokenTalk. (Each individual network must have only one type of physical link.)

Developers have used AppleTalk to provide a wide assortment of distributed applications, supporting the Apple Macintosh, the IBM PS/2 and PC-compatible computers, workstations running UNIX, and the Apple IIGS. These applications include file sharing, print spooling, printer sharing, and electronic messaging. In addition, gateways are available for linking AppleTalk networks with DEC mini- and mainframe computers.

The AppleTalk Protocol Suite

This section examines how the AppleTalk protocol suite fits into the OSI Reference Model. The application layer contains application programs using the AppleTalk network architecture.

The presentation layer contains the AppleTalk Filing Protocol (AFP), which enables users to share files across an AppleTalk network. The AFP uses the AppleTalk Session Protocol to establish a communications session with the remote computer.

The session layer includes the AppleTalk Session Protocol (ASP), the AppleTalk Data Stream Protocol (ADSP), Printer Access Protocol (PAP), and the Zone Information Protocol (ZIP). The AP enables an application to send a reliable sequence of transactions between a client and a server; the ADSP implements a reliable data-stream service.

The transport layer contains the AppleTalk Transaction Protocol (ATP), the Name Binding Protocl (NBP), the Routing Table Management Protocol (RTMP), and the AppleTalk Echo Protocol (AEP). The ATP provides a request-response service to applications, and the RTMP maintains the routing information tables within AppleTalk internetorks.

The network layer contains the Datagram Delivery Protocol (DDP), which i responsible for addressing and routing pckets through an AppleTalk internetwork.

The data-link layer contains protocols for each of the major local area network standards. These include the LocalTalk Link Access Protocol (LLAP); the EtherTalk Link Access Protocol (ELAP); and the TokenTalk Link Access Protoool (TLAP) for LocalTalk, Ethernet, and token-ring networks, respectively. It also contains the AppleTalk Address Resolution Protocol (AARP) which translates AppleTalk node IDs to physical addresses.

The physical layer contains the specifications for the hardware required to support LocalTalk, EtherTalk, and TokenTalk. Figure 5.2 illustrates the AppleTalk architecture.

OSI Layer	AppleTalk Protocols			
Application / Presentation	AppleTalk Filing Protocol			
Session	AppleTalk Data Stream Protocol	AppleTalk Session Protocol	Zone Information Protocol	Printer Access Protocol
Transport	AppleTalk Transaction Protocol	AppleTalk Echo Protocol	Routing Table Maintenance Protocol	Name Binding Protocol
Network	Datagram Delivery Protocol			
Datalink	LocalTalk Link Access Protocol	EtherTalk Link Access Protocol	TokenTalk Link Access Protocol	
Physical	LocalTalk	Ethernet	Token-Ring	

Figure 5.2:
The AppleTalk architecture.

AppleTalk Physical Protocols

AppleTalk supports three leading physical protocols: AppleTalk, EtherTalk, and TokenTalk.

LocalTalk

AppleTalk initially used shielded twisted-pair (STP) cabling for its physical link. The physical specifications enable data to be transmitted at a rate of 230.4Kbps; a network segment can be up to 300 meters long. As many as 32 nodes can be attached to a single LocalTalk segment. The topology of the network is a bus with terminators at each end of the network. The terminators are built directly into the AppleTalk connection modules and are self-terminating if unused. LocalTalk does not allow a ring topology—end connectors must therefore never be attached. The connection module enables a station to be added or removed from the network without disrupting the rest of the network, which is an important consideration in the plug-and-play design of AppleTalk.

The frame format of LocalTalk is the Synchronous Data Link Control (SDLC) format. LocalTalk uses a method of encoding bits on the media called FM-0, which encodes the bit data and the synchronization information together. Encoding schemes such as this are called *self-clocking*, because no external signal is required to keep the sending and receiving hardware in sync.

In this method, there is a signal transition at the beginning of each bit, which provides the clocking information and delineates the bit time. The value of 0 is encoded by adding an additional transition in the middle of the bit time. The value 1 is encoded without the additional transition. In comparison, Ethernet and IEEE 802.3 use Manchester encoding, in which a 0 is encoded by having a low level for the first half of the bit time and a high level for the rest of the bit time. Encoding a 1 is exactly the reverse of this process.

Because of the data-transfer rate and the cable segment restrictions, LocalTalk is well suited for small networks.

In addition to connecting Macs to a LocalTalk network, the LocalTalk PC Card (with appropriate software) enables IBM PCs and PC compatibles to exist as peers on the network.

EtherTalk

Ethernet was developed at the Xerox Palo Alto Research Center (PARC) in the mid 1970s. Ethernet supports a data-transmission rate of 10Mbps and supports several cabling systems, including thick coaxial cable (RG-8 and RG-11), thin coaxial cable (RG-58) and shielded or unshielded twisted-pair cabling.

Specifications exist for each of the cabling types that determine the length of network segments and the maximum data-transmission rate. When EtherTalk is used on an AppleTalk network, all regular restrictions associated with that type of cabling apply.

As described in Chapter 4, Ethernet uses a 48-bit address that is assigned to the network interface card at the time of manufacture. This is a permanent address that is guaranteed to be unique among all the Ethernet adapters in the world. AppleTalk, however, uses a system of dynamic address selection for network nodes. When a node comes up on an AppleTalk network, the software arbitrates a network address of it on the fly.

When EtherTalk is used on an AppleTalk network, the Ethernet and AppleTalk addresses need to be associated with each other. This is done by using a protocol called the AppleTalk Address Resolution Protocol (AARP). The EtherTalk Link Access Protocol (ELAP), which is an extension to the regular IEEE 802.2 Logical Link Control (LLC), makes use of the AARP to perform this mapping between addresses.

TokenTalk

Token-ring nodes, like their Ethernet conterparts, use a 48-bit address that is assigned to the network interface card at the time of manufacture. AppleTalk is required to map the address selected dynamically for network nodes to the 48-bit address used in the token-ring network.

TokenTalk, like EtherTalk, uses the AppleTalk Address Resolution Protocol (AARP) to perform this task. The TokenTalk Link Access Protocol (TLAP), which is an extension to the regular IEEE 802.2 LLC, also makes use of the AARP to perform this mapping between addresses.

AppleTalk's Data Link Protocols

AppleTalk's data link protocols serve two major purposes. They provide a way to transfer data between nodes (workstations and servers) on the same AppleTalk network. Additionally, because all devices on the network share the same physical medium, the data link protocols mediate the access to this common network link.

The data link protocol for LocalTalk is called the LocalTalk Link Access Protocol (LLAP). LLAP enables data to be transferred across the local network in a best-effort method. This means that the packet is not guaranteed to be delivered. Although packets that arrive damaged are dropped, LLAP guarantees that packets that are passed up to higher-level protocols are error-free.

LLAP mediates access to the shared network medium by a system called Carrier Sense Multiple Access with Collision Avoidance (CSMA/CA). A collision occurs when more than one station transmits over the communications medium at the same time. If this happens, the signal gets muddled and the packet is lost. CSMA/CA is similar to the system of CSMA/CD (Collision Detection) that Ethernet provides, but it is fundamentally different in the manner in which data-transmission collisions are dealt with.

In CSMA/CD, when the sending station wants to send data across the network, it uses the hardware in the network interface to sense the line (carrier sense). If the line is being used, the station waits. If the line is free, however, the station waits a period of time that is the sum of the Interdialog Gap (IDG) and some randomly generated time. In LocalTalk, the IDG is fixed at 400 microseconds. After this time, the sending station transmits a Ready To Send (RTS) packet to the destination and waits for a

Clear To Send (CTS) packet to return as an acknowledgment that it is safe to send. When the CTS arrives, the sending station knows that it can send the packet with little chance of collision.

Other stations on the network hear this "handshake" process taking place and hold off from trying to send. If no CTS packet is returned, the sender assumes that a collision has taken place and retreats to try later. This system works quite well because most collisions occur during the handshake, and only a small amount of time is wasted.

The format of the LLAP packet is as follows:

Destination node ID	1 byte
Source node ID	1 byte
Type	1 byte
Data	up to 600 bytes
Unnamed, used by high-level protocols	6 bits
Data length	10 bits
Data	up to 600 bytes

The fields are described in the following sections.

- ❖ **Source node ID** and **Destination node ID**. Numeric identifiers of the sending and receiving station on the network. Values in the range of 1 and 254 are valid node IDs. The ID 255 is used as the broadcast address.
- ❖ **Type**. Specifies the type of packet. LLAP makes use of two types of packets: *control packets* and *data packets*. Data packets use the range 1-127; control packets use the range 128-255. The type field for data packets is used to identify the type of process using the the data

link. It can be used to identify a protocol when multiple protocol stacks are used concurrently on the network station. This use of the type field is similar to the Service Access Points in the Logical Link Control (LLC) of the IEEE 802.2.

- **Data**. Carries the data between the source and destination nodes. The data field can be divided into three sections. The first six bits are unnamed and used by higher-level protocols. The next bits are used to specify the length of the data field in the packet. These two sections make up the first two bytes of the data field. The rest of the field is the actual data being transferred.

There are four types of control packets, which are used for:

- Dynamic node ID enquiry
- Dynamic node ID response
- Request to send a packet to a destination
- Response from a destination that it is clear to send a packet

The dynamic node ID enquiry and response packets are used to implement AppleTalk's dynamic selection process of the eight-bit node ID of the network station. As mentioned earlier, AppleTalk assigns an address to a station when it is powered up on a network. This process enables a network device to determine its own address without requiring the user to preconfigure it. The node ID can be thought of as a hardware address, similar to the 48-bit address used by Ethernet and token ring, except that the AppleTalk address is determined dynamically when it is attached to the network; Ethernet and token ring addresses are permanently configured at the time of manufacture. The AppleTalk "hardware" address of a station may be different every time it is removed and reattached to the network. The only guarantee is that the address is unique on the network.

The process to determine an AppleTalk address is straightforward. The station takes a guess at a value. It can be a random guess or it can be an earlier address that was stored in a nonvolatile region of RAM, such as the parameter RAM (PRAM) on the Macintosh. The station then sends several Enquiry Control packets using the node ID it guessed as the destination. If the ID is already in use, it should expect an Acknowledgment Control packet. If the station receives a result, it knows the ID is in use on the network and starts the process all over again, guessing at a new ID. It sends multiple packets to the destination—reducing the chance that an undelivered packet could be misinterpreted as a valid new address.

AppleTalk takes one extra precaution with the dynamic node ID selection process on a LocalTalk network. The node IDs on the network are divided into two groups. Node IDs between 1-127 belong exclusively to workstations; node IDs between 128-254 can only be servers (such as file servers or print servers). Node ID 255 is the broadcast address, which prevents a user workstation from incorrectly selecting the node address of a server. This would cause greater chaos on the network than if two workstations accidentally shared the same ID.

The EtherTalk Link Access Protocol and the TokenTalk Link Access Protocol are likewise concerned with the issues of frame transmission, network station addressing, and media access of the common network for their respective networks, Ethernet and token ring. Interestingly, the node IDs are not divided between workstations and servers when either Ethernet or token ring is used as the physical network. Servers on these networks are less likely to miss a node ID Enquiry Control packet because of the way they buffer incoming packets.

AppleTalk Address Resolution Protocol (AARP)

AppleTalk's data-link layer is capable of supporting multiple protocol stacks. Each protocol has its own addressing convention that may be incomprehensible to other protocols. When these protocols are used on an AppleTalk network, their addresses must be translated to AppleTalk node IDs in order to transfer packets to the proper destination. This process of address translation is known as *address resolution*. This service is provided by the AppleTalk Address Resolution Protocol (AARP).

For example, when the AppleTalk stack is used on an Ethernet network, the AppleTalk node ID must be translated into 48-bit Ethernet addresses in order for the data link to deliver the packet to the correct destination.

This section examines the AARP and how it provides address resolution. AARP defines a packet that it uses to perform resolution operations. There are three types of packets: AARP request packets, AARP response packets, and AARP probe packets. They share a common packet structure, the AppleTalk Address Resolution Protocol Packet structure, which is as follows:

Hardware Type	2 bytes
Protocol Type	2 bytes
Hardware Address Length	1 byte
Protocol Address Length	1 byte

Function	2 bytes
Source Hardware Address	Length specified above
Source Protocol Address	Length specified above
Destination Hardware Address	Length specified above
Destination Protocol Address	Length specified above

The fields are described in the following sections.

- **Hardware Type** and **Protocol Type**. Specify the data link type and the protocol stack respectively. From the earlier example, the Protocol Type can be AppleTalk and the Hardware Type is Ethernet.
- **Hardware Address Length** and **Protocol Address Length**. Because the AARP is designed to be open and independent of protocol or data link type, the length of the respective addresses must be supplied to help interpret the packet.
- **Function**. Specifies the function of the packet and can contain the following values:
    1. Indicates an AARP Request packet
    2. Indicates an AARP Response Packet
    3. Indicates an AARP Probe packet
- The **Source Hardware Address, Destination Hardware Address,** and **Destination Protocol Address** fields have a different meaning, depending on the type of the AARP packet.

Address mappings are stored, appropriately enough, in the Address Mapping Table (AMT) that is kept on each network station. This table contains entries associating protocol addresses with hardware addresses on a per-protocol basis. This information is kept locally throughout the network for quick lookup and resolution when a packet needs to be sent. If a desired mapping is not present, an AARP Request packet is broadcast through the network. When a reply is received, in the form of an AARP Response packet, the association is inserted into the AMT. The request is repeated until a response is received, after a maximum number of attempts, or until an error is reported.

AARP can also be used to build the AMT in the background by examining all incoming packets and extracting the hardware-protocol address mapping present in the packet.

AARP can also be used for the dynamic address selection process. Using this method, a potential address is selected and the AMT is checked for the address. If the address is found, a new address is selected without having to use network bandwidth. If the address is not found in the AMT, an AARP Probe packet is sent to the potential address.

An AARP Response packet from the address starts the selection process over again. If no response is received, the probe is sent several times until a maximum is reached and the address is accepted as unique and inserted into the AMT with the proper mapping.

Like many protocols that build addressing-information tables, AARP recognizes that old information is rarely reliable information in the context of a dynamic, ever-changing network. The AMT contains a timer field that enables the entries in the table to be aged. If the timer expires, the entry is removed. If the entry is updated, such as when a AARP Probe arrives, the timer is reset.

Datagram Delivery Protocol (DDP)

The Datagram Delivery Protocol (DDP) serves as AppleTalk's network layer protocol. As with other network layer protocols, DDP is concerned with the addressing and routing of packets through an internetwork. DDP provides a "best-effort," (though unreliable) process-to-process delivery of datagrams between network applications.

DDP allows one or more 16-bit network numbers to be assigned to a single AppleTalk network. The set of numbers used to identify a network cannot overlap with the network numbers from any other network. In addition, DDP uses an eight-bit socket number to represent the process requesting delivery services from DDP. Together with the node ID that was examined earlier, the network and the socket numbers form a complete internet address and uniquely identify a process on the internet.

Socket numbers on a node can be determined statically or dynamically. The static sockets have values between 1 and 127. These sockets are reserved for well-known processes or protocols, such as the Name Binding Protocol (NBP) and the Routing Table Maintenance Protocol (RTMP), and for experimental protocols.

Dynamic sockets are established when a process requests datagram delivery from DDP; they are identified by having the number range of 128 to 254.

A process that wishes to transfer data using DDP opens a socket for sending datagrams and assigns a process called a *listener* to receive packets that are sent to the socket.

The structure of the Datagram Delivery Protocol packet is as follows:

(Unnamed)	6 bits
Length	10 bits
Destination Socket Number	8 bits
Source Socket Number	8 bits
Type	8 bits
Data	up to 586 bytes

The first six bits of the short DDP header are set to zeros. The following 10 bits encode the length of the datagram. The maximum length of data that can be transferred by using a single DDP packet is 586 bytes. The source and destination socket numbers identify the communicating processes sending and receiving the datagram and the type field.

DDP defines two type of headers, a *short header* and an *extended header*. The short header is used when the source and destination of the packet are located on the same network. Extended headers are required when the source and destination have different network numbers. In addition to the information in the short header, the extended header includes the source and destination network numbers and node IDs, along with a checksum and hop count field. The short header is five bytes long; the entended header is 13 bytes long.

Like other network layer protocols, DDP routes packets through the AppleTalk internet. When data needs to be transferred, DDP examines the network number of the destination. If the number is within the range of the local network, DDP constructs a short header and instructs the data-link layer to send the packet directly to the desination node. If the destination network number is not within the local network, DDP constructs an extended header and sends the datagram to an Internet Router (IR) attached to the network. Internet Routers are used to connect networks together to form AppleTalk internets.

In the AppleTalk scheme, not every node is required to have a routing capability. Each node is required, however, to know its range of network numbers and the node ID of any IR attached to the local network. Once the datagram arrives at an IR, a routing table is consulted and the datagram is transferred from IR to IR through the internet in a store and forward manner.

The routing tables are maintained by the Routing Table Maintenance Protocol (RTMP). This is done by periodically exchanging routing-table information between the routing entities on the AppleTalk internet. Each entry in the routing table contains the shortest known path to the destination network. The entries contain information concerning the number range for each network, the next Internet Router on the path, the distance measured in hops through IRs on the path, and the port to which the next IR is attached. In addition, a field is used to indicate the state of the information; either good, bad, or suspect.

AppleTalk Transaction Protocol (ATP)

The AppleTalk Transaction Protocol (ATP) is a transport layer protocol that provides a request-response service to client processes. ATP efficiently implements a client-server model of process interaction, in which a network client requests a service provider (server) to perform an action and return a response. Because a great deal of network data exchange is exactly of this nature, ATP provides this service model with very little overhead.

With ATP, client processes request a service and wait for a response. Each transaction is handled separately from all others.

ATP provides the client with a reliable tranaction system by resending any request for which a response has not been received in a timely manner. ATP resends the packet until a maximum is reached. At that point, the client in informed of the failure. A tranaction identifier is used to match responses to requests.

Although each ATP request must be contained in a single packet, the response to a request may span up to eight packets. Because a packet may be resent, two copies of the request may arrive at the destination. For some applications, such as those determining the status of a server, this has little consequence. However, if the request is to debit a bank account, the results can be unfavorable.

ATP provides a service whereby the requesting application can specify that the request should be executed exactly once (and that it cannot execute more than once). ATP implements this by maintaining a list of recent responses; if a duplicate request arrives, the response from the list is returned.

The AppleTalk Transaction Protocol packet is as follows:

Control Information	8 bits
Bitmap/Sequence Number	8 bits
Transaction Identifier	16 bits
User Bytes	32 bits
Data	up to 578 bytes

The fields are described in detail in the following sections.

- **Control Information**. Indicates whether the packet is a request, response or release message. The field also indicates whether the request is an execute-exactly-once operation and whether the packet represents the final part of a response from a service.

- **Bitmap/Sequence Number.** Used by the request packet to indicate the number of packets of response it is expecting. The service provider uses this field to sequence the packets if the response involves multiple packets.
- **Transaction Identifier.** Used to match received responses to the corresponding requests for a service. The ID is 16 bits long to reduce the possibility that the field will wrap-around and an active transaction ID will be reused.

AppleTalk Session Protocol and AppleTalk Data Stream Protocol

The AppleTalk Session Protocol (ASP) enables a process on a client workstation to establish a reliable communications session with a network server process. The ASP is a session layer protocol and uses the services of the ATP. Because ATP is a transaction-oriented protocol, ASP enables the communicating stations to exchange an ordered sequence of transactions without duplicates. ASP ensures that sessions are properly distinguished by means of a session identifier. Each session of a network node has a unique session ID.

ASP supports several type of operations, including the following:

- Opening and closing of communications sessions
- Sending of ordered requests by a client workstation to a server
- Sending of a response by a server

- Determination of the server status
- Sending of an message from the server to the client workstation announcing a request for attention

The ASP is transaction-oriented and does not implement a data stream on the session between the client workstation and the server. For this service, the AppleTalk Data Stream Protocol (ADSP) is required.

The ADSP provides a reliable, full-duplex data-stream service between applications that are attached to sockets on the network. Unlike the ASP, which permits sequenced transaction-based communications between a client and a server, ADSP provides a data stream between applications by using sequence numbers to preserve the data order and to remove duplicate packets from being delivered to the application. The data stream can be thought of as a *data pipe*. The concept of a pipe as a form of Interprocess Communications (IPC) is a well-established model that enables either process to read and write to the connection, which then "pipes" the data in order to the other side.

Like the ASP, ADSP requires the sending process to open and ultimately close a connection with another process. These connections are identified by connection IDS. Data can flow in both directions simultaneously along the data pipe and ADSP implements a flow-control mechanism that prevents one process from overrunning another by sending too fast. Also, unlike ASP's client-server model of interaction, ADSP is a peer-to-peer protocol that enables either end to initiate the connection. ADSP includes a mechanism by which either process can send attention signals to each other "out-of-band" from the regular data transmission.

Understanding TCP/IP

Since the late 1960's, the U.S. (Defense) Advanced Research Projects Agency (ARPA, now DARPA), has funded research into the building of very reliable networks that link heterogeneous computing systems. The results of these efforts include the ARPANET, an early packet-switching network, the Transmission Control Protocol (TCP), the Internet Protocol (IP), the File Transfer Protocol (FTP), and others. The ARPANET was later succeeded by the Internet, a massive worldwide network with thousands of computers and millions of users.

The Internet protocols are designed to facilitate the multiple processes on host computers that communicate with each other by network media. The only requirement is that the computers are connected using a packet-switched network. No assumptions are made as to the nature of the underlying media or to its reliability in terms of packet delivery. In the model, host computers are attached together to form networks, generally within a confined geographic area, such as a building or campus of buildings. Networks are connected together by means of devices called gateways. *Gateways* are computers that have been dedicated to the task of switching and routing packets between connected networks.

The goals of the Internet suite of protocols were considerably different than those based on the OSI Reference Model or other network architectures, such as IBM's System Network Architecture (SNA) or Digital Equipment Corporation's DECnet. The Internet protocols were envisioned to be used for military computer communications, in which networks and systems had to be available and secure, especially during times of crisis. In addition, the networks would remain reliable, even when faced with packet congestion.

The emphasis of the Internet protocols is the efficient and reliable internetworking of dissimilar computer systems residing on heterogeneous network environments. The glue connecting these systems is the Internet Protocol, the now familiar IP. The Internet Protocol provides a connectionless, unreliable datagram-oriented service that higher-layer protocols, such as the Transmission Control Protocol (TCP) can use to provide additional services. In the case of TCP, this includes a reliable, connection-oriented service.

The Internet protocols are organized into four layers that, borrowing terms from the OSI Reference Model, can be described as the application layer, the transport (or host-to-host) layer, the network (or internetwork) layer, and the data-link and physical layer (grouped into one layer for the purposes of the Internet protocol suite). A brief description of each layer follows.

- **Application layer**. The layer containing the network applications. Examples of Internet network applications include programs for interpersonal communications, such as electronic mail and bulletin boards, virtual terminal emulation (TELNET), and file transfer (File Transfer Protocol, or FTP). This is in slight contrast to the application layer in the OSI Reference Model, which contains groups of application-service elements that can be combined with application-specific elements to form an application context (the network application).
- **Transport layer**. The first layer responsible for true end-to-end connections. It is at this layer that programs or processes on different computers ultimately connect and speak directly to each other. The two protocols defined at this layer in the Internet suite are the Transmission Control Protocol (TCP) and the User Datagram Protocol (UDP). TCP provides a connection-

oriented virtual circuit model for network communication; UDP provides a connectionless model that is essentially the datagram service provided by the Internet Protocol (IP) below it.

- **Network layer.** Enables multiple networks to be connected into a internetwork. The protocol defined at this layer is called the Internet Protocol (IP). IP provides a connectionless, datagram service to higher-layer protocols. It is an unreliable service. Being at the network layer, IP provides routing services to the computer and is the glue that ties networks and computers together on the Internet. Internet routers are also called gateways.
- **Media Access layer.** Provides access to the communications media with optional flow control and error detection and correction. The Internet suite can use the X.25 packet protocol for wide area networks and the IEEE 802 specifications (such as 802.3 Ethernet and 802.5 token ring) for local area networks.

Addresses used by the TCP/IP protocol suite are called *internet addresses*. These addresses are 32-bit values that can be segregated into a network number and a host number. The designers of internet addresses created three classes of addresses. Class A addresses have the high-order bit set to zero, with the next seven bits identifying the network and the final 24 bits specifying the host. In Class B addresses, the first two bits are set to 10, the next 14 bits identify the network, and the last 16 bits identify the host. In the Class C address, the first three bits are set to 110, the next 21 bits identify the network, and the next eight bits specify the host.

The designers chose these three classes of addresses because they felt that different network configurations would be better served by a variety in addressing structure. They believed that there would be a small number of networks (seven bits, maximum 127) with a very large number of hosts, a fair number of networks with a moderate number of hosts, and a large number of small networks. Figure 5.3 shows the internet address classes.

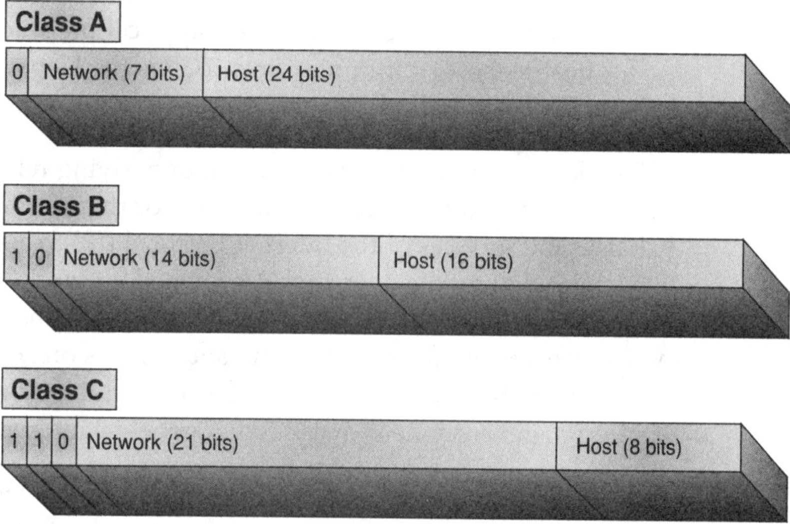

Figure 5.3:
Internet address classes.

A simple illustration of data flow is as follows. The user application passes data to TCP using an Application Program Interface. TCP then creates a connection to the remote process and relies on IP to route and transfer the data packets to the remote computer. TCP does this by passing the data, source, and destination addresses and control information to IP. Upon receiving the data, the remote IP passes the data up to TCP on the remote computer, which places the data for the application in a buffer. The remote application reads this data from the connection, and then the transfer is complete.

Transmission Control Protocol (TCP)

The Transmission Control Protocol provides a reliable connection-oriented virtual circuit service for application processes to use for host-to-host communications. TCP is the Department of Defense (DOD) standard for inter-process communications.

TCP makes few assumptions about the underlying reliability of the communications services in the layers or the media below it. TCP uses the services of the Internet Protocol (IP) to send variable-length datagrams over packet-switched networks and internetworks. TCP is concerned with ensuring a reliable, host-to-host, stream-oriented connection, and it relies on IP to take care of the matter of fragmentation and reassembly that may be required to get a segment over a heterogeneous internetwork.

Applications that require a reliable, stream-oriented connection to an application on another computer make use of TCP's services. These network applications interface directly with TCP through an Application Program Interface (API) that is provided by the protocol implementation. Depending on the host operating system, this API may be made an integral component of the OS. The application makes familiar I/O calls such as open, close, read, write, and calls to get the status of the connection.

TCP, being a connection-oriented protocol, requires that a connection be established between the two communicating processes. This requirement necessitates that a certain amount of time and effort needs to be expended at the beginning and end of a session to affect connection establishment and teardown. During this connection establishment, fundamental parameters that will be used throughout the connection are established, including the sockets used, the sequence numbers for data, and the window sizes for flow control.

The end point of a TCP connection is called a socket. A *socket* is a combination of the network address, the host address, and the port number on the local host. The *port* is a logical concept that enables multiple-application processes to use the transport services of TCP on the same machine. Sockets identify the end points of the connection on the sending and the receiving computer. Therefore, a pair of sockets uniquely identify the connection.

TCP uses a *three-way handshake* for connection establishment, which uses three messages to make the connection. The packets sent have control flags set to indicate the stage of progress. In particular, the synchronize (SYN) and acknowledgment (ACK) control flags are used in the following manner:

1. Computer 1 sends a SYN and a sequence number to computer 2.
2. Computer 2 sends an ACK and SYN (both sent in a single message) to computer 1 with the sequence number.
3. Computer 1 sends an ACK of the sequence number to computer 2.
4. Connections are terminated by exchanging segments with the FIN control flag set.

Data transfer involves moving a stream of data between processes running on two computers. Application programs call the send function to move data from the application into the transport buffers. By issuing this call, however, the application process has no control over when the data actually get transmitted to the remote process. In general, TCP waits for its send buffer to fill for a more efficient use of the network.

In some cases, an application may want to signal TCP to send the data immediately. TCP indicates this by the use of the optional PUSH flag, which pushes the data through the connection and, at the receiving process, signals that the data should be presented to the application without delay.

One of the most important services that TCP provides is to take the unreliable datagram service provided by IP and create a reliable stream-oriented, data-transfer mechanism. Even as network hardware and communications media become more and more reliable, packets may still become damaged, duplicated, or lost entirely. Additionally, packets comprising a TCP segment may arrive out of order.

To protect against damaged segments, TCP provides a checksum field to enable the receiving end to ensure the integrity of the data. If a packet arrives and is determined to be damaged (by comparing the new checksum computation with the one in the segment), TCP drops the packet, thereby forcing a retransmission of the data at the sending host.

TCP also requires that segments be acknowledged by the receiving host. A sequence number is used to implement the acknowledgment mechanism. After a segment is sent, the sender starts a timer. If an acknowledgment is not received for the segment before the timer expires, it is retransmitted by the sender. Conceptually, the TCP acknowledgment process is identical to the process used by the other protocol suites, such as XNS. The sequence number can also be used to reorder segments that are delivered out of order.

To increase the efficiency of the TCP acknowledgment process, a single ACK can be used to acknowledge several segments. It does this by simply returning the largest sequence number it has received plus one (indicating the next segment it expects to receive). This assumes that it has received all the segments prior to the last acknowledged in an undamaged state.

Flow control is important, so that a fast-sending host does not overwhelm a slower receiving host. Flow control is implemented in TCP in a simple and elegant manner. Each acknowledgment returned also contains the new window size of the receiver. This window size tells the sending process the number of unacknowledged segments that the receiving process can handle before it starts dropping them because of buffer and processing limitations. When the sending process hits this window limit, it stops sending new data until some of the previous data is acknowledged as properly received or until the receiver indicates that it has allocated more resources to receiving data and has increased its window size.

TCP enables multiplexing of data transfers. Multiplexing is done through a port, in which many processes may communicate using different port numbers on the local host. Because a TCP address is uniquely identified by a socket (the network and host address) and the port number, the use of multiple ports on a host enables multiple simultaneous communications to take place.

Each host is responsible for determining the port numbers used for a connection. In most cases, this number is determined dynamically at the time of connection establishment. However, for several well-known services that have a very broad audience, so-called port numbers have been defined. This enables a process to initiate a connection to the service without additional overhead. An example of a well-known port number is the one for the Simple Mail Transfer Protocol (SMTP), which is used to implement electronic mail transfer on the Internet. SMTP makes use of the well-known port number of 25. If an SMTP agent is running on a host, you can count on it using port 25.

Other services include TELNET (virtual terminal service), the File Transfer Protocol (FTP), and Echoer. TCP also has fields enabling information about the precedence and security of the data transferred on the connection.

In order for the peer processes to communicate by using TCP, they must agree on an initial 32-bit sequence number. If a connection is aborted, packets belonging to the connection may still be in transit on the network. The initial sequence number should be unique, in order to prevent packets belonging to the new connection from being mistaken for the packets from the aborted connection. One method for assigning a unique initial sequence number is to base it on an internal clock, which reduces the possibility that any packets will still be on the internet when a duplicate sequence number is selected.

The general model for an application using a TCP connection is the performing of stream file I/O. A connection is opened and a data structure is maintained to keep track of the connection status, much like the file I/O structure.The remote socket must be specified when the connection is opened (well-known network processes may open a passive connection that does not explicitly specify the remote socket, however). Opening a passive connection enables it to accept connections from unknown processes.

After a connection has been successfully opened, the octets of data are placed in a TCP segment and assigned a sequence number, corresponding to the data being sent. After the data is transmitted, a timer is started to determine whether the segment needs to be retransmitted. If an acknowledgment is received before the timer expires, the segment is deleted from the buffers. If not, the segment is retransmitted to the destination process. The TCP header is shown in figure 5.4.

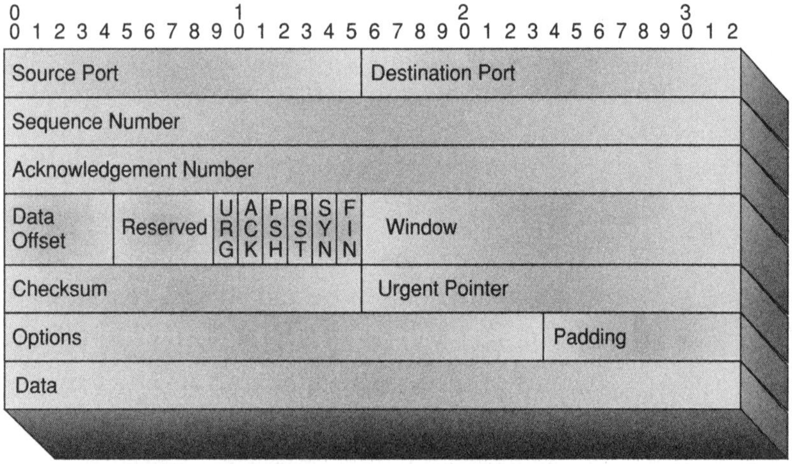

Figure 5.4:
The TCP header.

The TCP segment is placed in an IP datagram for transfer over the internet. Because IP is concerned with getting the packet to the destination host and network, these addresses are contained in the IP header, not the TCP header. Likewise, because the port is a TCP concept, the Source Port and Destination Port numbers are stored in the TCP header. The source and destination port numbers are 16-bit values.

Sequence numbers are 32-bit values that contain that sequence number of the first octet of data in the segment. When the connection is being established, this field contains the initial sequence number and the SYN control flag is set, as described earlier. When the ACK control flag is set, the Sequence Number indicates the next octet of data that the receiving process is expecting. This also has the effect of acknowledging all data received up to the sequence number, minus one.

The Data Offset is an offset from the beginning of the header to indicate where the data begins. The next six bits are reserved for future use and must contain zero values.

The field for the control flags is six bits long and attaches the following significance to the corresponding bits:

- **URG**. Indicates that the the Urgent Pointer field contains a meaningful value and should be used
- **ACK**. Indicates that the Acknowledgment Number contains the sequence number to acknowledge
- **PSH**. Indicates that the data should be pushed through immediately and not buffered before transfer
- **RST**. Informs TCP that the connection should be reset
- **SYN**. The control flag used to establish a connection and synchronize the sequence numbers
- **FIN**. Indicates that the sender has no more data and wishes to terminate the connection

The Window is a 16-bit field that contains the number of octets that the receiver can accept, after the acknowledgment sequence number, before it starts to overflow its buffers and drop data.

The Checksum is a 16-bit value that contains a computation that ensures that the data was transferred without damage. RFC 793, the Transmission Control Protocol DARPA Internet Program Protocol Specification describes this field best as "the 16 bit one's complement of the one's complement sum of all 16 bit words in the header and text."

It is imperative that the TCP header end on a 32-bit boundary; a padding field is provided that must be filled with zeros.

User Datagram Protocol (UDP)

The User Datagram Protocol uses the Internet Protocol to provide application processes with an unreliable datagram protocol at the transport layer, enabling applications to communicate without the overhead of connection establishment and teardown. Like IP, the UDP does not guarantee packet delivery, nor does it provide packet sequencing or packet duplication suppression. Applications that require these services should consider the Transmission Control Protocol (TCP).

The UDP is useful for applications that may have special reasons for implementing their own packet-delivery sequencing and reliability. In these cases, the services provided by TCP may go unused while adding considerable overhead. The format of the UDP header is illustrated in figure 5.5.

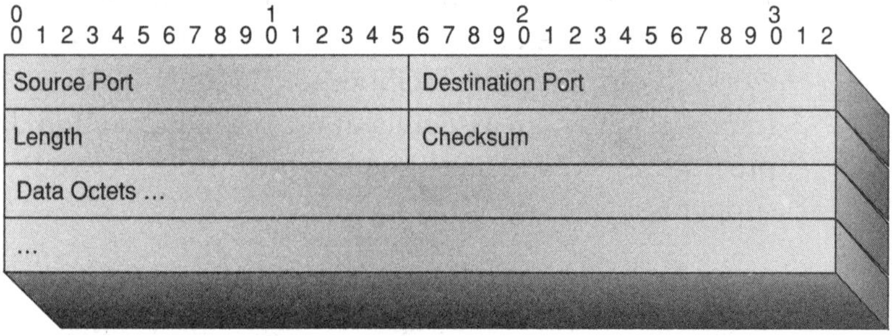

```
0                   1                   2                   3
0 1 2 3 4 5 6 7 8 9 0 1 2 3 4 5 6 7 8 9 0 1 2 3 4 5 6 7 8 9 0 1 2
```

Source Port	Destination Port
Length	Checksum
Data Octets ...	
...	

Figure 5.5:
The User Datagram header.

- **Source Port** and **Destination Port**. Specify the ports of the sending and receiving application processes, respectively.
- **Length**. The length of the user datagram packet, including both the header and the data.
- **Checksum** .A 16-bit computation that can be checked to ensure that the data was transferred without damage. From the RFC 768 User Datagram Protocol, the checksum "is the 16-bit one's complement of the one's complement sum of a pseudo header of information from the IP header, the UDP header, and the data, padded with zero octets at the end (if necessary) to make a multiple of two octets."

Sun Microsystem's Network File System (NFS), a distributed file system that is available on many UNIX and non-UNIX computers, uses the UDP for data transfer.

The Internet Protocol

The Internet Protocol (IP) provides an unreliable, connectionless datagram service for switching data over packet-switched networks. It also provides facilities for fragmenting large packets for transmission and reassembly at the receiving station. IP does not provide any flow control, sequencing, or duplication supporession.

IP is used by both TCP and UDP to route and deliver packets across the internetwork. The TCP segment (header and data) is placed in the data section of the IP datagram. The Internet protocol must be implemented in every host that is connected to the internetwork and that is capable of routing packets on the local network. Internet gateways connect networks together and route and deliver packets between them.

IP uses the hierarchical structure of the internet address and routes each datagram independently of others. Figure 5.6 shows the Internet datagram header.

Bits 0–7	Bits 8–15	Bits 16–23	Bits 24–31
Version / IHL	Type of Service	Total Length	
Identification		Flags / Fragment Offset	
Time to Live	Protocol	Header Checksum	
Source Address			
Destination Address			
Options			Padding

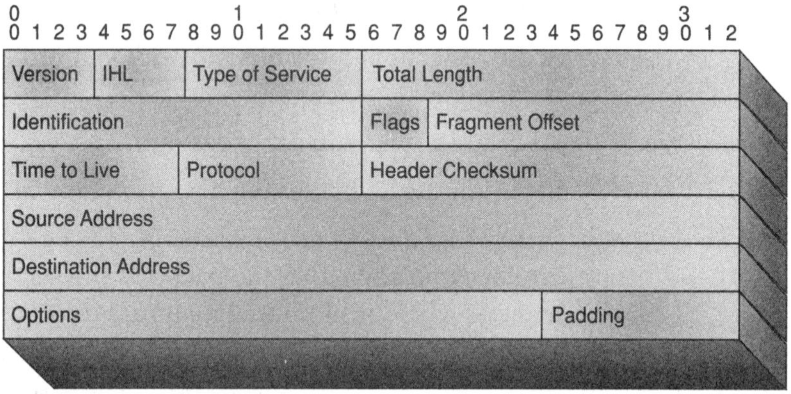

Figure 5.6:
Internet datagram header.

The fields are described in the following sections.

- **Version**. Denotes the internet header format.
- **Internet Header Length (IHL)**. Points to the beginning of the data. The value in this field is multiplied by 32 bits to indicate the offset value.
- **Type of Service**. An eight-bit field that contains values to affect the quality of service provided in certain networks. One example of a type of service is *precedence*, which gives priority to select packets.
- **Total Length**. A 16-bit field that contains the length of the header and the data together. The 16-bit field width places a maximum limit on the size of a datagram at 65,535 octets. In general, however, most

implementations of the Internet protocol limit the maximum length of a datagram at 576 octets to ensure that it can pass across any gateway on the internet.

- **Identification**. Used by the receiving computer to reassemble fragmented datagrams.
- **Flags**. A field that is three bits in width and indicates the fragmenting of datagrams:

  Bit 0 is reserved and set to zero

  Bit 1 indicates whether the datagram may be fragmented or not

  Bit 2 indicates whether the packet is the last fragment or whether more fragments are due
- **Fragment Offset**. A field that is 13 bits in width and shows the proper location of the fragment in the datagram. The value in this field is multiplied by eight octets to determine the octet offset of the fragment in the datagram. A datagram is fragmented when it must pass through a network that has a maximum packet size smaller than the datagram size. The datagram will not be fragmented if the Don't Fragment flag is set. In this case, the datagram will be discarded and an ICMP report (discussed in the next section) will be sent back to the source.
- **Time to Live**. A field that is eight bits wide and specifies the maximum time that the datagram can exist in the internet before it is caught in a loop in the network and destroyed. The unit of time is in seconds; the field is intended to prevent a datagram from bouncing around the network indefinitely.

- **Protocol**. An eight-bit field that specifies the protocol that created the data that the datagram is delivering to the remote host. A list of values for this field can be found in RFC 1060, "Assigned Numbers."
- **Header Checksum**. A 16-bit field that is a checksum for the header only. From RFC 791, Internet Protocol, DARPA Internet Program Protocol Specification, "The checksum field is the 16 bit one's complement of the one's complement sum of all 16 bit words in the header. For purposes of computing the checksum, the value of the checksum field is zero."
- The **Source Address** and **Destination Address**. Fields that are each 32 bits wide and contain the internet addresses for the local and remote hosts.
- **Options**. A variable-width field that is optional in a datagram. However, every host and gateway that implements IP must support it if it is present.

Internet Control Message Protocol (ICMP)

The Internet Control Message Protocol (ICMP) is used to report errors that occur during the delivery of datagrams through the internet. Generally, the destination host or an intermediary gateway is the originator of the message. This device may report that the destination is unreachable or that a gateway did not have sufficient buffers to store and forward the datagram. The message may also contain information informing the sender of a shorter route to the destination.

The ICMP is required by every device that uses IP and is an essential part of IP. ICMP uses IP to perform the delivery of its control messages, however. This reliance on IP makes the ICMP itself inherently unreliable—delivery of control messages are therefore not guaranteed. For this reason, no control messages are generated about errors with ICMP datagrams.

ICMP messages are distinguished from one another by the value of the first octet in the data portion of the IP packet, and they enable the ICMP module to interpret the meaning of the message.

When the IP header is constructed, the gateway (or host) that is reporting the error is used as the source address. The destination is the address where the message is being directed.

The following table outlines the types of ICMP messages:

IMCP Message	*Type*
Echo Reply	0
Destination Unreachable	3
Sourch Quench	4
Redirect	5
Echo	8
Time Exceeded	11
Parameter Problem	12
Timestamp	13
Timestamp Reply	14
Information Request	15
Information Reply	16

- **Echo Reply**. Returns whatever data the sender has in the Echo message. The sequence number can be used to determine which echo request is being replied to.
- **Destination Unreachable**. Conveys information about one of the following conditions: the network was unreachable, the destination host was unreachable, the destination port was unreachable, or a packet was not allowed to be fragmented. Many of the messages return the IP header and the first 64 bits of the data field of the datagram that initiated the ICMP message.
- **Source Quench**. Sent by a gateway or destination host to indicate that datagrams are coming in faster than it has buffer space or processing power to handle. The message to the sending station is to reduce its rate of sending packets.
- **Redirect**. Sent by a gateway when it discovers a shorter route to the destination in its routing table. This message is not sent if the datagram is using source-routing information.
- **Echo**. A request for the destination to return an Echo Reply message. This reply is an acknowledgment that a datagram can be delivered to the destination.
- **Time Exceeded**. Sent by a gateway if it notices that the Time to Live field in the datagram has expired. The gateway uses this message to inform the sender that it has discarded the datagram. A host may also send this message if it is unable to reassemble the fragments of a datagram in time.
- **Parameter Problem**. Sent by a gateway or host that was forced to discard a datagram because it found something critically wrong with the datagram header.

The message also contains a pointer indicating the location of the error in the header.

- **Timestamp**. Collects information about the time required to reach a destination. The sender fills in a 32-bit timestamp (measured in milliseconds) of the current time, using midnight UTC (Universal Time Coordinated) as the reference time.
- **Timestamp Reply**. A reply to the timestamp message; contains a timestamp of when the datagram was received at the destination and a timestamp of when the reply was sent. The client application is free to use this information in any way.
- **Information Request** and **Information Reply**. Used by hosts to determine the network number that they are attached to. These messges are defined in the protocol specification but are not generally implemented.

Routing Information Protocol (RIP)

As mentioned earlier, IP-based internets are made up of separate networks connected together by means of gateways. These gateways are responsible for routing messages between the networks when the destination host is not attached to the local network. The gateway's task is to find a path to bring the packet closer to the destination.

To do this, internet gateways maintain a routing table. The routing tables are maintained by using the Routing Information Protocol (RIP) to exchange information between gateways.

The RIP is based on the Bellman-Ford algorithm, which is in a class of algorithms known as "distance vector algorithms." The program "routed," which is part of the Berkeley Software

Distribution (BSD) 4.3, is perhaps one of the most popular implementations of the RIP protocol.

The Internet RIP is very similar to the Xerox Network Systems' (XNS) Routing Information Protocol (RIP). The XNS RIP itself is based on the Gateway Information Protocol, which was a component of the PUP protocols suite.

The RIP Protocol has the advantage of exchanging a minimum of information to maintain the routing tables. RIP has the limitation of allowing only a 15-hop maximum as a metric for measuring the distance to a network. For the purposes of the RIP, 16 hops represents infinity. An additional limitation is that RIP does not take into account real-time network conditions such as congestion or other delays when calculating the "distance" between networks.

Networks that have been determined to be inaccessible are given a distance value of 16, meaning infinity. Each entry in the routing table contains the following information:

- **IP Address.** The address of the destination.
- **Distance**. Measures how far away the destination is from the current host or gateway, and measures the cost of getting the datagram to the destination. In most implementations, the distance is a measure of the number of hops (or gateways) that the datagram must traverse in order to reach the destination.
- **Next Hop**. The IP address of the next gateway to which the datagram needs to be sent in order to get it closer to its final destination.
- **Change Flag**. A flag indicating that there has been a modification to the routing information for this entry.

- **Interface**. The network interface that should be used to send the datagram to the next gateway (or destination host).
- **Timers**. Used to age the route entries in the table. There are two timers for each entry. The first indicates the time left before the entry will be considered out-of-date and marked for deletion. Generally, this value is set to 180 seconds when the entry is created or updated. The second is a timer controlling when the outdated route is actually removed from the table.

The RIP uses the User Datagram Protocol (UDP) for exchanging information. Both the sending and the receiving process use the well-known port number of 520. Some devices, such as hosts, may choose to have a process listen on this port and build a routing table from the information that it overhears.

RIP propagates the information in the rouuting table to every directly connected gateway every 30 seconds. In addition, it responds to explicit requests for routing information. Finally, when the distance metric has been updated for an entry, RIP causes the change to be sent to connected gateways. The RIP packet is structured as follows:

Command	1 byte
Version	1 byte
Unnamed (must be zero)	2 bytes
Address Family Identifier	2 bytes
Unnamed (must be zero)	2 bytes
IP Address	4 bytes
Unnamed (must be zero)	4 bytes
Unnamed (must be zero)	4 bytes
Metric	4 bytes

The RIP packet may contain up to 25 entries of routing information.

Using the Command field in the RIP packet, a system can request all or part of a routing table to be transferred and can respond to a routing information request by sending part or all of its routing table.

The Address Family Identifier specifies the protocol that the routing information refers to. This enables RIP to be used for protocols other than the Internet suite.

To request a gateway to send its entire routing table as a response, the sender prepares a RIP packet with one entry by using an address family identifier of 0 and specifying the metric to be 16 (infinity).

Summary

Network protols and connecting schemes have grown significantly since their introduction, and attempts to standardize how computers talk with each other have led to a number of now widely-accepted methods and models. This chapter has given you an overview of the more protocols most commonly in use today.

This chapter introduced you to five major LAN protocols: Xerox Network Systems (XNS), Novell's IPX/SPX, NetBIOS, AppleTalk, and the TCP/IP protocol suite. You learned how each of the protocols relate to the OSI Reference Model, including which protocols are implemented at each layer. The chapter also discussed each protocol, including how headers and data are structured. Finally, you learned how data packets are routed between computers connected to internetworks.

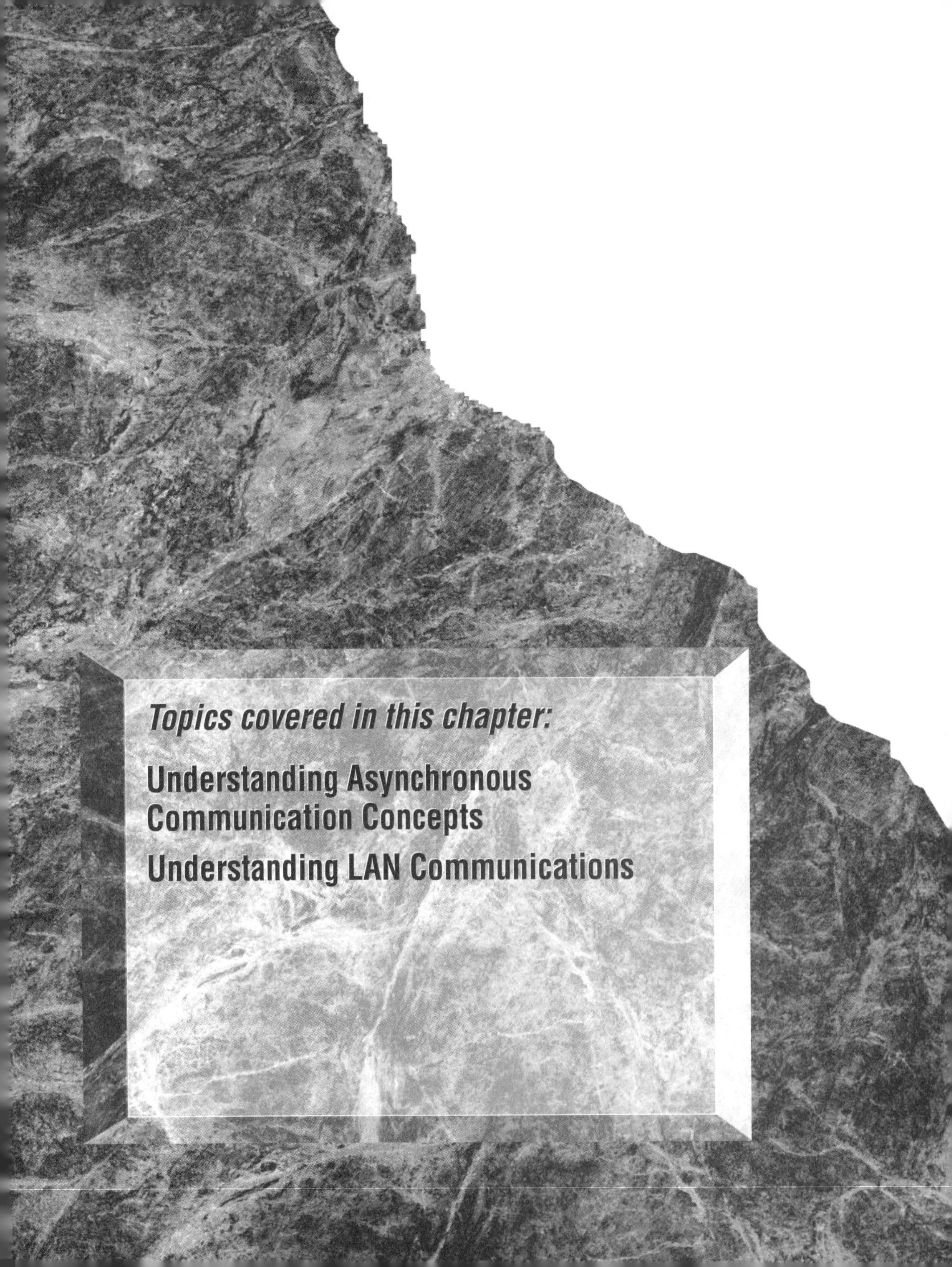
Topics covered in this chapter:
Understanding Asynchronous Communication Concepts
Understanding LAN Communications

Chapter 6

Network Asynchronous Communication Services

One of the basic reasons for implementing local area networks is its capability to share resources on the network, whether they are hardware components or data. Networks were first used for sharing files and printers. That use has grown and now enables the sharing of mainframe and minicomputer connections. This chapter discusses the capability to share asynchronous communications devices across the network.

Asynchronous communications enable network users to share modems. Typically, modems are shared as follows:

- *Dial-in*, in which you which you dial into the network from a remote location and access the network resources
- *Dial-out*, in which you dial out of the network to access resources beyond the network itself

Although both of these situations use the same concepts in asynchronous communications, the way in which they operate at the operating system level are two different things. This chapter discusses the difference between dial-in and dial-out as well.

The basic concepts you need to understand are the foundation of asynchronous communications: communication elements, serial-communication concepts, modems, and modem standards. After discussing these concepts, this chapter moves to a discussion of the implementation of these concepts in a network environment.

Understanding Asynchronous Communication Concepts

The first thing you need to know about asynchronous communication is how it fits into the way computers are used to communicate. The two basic methods used in the computer field are *parallel* and *serial communications*.

Parallel Communications

Data in a computer travels in parallel. In other words, bits are transmitted from one place to another along multiple lines, such as in a data bus. The basic principle of *parallel communication* is that all the data bits leave one location simultaneously and arrive simultaneously at another location. On the data bus, for example, 16 bits may be transmitted from a 16-bit interface card to the CPU, all leaving the interface card along separate lines of the bus and arriving at the CPU through multiple lines in the same bus. Parallel communications are fairly simple to do because the physical distances in the computer are constrained. The bits travel less than a foot in most cases. Even parallel-connected printers typically are less than 20 feet away the computer.

Serial Communications

Serial communications are used when data must travel more than a few feet because, when data is communicated over a cable, differences in the *impedance* (resistance) in the individual strands of wire vary enough so that bits transmitted in parallel do not arrive simultaneously at the destination. Because internal communications in the computer are in parallel, some method or means is needed to be able to convert individual bits of data and transmit them serially. The way conversion between parallel and serial communications is done is discussed later in this chapter.

Serial communication differs from parallel communication because it sends data in packets or bits over a single line, serially.

Another problem is that computers must be able to communicate over extremely long distances—across the state, country, or world, for example—and they must be able to communicate across media that sometimes are less than desirable. Because of undesirable conditions, there is a need for error correction, as well as for the communicating systems to be able to deal with problems when they occur. These ideas also are discussed shortly.

Representation of Data

Data may be transmitted in one of two forms: character-based or binary.

As you may know from reading other books about microcomputer systems, *character-based data* is represented in a seven-bit code called *ASCII* (American Standard Code for Information Interchange). The seven bits may be arranged to represent the letters (both upper- and lowercase) of the alphabet, numbers (0-9), punctuation, and some special control characters (such as tabs, form feeds, and carriage returns). Because each word in a 8088, 80x86 microcomputer is sixteen bits long, representing two bytes, one character may be represented in a single byte, using the first seven significant bits.

Binary data, which consists of code instructions in an application, is based upon the pattern of the bits.

For all forms of serial communications, the form of the data must be preserved during transmission. Otherwise, a character-based document that is transmitted may not be readable or, in the case of binary data, the application may not function properly after it is received.

Synchronous and Asynchronous

Basically, today's computer systems use two forms of serial communications: synchronous and asynchronous.

Synchronous communications typically are used by mainframe and minicomputer systems. The name *synchronous communications* implies that both the sending and receiving devices are in sync, that they operate together. The problem with synchronous communications is that both systems on either end of the communication must stay in sync over the course of the transmission. Because a great deal of communication takes place over normal, voice-grade telephone lines, this may be very difficult; this inability to stay in sync is why most synchronous communications take place over higher grade, or *dedicated*, communications lines.

Asynchronous communications, on the other hand, do not rely on hardware at both ends of the communication to stay in sync. Instead, the data to be transmitted, whether character-based or binary, is broken into smaller chunks of information called *packets*.

The data is broken into packets internally by a UART (Universal Asynchronous Receiver/Transmitter). This device is specifically responsible for the conversion of data from parallel to serial communication. These packets of information are then *framed* by placing a header and a trailer on each packet. The header of the packet consists of a start bit; the trailer contains a stop bit. Thus, a packet of data being transferred by means of a modem consists of 10 bits: the start bit, eight data bits (which usually include the parity bit), and a stop bit.

Actually, the number of data and stop bits can vary. A packet can contain seven or eight data bits and 1, 1.5, or 2 stop bits. It is very important that both of the communicating devices be configured in the same way.

The RS-232 Connector

In the Intel-based microcomputer world, an RS-232 interface is usually employed as the serial connection on a computer. The RS-232 connector is usually a 25-pin connector, sometimes called a DB-25. (Note that many newer computers use the DB-9 connector rather than the 25-pin connector.)

There are two different types of serial connections: Data Terminal Equipment (DTE) and Data Communications Equipment (DCE). The difference between them is pin 4. DCE sends a signal for RTS that it wants to send data; DTE receives the signal on pin 4.

Pins on the connectors have special functions that control the operation of the serial communications occurring between the pins themselves and the corresponding pins at the other end of a communication link.

Table 6.1 presents a synopsis of the pins and how they function on this connector:

The RS-232 connector is the point at which the PC and modem interact. Each of these pins communicate the status information (of the modem) back to the serial communications port on the PC. While the modem is in operation, communications status changes rapidly to reflect what is happening between the local system and the remote system.

The process of a call goes like this: when a modem is connected to the PC and the serial port determines that a modem device is ready and waiting, the DTR and RTS pins are already high (active). (Engineers often refer to pin signals in terms of the voltages rather than the logic of what the voltages mean. *High* simply means that a standard voltage has been applied to the pin and it indicates an active status.)

When the command is given to the modem to dial, the telephone line goes *off-hook*—basically, the modem hears a dial tone. The dial tone is a reminder of the telephone origins of asynchronous data communcations: a telephone goes active when the handset is lifted and the telephone goes off-hook. At this point, the DSR pin *goes high*, or becomes active. The number is dialed by the communications software sending the appropriate commands to the modem. (More often than not—99 percent of the time—Hayes Smartmodem commands, or commands based on the Hayes standard for smart modem communications, are used.)

Table 6.1
Pin Assignments for RS-232 Connectors

Pin Number	*Abbreviated Pin Name*	*Pin Name and Function*
2	TD	Transmit Data; the line over which data is transmitted
3	RD	Receive Data; the line over which data is received
4	RTS	Request to Send; sender signals the receiver that it is ready to send data
5	CTS	Clear to Send; receiver signals that sender can transmit data
6	DSR	Data Set Ready; indicates to the terminal that a modem is ready to receive data
8	DCD	Data Carrier Detect; detects that modem (or other device) is on-line
12	SI	Speed Indicator
20	DTR	Data Terminal Ready; signals that terminal system is powered up and ready to communicate; also handles Auto Answer
22	RI	Ring Indicator; detects that telephone is ringing and that modem should answer it

When the telephone number is dialed, a "ringback" signal is sent by the other system (the one to which you want to connect). The sound you hear in the handset sounds like the other telephone ringing. At this point, if you receive a busy signal from the other system, your modem receives and interprets this frequency and tells you that the system is busy. If the other system is not busy, it answers the telephone. At this point, a handshaking occurs between the two systems; the DCD pin becomes active because of the carrier detect signal.

On the answering end of the connection, the modem's RI pin goes high to indicate that a ring has been detected. If the DTR is active, signifying that the modem is active and ready to be used, the modem's DSR line goes active and the modem answers the telephone and starts handshaking with the system calling it.

Handshaking is the protocol by which two modems decide to communicate. There are two methods of handshaking: software and hardware.

Software handshaking involves the use of the Xon/Xoff (pronounced "ex-on-ex-off") protocol. This protocol is rather simple, involving a software command between the two systems so that one can tell the other when to start and stop communications. Suppose, for example, that a modem is receiving a file transfer from a remote system. At some point, the buffer fills and the receiving system has to write the information to a disk file. During this time, data is lost if the sending modem does not stop transfer (because modem communication is stopped on the receiving end while the disk file is written). Using Xon/Xoff, the receiving system issues an Xoff, writes the file to disk, and then issues an Xon to start the transfer again.

Hardware handshaking involves the use of the CTS/RTS pins on the RS-232 interface. Instead of issuing a software command, the pins alternate between active states. Hardware handshaking, which is much faster than software handshaking, is used by much faster modems (faster than 2400 bps). The one item to remember about hardware handshaking is that you must make sure the proper cable is between the RS-232 connection and the modem. Many older systems tied the CTS line to the DSR line, and therefore did not allow these two lines to operate independently.

Modems

Data that is to be communicated may be transmitted in either of two methods: digital or analog.

Digital communications are discrete by nature, which means that they have a limited number of distinct representations. In the computer, each bit of information is represented by an electrical signal corresponding to one or zero (1 or 0), which represents on or off, respectively.

The values represented in *analog communications* are infinitely variable. If the analog signal were represented on an oscilloscope, it would represent a wave pattern. An example of an analog wave pattern is the human voice, electrical transmission over a power line, or an editor screaming because the author is so late with this chapter.

Telephones transmit signals in an analog form. When you speak into a telephone, it acts as a modulation device, converting the tone of your voice into an electrical signal that is passed over the wire and then converted back into a tone on the receiving telephone. Because computers transmit data in digital format, some sort of device must be used to modulate the digital format into an analog signal and transmit it over a telephone line. At the receiving end, another device must be present to demodulate the signal, converting it back into digital format the computer can understand. Modems are responsible for the conversion that takes place between the computer and the telephone line.

Modulation/Demodulation

As stated, a signal transmitted in analog form represents a wave. A *wave* consists of frequency and amplitude. Frequency is represented in *hertz* (Hz), the number of times-per-second the wave form repeats itself. A voice-grade telephone line has a usable bandwidth of about 3Khz. Any signals transmitted must be within the range of about 300-3,300Hz (the wave being transmitted can repeat itself anywhere from 300 times-per-second to 3,300 times-per-second).

Without going into great technical detail (remember all that high-school physics?), this means that the bandwidth of a voice-grade telephone line is not high enough to transmit data at a high rate. Some means of converting or changing the signal being transmitted is needed to enable the passage of higher rates of transmission. The passage of higher rates is done by modulating the signal in different ways.

Modulation is the capability of the modem to change the frequency, amplitude, or phase of a transmitted wave, which makes achieving higher rates of transfer possible. Just as modem speed varies with different types of modulation, different types of modems use different types of modulation. For this reason, many modems of a certain standard may not communicate properly with other modems not of the same type.

Bps versus Baud Rate

Most people mistakenly use the term "baud rate" to mean the transfer rate in bits-per-second (bps). Using "baud" and "bps" interchangeably is incorrect because a modem operating at 9,600 baud may be capable of transmitting 38,400 bps.

Baud rate refers to the number of signal changes taking place during a specified time period. Baud rate also has to do with the way the modem modulates the signal. A modem operating at 2,400 baud changes the signal 2,400 times per second. The number of actual signal changes that the modem makes does not correspond directly to the number of bits it is transmitting because some modulation techniques allow more than one bit to be transmitted with one signal change. Therefore, using the terms interchangeably is improper (but accepted by most people).

Duplexing

Another term used with respect to modem communications is *duplexing*. The terms used are half-duplex and full-duplex.

Half-duplexing means that the modem can communicate in only one direction at any time. Essentially, this means that the modem must send a transmission, then wait for the other end to "turn the line around" (this is an old telegraph expression) or to send communications in the other direction.

Full duplexing means that the modem can communicate in both directions at the same time. The resulting communications are much faster.

Note also that, in many communications programs, the term "duplex" refers incorrectly to the modem's ability to echo characters back to the screen. This is not the same thing as the modem's inherent duplexing capabilities.

Modem Types

A variety of types of modems are available. Over the past few years, vendors such as Hayes, Telebit, and Microcom tried to establish de-facto standards for high-speed modems (9,600 baud). As a result, many people bought a Hayes HST or a Telebit Trailblazer modem that could communicate at high speed only with another modem from the same manufacturer. Although the modems might "drop down" in speed and communicate properly at a lower rate, the advantage of a higher speed modem was then effectively lost.

Vendor-independent standards created by the CCITT (International Consultative Committee on Telephone and Telegraph) enable modems from different manufacturers to communicate with each other, provided that they follow the same standard. Some of these standards follow or correspond to a manufacturer's defacto standard for a modem type, such as the Bell 103 (described next), which closely follows the V.21 standard.

One of the first standards set for modems was the Bell 103/V.21 standard. This modem was capable of transmitting data at 300 bps or 300 baud which, by today's standards, is extremely slow. The Bell 103 is obsolete because today's modems operate at much higher transfer rates. Comparable to this was the Bell 212A standard, which is capable of transmitting data at 1,200 bps. Again, by today's standards this is slow. The Bell 212A may be fine for systems that do not need to handle high rates of traffic; otherwise, it should be replaced with newer, faster modems.

The V.32 standard established by the CCITT describes the methods by which modems operating at 4,800 bps and 9,600 bps communicate with each other. Following this standard ensure that other modems can communicate properly at high speed, regardless of the manufacturer. V.32 uses a modulation method called *trellis encoding*, which adds a check bit to improve the modem's performance over a public switched network. Trellis encoding also pushes the modem's modulation frequency past the standard range for a voice-grade lin, which is one reason that some higher-speed modems may have problems communicating at high speeds over lower-grade voice lines.

The V.32 standard does not include any method for error correction. Because these modems are communicating at higher rates of speed over possibly low-grade lines, error correction becomes increasingly important. The need for the error-correction standard resulted in the implementation of the V.32bis standard. V.32bis also added faster rates of 7,200 bps, 12,000 bps, and 14,400 bps to the V.32 standard.

These standards involved the way the modem modulated the line—in other words, the way the modem manipulated the electrical transmissions to achieve higher transfer rates. Newer standards involve the modem's capability to compress data, which results in even higher transfer rates.

The CCITT developed a newer standard, V.42, which uses the Link Access Procedure for Modems (LAPM) to do error correction in hardware. The V.42 standard resulted in faster transfer rates but still did little with data compression.

Because data compression was another technique by which the modems could transfer data at a higher rate, the V.42bis standard was created. V.42bis uses Lempel-Ziv compression techniques to "compact" data before it is transmitted over the line. Modems that follow the V.42bis standard can transmit data at a rate of up to 38,400 bps.

At about the same time that the CCITT was becoming more involved in setting standards for high-speed modems, Microcom was developing its own proprietary standards for modems, called MNP (Microcom Network Protocol). MNP has different levels, some of which are comparable to the CCITT standards.

The different levels of MNP have to do with error correction and data compression. MNP Level 4 is an error-correction technique that may give a modem a higher transfer rate.

MNP Level 5 is a data-compression standard, in which the MNP design tries to compress data before the data is transferred over the line. MNP Level 5 is comparable to the CCITT standard V.42bis (in fact, MNP Level 5 is the secondary protocol in the V.42bis standard).

What Does It All Mean?

The following section is a layman's explanation of modem types.

The number of standards and different types of modems confuse most people—and for good reason. Essentially, to have high-speed modems work, you need to have the same standard implemented in each modem at the ends of the connection. When the modems begin to "talk," they discover at what level they can both communicate. Modems involved in communication "drop down" to the lowest common denominator between them.

Suppose, for example, that your modem follows the V.42bis standard. If you connect to another modem that also follows the V.42bis standard, both will use this standard to communicate. If not, your modem will try to detect the level at which the other modem is capable of communicating and will "drop" to that level.

The My V.42bis modem also supports MNP Level 5. If the other modem is not of a V.42bis standard, but supports MNP Level 5, both modems should communicate at this level. If the other modem is a simpler, older modem capable of 2,400 bps, your modem should drop to 2,400 bps and turn off any error-detection or data-compression scheme the other modem does not have. Then they can communicate properly at 2,400 bps.

Please note that some modem functions can be set by communications software. If you experience problems when communicating with another modem, for example, you may need to disable error correction or data compression through the communications software you are using.

In short, to take advantage of high-speed modems, you need high-speed modems—both of which support the same standards—at both ends of the connection.

Understanding LAN Communications

The communications concepts discussed thus far remain the same, even in a network environment, because the same type of communications software and modems are used. The biggest change at the network level is that the asynchronous communication is routed across the network, instead of through a modem attached to the serial port in the local PC.

The next two sections—dial-in and dial-out—reflect the basic need of asynchronous communications across networks.

Dial-In Services

Dialing into the network is the capability to attach, via modem, to the network from a remote location and access the resources of that network. Typically, dialing-in includes the capability to access file information or to run applications that may be located on the network. An example of dialing-in is a person who wants to run a sales report through a database system on his network while he is at home at night or on the weekend.

If simple file access is the resource required, something like a bulletin board system (BBS) often does the job easily. Although a complete discussion of BBSs is beyond the scope of this chapter, the basic function of a BBS is to have access to files and messages. A BBS typically is a stand-alone operation, not tied directly to network services. Because the BBS typically is managed separately from the network, information on the BBS typically is placed there by an administrator. Because additional administration is required, all files needed by a remote user may not be accessible through a BBS.

If the required resource is an application or interaction with data stored on the network, the scenario changes dramatically. The hardware and software needed to have remote dial-in access are widely misunderstood by many people. The following pages offer a reasonable explanation of dial-in access.

When dialing into the network to use an application, you need to start up a DOS session on a machine local to the network.

Consider how applications function. To be executed, they must be loaded into memory from a storage place (the network's hard drive). If the loading were to take place across a communication line, even at 38,400 bps, loading an application such as Wordperfect or Lotus would take several minutes. Whenever the application needed to overlay itself, or load another piece of itself into memory, the response time wouuld drop dramatically. Such a system would be unusable.

In a better implementation, the application would be loaded into the memory of a PC attached to the network, after which screen updates and keystrokes would be passed across the communications lines between the local PC and the remote PC. Screen updates and keystrokes would represent a small amount of traffic (at least when compared to transfer of the entire application). Thus, a system such as this would be extremely usable.

All that is needed to implement this type of system is some type of remote-control software for the host (local to the network) and remote PCs. Many software applications—such as pcAnywhere IV, Carbon Copy, Triton's Co/Session, and Norton-Lambert's Close Up—are available to perform the remote-control tasks.

Suppose, for example, that you want to use pcAnywhere IV to implement this type of system. Both the host and remote versions of the software come in one package. The host version of the software is installed and loaded on a workstation attached to the network. At the workstation, the appropriate modem is attached to a dedicated telephone line, and pcAnywhere IV is set up to wait for an incoming call.

At the remote workstation, the remote version of pcAnywhere IV is loaded. When users want to dial into the workstation attached to the network, they simply use the remote version to dial and connect, then they log in to the network as if they were sitting at the local PC. The DOS session is running on the local PC. Only the keystrokes and screen updates are transmitted over the modem line. A key point to keep in mind is that because the applications will run at the speed of the local PC, you must dedicate a 80386 if you expect the application to execute at 80386 speed.

Performance becomes most critical with graphic applications such as Microsoft Windows. A bit-by-bit transfer of a graphic screen takes a long time at modem speeds. Most advanced PC remote-control programs are capabable of operating more intelligently, however. Programs optimized for Windows will transfer the Windows control information, rather than the screen-display bit patterns. This control information is more compact than the screen-image data. Close-Up is an example of a program that contains advanced features for optimizing performance under Windows.

This type of implementation is fine for smaller networks in which only a few users want to access the network from a remote site. In fact, this solution is more stable than many other dial-in implementations; if you have more users and can afford to dedicate more PCs, more copies of the remote-control software, and more telephone lines, this solution is quite desirable. In most cases, people are not willing to dedicate many PCs to function for dial-in use only, especially if the PCs are powerful (a 80386 or 80486, for example).

This type of implementation is desirable also for users who want to access their workstations after hours. When users leave the office, they simply load the remote-control software, thus making their system accessible to them while they are not using it at work. This method often is not desirable in larger installations because, again, it requires a dedicated telephone line and modem for each workstation attachment.

Dial-In Dedicated Servers

A more realistic situation is to use a dedicated server that can enable multiple DOS sessions through one dedicated PC. The most popular type of this system is Novell's NetWare Access Server (NAS).

Novell's NetWare Access Server

With Novell's NAS, many users can dial in to the same dedicated PC. This dedicated PC must be a 80386 or 80486 with a minimum of 3.6M of memory—enough memory to allow one user session and an operator session. NAS allows a maximum of 16 users per dedicated PC. Additional memory is required beyond the original 3.6M for each additional session desired. You must add 1M per session, as well as even more memory for any session requiring expanded memory. The maximum amount of memory NAS will access is 16M.

A modem line is required for every user that will access the NAS system simultaneously. NAS uses multiline communications adapters (a single board with several modem attachments available), such as the WNIM+ board described in the following paragraph. Novell has certified a few other multiport boards that may be used with NAS, such as IBM's ARTIC (Realtime Interface CoProcessor Adapter) and Newport System's Solution Adapters.

The WNIM+ (Wide-Area Network Interface Plus) adapter is available from MicroDyne Corporation. It is a four-port intelligent communications adapter, capable of speeds of up to 38,400bps per port. It is the board most widely used with NAS. Note that because the WNIM+ uses a 64K RAM buffer, no other devices must conflict with this address. If multiple WNIM+ boards are installed in a NAS server, they all must be configured to use the same address space.

NAS operates by using the multiple-8088 mode of the 80386 (80486) chip to simulate several different DOS sessions. These DOS sessions are running in real mode, not in protected mode. Keep in mind that applications written specifically for use with 80286 or 80386 software do not work in a DOS session under NAS.

Historically, NAS has been a tricky system to implement properly. The implementation requirements should be based upon the types of applications you plan to run through the NAS system.

NAS is booted from DOS versions 3.x or 4.0x only. DOS version 5.0 is *not* supported. Once booted, NAS is loaded into memory and a special version of the NetWare shell is loaded, which allows multiple DOS sessions to be used with only one copy of the NetWare shell loaded.

Some of the applications you run on NAS require more memory than others. In such a case, you may want to use a CGA adapter, rather than VGA or monochrome. CGA takes much less memory than other graphics adapters.

Here is what happens in the NAS system to the video adapter: NAS must keep in memory a copy of the screen for each user logging in to the system. Because VGA requires more memory for a higher-resolution screen, this memory effectively is taken away from the DOS session for that user.

Something else to consider when choosing which video adapter to install in the NAS is that this determines the highest resolution graphics available to the user. A VGA adapter takes memory away from the DOS session but enables the user to use VGA graphics, whereas a CGA adapter only enables the user to display CGA graphics. For this reason, the decision of which video adapter to use depends largely on what type of application users will be running on the NAS. The maximum resolution available through NAS is 640×480.

NAS supports a variety of connections. Typically, NAS users connect through modems, but they may also connect through multiplexer, null modem cable, and X.25 PDN attachments. When attaching users through a modem, you must choose also which modems you will support. NAS supports modems with the V.32 protocol and speeds of up to 38,400 bps.

To attach to the NAS, PC users will use the OnLan/PC application (basically, a modified version of the remote version of pcAnywhere IV). When OnLan/PC users are attached to the NAS, they do not have access to their local drives. OnLan/PC does allow file transfers. Users attaching in this manner will be able to use either their own printers (by redirecting the output of the application running on the NAS) or the printers attached to the local network. They cannot use a printer that is attached directly to the NAS, because use of the printer or serial ports directly on the NAS is not supported.

Dumb terminals may be attached to the NAS by null-modem cables, thereby enabling users to use network applications while using only an inexpensive dumb terminal.

Macintosh users may connect to the NAS by using OnLan/Macintosh, a version of OnLan/PC for the Macintosh, which does terminal emulation, as does OnLan/PC. This supports up to VGA graphics on the Macintosh workstations, and enables Macintosh users to access directly DOS applications that reside on the server. This connection may come either through a dial-up connection by modem, or be directly attached across the network.

Performance is another issue with the Access Server. If only one user is attached to the NAS, performance obviously will not suffer. Performance declines slowly as other users are attached simultaneously, because they effectively divide the use of the NAS processor between them.

NAS also provides *dial-back service*, the capability of the remote system to call the NAS system, hang up, and have the NAS call the user back. Dial-back service provides additional security because the NAS will call back only a limited number of predefined telephone numbers. It also provides the capability to have telephone charges paid by the server's company, which can be beneficial for remote sales offices.

Novell provides a document, called "Rules of Thumb," which may be found in the NETWIRE forum on CompuServe. Anyone who is considering installing this system should download this document and read through it *before* installation of the NAS. The document contains a list of supported hardware, such as modems and dumb terminals, as well as applications that are supported under NAS.

MicroDyne

MicroDyne Corporation, which has taken over support for the NetWare Access Server, has released a "plug-and-play" version of Access Server—essentially, a dedicated 80386 with the Access Server software preloaded and ready to use.

This version of the Access Server comes in four- and eight-port versions. The 80386 comes equipped with the necessary communications adapters and either four or eight modems, obviously dependent upon the version of the Access Server you purchase. The server also comes equipped with a network interface card.

Dial-Out Services

To accomplish dial-out services, the serial communications that are intended to be passed to the serial port are redirected across the network to a shared modem device.

Dial-out services are accomplished by a few basic methods, which follow:

- Software-only solutions, by which a modem is shared throughout the network by loading a TSR at a workstation that makes the modem a shared device

- Dedicated modem pooling servers, which consist of a dedicated PC running modem-sharing software
- Devices that are shared modems attached as a network device, such as the Shiva Netmodem/E

Dial-out services require two correctly configured "ends." At one end of the desired communication is the user's workstation. This end uses a redirection technique to direct signals from the PC's modem port through the network to the communication server. Redirection options are explained a little later in this chapter.

At the other end is the shared modem, which also requires appropriate hardware and software to be loaded, depending on which modem-sharing method is chosen. This hardware and software receives the modem signals redirected from the user's PC and passes them on to a modem. The result of this process is that the shared modem appears to the user to be directly connected to his own PC's serial port.

When any modem-sharing device is installed, regardless of whether it is on a dedicated server or a shared modem in a workstation, it is given a name. When a user loads the sharing software, the software looks across the network for available shared modems. When it finds one, a "virtual circuit" is established between the user's workstation and the shared modem device. This virtual circuit should remain intact until the user has finished using the shared modem device. When the modem is in use, the modem device is unavailable to other users throughout the network.

Redirection of Serial Communications

As stated, the serial communications must be redirected across the network to the shared modem device. Redirection is done by either of two methods, depending on which type of modem-pooling software and hardware is chosen: Int14 and NASI.

Int14

Int14, a serial communications redirection standard, operates with BIOS redirection by using Interrupt 14, which is the IBM ROM BIOS serial port interrupt. A TSR is loaded that intercepts calls made to Interrupt 14, and these calls are redirected across the network. In turn, because the proper return codes also are made by the redirection TSR, the workstation application sees what it expects to see.

Before you can use the Int14 interface to redirect communications, you must load a TSR and the communications application. (You can unload the TSR after you exit the communications software.) Typically, this TSR is configured to look for a specific server name and log in to a communications server with a specific user name and password.

NASI

Novell has developed NASI (NetWare Asynchronous Services Interface), another method of serial communications redirection.

Because NASI interfaces directly to the NetWare shell and does not use the computer's BIOS, it performs better at higher communications speeds.

Like Int14, NASI consists of a TSR that must be loaded before the communications application (which must also support NASI) is loaded. After the communications are completed, the NASI TSR may be unloaded.

NASI is operated in of two modes: basic and advanced. In the *basic* mode of operation, the NASI command interpreter is used to send and receive commands from the NASI TSR. *Advanced* mode is used more often because it is application-driven (applications are programmed to use it) and—in this mode—NASI runs within the application, unseen by the user.

In advanced (or application) mode, NASI requires the use of a NASI-compatible communications software package (see Table 6.1).

Products for Dial-Out

Here is a sample of some products that support network dial-out services. These products vary greatly in sophistication and cost. At the low end are software products that run on a standard PC using conventional serial ports; some systems often are capable of running in the background so that the PC supporting the modem can be used for other work. At the high end are systems that require special hardware that may improve performance or capability.

Table 6.1
NASI-Compatible Communications Software

Software	*Publisher*
Ascom/IV, Network version	Symantec
Blast Professional	US Robotics
Citrix Remote Link	Citrix Systems
Citrix Multiuser	Citrix Systems
CO/Session Lan II	Triton Technologies
Crosstalk Mk 4	Digital Communications
Crosstalk for Windows	Digital Communication
DynaComm Asynchronous	Future Soft
Lexus 2000 LAN	Mead Data Central
On/Lan PC	Novell
PcAnywhere IV/Lan	Symantec
poly-START	Polygon Software
Procomm Plus Network	DataStorm Technologies
Reflection/7	Walker, Richter & Quinn
RELAY Gold Lan	MicroCom, Inc.
Smartcom Exec	Hayes Microcomputer Products
SmarTerm 340	Persoft
Softerm PC	Softronics
VsComm/Lan	The M/H Group
WestLaw/Westmate	West Publishing Co.
Zstem 340, Lan Version	KEA Systems, Ltd.

Instant Information Inc.'s InstantCom //CS

The InstantCom Communications Server (ICS) is a software-only package that may be used to share a modem attached to a user's workstation. Because it is software only, it does not require a dedicated PC to function as a communication server. It is therefore less costly for installations in which fewer connections are needed. ICS supports both NetBIOS and NetWare networks, using the Int14 redirection at the user's workstation.

ICS is sold in 1-, 2-, 4-, 8-, 16-, 32-, and 64-port versions, thereby enabling a system to grow into a large number of shared modems throughout a network. Up to eight ports can reside on one server, by using one of the communications adapters listed in the next sentence. To alleviate the problems associated with high-speed communications, ICS also supports several intelligent adapter boards, such as the Digiboard PC series, Specialix Corporation's Specialix Xi series, and Star Gate Technologies' Star Gate ACL series.

ICS consists of a number of smaller programs. ICM, the Manager program, is responsible for the creation of groups and users, the groups and users may be used to determine the proper security access for a single modem or a pool of modems. Please note that the group "EVERYONE" is created automatically upon initial installation. If no security is needed, users can use the "EVERYONE" group to attach to ports with no additional configuration of the groups or users.

Before ICS can be used, it must be configured, giving the servers names by which they can be referenced and defining the modems they are sharing. When ICS is installed, one server name (ComServer) is preconfigured. Individual shared ports must be configured following the installation of the software, which copies the ICS software to a storage place (the network hard drive). For each port, a name and a hardware configuration are chosen. The hardware configuration reflects the interrupt and memory address at which the port is installed. A *connect mode* is chosen also. The connect mode reflects whether a particular port is "normal" or in X.PC mode.

X.PC is a protocol with which users simultaneously can use the same telephone line attached to the same system. If an X.PC line were active and attached to Easylink, for example, another user on the network could opt to attach to Easylink through the same telephone line (and modem) while the first session was still active. The number of simultaneous users is determined by the connect mode you select. A port configured with X.PC mode can still be used in normal mode.

After the ports have been defined, groups and users must be defined by using the Manager program, ICM.EXE. Clearly, users are defined individually, in much the same way as regular users on the network. ICS does not access the binderies in a Novell network. You do not have to use an individual name for every user. You may simply share the same name. After groups and users are created, they can be assigned to the ports. Groups or users can grant exclusive rights to certain ports, or the ICS can be left wide open, with little security access. Security access is recommended, especially with respect to high-speed modems. A maximum of 255 users and 32 groups can exist.

Users who can access an X.PC modem have an additional level of access. These users may configure it so that when they are attached to a specified X.PC port, they do not have to share that X.PC session with anyone.

ICS is loaded as a TSR at a user's workstation. The TSR effectively makes the modem at that workstation available to other users on the network. This TSR requires 48K as a base. For each normal port that is configured, an additional 8K is required. For each X.PC port, 32K is required. The TSR may be loaded high, depending on the configuration of the workstation. Please note that because this TSR is handling the serial communications at that workstation, workstation performance may suffer if the port is being used at high speeds. If many modems are shared at one workstation, that workstation realistically should be made a dedicated workstation, because of the high amount of memory additional modems take and the workload they place on that specific workstation.

The ICS TSR is loaded in the form "ICS-S <Server Name>" for a standard serial port (not using an intelligent communications adapter). The command used reflects which type of communications adapter is being used. Other forms of the command must be run, depending on the communications adapter being used. The ICS TSR may also be unloaded by using the command-line parameter "/u". The TSR may also be loaded into high DOS memory, saving precious RAM for the user's workstation.

After the communications server has been defined, the Int14 interface, which is to be used by a connecting user, must be configured. The name of the user, password information, server name, and port information are configured in the Int14 interface. This configuration information is stored in a file called INT14.CFG; it is loaded automatically whenever the user loads the Int14 TSR.

Advanced and technical configurations may be done with the Int14 configuration program. Baud rate and communications options, such as parity and the number of data and stop bits may be configured. *Technical configuration* gives the user the ability to do the following:

- ❖ Choose whether communications may be monitored.
- ❖ Enable Xon/Xoff software flow control.
- ❖ Disable RTS/CTS hardware flow control.
- ❖ Set the interactive mode escape character. (By entering a network interrupt number, you enable some background communications processing on a workstation without otherwise interrupting the use of the network.)

Use of the Int14 driver with a communications application is either automatic or interactive. In *automatic mode,* the user simply loads the Int14 TSR and attaches to a particular port. This works well if the port is not currently in use; otherwise, the TSR does not connect to a port. Remember, however, that the Int14 configuration file, INT14.CFG, is not likely to be shared in this case. Rather, a different copy is made for each user needing access to ICS. By making a specific copy for each user, the network administrator does not have to worry about technical support calls when a particular user forgets his or her name, password, or any other configuration information.

Interactive mode enables the user to dynamically select a communications server and port. The user name and password may be entered at start up, along with the user's choice of whether to allow X.PC sharing. Interactive mode can be used only when the INT14.CFG file has no user name. First, the Int14 TSR is loaded, followed by the communications program. When the communications program is loaded, the Int14 TSR prompts you to enter a user name, password, server name, port name, service (the name of the service to which you will connect), and your choice on X.PC sharing.

With interactive mode, any number of users on the network may share the INT14.CFG configuration file. If any changes are made to the INT14.CFG file, the network administrator has to update only one copy of that file. Because of this feature, you may prefer interactive mode to automatic mode, in which every user who has access to ICS has a copy of the configuration file, each of which has to be updated by the administrator.

The capability to monitor a communications port is included in the Manager utility, ICM.EXE. With this capability, an administrator can watch the communications taking place over the communications server port. (Some people may consider this a security breach.) Monitor enables the administrator to determine the current user and status of the mode. Also, a communications session can be recorded so that the administrator can debug any repeatedly occurring problems.

The Manager utility also creates a log of system use. This log is especially useful for showing your managers or financial people that the system is actually being used or for tracking possible connection problems in the system. A new log entry is created whenever the server is used. Each entry tracks the user's name, the server to which the user attached, the port to which the user attached, the service, and the time on (connected) and off (disconnected).

The log can hold a maximum of 16,384 entries. The server administrator may choose (through Manager configuration) how often a new log file is generated and how many log files may exist at any given time. Suppose, for example, that the administrator chooses to create a new log file every day and have a maximum of three logs. A new log file is created every day, the old log files for the preceding day and the day before that are saved, and all previous log files are deleted.

A diagnostics utility, ICTEST.EXE, is provided with the package. After the ICS TSR has loaded and provided the network with a shared modem, Int14 is loaded. Then ICSTEST is run. ICSTEST enables you to select a port, change baud rates, parity bits, stop bits, data bits, and send 50,000 alphabetic characters to that particular port to test it. ICSTEST displays modem status and line errors (such as parity, framing, timeout, and flow-control errors).

ICS also comes with an Int14-compatible communications program, called the Connector program (ICC.EXE). ICC is a fairly decent communications program. It is not elegant but does provide enough features to get the job done. ICC includes a fairly robust scripting language with a learn mode. Learn mode allows a user to create a script while logging on to a system. By recording the screen prompts (of the service to which you are attached) and your input to the screens, ICC can save the script to automate your next log-in.

ICC provides the items you normally expect from a communications program: a telephone book, file transfer (supported protocols are ASCII, Xmodem, Xmodem Batch, Ymodem, Ymodem-G, and Kermit), the ability to create macros, keep a capture buffer, and so on.

ICS is a good product for sharing up to eight modems. You may find that, at speeds greater than 2,400 bps, data may be lost (which probably is true for *any* product of this sort) unless you are using an intelligent communications adapter. If your shared workstation has an 8250 UART installed, it may be swapped with a 16500 UART, which handles a better rate of throughput and should therefore solve the problem.

Novell's NetWare Asynchronous Communications Server

Novell's NetWare Asynchronous Communications Server (NACS) is another modem-sharing communications server. The two versions of NACS function in completely different ways and require different hardware configurations as well. Figure 6.1 shows the Novell Access Server configuration.

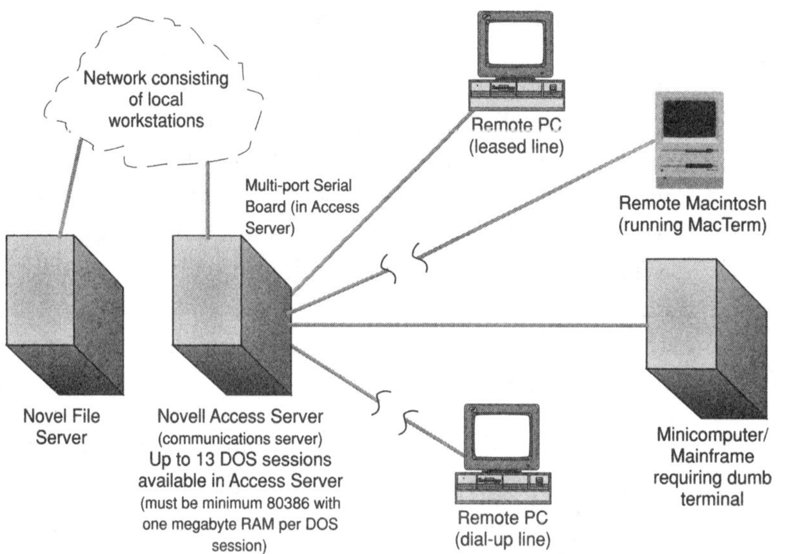

Figure 6.1:
Novell Access Server configuration.

The older version of NACS (Version 2.x) requires a dedicated PC to function as the communications server. The dedicated PC requires the installation of an intelligent communications adapter, such as the WNIM+, discussed earlier in this chapter in the section on dial-in systems. Note that the dedicated PC does not have to be a 80386 system, as is required by NACS version 3.0 (discussed next). This older version of NACS is still available (as ACS2) from the original developer, Network Products.

A newer version of NACS (at time of this writing, version 3.0) is available. NACS version 3.0, which is NLM-based (NetWare Loadable Module), enables users to share modems that are attached directly to a NetWare 3.11 (or above) server. Thus, NACS requires at least an 80386 PC with at least 6MB of RAM available. Because it is installed directly on a NetWare 3.11 file server, version 3.0 alleviates the need for modems spread throughout the network—but it has some drawbacks.

Modems that are attached directly to the file server then become available to all users throughout the network. Instead of requiring an intelligent communications server, NACS is able to use the serial ports on the NetWare 3.11 file server. This works fine, provided that you are not using high-speed communications with these serial ports.

NACS is sold in two-port, eight-port, and 32-port configurations. Typically, the two-port version is for use with systems that will share modems attached directly to the file server's serial ports, but the two-port version does allow the use of intelligent communications adapters. The eight-port version is able to use as many as five serial ports on the file server, combined with as many as three ports on an intelligent communications adapter. The two-port, eight-port, and 32-port configurations can support their respective number of shared connections concurrently.

NACS version 3.0 supports speeds of up to 115.2Kbs-per-port, depending on the capabilities of the communications adapter being used with NACS. Several intelligent communications adapters are available for use with NACS. (One example is the

WNIM+, discussed in this chapter's "NetWare Access Server" section.) Other products being tested for use with NACS are:

- ❖ Digiboard's PC/Xe Adapter, which comes in four-port, eight-port, and 16-port versions. The PC/Xe is capable of communications at speeds of up to 115.2Kbps.
- ❖ Newport Systems Solutions Asynchronous Communications Interface (ACI), which provides eight ports at speeds of up to 38.4Kbps.
- ❖ Newport Systems Solutions X.25 Communications Interface (XCI) for attachment to an X.25 network at speeds of up to 38.4Kpbs per port.

At the time of this writing, Novell has certified only the Digiboard product.

The problem with using NACS on a NetWare 3.11 file server is that serial communications are interrupt-driven. This means that performance of the file server may suffer if high-speed modems are used, because the server operation is constantly being interrupted by the serial port communications.

There are two ways to overcome this problem. The first way is to use NACS with an intelligent multiport serial board, such as the WNIM+. Boards like these have additional processors that are dedicated to handling the serial communications, and therefore are much less likely to be overrun by high-speed communications requirements.

Another method is to use a dedicated NetWare 3.11 Runtime server, which is shipped with the eight- and 32-port versions of the package. The NetWare 3.11 Runtime server is a special version of the standard 3.11 NetWare version, without file or print services. Typically, NetWare 3.11 Runtime is used for dedicated communications servers such as NACS or NetWare for SAA. Increased performance for both servers results from using Runtime on a dedicated server, instead of placing NACS directly on a file server. Because your file server is not interrupted by the serial communications processes, it does not see the performance decline for file access. Conversely, because Runtime does not have file or print services, the communications processes are not slowed down by file access on the communications server. Note also that a Runtime server may be used for different types of communication at the same time. A Runtime server may be running both NACS and NetWare for SAA simultaneously, for example.

NACS consists of several NLMs (NetWare Loadable Modules), loaded directly on a functional NetWare 3.11 server. Although the first set of NLMs, called the Communication Executive NLMs, is not exactly part of the NACS software, it is a standard set of NLMs that provides communications services on the 3.11 server. The Communications Executive NLMs are used with other communications products running directly on a Novell server (they are included with NetWare for SAA, for example).

The first step in installation is to use the CSINSTAL.NLM utility to copy the NLMs to the file server. This utility copies the Communications Executive NLM and the NASI interface for the user's communications software. The Communications Executive is the COMMEXEC.NLM. The software is installed in the directory SYS:\PUBLIC\NASI3. Remember that if you are using the NetWare Runtime version, this software must be copied to your file server, because the Runtime version provides no file services.

Otherwise, your users will not be able to access the software. Note also that security access to these directories must be given so that users can read them.

Three standard (meaning that they come with the NetWare 3.11 software) NLMs must be loaded before the COMMEXEC.NLM and NACS NLM files. These three standard NLMs are the CLIB.NLM, an interface library for running NLMs in the NetWare 3.x environment; SPXS.NLM, which provides support for the connection-oriented SPX protocol; and the BTRIEVE.NLM, a file manager that the Communications Executive uses internally.

After these standard NLMs have loaded, you load the AIO.NLM, which provides control for asynchronous communications. AIOCOMX provides the support needed for using the COM ports directly on the NACS (the serial ports that are directly on the server, not the communications adapter, if you have one). If you are using a WNIM+ board, AIOWNIM.NLM is loaded. Any other communications adapter needs the appropriate NLM to provide an interface between itself and the NACS NLM. When loading the AIOCOMX or AIOWNIM NLMs, memory-port information must be provided, as in the following:

```
Load AIOWNIM port=0280 mem=D0000
```

If multiple WNIM+ boards are installed, you must load this NLM for each of them. Each board will have a different base I/O port but the same buffer memory address. The following line, for example, loads the NLM for the second WNIM+ board:

```
Load AIOWNIM port=0290 mem=D000
```

This command provides the NLM with the address information so that it can communicate properly with the board. If this information is incorrect, the NLM simply will not load.

After these have loaded, the COMMEXEC.NLM must be loaded. As explained earlier, the COMMEXEC.NLM provides the basic level of communication services. The COMMEXEC.NLM prompt on the NetWare 3.11 server is different from the standard DOS prompt because it provides its own set of commands. The prompt looks like the following:

```
CS>
```

Type the following to load the NACS NLM:

```
CS> csload NACS
```

Now the NACS must be configured. The command that brings forth the status windows for communications services is the following:

```
CS> csstatus
```

After you select the NACS service, you are asked to enter a password. If this is the first time you have done this, the default password is NEWPASS.

By editing the system's AUTOEXEC.NCF file to include the exact steps for loading the NACS NLMs, the NLMs are loaded in sequence and with the correct parameters each time the server restarts.

Configuring the NACS is like configuring the InstantCom. You must enter a name for the NACS (otherwise, the system creates a name), a password, and the NASI prompt. And you must choose whether to implement security. The NASI prompt is the one shown to users whenever they enter NASI command-interpreter mode. (This mode is reached whenever the user loads his or her NASI-compatible communications software at the workstation.)

The following items are configuredwhen you reach the NACS configuration screen:

- `Specific name`, a name given to each NACS port so that users can access that specific port
- `General name`, a name that can apply to more than one port; given so that users can access ports on a pooled basis, instead of trying to connect to one specific port
- `Port State` reflects the current status of the port. On installation, the port should be IDLE. If it is DOWN, you must add it as a NACS port.
- `Baud Rate`, the speed at which the port operates. This speed depends on the driver (such as AIOWNIM.NLM, mentioned earlier).

Configuration for the data bits, stop bits, and parity bits must also be entered for each port.

If `Trace` is chosen, data transmitted through the port is written to a trace file. The *trace file* contains information about the amount of data passed through the port.

If security was set on, it must be configured. Security is important with any shared devices, simply because resources may be limited. This is especially true if you have installed a set of modems, some of which are higher speed (essentially more powerful than others). Your users, when they find out, won't want to use the slower modems, even though they may not need the faster ones. For this reason, most packages that allow modem sharing also provide some sort of security. (This is similar to the groups and users discussed with ICS.)

Because the NACS is built directly on top of NetWare, it uses the NetWare bindery files for security information. Therefore, to add security to the NACS you must use the standard Syscon utility. Security can be configured either by NACS name (by server, essentially) or by individual port.

To configure security by NACS name, a group must be added in Syscon's group-information section. The group name must be the word SECURE, followed by the name of the NACS. If you have just installed a NACS in the accounting department of your company, for example, you may want to name the NACS server ACCTG. To configure security access for this, create the group name SECUREACCTG. When you add NetWare users to this group, they will have access to the ACCTG NACS server.

To configure security by port number, a similiar method is used. The group name must begin with the word SECURE, followed by the number of the port to which you want to grant access. In an extension of the preceding example, suppose that you want to give a certain set of users access to port three. You create a group called SECURE003ACCTG, and then add these users to that group.

Like ICS, NACS includes a monitoring utility. A selection under the NACS console screen (the same utility used to configure NACS) enables the administrator to look at the statistics for each port. These statistics include characters input and output, packets input and output, communications errors, port signals (CTS, DSR, and DCD may be used for diagnostic purposes), User ID (if port is not IDLE), NetWare Server, the address of the workstation currently connected to the port, and the current connection time. Because this monitoring utility runs on the file server, an administrator may be able to get to it by running Rconsole, Novell's Remote Console utility.

Also like ICS, NACS keeps a log file that tracks pretty much the same information. The log is cleared whenever NACS is started.

For proper communications to be established, the NASI TSR must be loaded at the other end of the connection, the user end. This is done by running the NASI3 command. (This can also be unloaded by running NASI3 /u.)

A diagnostic utility, called NASIDIAG, is provided with NACS. This utility is capable of doing loopback tests with the communications server, as well as performance testing. To perform the loopback testing, you must disconnect the modem attached to whatever port you want to test, and instead attach the loopback plug provided with the NACS package.

Telebit Asynchronous Communications Server

The Telebit Asynchronous Communications Server (TACS) is another communications server that is comparable to Novell's NACS. TACS requires a dedicated PC with 512K of memory (no more conventional memory than this, however). 512K is required because the multiport communications adapter uses the memory range of 512-640K for buffer space. Figure 6.2 shows the Telebit TACS configuration.

TACS supports both NetBIOS and native NetWare IPX/SPX protocols. The protocol you are using on your network will be chosen at installation time. IPX/SPX can be supported across bridges and routers, due to the nature of the protocol, but NetBIOS cannot.

Unlike most communication servers, TACS supports both the Int14 interface and NASI, as well as a third—the Telebit API. TSRs are provided for each of these interfaces. These interfaces may be used simultaneously by users throughout the network. One user may load an Int14 terminal interface to a mainframe, for example, while another uses a NASI-based communications package to connect to CompuServe.

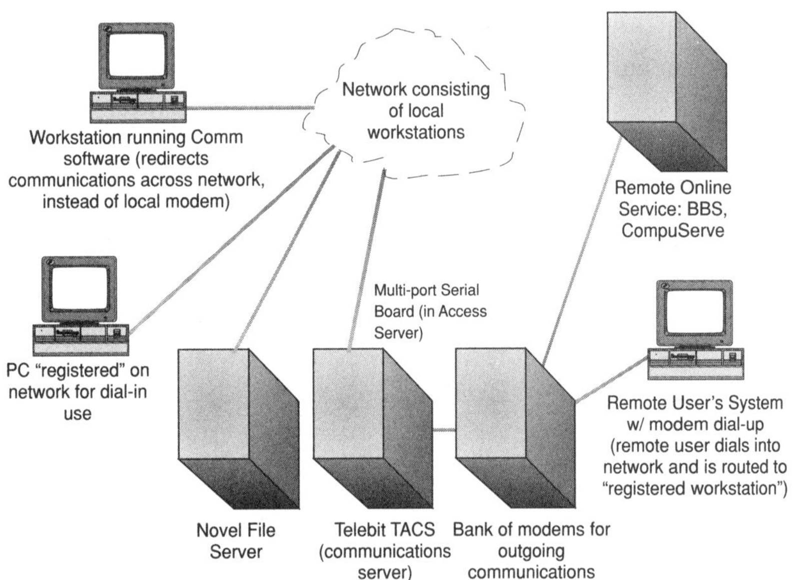

Figure 6.2:
Telebit TACS configuration.

The intelligent communications adapter is typically sold along with the TACS software. Three cards—PACS-ISA, ASYNC-ISA, and ASYNC-MCA are supported. (ISA is for the standard bus and MCA is for IBM's Microchannel bus.) Because TACS does require the use of a 16-bit bus, the machine used as the communications server must be at least an AT and must be operating DOS version 3.x.

Installation of the communications adapter requires careful attention to the network interface card in the TACS server. The communications adapter cannot be in the same system with another card that is using interrupts 2, 9, 10, or 11. It must not conflict with certain specific hardware addresses, as evidenced by the fact

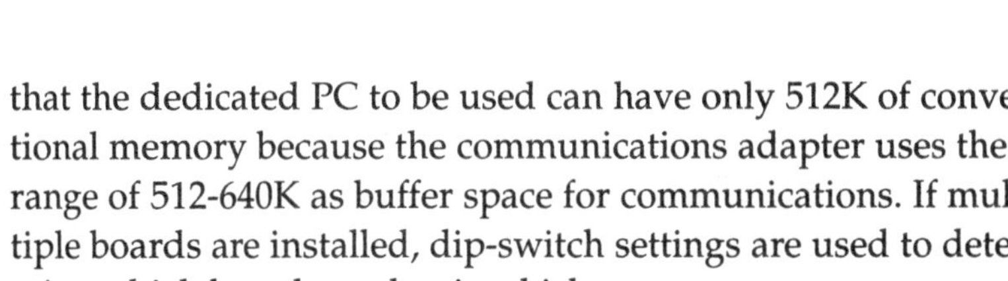

that the dedicated PC to be used can have only 512K of conventional memory because the communications adapter uses the range of 512-640K as buffer space for communications. If multiple boards are installed, dip-switch settings are used to determine which board number is which.

The INSTALL program is used to copy the TACS software onto the file server and to create the appropriate directories. Directories are created for the TACS executables (\ACS\EXECUTE), server configuration (\ACS\SERVER\name), and users if using the Int14 interface (\ACS\USERS). Remember that security access must be provided for the correct directories on the file server.

The TACS, like the other communications servers discussed in this chapter, must be configured. Again, the same concepts are applied. Configuration is accomplished with a utility called PDGATCF.EXE. As with other communication servers, the TACS must be given a name which, if multiple servers are installed, must be unique.

PDGATECF is used to configure each board and each port setting with respect to baud rate, parity bits, stop bits, data bits, and the type of handshake. Modem strings, used for initialization of the modem attached to that port, may be entered here.

Pool names, which specify which ports are to be used in a pool of modems, are created. Users may then be given access to a certain pool. One special pool, REGISTER, is used for dial-in capabilities (discussed later in the chapter). When using this pool, a dedicated PC may register as a dial-in system.

Load balancing may be used if multiple boards are installed in the server. This feature balances the load of communications between several boards. If three users are connected to one board and two users to another, for example, the next user will be connected (provided that the pooling and security allow it) to the board with only two users attached.

The TACS server is loaded by issuing the command **PDGATE.EXE** (for Novell's SPX) or **NBGATE.EXE** (for NetBIOS). A command-line parameter may be used to specify the number of seconds between screen updates on the TACS. A separate command-line option may be used to start a trace facility, which may be used to diagnose problems with communications sessions. A trace file (appropriately called PDGATE.TRC) is created. Because of the overhead, the trace facility is meant for diagnostics, not for everyday use, as it will harm performance.

Auditing may be specified with another command-line parameter, which logs the communications sessions, including the user's name and workstation address, time on, packets transferred, and time off.

Like other packages, TACS provides a management console, which provides information in several separate areas, including the following:

- **Server information**, consisting of such basic information as name and time started; active user information, which shows all active server sessions and information about them, such as time connected to which board and port number, and the status of that port, as well as packets transferred in and out of the port.
- **Server activity statistics**, which show the maximum concurrent sessions, total sessions since last start, total packets routed to and from workstations, and a

queued number. The queued statistic, which reflects the number of times an event was queued instead of being processed immediately, is a function of system load. An extremely high number reflects the fact that server hardware is being overrun by communications. `Connects queued` reflects the number of times a user tried to attach to a port and could not because it was in use. `Sends queued` and `receives queued` reflect the number of times a message was being sent to or received from a workstation. This reflects whether the TACS is operating efficiently or slowing down communications across the network.

- **Port status information** shows such port statistics as parity, framing, and overrun errors, as well as the status of Pins corresponding to the RS-232 connector. It also shows the total number of packets routed to and from workstations. Queue statistics specific to this port also are shown, aiding in further diagnostics as to performance of the TACS server.
- **Registered workstations** (discussed later) are shown, which lists the workstations available on the dial-in pool. It displays their CPU type (80286, 80386, and so on), DOS version, video-adapter configuration, as well as the amount of total conventional memory and how much of that memory, is free.

A remote console utility is provided (PDVIEW or NBVIEW, depending on whether you are using the SPX or NetBIOS version, respectively.

At the workstation level, the TSR loaded depends on whether the network is SPX-based (Novell), or NetBIOS-based. These TSRs are PDWSINF.EXE and NBWSINF.EXE, respectively.

If Int14 is to be used as the workstation interface, it (like the other communication servers) must be configured to recognize the TACS server and choose a port or pool to use. INT14.EXE is a TSR which is loaded over the top of either PDWSINF or NBWSINF. INT14CF.EXE is used to configure the Int14 interface for the TACS. In INT14CF, the administrator must supply the name of the terminal-emulation program (or communications package) that will be used with Int14. The name of the communication software is used so that the communications package is loaded automatically along with INT14.EXE, whenever the TSR is loaded.

You must supply the server's name also. Instead of placing the entire server's name in the Int14 configuration, you can use the DOS wildcard characters (? and *). To find all TACS servers automatically, for example, enter an asterisk (*). The COM port that is to be redirected in the workstation must be entered. The Int14 interface will redirect COM1-COM8 across the network. Note that COM1-COM8 do not have to be physically installed in your workstation because they are being redirected by software.

A session-allocation method (whether the user's session is to be chosen from one of the pools the administrator configured, or by specific port) is specified. If you choose to use a specific port, you can enter the gateway board number—the number of the communications adapter in the TACS. Doing so ensures that you get to a specific modem.

The Int14 configuration file is named by the administrator and has the extension .I14. You may configure this file, like other communications servers, so that it may be shared by many different users or be specific to each. Remember—updating the configuration files is much less painful if they are shared and not specific to each user.

If the NASI interface is chosen, a TSR called PNASI.EXE is loaded, after which a communications package is loaded. To start communications with the communications server, the NASI interface asks the user for the name or location of the server. The response may be entered, according to the following syntax:

```
<Server-name>%<Pool-Name>
```

This enables attaching the session to a pool specified on the communications server. If you have a TACS server named ACCTG, for example, and a pool (named 9600) that contains all 9,600 bps modems, the form of the command is the following:

```
ACCTG%9600
```

Another form of this response is used to attach to a specific port:

```
<Server-name>%G<Gateway-Board-Number>-P<Port
Number>
```

To attach to the ACCTG TACS server, finding a specific port on the ACCTG server is done with the following:

```
ACCTG%G1-P6
```

This command attaches the user to the modem located on the sixth port of the first gateway board.

Like other TSRs mentioned, the PNASI TSR can be unloaded by specifying a **U** on the command line behind PNASI. The command to unload the TSR is as follows:

```
PNASI U
```

TACS can dynamically configure ports that may be used for either incoming or outgoing access. Thus, these ports can be available to network users using the dedicated modems for dial-out access, while simultaneously, without any reconfiguration, being used for dial-in access to a dedicated PC.

Using these dynamically configured ports, dedicated PCs running PC anyWhere IV may be configured. When a call is placed into the TACS, the TACS answers and routes the call to one of the dedicated PCs. At this PC, PC anyWhere IV takes over and allows the remote user to control it and therefore have access to the resources of the network. The remote user must have proper access before this is accomplished. Dialback is supported in newer versions of the TACS, allowing the communications server to be used as both a dial-in and dial-out system.

TACS, which comes with Digital Communication's Crosstalk Mk IV software as a communications package, is also bundled with PC anyWhere IV for inbound remote control of a dedicated PC.

When setting up Crosstalk for use on the system, the adminstrator firsts specifies which COM port will be redirected across the network. In this configuration, the administrator then specifies the TACS port to which this COM port will be redirected. (To do so, the administrator uses the command syntax shown earlier—if using PNASI.) Each of these COM ports may then be specified in a telephone book entry (or service entry). If the administrator knows that the user will be connecting to a service that has only a 2400-baud modem, for example, he or she may want to specify that the user's port attachment is 2400 baud maximum, and not allow the user to attach to a 9600-baud modem when using this service. (Why waste the faster resource?) If the administrator knows that the user will need a 9600-baud modem for another service, he or she can simply specify the correctly configured COM port (at the workstation level) and then have that COM port attach to a 9600-baud modem.

TACS is a good choice for a communications server, especially if you like the dynamic dial-in capabilities.

Banyan VINES Serial Communications Options

Banyan has a long history of supporting wide area communication with local area networks. The company has developed a comprehensive family of asynchronous communication products that install in a VINES server. These services are described in the VINES section of Chapter 8.

VINES servers are especially suited to supporting asynchronous communication. As mentioned in the discussion about the NetWare NACS, asynchronous communications rely heavily on interrupts, which are used to notify the operating system that communication services require attention. VINES runs over the UNIX operating system, which features preemptive multitasking. Preemptive multitasking enables communication services to receive the attention they require without adversely affecting server operation.

Communications Packages

You must make sure that your communications package is compatible with the proper interface on the communications server.

Here is a list of some packages that are available for each interface. Please note that this is not an exhaustive list.

NASI-Compatible Software

Table 6.2
NASI-Compatible Communications Software

Software	*Publisher*
Ascom/IV, Network version	Symantec
Blast Professional	US Robotics
Citrix Remote Link	Citrix Systems
Citrix Multiuser	Citrix Systems
CO/Session Lan II	Triton Technologies
Crosstalk Mk 4	Digital Communications
Crosstalk for Windows	Digital Communications
DynaComm Asynchronous	Future Soft
Lexus 2000 LAN	Mead Data Central
On/Lan PC	Novell
PcAnywhere IV/Lan	Symantec
poly-START	Polygon Software
Procomm Plus Network	DataStorm Technologies
Reflection/7	Walker, Richter & Quinn
RELAY Gold Lan	MicroCom, Inc.
Smartcom Exec	Hayes Microcomputer Products

Table 6.2—continued

Software	*Publisher*
SmarTerm 340	Persoft
Softerm PC	Softronics
VsComm/Lan	The M/H Group
WestLaw/Westmate	West Publishing Co.
Zstem 340, Lan Version	KEA Systems, Ltd.

Summary

Asynchronous communication gives networks the capability to share modems on a dial-out basis, and can give users remote access to network resources on a dial-in basis. As networks become more complex, the use of asynchronous communications in conjunction with networks is becoming more commonplace.

Using asynchronous communications gives you the capability to share resources, which makes them cheaper, easier to control, easier to maintain, and more available to users on the network.

Asynchronous communications systems that are installed on networks can be difficult to install, but if you know the concepts, you will find them not much more complex than general networks.

This chapter discussed these concepts, as well as telling you about some of the products that are currently available.

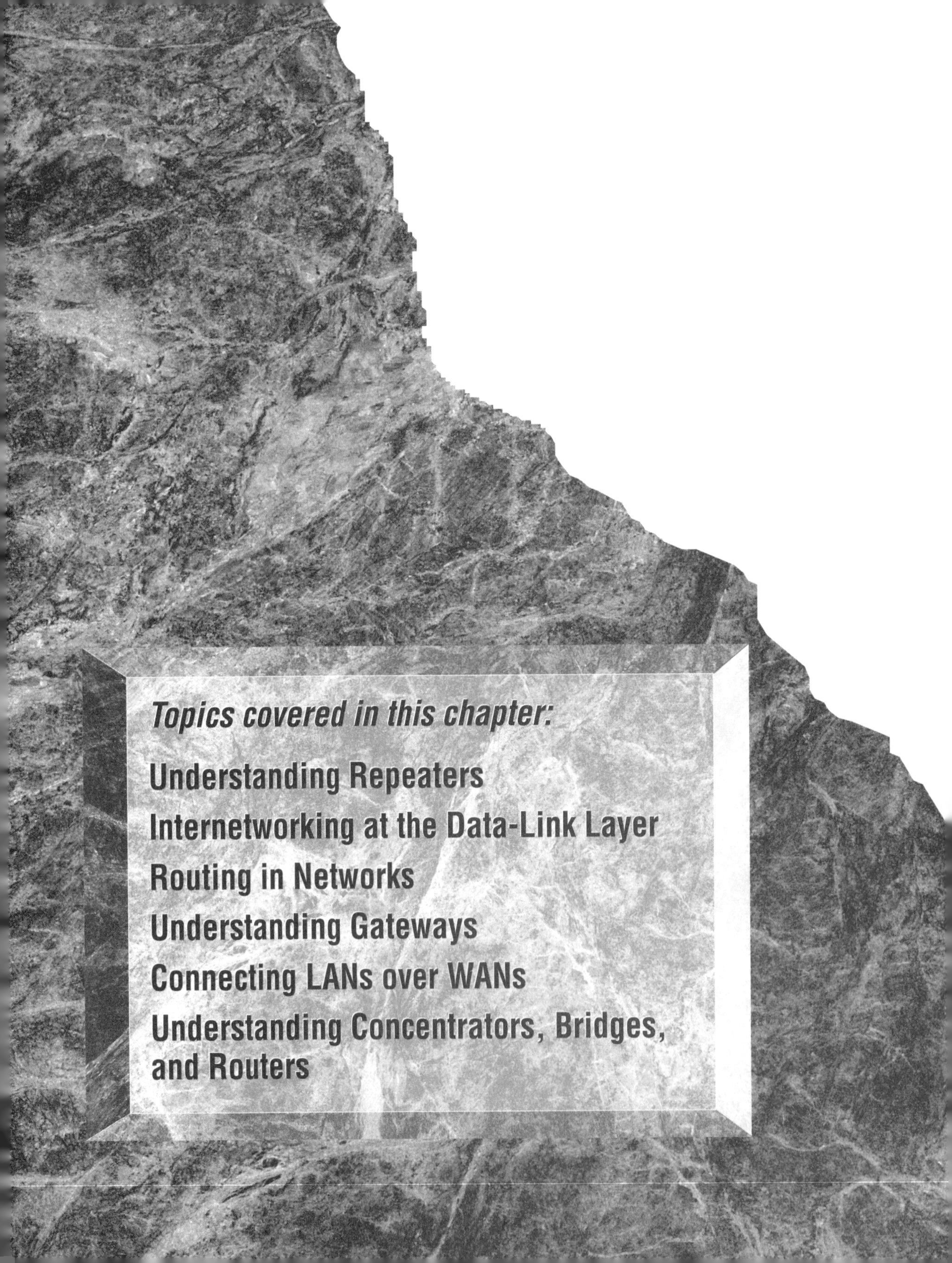
Topics covered in this chapter:
Understanding Repeaters
Internetworking at the Data-Link Layer
Routing in Networks
Understanding Gateways
Connecting LANs over WANs
Understanding Concentrators, Bridges, and Routers

Chapter 7

Interconnecting LANs

With the rapid proliferation of local area networks in the 1980s came the need to interconnect LANs and to tie them into the computing infrastructure as a whole. This trend, called *internetworking*, gave rise to the notion of a single network that encompasses an organization's LANs and minicomputer and mainframe networks. The building blocks of these "enterprise" networks are internetworking devices such as bridges, routers, and gateways.

Hand-in-hand with tying LANs together is the need to organize the resulting larger networks into a hierarchy of manageable units. Internetworking devices are used not only to link LANs but also to create a network structure that provides a reasonable level of performance and can be managed with reasonable effort.

Initially, internetworking was needed to link all computer users in an organization, providing organization-wide communications. Electronic mail is still the primary application for corporate networks. Because the marketing slogan "the network is the computer" is slowly but surely being realized, however, the importance of building a sound network infrastructure is growing. Computer industry observers have declared that the future is *distributed computing*, a style of computing in which individual applications run simultaneously on more than one computer over the network.

There is no set formula for building an organization-wide network. You begin with an installed base of applications, network operating systems, protocols, computers, and cabling, add what you expect the installed base to be in five years, and strain the resulting mix through your budget.

Several factors determine the numbers and types of internetworking devices you will use and where you deploy them. The principal factor is network traffic: which protocols make up the traffic, where the traffic flows, and how it is to be controlled.

Because organization-wide networks frequently encompass different protocols and types of computers, having a common frame of reference is important . Network protocols in the TCP/IP, IBM SNA, DEC DECNET, and PC LAN environments have multiple layers that can be mapped to the OSI seven-layer reference model. Similarly, internetworking devices correspond to specific layers in the model (see fig. 7.1).

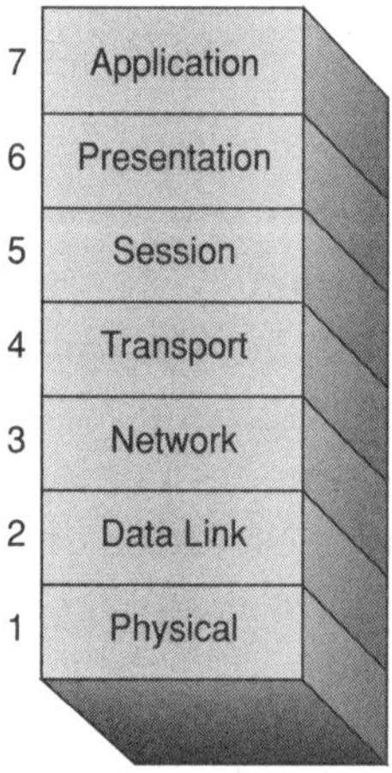

Figure 7.1:
The OSI seven-layer model.

Understanding Repeaters

The lowest layer of the OSI reference model, the physical layer, covers cabling and electrical signaling. The device that operates at the physical layer is called a *repeater.* Repeaters, which receive a transmission on a LAN segment and regenerate the signal, are used to boost weakened transmissions, so that LAN segments can be made longer.

In Chapter 4, it was explained that an Ethernet can consist of two types of segments: coax segments and link segments. The link segments utilize repeaters (actually, half-repeaters—they are used in pairs) to extend the range of the network by connecting several coax segments. An Ethernet consisting only of coax and link segments is a *logical segment*. It can be considered to be a single Ethernet.

Repeaters are not actually internetworking devices because they only extend individual LAN segments. They can be used to connect pieces of cable, but the connected cables remain part of the same logical LAN segments. Ethernet supports a theoretical maximum of 1,024 nodes per logical segment, for example, and that number can be exceeded only by using more than one segment. No matter how many repeaters are used or how big a segment becomes, the node limit still applies. More important, repeaters do not run any software and can offer no means of affecting LAN traffic beyond boosting the raw electrical signal.

Repeaters should be considered part of your cabling scheme, rather than part of your internetworking plans. You should use repeaters, for example, when nodes you want on a single Ethernet segment are farther apart than the 500-meter maximum cable length allowed by the Ethernet standard for thick Ethernet. The delay introduced by repeaters limits the number of cable segments that can be strung together, however. In the case of Ethernet, no more than four half-repeaters can separate nodes on a logical segment.

Internetworking at the Data-Link Layer

Internetworking comes into play at the second layer of the OSI model, the data-link layer. The data-link layer covers communications between adjacent nodes. Each data-link address corresponds to the address for a particular node to the network.

At the data-link layer, the bit stream formed by electrical pulses at the physical layer is organized in packets.

The three major LAN types (Ethernet, token ring, and FDDI) are defined for the most part by their data-link layer characteristics. Internetworking at the data-link layer is confined largely to linking networks of like LAN types, although the most recent generation of technology includes products that tie FDDI to Ethernet and to token ring.

Ethernet, a form of a Carrier Sensing Multiple Access/Collision Detection (CSMA/CD) network, is a broadcast medium in which all nodes "listen" to every transmission on the wire. A node ready to transmit senses the wire and, if no transmission is occurring, begins sending. If two or more nodes attempt to transmit at the same time, the transmissions collide. The sending nodes detect the collision and wait a random interval of time before trying again. Ethernet operates at 10 megabits-per-second.

Token ring utilizes media arranged as a loop, on which a token is passed from node to node. A node that is ready to transmit waits for the token to arrive. Only the node in possession of the token can transmit. The receiving node marks the transmitted packets to indicate that it has copied the transmission. When the packets return to the sending node with the acknowledgment of receipt, the sending node removes them and returns the token to the ring. Packets must be removed from the loop because the first bits of the packet returns to the sending station before the last bits of the packet have been transmitted. There are two standard versions of token ring: one operates at four megabits-per-second, the other at 16 megabits-per-second.

FDDI is also a token-passing network. Unlike token-ring networks installed in a typical PC LAN environment, however, FDDI operates at 100 megabits-per-second and has two rings for redundancy. FDDI was designed to operate over fiber optic cables, allowing distances between nodes as great as two kilometers.

The internetworking device used at the data-link layer is called a *bridge*. Bridges consist of media interfaces, buffers, address tables, and one or more processors. Bridges are store-and-forward devices. They receive packets, store them in a buffer, look up a packet's address in the bridge's address table and, depending on whether the source and destination addresses are on the same segment, either discard the packet or forward it to another LAN segment (see fig. 7.2).

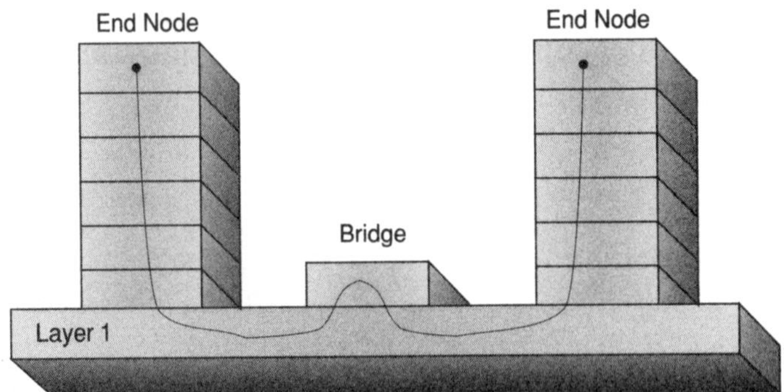

Figure 7.2:
End nodes communicating across a bridge.

Bridges range in size from those with only two LAN-segment ports to those with several wide-area ports and dozens of LAN-segment ports. Generally, bridges with more than two ports have bus-based internal architectures, although higher-performance switch-based bridges are now becoming available.

Bridges can be translating, encapsulating, transparent or, in the case of many token ring bridges, source routing. Translating and encapsulating bridges are used between dissimilar LAN types. *Translating bridges* convert packets from one LAN-type packet format to the other. *Encapsulating bridges* encapsulate packets or fragments of packets from the sending node's LAN type within packets of the receiving node's LAN type.

Communicating with Transparent Bridges

Most bridges, including almost all Ethernet bridges, are transparent. They are called *transparent* because bridges of this type can be installed in the network without hardware, software, or addressing changes to any device. A transparent bridge monitors all traffic that passes through it and dynamically builds and maintains routing tables. With transparent bridging, end stations communicate across segments without seeing the bridges. Transparent bridging leaves much of the control of networks to network and transport layer protocols.

If transparent bridges simply learned how to route packets between LAN segments, they would be limited. Such simple bridges could not be used in any network configuration in which multiple paths between nodes exist. Multiple copies packets might be routed to a reciever or packets might be routed around the loops formed by the multiple routes. This situation can result in explosions of duplicate packets.

To prevent these explosions, networks must be configured by using a *spanning tree*, which requires that only a single path exist between any two nodes. The disadvantage of spanning-tree networks is that they do not allow for backup paths. If a bridge between two nodes fails, communication between the nodes becomes impossible.

To enable multiple paths while avoiding loops, transparent bridges configure networks into a logical spanning tree. The bridges exchange routing information and configure themselves to route packets through the most efficient path. The protocol runs automatically, enabling the network to reconfigure, in case of a failed link. Some bridge makers have adjusted the protocol to switch between physical links, which enables you to use idle links and perform load balancing. Figure 7.3 illustrates the way transparent bridges can overlay a logical spanning tree onto a complex network.

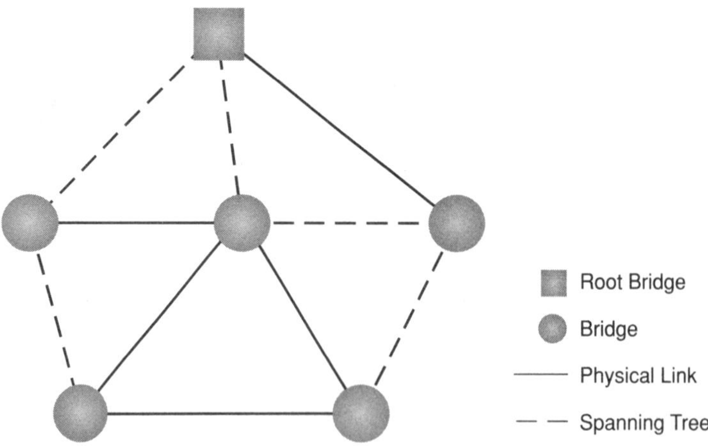

Figure 7.3:
Network paths determined by spanning tree protocol.

As data-link layer devices, bridges usually examine only a packet's data-link source and destination addresses. But many bridges are capable of looking deeper into a packet to determine its network layer protocol or even the contents of its data field.

A bridge capable of determining a packet's network layer protocol can prioritize network traffic. Bridges with this capability can process protocols that are sensitive to delays before processing other traffic.

A bridge's capability of looking into a packet's data field, usually referred to as *logical filtering*, gives you a great deal of control over network traffic. You can use bridges to keep your accounting department's traffic off the rest of the network, for example, without having to restrict the accounting department's computers to a specific LAN segment or set of segments.

One note of caution: a bridge's capability to prioritize or perform logical filtering can mean a performance tradeoff because the bridge has a greater processing load. If the filters are implemented in hardware, there is virtually no performance loss, but the performance hit can be considerable if the bridge's CPU performs the filtering. Although many newer bridges have RISC CPUs that can handle heavier processing loads, be careful when burdening low-end and older model bridges with added functions like prioritizing and logical filtering.

Using Source Routing

Some token-ring networks, as well as other networks, use transparent bridging. IBM's System Network Architecture (SNA) does not use protocols that correspond to the network and transport-layer protocols used by TCP/IP, OSI, DECnet, and many of the PC LAN network operating systems. Consequently, many of the functions performed by those protocols are handled at the data-link layer in IBM's token ring.

IBM's implementation of token ring uses *source routing*, which requires end stations to learn routes to other end stations by discovering the bridges in the path. Source routing requires end stations to "see" bridges to learn routes to other end stations. When one end station communicates with another, it first sends out discovery packets that travel across the network. Each time a discovery packets crosses a bridge, the bridge marks it. When a discovery packet comes to the receiving station, the station looks at the marks from the bridges to determine the route the discovery packet took.

The receiving station informs the sending (source) station of the route. The source station puts the route information in the Source Routing Information field in the header of each packet. When a packet comes to a bridge, the bridge looks at the Routing Information Field of the packet to see whether the bridge is part of the route.

By definition, source routing cannot extend across transparent bridges. Source routing has to exist in a separate domain within an internetwork. Some vendors offer source-routing drivers for end stations, thus enabling source routing to coexist with routing protocols. Many router makers encapsulate source-routing packets in IP to allow source routing to cross TCP/IP backbones.

A new type of bridge, called *source routing transparent* (SRT), is now becoming available, however. SRT bridges are hybrid devices that allow source routing and transparent bridging to coexist.

As a packet enters an SRT bridge, the bridge looks at the first bit of the source address. If the bit is 0, the bridge handles the packet by using its transparent-bridging module. If the bit is 1, the bridge handles the packet by using its source-routing module. The SRT bridge also executes the spanning-tree algorithm, including all SRT and transparent bridges in the network.

Transparent traffic follows the tree, and source-routed traffic follows whichever path the protocol has calculated. SRT is not compatible with source routing, however.

Ethernet and Token Ring Incompatibility

Although bridging in general is fairly simple, bridging between Ethernet and token ring is rarely attempted for many reasons.

One of the most obvious reasons is that Ethernet and token ring have different throughput rates. Congestion can be a problem when a bridge attempts to forward packets from a 10-megabit-per-second Ethernet to four-megabit-per-second token ring, or from a 16-megabit-per-second token ring to Ethernet.

Another readily apparent difference is packet formats. Any bridge between Ethernet and token ring must reformat packets, but packets at the data-link layer include a checksum as a means of error control. When packets are reformatted, a new checksum must be calculated. This leaves data vulnerable to errors caused by the bridge itself (see fig. 7.4).

Packet size is another issue. Ethernet has a maximum packet size of 1,518 bytes. 16-megabit-per-second token ring has a maximum packet size of 8K; four-megabit-per-second token ring has a maximum packet size of 5K.

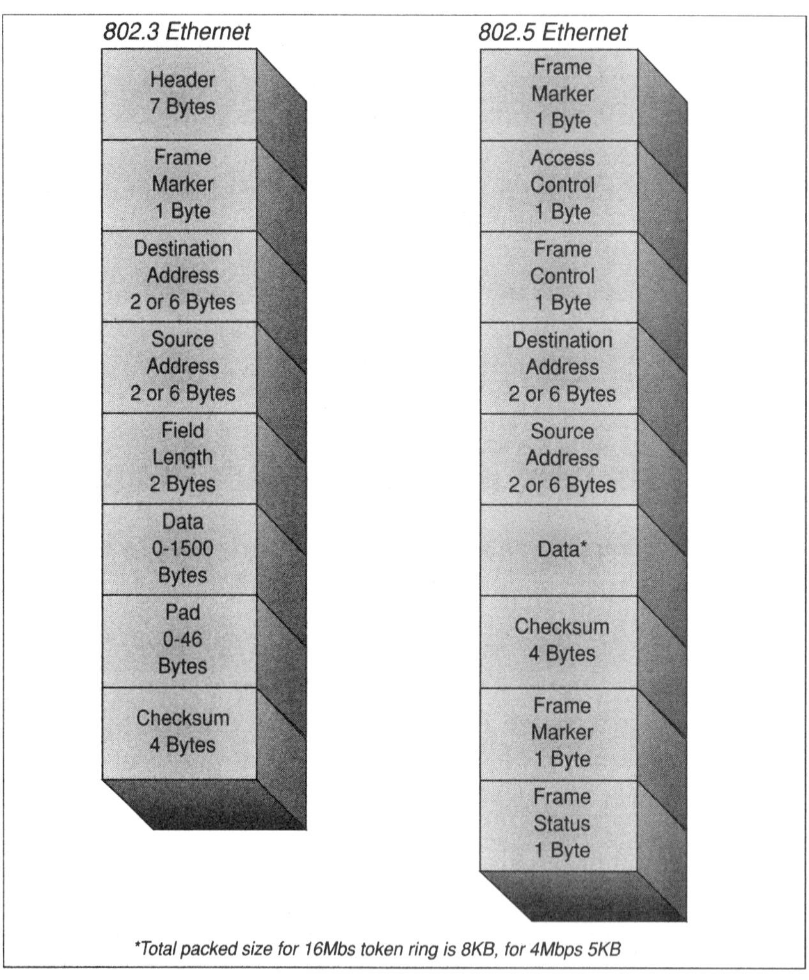

Figure 7.4:
IEEE 802.3 and 802.5 packet formats.

Although the difference in packet sizes does not pose a problem for traffic going from Ethernet to token ring, traffic from token ring to Ethernet requires packets to be segmented. Higher-level protocols can segment packets, but there is no standard method for segmentation. The bit order used in Ethernet is least-significant bit first; the bit order used in token ring is most-significant bit first. The different bit orders pose a problem when addresses are sent between stations on the different LAN types. The bit order of the address in the header of each frame must be flipped as the packet is passed from one side to the other through a bridge.

Flipping the bit order of the address is relatively simple because the bridge has to examine the header of each packet anyway. Handling data-link addresses used by higher-level protocols is a greater challenge. Those addresses are carried in the data field of the data-link layer packet, a field that bridges do not ordinarily examine. An example is the Address Resolution Protocol (ARP) of the TCP/IP suite. ARP is used to match IP addresses to data-link layer addresses. When ARP messages are passed from Ethernet to token ring or vice versa, the bridge passes along the data link address in the wrong bit order. IBM's 8209 bridge, designed specifically to bridge Ethernet and token ring, handles the ARP problem by looking into the data field of each packet to determine whether it is a TCP/IP packet and, if it is, whether there are any ARP messages.

One of the more problematic differences between Ethernet and token ring is the issue of broadcast addresses. Ethernet enables 2^{47} multicast addresses. The equivalent in token ring, functional addresses, is limited to 31 possible values. The problem is mapping between the two in a consistent way.

Five of the 31 functional addresses are globally administered; that is, they have been assigned for all networks. The remaining 26 can be used for mapping multicast addresses. The problem is that vendors and users can map to those addresses at will, leaving room for conflicts when multiple protocols are used. Apple, for example, uses all of the available addresses for mapping AppleTalk multicasting.

When a token-ring node removes from the ring a packet it has sent, it notes whether the receiving station was active and whether it copied the packet. This provides a means for end stations to receive acknowledgment that their transmissions have been successful. Some applications depend on the acknowledgment.

The method of acknowledgment is known as *setting the A and C bits*. The receiving end station sets the Address Recognized Indicator, or A bit, to tell the sending end station that it is active on the ring and notes that the transmission was intended for it. The receiving station sets the Frame Copied Indicator, or C bit, to tell the sending station that it has successfully copied the packet.

The difficulty is handling A and C bits when crossing bridges, and the problem applies to token ring-to-token ring bridges as well as to Ethernet-to-token ring bridges. Because the sending station strips the packets off the ring as they return (in order to clear the ring and provide a reasonable level of performance), it is impossible for the sending station to wait for a bridge to forward any acknowledgment from the receiving station on the other side.

One option for handling A and C bits in bridging is to have the bridge always set the bits. In other words, have the bridge send the acknowledgment whether or not the packet was actually received by the end station on the other side. If the packet is lost or corrupted, the receiving station will time out but the sending station will be unaware of the problem.

Another option is to have the bridge always leave the bits unset. The result is that the sending station essentially receives a negative acknowledgment, which can cause problems, depending on the application.

Other options involving a greater level of intelligence on the part of the bridge are under consideration by the IEEE. Having the bridge accurately set the A bit can involve a performance penalty, however, because the bridge hase to scan its address table before setting the bit.

Priority and token reservation are two other features of token-ring networks that Ethernet does not support. An Ethernet end station transmitting across a transparent bridge to a token ring end station must know to generate a fictitious priority to ensure reasonable access to the ring. Ethernet end stations also lack a means of reserving tokens, which can also restrict access to the ring.

Where Bridges Fit

You would be hard-pressed to build a cost-effective, organization-wide network without using bridges. On the other hand, you can build a network using only bridges. Generally, however, the advantages and disadvantages of bridges make it advisable to use routers and gateways with bridges.

Bridges are best used to segment a network and to control traffic between workgroups and the network backbone. When the traffic load on a LAN segment begins to cause performance problems, the easiest solution is to reduce the load. The best way to reduce the load is to reduce the number of nodes on the LAN segment.

Segmenting networks with bridges—that is, using bridges to divide the network into addditional segments—becomes increasingly necessary as more users come on line and as new applications use more network resources. Before you segment your network, you should map your traffic patterns to determine who talks to whom and who uses which resources.

The most widely recommended guideline for populating segments is the so-called 80-20 rule, which calls for about 80 percent of network traffic to remain local and not cross the bridge. This will help you optimize the performance of each segment. You should adhere strictly to the 80-20 rule if your traffic will cross a wide-area link at any point, because wide-area links are slower and much more expensive to use than local area networks.

Segmentation is a tactical operation in which bridges are deployed in reaction to a problem. Bridges are perhaps more useful as strategic tools when you plan a network or an extension to a network.

Bridges should be used to control workgroup access to the backbone, the segment that links all of the LANs across your organization. The backbone, which serves as the network's foundation, can also be an Achilles heel. If the backbone is swamped with network traffic, organization-wide communications are threatened. But if only internetworking devices and a few large servers are directly connected to the backbone, the number of user, application, and hardware errors that effect the backbone is greatly reduced. Many Ethernet bridges, for example, can squelch broadcast storms (see fig. 7.5).

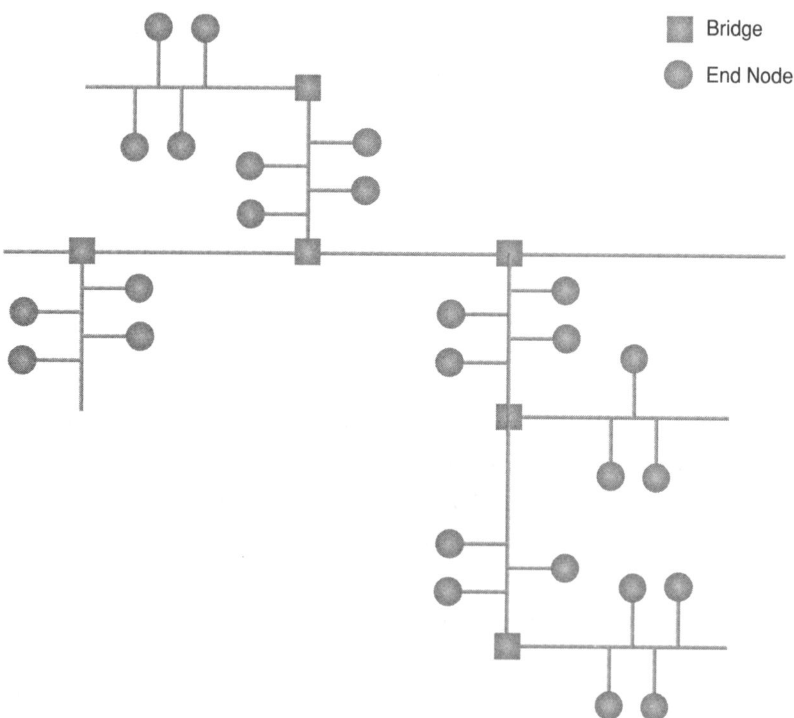

Figure 7.5:
Segmenting and isolating workgroups with bridges.

Increasingly, network managers are turning to multiport bridges in place of distributed network backbones. Interconnecting LAN segments with a multiport bridge serves the same function as tying them together with a central segment. Models with many ports can have aggregate throughput rates that are higher than the throughput of an FDDI backbone. Multiport bridges also are easier to manage than distributed-backbone networks, which have to be configured with multiple internetworking devices.

You can use bridges to build a considerably stratified network—to connect the backbone to your wide-area network, to connect workgroups to the backbone, and to segment workgroups. There are limits to the size of bridge-based networks, however. Each time a packet crosses a bridge it is delayed. If a packet crosses too many bridges, the delay can be enough to cause the receiving station to time out and request retransmission. The number of bridges a packet crosses is called the *hop count*.

The size of the network also can affect a bridge's performance. The larger the network, the larger the bridge's address table, and the slower the process of looking up each address. Transparent bridges "learn" addresses by observing the source addresses of the packets it handles. If a new node is added to the network, a bridge can encounter destination addresses it does not recognize.

In a network of transparent bridges, a bridge handles unknown destination addresses by flooding the network. In a very large network, this can cause congestion. The problem is worse, however, for networks of source-routing bridges. Because source routing allows for loops, more than one bridge can be connected to each LAN. When a node issues a discovery packet, each bridge copies the packet onto the next LAN. In a mesh network, discovery packets are copied exponentially, causing a *frame explosion*, which results in a heavily congested network.

On the whole, however, today's bridges rarely are the source of network performance problems. Ethernet bridges, in particular operate at rates approaching the theoretical maximum of the Ethernet standard. Summarizing the results of tests performed at Harvard University by the Internet Engineering Task Force (IETF) in the fall of 1991, Scott O. Bradnor, chairman of the IETF's Benchmarking Methodology Working Group, said that performance is no longer a point of differentiation between Ethernet bridges.

According to a report of the Harvard study that was published in the February, 1992, issue of *Data Communications*, six commercially available dual-port local Ethernet bridges had throughput rates ranging from 6,619 to 14,753 64-byte packets per second. The report states that only bridges with throughput rates below 5,000 64-byte packets-per-second risk hindering network performance.

Because most commercially available bridges offer at least that level of performance, the report recommends that you base your purchasing decision on a range of criteria, including some fairly obvious ones like price, configuration, network management, and vendor credibility and support. Some less obvious criteria include security, user interface, reliability, and the capability to boot and to receive updates from a remote node.

A general note of caution about using only bridges to build a network: because most bridges are transparent (and by definition cannot be "seen" by end stations), the devices handling your network traffic are unable to influence the sources of the traffic.

LAN Switches

A new class of data-link layer internetworking devices has emerged. These devices bring connection-oriented switching technology, ordinarily associated with telecommunications, to the traditionally connectionless datagram LAN environment. LAN switches, which have the same application as multiport bridges, create virtual links between individual nodes on different segments and allow multiple simultaneous connections.

Switches are cut-through devices, not store-and-forward devices (they forward packets without first buffering them). Because switches do not buffer packets, they cause minimal delay. The latency of LAN switches is in microseconds, whereas the latency of bridges can be as much as a millisecond.

Low latency is important for protocols or applications that have a very small acknowledgment window size. A small window size implies that the acknowledgment is received before additional packets may be sent.

Older versions of Novell's NetWare, for example, require that the acknowledgement for each packet be received before the next packet is sent. This can cause problems in an extended bridge-based network, especially if a great deal of cross traffic exists. Using switches in a NetWare LAN makes separating servers from workgroups an easier process. Separating them is useful for a configuration in which all servers are concentrated on a single segment for security or management purposes.

Cut-through devices like switches forward all packets without stopping. One drawback to this is that bad packets are forwarded with good packets. Because bridges buffer, they can discard mangled packets.

Because switches create virtual circuits, they essentially make shared LAN media unshared. By removing the problem of contention between nodes for access to the LAN, switches make LANs more determinate. This is necessary for applications, such as video conferencing, that require a relatively constant, low rate of delay. The irregular bursts of traffic that are typical of LANs make carrying real-time traffic difficult.

Routing in Networks

The internetworking device that corresponds to the network layer is the *router*. Individual networks can contain from a handful to thousands of nodes. Most router-based networks of moderate to large size are hierarchical, with some routers defining the borders between zones, levels, domains, or groups of networks.

Just as bridges handle such specific data-link layer protocols as Ethernet and token ring, routers handle specific network-layer protocols used by end nodes to communicate with each other. Some routers are programmed to handle only one network-layer protocol, whereas others handle more than a dozen. Many network-layer protocols exist—at least one for every type of operating system and several that work with multiple operating systems. Figure 7.6 shows how a router manages packets between modes. Because the router examines packets at the network level, it operates independently of data-link protocols such as Ethernet or token ring.

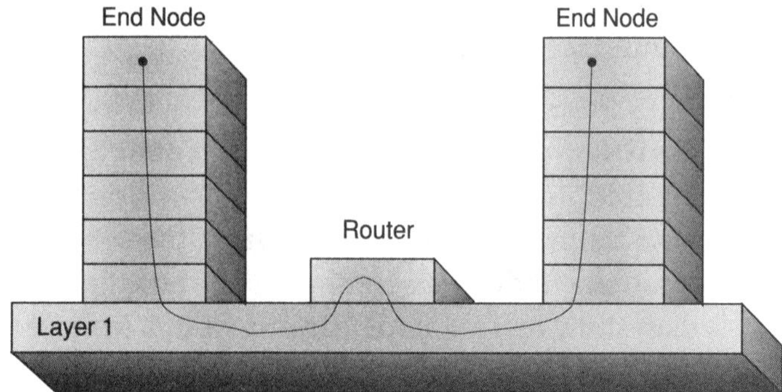

Figure 7.6:
End nodes communicating across a router.

The Internet Protocol (IP) of the TCP/IP protocol suite and Connectionless Network Service (CLNS) and Connection Oriented Network Service (CONS) of the Open Systems Interconnect (OSI) protocol suite evolved in the UNIX world but have been extended to various operating systems. Many of the PC LAN network operating systems use adaptations of the Xerox Network System (XNS) protocols. Microsoft's LAN Manager and Ungermann Bass' Net One use XNS. Novell's NetWare uses the Internet Packet eXchange (IPX), a derivative of the XNS network layer protocols. Banyan Systems' Virtual Network System (VINES) uses the VINES Internet Protocol (VIP), which is also a derivative of the XNS network-layer protocols. Other significant protocol suites tied to proprietary operating systems include Apple's AppleTalk and Digital Equipment Corporation's DECnet Phase IV.

As network layer devices, routers do not connect at the data-link layer. As a result, a router can connect dissimilar LANs, as long as it has interfaces to more than one LAN type. Using routers remains the simplest way to connect token ring and Ethernet. If you have a token-ring LAN running Novell's NetWare and an Ethernet LAN also running NetWare, for example, the simplest way to link them is to use a router that has Ethernet and token-ring interfaces, and supports IPX.

Because routers, unlike most data-link layer devices, are "visible" to end stations, they can perform flow control. *Flow* means the flow of traffic from the sending node to the receiving node. If a sending node transmits packets faster than the receiving node can store them in its buffer, the transmission can cause congestion. Routers can signal the sending station to halt or slow transmission, thereby controlling the flow and avoiding congestion.

The basic function of a router is to forward packets between networks. Because networks usually have more than one path between them, routers must find the best path along which to send the packets. The best path is determined by routing algorithms, a variety of which have been developed over the last 30 years.

What constitutes the best path varies, depending on a range of criteria including distance, hop count, bandwidth, and load. Distance determines a packet's travel time across a link, called *propagation delay*. Hop count determines the delay introduced by each internetworking device. Also, some packets have a maximum hop count at which they are discarded. Bandwidth measures how much traffic a link can carry. The load of a link is derived from queue depths at each end and, assuming unlimited bandwidth, determines how much traffic the link can carry. These criteria are sometimes referred to as the *route path cost*, and the best path is sometimes referred to as the *least cost path* (see fig. 7.7).

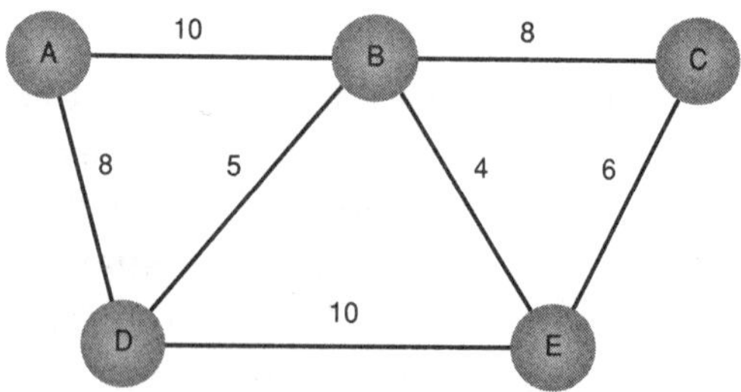

Figure 7.7:
Determining the best path.

Types of Routing Algorithms

There are five categories of routing algorithms: static, dynamic, centralized, local, and distributed. The simplest algorithms are static and local. The algorithms commonly used today are dynamic and distributed.

In *static* routing, you must determine the routes in advance and build the tables yourself. Static routing assumes no changes in the network, including link or node failures. Any changes require an update of the tables. Clearly, static routing should not be your preferred method of routing. In fact, to find a commercially available router that supports only static routing.

Dynamic, or *adaptive*, routing algorithms are capable of recognizing changes in the network and updating routing tables to reflect those changes. Dynamic routing algorithms can calculate the best path, based on such rapidly changing factors as average traffic and measured delay.

In *centralized* routing algorithms, all of the routers forward information to one central router or node that determines the best paths between all the routers. This centrally-maintained routing table is then disseminated to the routers. Centralized routing should not be your first choice of routing schemes—especially if you have a large network—for several reasons. The most obvious is that if the central router fails, the entire network crashes. Another problem with centralized routing is congestion on the links nearest the central router from routing information traffic.

Local routing algorithms, also known as *isolated* routing algorithms, rely on each router to forward packets without knowledge of the network, or to learn routes by tracking the source addresses and hop counts of passing packets. Local routing algorithms can be adaptive, but only to a degree. Because at most they track source addresses and hop counts, the only means local routing algorithms have of determining the best route is distance measured by hop count. One local routing algorithm, Baran's hot potato, tracks only the queue depth of outgoing links. *Flooding* (forwarding packets through all or a set of ports) is the most basic local routing algorithm.

In *distributed* routing schemes, each router keeps track of its immediate neighbors and the paths to them, and forwards this information to all other routers in the network. When all of the pieces of the network picture come together in each router, the algorithm is said to *converge*. Because distributed routing algorithms require each router to send updates to every other router, usually by flooding, they can add to network overhead. Stability is also an important issue. If an algorithm updates frequently and is highly sensitive to changes in the network, it becomes difficult for the algorithm to converge. When an algorithm fails to converge it is said to *oscillate*.

Two commonly used distributed routing algorithms are link state and distance vector. *Distance vector* routing is based on sharing routing tables built using the calculated delay between routing nodes. Every router calculates the delay on the links to each of its neighbors and builds a routing table that determines the delay to every destination via each adjacent router. Each router broadcasts its routing table to the other routers. When a router receives an update from an adjacent router, it calculates the delay to the updating router and adds the result to the reported delays in the update.

In *link state* routing, every router maintains a map of the whole network, in addition to tracking the delay on the links to its neighbors. Routers update each other about the condition of their links and use the updates to revise their maps of the network. Routers use their maps to determine the best path to forward packets. Link state, is favored over distance vector routing because each router has a more complete picture of the network. Also, because updates in link state contain only reports of a router's links and not whole routing tables, the algorithm produces less overhead.

The original routing protocol used in the TCP/IP suite in the Internet, the Routing Information Protocol (RIP), uses a distance vector algorithm. Other network protocol suites, such as XNS and NetWare, define their own routing information protocols. RIP has serious limitations, not the least of which is its 16-hop limit. The routing protocol gaining favor in the Internet community, called Open Shortest Path First (OSPF), uses a link state algorithm. The routing protocol used in OSI, called Intermediate System-to-Intermediate System (IS-IS), uses a similar link state algorithm.

Hierarchical Routing

Large router-based networks are organized hierarchically, with the network divided into groups, areas, or zones (see fig. 7.8). These subdivisions are shielded from each other, enabling the same network address to be used repeatedly. Some protocols support a limited number of addresses; to use them in large networks, you often have to reuse addresses. Routers communicate within the subdivisions in order to route packets from end station to end station. A subset of the network's routers are used to communicate across the borders of these subdivisions. Different routing protocols often are used at these different levels. In the TCP/IP world, routing protocols used within the subdivisions (called *autonomous systems*) are called *interior gateway* protocols. Not surprisingly, protocols used across autonomous systems are called *exterior gateway* protocols .

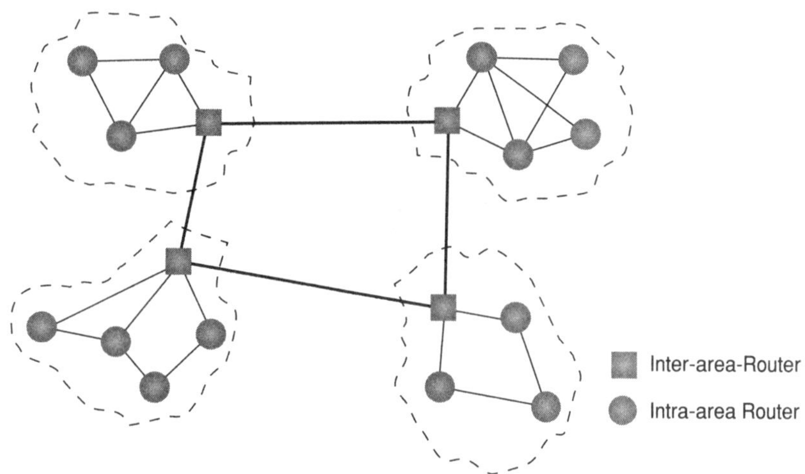

Figure 7.8:
Hierarchical routing.

One note of caution: just because multiprotocol routers from different vendors support the same routing protocols, such as OSPF and IS-IS, multiprotocol routers from different vendors do not necessarily work together. If you intend to buy multiprotocol routers, but you do not want to be locked into buying any one vendor's routers every time you add to your network, you must weigh the benefits of the unique features and implementations of each brand of router against the inability to extend those features to other brands.

Router Hardware

The original routers were mainframes or minicomputers, *running* routing software as one of several applications or as dedicated routers. Host-based routing evolved on the Internet, in which a university's computer was attached directly to the network. Host-based routers on the Internet are called *gateways*; today, however, that term is used to describe a different class of device, discussed later in this chapter. Specialized systems built for the purpose of routing became necessary because host computers are expensive and usually are not optimized for handling network traffic.

Although the software used in today's routers is different and considerably more complex than the software used in bridges, the hardware is quite similar. In fact, many router makers have added bridging to their products over the last few years. Combined bridge-routers, sometimes referred to *brouters*, are becoming the rule rather than the exception. Bridge-routers route any protocols they support and bridge the rest. Routing some protocols and bridging others is especially useful for networks running protocols that cannot be routed, such as DEC's Local Area Transport terminal-to-host protocol.

Routers range from simple dual-port local models to models with wide-area network interfaces and a dozen or more ports. Some routers have multiple communications boards, each with a processor, attached to a bus or switch. Each communications board processes a network protocol.

According to the Harvard bridge and router performance study, virtually no difference in performance exists between similarly configured bridges and routers. As with bridges, the study found that routers are capable of operating at wire speed. In deciding which router to buy, the report recommends using the same criteria listed earlier for selecting bridges.

Multiprotocol Routing and SNA: Oil and Water?

One aspect of interconnecting LANs that has gone from the impossible to the merely difficult is combining multiprotocol routing with IBM SNA traffic. Until recently, the only connection possible between the multiprotocol LAN environment and the SNA environment was through a gateway. SNA traffic can be encapsulated in token-ring or Ethernet packets, but the two worlds diverge at the network layer.

SNA is hierarchical, with minicomputers and personal computers communicating through mainframes. Each mainframe and its associated computers and devices is called a *subarea*. SNA uses subarea routing, which involves dynamic allocation of node addresses and the creation of virtual routes.

In order to fully integrate multiprotocol and SNA routing, routers have to emulate IBM front-end processors, called *Type 4 devices*, which are used with mainframes to handle SNA traffic. Although some router makers once indicated that they eventually would offer Type 4 device emulation, they have since backed away from their proposals because of the technical challenge and the added overhead SNA routing would add to their products.

Instead, most router makers appear to be waiting for IBM's Advanced Peer-to-Peer Networking (APPN) scheme to gain favor with SNA users. APPN is a distributed, host-independent networking scheme similar to OSI, TCP/IP, and DECnet. APPN routing is similar to the source routing used in IBM Ttoken Ring bridging. It will be years, however, before APPN will dominate IBM networks.

In the meantime, router makers support SNA with two sets of features centered on source routing and synchronous communications. As mentioned earlier, some router makers support source routing and offer IP encapsulation for carrying source-routing traffic across IP backbones. Some routers are also capable of responding to discovery packets without forwarding them across the backbone, by maintaining an address table of remote source-routing nodes.

Many SNA devices use synchronous communications protocols that require the establishment of virtual circuits between front-end processors. To support virtual circuits, some router makers offer synchronous passthrough which allows virtual circuits to extend through their routers.

Where Routers Fit

Routers are a requirement for building large networks or for participating in a major network like the Internet. To build an organized hierarchical network, rather than a simply stratified one, you need the more sophisticated traffic-handling that routers provide.

The router's complexity, compared to bridges, can be a disadvantage. The more complex the routing algorithm, addressing scheme, and protocol handling, the greater the chances of complications or failures. The greater complexity also means that your staff needs a higher level of training and experience. Although bridges are rapidly approaching the status of plug-and-play devices, routers continue to require attention. If a duplicate IP address pops up or a routing algorithm fails to converge, the average workgroup administrator or computer room operator is not likely to know how to correct the problem.

You can build a network by using only routers. Today, because low-end local routers are not much more expensive than local bridges, you can use routers to isolate workgroups from the backbone. If you have a router for every couple of workstations, however, your network is unnecessarily complicated.

For most networks, a combination of bridges and routers will yield the best results. In general, try to use bridges to isolate and segment workgroups and use routers to create your backbone network. Because most current multiport, multiprotocol routers also perform bridging, few penalties exist for using routers instead of bridges to build your network infrastructure (see fig. 7.9).

You may want to avoid routers if your network has only a few hundred users and your network staff has limited experience with routing and protocol handling. If your network will become part of a larger network (through a corporate merger or acquisition, for instance), or is expected to grow significantly, you should be prepared to develop a router-based network.

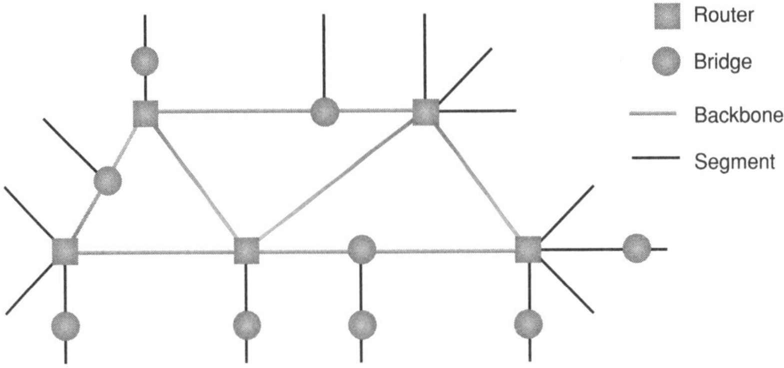

Figure 7.9:
Network consisting of bridges and routers.

Understanding Gateways

The next category of internetworking device, gateways, corresponds to the session and application layers. *Gateways* are not so much internetworking devices as bridges (in the generic sense of the word) between different environments. Gateways usually are used between quite different networks, like SNA and DECnet or NetWare. You would use a gateway to link two or more unrelated networks, not to build a network.

Usually, a gateway is a computer that exists as an end node in each network or as an end node in one network and a peripheral device to a host system in the other. Gateways are not transparent to other end nodes on the network. A workstation in one network, needing access to an application on a server or host in the other, first establishes a session with the gateway. The gateway then establishes a session with the system on the other network. The gateway takes the data stream from the session on one side and maps it to the session on the other side (see fig. 7.10).

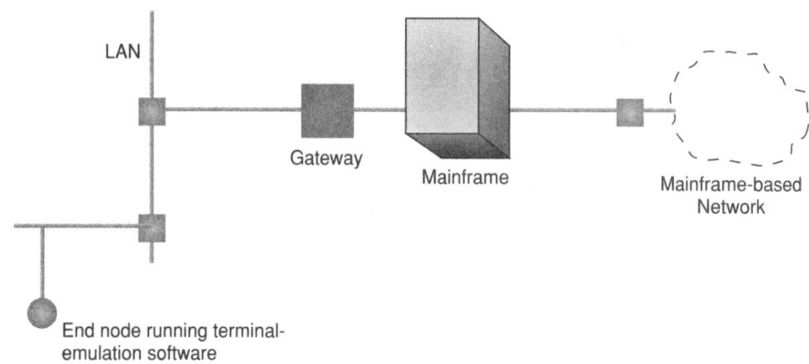

Figure 7.10:
Gateway, linking a LAN to a mainframe.

Another class of devices that can connect vastly different systems is that of protocol converters. *Protocol converters* are applications or software routines that convert a data stream from one set of formats and protocols to another. An example is a program that converts TCP/IP-based Telnet terminal communications to IBM 3270 terminal communications. Protocol converters can run on the gateway or on the end node or terminal server initiating the session with the gateway.

It is usually clear when you need a gateway. If you have users in one environment who need access to an application in another, you can give them each two terminals on their desks or you can use a gateway.

But if you want to connect two LANs of one environment across a backbone network of a different environment, gateways are an expensive option—one you should avoid if you can. Your first choice should be to encapsulate the LAN traffic in the backbone traffic. In some cases, encapsulation is not available and gateways are your only choice.

Connecting LANs over WANs

Tying together all the LANs that have sprung up around an organization often means spanning remote sites. Wide-area links once used primarily to ship data to a central mainframe are now carrying significant amounts of LAN traffic. But LANs and wide-area networks are different animals, and getting them to coexist peacefully is a challenge.

LANs typically are connectionless, whereas wide-area networks are mostly connection-oriented. The major costs of a LAN are hardware, installation, and maintenance. The major costs of a wide-area network are recurring monthly carrier charges and usage fees. The protocols used in each are very different; unfortunately, finding a single network manager versed in both is rare.

LANs are high bandwidth, ranging from the 230 kilobits-per-second of Apple's LocalTalk to the 100 megabits-per-second of FDDI. Typical LAN bandwidths are about 10 megabits-per-second. The current generation of wide-area networks ranges in bandwidth from 19.2 kilobits-per-second to the 45 megabits-per-second T3. Typical wide-area network bandwidths are 56 kilobits-per-second and 1.544 megabits-per-second.

Three common types of wide-area networks that are used to link LANs are private T1 networks, carrier-based switched 56 networks, and X.25 networks. LANs connect to the wide-area network through an internetworking device, either a bridge or router, linked to a wide-area switch. In X.25 networks, the internetworking device connects to a packet assembler/disassembler (PAD) that encapsulates the LAN traffic.

In the past year or so, a few internetworking devices that combine bridging and routing with T1 switches or other wide-area devices have come on the market. These devices were developed in response to the need to link LANs over wide-area networks. Nevertheless, these devices are part of a wide-area network infrastructure. From the LAN perspective, they are functionally no different from separate devices.

Perhaps more significant are emerging technologies for linking LANs over large distances. *Frame relay,* which uses variable amounts of bandwidth, is connection-oriented and uses permanent virtual circuits in the wide-area network. The frame-relay specification defines the connection between a LAN internetworking device, such as a router, and a switch at the local end of the wide-area link (see fig. 7.11).

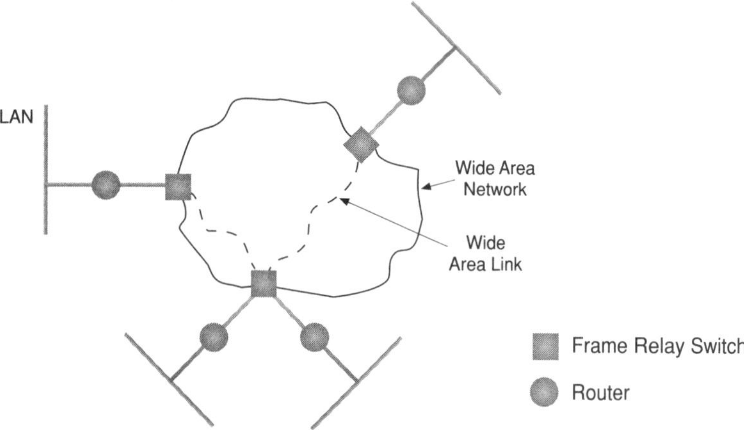

Figure 7.11:
Frame relay.

SMDS is a metropolitan-area network service designed by Bellcore that regional Bell operating companies are expected to offer soon. SMDS defines a connectionless datagram service over a fiber-optic ring, operating at rates of 1.544Mbps (and eventually 45 Mbps). The datagram service operates over a cell-relay layer, defined in the specification as Asynchronous Transfer Mode (ATM), which is controlled by a central office switch called the Metropolitan Switching System.

In addition to the particular wide-area network technology, other issues to bear in mind when you link LANs over wide-area networks have to do with the LAN traffic itself. Protocol suites such as TCP/IP, OSI, SNA, and DECnet, were designed with the expectation that wide-area links would be part of the network; most PC-LAN network operating systems, on the other hand, were not.

Problems with Connecting PC LANs over Wide-Area Links

Because PC-LAN protocols evolved in an environment in which bandwidth is virtually free, they are not the most economical consumers of bandwidth. Such PC-LAN protocols as Novell's NetWare and Apple's AppleTalk produce a great deal of overhead through arguably excessive use of broadcast messages.

The routing tables of the PC-LAN protocols are updated with broadcast messages. AppleTalk and NetWare use variations of the Routing Information Protocol (RIP) which, in larger networks, sends large updates.

NetWare also uses broadcast messages, called Service Advertising Protocols (SAPs), with which servers and printers make their availability known to end stations. The timers for SAPs and routing table updates can be adjusted but usually are set for 30-second intervals, so that every 60 seconds there is a burst of traffic over the wide-area network.

Many of the router vendors restrict broadcast messages from going over the wide-area. Because the network updates are too frequent and NetWare SAPs are useless over a wide-area link, the router vendors use filters to control SAP and RIP messages.

If all vendors—including Novell and Apple—supported one routing protocol such as IS-IS, for their protocol suites, some of the traffic across the backbone could diminish. Several alternatives exist to extending PC-LAN protocols across wide-area links. One alternative is to encapsulate PC LAN protocols in other network protocols. Encapsulation simplifies handling traffic over wide-area links but does not necessarily reduce overhead from broadcast traffic. The main penalty to using encapsulation is reduced performance. The process of encapsulating packets at one end and stripping off the encapsulation at the other end is added work for the internetworking devices.

The most effective way to reduce the impact of PC-LAN protocols on wide-area links is to contain the protocols on the LAN. You still have to get data from the LAN to the rest of the network, however.

You can use gateways or run multiple protocol stacks on the end stations. By running dual network protocol stacks on end stations, users can employ the end stations as protocol converters or run applications that use only one of the protocol stacks (NetWare for local file access, for example, and Telnet for accessing a remote host).

Because of the additional system resources (especially memory) required to support two protocols, running two protocol stacks on a PC is not always efficient. Also, running a second protocol stack on every PC can be costly.

Even though running PC-LAN protocols across wide-area links can eat up a great deal of expensive bandwidth, it is the easiest way to connect remote LANs. No right answer exists for every network. For some, the added cost of carrying PC-LAN protocols across wide-area links will be lower than the cost of alternatives. Over time, the effect PC-LAN protocols have on wide-area links will diminish. PC-LAN network operating system vendors (Novell, for example) are updating their products with wide-area connectivity in mind.

Understanding Concentrators, Bridges, and Routers

The rise in popularity of structured wiring has led to an increase in the integration of network devices. The key element of structured-wiring schemes is the *concentrator*, and during the past few years increasing numbers of devices have been configured as modules for concentrators. Internetworking devices are no exception. Today, most of the major concentrator vendors offer bridge and router modules developed by many of the leading internetworking vendors. An intelligent concentrator is shown in figure 7.12.

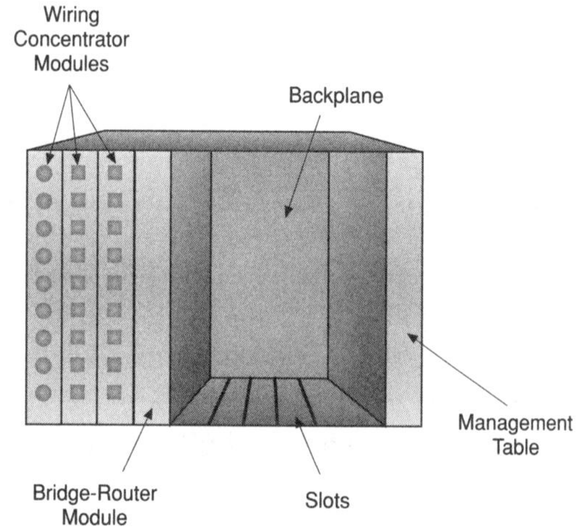

Figure 7.12:
Intelligent concentrator.

Instead of separate devices with their own enclosures, power supplies, and network interfaces, concentrator-based bridges and routers are little more than circuit boards that plug into a concentrator's backplane.

Putting bridges and routers in concentrators makes managing them easier and can also provide some degree of fault-tolerance.

One of the benefits of concentrators is integrated network management. Cabling, concentrators, and internetworking devices can all be managed together through a single management module. Because concentrators concentrate almost all of a network into one box, concentrator designers have had to make sure that their boxes are as close to fail-safe as possible. Hubs are often equipped with redundant components that help keep anything in them running.

Also, by more closely linking internetworking devices with wiring hubs in concentrators, some concentrator manufacturers are working on schemes to enable bridges and routers to control traffic (through port-mapping) down to the level of individual nodes rather than just among segments and networks.

Some manufacturers are extending the integration of internetworking functions even further. Several of the newer concentrators on the market have extremely high speed, often switch-based, backplanes that are used to link FDDI, Ethernet, and token-ring segments built into the concentrators.

One vendor coalition foresees this integration trend culminating in the merger of two types of devices: multiport routers and concentrators. Router-maker Cisco Systems, Inc., structured-wiring system maker SynOptics Communications, Inc., and workstation-maker Sun Microsystems, Inc., have outlined a project to develop a routing concentrator, called RUB. RUB essentially makes the concentrator an oversized router with slots for wiring concentrator modules, in place of cable ports. In a RUB, concentrator routing is supported on the backplane itself, as opposed to relying on passive backplanes that require a separate routing module to support routing.

One drawback to concentrator-based internetworking is that, because the manufacturers use different backplanes, bridge and router modules of one brand of concentrator cannot be used with another. If you use concentrators from more than one vendor, you can end up having to use router modules from different router vendors. Even if you use different brands of concentrators, you do not have to use router modules from different vendors.

If you already have a structured-wiring environment, there are only two reasons to use a stand-alone bridge or router rather than a bridge or router module: either you do not have an available slot in your concentrator or you need a higher performance bridge or router than what is currently available in module form. If you do not have a structured-wiring environment, internetworking issues should not be the most important factors in your decision to move to one. Structured wiring is first and foremost a cabling issue.

Summary

Internetworking is one of the last steps in building the computing infrastructure—it is addressed where planning from the top down meets planning from the bottom up. To oversimplify the situation: the task determines the application, which determines the computer, which determines the operating system, which determines the network protocols, which factor into the internetworking equation. In the other direction: the office layout determines the location of the computers, which determines the network topology, which factors into the internetworking equation.

Determining how to interconnect your LANs depends on how many LANs you have, what types they are, where they are located, what protocols and how much traffic they carry, whether they are configured in a structured or distributed-wiring scheme, and how all of the above may change over the next five years.

As with most aspects of computing, compatibility is the key to choosing a particular brand of internetworking device. Can you manage it with your network management system? Does its implementation of a particular protocol work with those already in your network? Do its unique features work in your network? Do they interfere with any aspect of your network? Although some of these questions can be answered only after you try the device in your network, you should ask the vendor anyway and then carefully document any incompatibilities.

Internetworking devices are becoming more reliable and easier to use. Nevertheless, you should carefully consider the vendor's service and support programs. Does the vendor have a 24-hour hot line? Does the vendor provide on-site spares? If not, does the vendor provide replacements overnight? The same day? Within an hour? Even if the vendor can answer these questions to your satisfaction, is an inordinate amount charged for support and service?

Most internetworking vendors probably will be able to meet most of your requirements for function, compatibility, and service. Also, because no single vendor in the internetworking market has a lock on any critical capabilities, you can weigh price heavily in your purchasing decision.

Part Three: LAN NOS Local Connectivity Support

Novell NetWare

Microsoft LAN Manager

Banyan VINES

Topics covered in this chapter:
Understanding Communications Protocols
Providing Local Area Support
Examining LAN Standards
Providing Asynchronous Communication Support

Chapter 8

Novell NetWare

Novell's NetWare v.3.11 is an advanced, 32-bit network-operating system that includes comprehensive support for every major desktop operating system, including DOS, Windows, Macintosh, OS/2, and UNIX. Besides providing extensive support for local area networks, NetWare includes support for asynchronous wide area communications, enabling users to build sophisticated enterprise-networking systems. In this chapter, you learn about Novell's support for local and wide area asynchronous connectivity.

Understanding Communications Protocols

The Novell protocol suite was greatly influenced by the design and implementation of the Xerox Network Systems (XNS) protocol architecture. XNS was developed at the Xerox Palo Alto Research Center (PARC) in the 1970s and released in 1981.

IPX/SPX and the NetWare Shell

The *Internetwork Packet Exchange* (IPX) is a network-layer protocol that is responsible for packet addressing and routing. The *Sequenced Packet Exchange* (SPX) is a transport-layer protocol that provides an application with peer-to-peer communications across a network. The *NetWare Shell* is a service protocol that controls the interaction between the network workstation and the NetWare file server.

This section covers Novell's IPX and SPX protocols and the Transmission Control Protocol/Internet Protocol (TCP/IP) protocol stack, along with the Open Data Link Interface (ODI) that decouples the LAN driver from the protocol stack. The relationship between the IPX/SPX protocol stack and the OSI Reference Model is also examined.

IPX

The Internetwork Packet Exchange (IPX) is a connectionless datagram protocol that delivers packets across an internet in a "best-effort" manner. This network-layer protocol provides NetWare workstations and file servers with addressing and internetwork routing services. The IPX protocol is closely related to the XNS Internetwork Datagram Protocol (IDP).

IPX, being an unreliable protocol, relies on higher-layer protocols to ensure data delivery, sequencing, and flow control. IPX interfaces directly with the data-link layer and relies on it to perform the actual transfer of data across the network.

IPX addresses consist of three components: a 32-bit network number, a 48-bit host number, and a 16-bit socket number. All three components are required to form a complete internet address. The entire address unqiuely identifies a computer application running on an internetwork of computers.

Software that implements the IPX protocol must be loaded on all stations that want to participate on an IPX network. On the file server, IPX is built into the network operating system, enabling the server to communicate with workstations and other NetWare servers. IPX must be loaded on network workstations before the workstations can use IPX to transfer packets through the network.

IPX transfers datagram packets across the network. A *packet* is composed of a header (containing control information) and the data being transferred. A packet's total size is 576 bytes: a header is 30 bytes long, and has as many as 546 bytes of data.

Higher-layer protocols, such as SPX, NCP, and the Service Advertising Protocol (SAP), use IPX to transfer data. They do this by encapsulating the data and any protocol-specific headers in the data portion of the IPX datagram.

The other important service that IPX provides is the internetwork routing of packets. A full IPX router is built into each NetWare file server, which enables any NetWare server to act as a connecting point between two or more networks. The server must have a network connection (a separate network interface card) to each of the networks between which it wants to transfer packets.

The router passes packets between networks in a store-and-forward manner. Memory is set aside in the router to buffer incoming packets until they can be forwarded along the proper network. Packet-routing decisions are made by consulting a routing table maintained in each router. The routing table contains, among other information, a list of network addresses and the addresses of routers that can get the packet closer to it destination. The routing tables are maintained by the Routing Information Protocol (RIP). Novell's implementation of RIP is a slightly enhanced version of the Routing Information Protocol used in the XNS.

The IPX protocol is implemented in the DOS program IPX.COM. For workstations using the Open Data Link Interface (ODI), the program name is IPXODI.COM. ODI is described in detail in a later section.

IPX.COM must be generated by linking the generic IPX.OBJ, supplied by Novell, to the LAN driver supplied by the manufacturer of the network interface card. The Novell program WSGEN is used to create the IPX.COM, by using the hardware settings on the adapter supplied by the user. This IPX.COM must then be used by workstations with the same LAN adapter settings.

Alternatively, workstations may use ODI, which provides a more general protocol architecture. IPX.COM no longer needs to be generated for workstations. Rather, a common IPXODI.COM is used for all ODI workstations on the network. For IPXODI to load and function, however, the Link Support Layer (LSL.COM) and network adapter driver (NE2000.COM, for example) must be loaded before IPXODI. The network adapter driver, although still supplied by the manufacturer, no longer needs to be linked to the IPX program. Rather, the manufacturer needs to follow the ODI specification to ensure compatibility.

IPX.COM and IPXODI.COM both implement SPX and the Remote Diagnostics Responder, as well as IPX.

SPX

Sequenced Packet Exchange (SPX) is a connection-oriented protocol that provides a reliable peer-to-peer data stream between communicating network applications. SPX, a transport-layer protocol, enables the sequenced exchange of data while maintaining flow control and preventing the delivery of duplicate copies of a packet. SPX uses the internetwork datagram delivery service provided by IPX, Novell's network-layer protocol. The SPX protocol was derived from the XNS Sequenced Packet Protocol (SPP).

SPX encapsulates its data and header-control information in the data section of the IPX packet. The SPX header, which is 12 bytes long, includes the following information:

- Connection control
- Datastream type
- Source connection ID
- Destination connection ID
- Sequence number
- Acknowledgment number
- Allocation number

The connection-control field controls the flow of data over the connection. The datastream type is used by higher-layer protocols to indicate the type of data in the packet.

The source and destination connection IDs uniquely identify the connection between peer processes. Using connection IDs also enables multiplexing connections over a single IPX socket.

The sequence number and the acknowledgement number are used to implement SPX's reliable data-transfer service. Together, they regulate data-flow control, packet sequencing, and suppression of duplicate packets.

The allocation number also plays a part in ensuring reliability by informing the sender about the number of buffers available for receiving packets. This information helps prevent a fast sender from sending data faster than a receiver can process it. Following the header information is the data.

The NetWare Shell and the NetWare Core Protocol

The NetWare Shell interacts with the applications on the client workstations. When an application program makes an operating-system request, the NetWare Shell determines whether the request is for a local resource, such as a file on the local drive, or a printer attached to the workstation and, if it is for a local resource, passes the request to the host operating system for processing. If the request is for a networked resource, the NetWare Shell encapsulates the request and redirects it via the network to a NetWare server.

The protocol used to request network resources and services is called the NetWare Core Protocol (NCP). The NCP controls the interaction between the workstation and the file server by establishing connections between them and processing requests for services from the file server. The workstation, for example, may request the server to open and read data from a file on the server. Interestingly, NCP implements its own connection management instead of relying on SPX to provide this service.

NCP provides a client with access to a number of services including file, print, and named-object management. Because the NetWare operating system enables several workstations to have simultaneous access to shared resources, NetWare provides a means for synchronizing access to a file, in addition to record and file-level locking.

The NCP also enables objects to be named and to have values associated with one or more of the object's properties. This information is stored on the NetWare file server in a database called the Bindery. The Bindery contains information about users, groups, servers, and more. Through the Bindery, NetWare and NCP are able to implement a comprehensive system of resource naming, accounting, and network security.

NCP uses a connection number to identify the session between a client workstation and a NetWare server. This connection number, which is unique on the server, is used to keep track of the server requests made by the client, along with the resources used. NetWare also uses the connection number to maintain system security, enabling access only to the services and resources for which the client is authorized.

The NCP packet includes information detailing the particular service requested by the client.

As a result of the interaction between the NetWare Shell and the services provided by the server through NCP, access to a network resource is transparent to the application on the workstation. (The application "believes" that it simply is using a local resource.)

The NetWare Shell is implemented on the workstation as a terminate-and-stay-resident (TSR) program. For the shell to load and function, IPX must be present on the workstation.

The shell relies on IPX being present on the workstation in order to load and function.

The NetWare Shell for DOS workstations comes in three types. NETx.COM is used in workstations with conventional memory (less than or equal to 640K). XMSNETx.EXE can be used with expanded memory that is compatible with the LIM 4.0 EMS standard. Finally, EMSNETx.EXE is used with extended memory compatible with XMS 2.0. In all cases, the *x* in the title refers to the version of DOS with which the shell is used (replace *x* with 3, 4, or 5 to indicate DOS 3, DOS 4, or DOS 5, respectively).

Novell now supplies a series of generic shells that work with all versions of DOS mentioned in the preceding paragraph. In the following cases, the letter *X* is a literal X, not a placeholder for a version number. The corresponding NetWare Shells are called NETX.COM, XMSNETX.EXE, and EMSNETX.EXE.

The shell for OS/2 workstations is called the *NetWare Requester for OS/2*.

When the NetWare Shell is loaded, it uses the Service Advertising Protocol (SAP) to request the location of the nearest NetWare file server. A connection is established with the first server that responds, and the workstation's network drive is mapped to the

LOGIN directory on that server. The user can now use the LOGIN.EXE command to log in to any file server on the network.

Through the preferred server option in the SHELL.CFG file, the user can specify an alternative file server to which the NetWare Shell should try to attach when it is loaded. If a preferred server is specified, the NetWare Shell performs the same steps as outlined earlier, using the SAP to locate a server. If this server happens to be the preferred server, the search is complete. Otherwise, the NetWare Shell checks the Bindery of the server to find the preferred server and then attaches directly to the preferred server.

Each connection to a NetWare server is identified by a connection number. The shell can maintain eight server connections simultaneously. It does this by using a connection table that contains the server's name and address as well as the connection number, the packet sequence number, and timeout values. When the shell is unloaded from the workstation, all active connections are closed.

Open Data Link Interface (ODI)

The *Open Data Link Interface* (ODI) is an architecture that enables multiple protocol stacks to be used with one or more LAN adapters in a workstation on the network. Originally, the ODI specification was a joint design by Apple Computer and Novell, known for a short time as ODLI. Today, ODI is supported by most major manufacturers of network adapters.

By using an ODI network adapter and drivers written to the ODI specification on a workstation, a user can load several protocol stacks concurrently and access file servers and hosts by using the different protocols. A user can have both the NetWare Shell and

Novell's LAN Workplace for DOS loaded at the same time, for example. By loading both programs (the Shell and LAN Workplace), the workstation can use the IPX/SPX protocol stack, along with TCP/IP, to conduct communications sessions.

An extra advantage to using ODI adapters and drivers is the relative ease of installation and maintenance of the protocol software on the workstations. Before ODI, it was necessary to create an IPX.COM file by linking the adapter-card files, provided by the card's manufacturer, with IPX.OBJ supplied by Novell. The program WSGEN was used to link the files using the network adapter settings. This procedure was time-consuming and prone to error. ODI simplifies this by enabling the user to configure the network-adapter settings in a file called NET.CFG. The components of the ODI architecture can then be loaded without needing to build an executable IPX module.

Figure 8.1 presents the overall structure of the Open Data Link Interface. At the top of the stack are the network applications, including the NetWare Shell (NETx.COM), the File Transfer Protocol (FTP), virtual terminal emulation (Telnet), Remote Copy (RCP), and others. These network applications use transport and network protocols on the workstation, such as Novell's SPX/IPX (IPXODI.COM), and the Internet and UNIX standard TCP/IP (TCPIP.EXE).

The network layer uses the Multi-Protocol Interface (MPI) to interface with the Link Support Layer (LSL). The LSL is the entity responsible for decoupling the higher-layer protocols from the LAN drivers in the ODI specification. On a NetWare workstation, the Link Support Layer is implemented by the program LSL.COM. The LSL provides a common interface between the protocol stack (SPX/IPX, for example) and the LAN adapter.

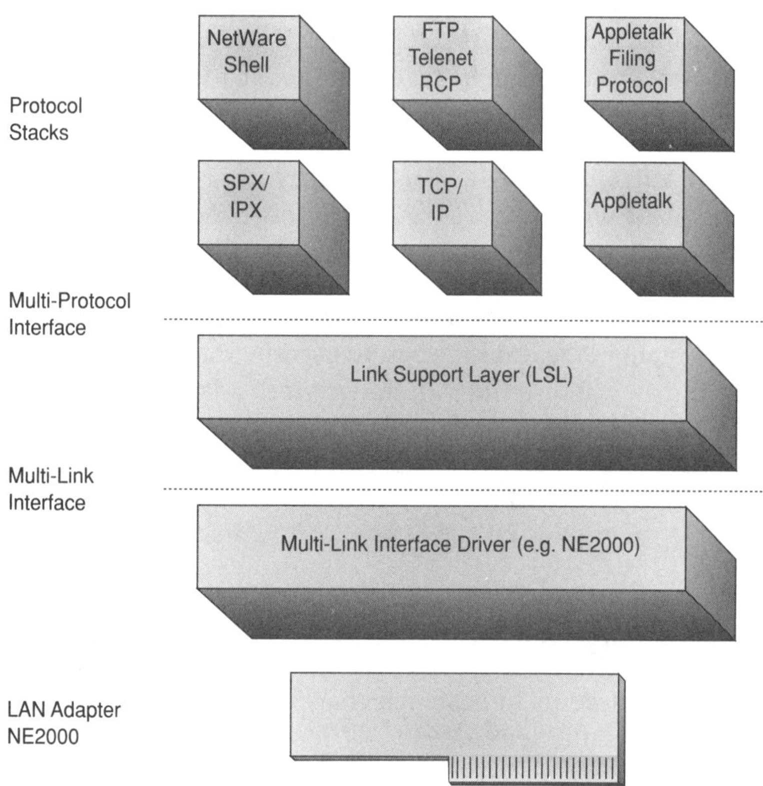

Figure 8.1:
The Open Data Link Interface.

Because the LSL interface is fixed, multiple protocol stacks that follow the ODI specification can be used on the computer, independent of the ODI-compliant LAN adapter used. The LAN driver uses the MLI as the interface to the LSL. A LAN driver written to the ODI specification is known as a Multi-Link

Interface Driver (MLID). Using the MLI, any adapter-specific information can be placed in the NET.CFG file without having to statically link a protocol stack to an adapter.

An example of an ODI LAN driver is NE2000.COM, which is used with Novell's NE2000 Ethernet Adapter.

NET.CFG, an ASCII file, contains information about and parameters for the Link Support Layer, the protocols used on the workstation, the frame structure used by the data link, and the LAN driver and settings on the network adapter. Each section is preceded by the following headers:

- Link Support
- Protocol
- Link Driver
- Frame

The headers indicate which aspect of the communications process is affected.

The Link Support section enables the user to specify the memory pool buffers and the number of communications buffers used to receive data. Although IPXODI ignores the values given here, other protocol stacks (such as TCP/IP) can use these values to tune performance.

The Protocol section enables a protocol stack to be bound to the LAN adapter, which enables network applications on the workstation to use the protocol. In addition, the number of concurrent sessions applications can use with the protocol is specified.

The Link Driver section enables the user to specify the settings on the network adapter without having to statically link the driver with any particular protocol stack. This section enables several configuration parameters to be established, including the following:

- Interrupt number
- DMA channels
- Memory addresses
- I/O port number
- Hardware address of the adapter (if allowed)
- The number of the slot where the adapter is located

For the LAN adapter and the protocol stacks to operate properly, these values must match the settings on the adapter itself.

The Frame section tells the data link what type of frame is used on the network to which the workstation is attached. Possible values for this section include the following:

ETHERNET_802.3	TOKEN-RING
ETHERNET_802.2	TOKEN-RING_SNAP
ETHERNET_II	IBM_PCN2_802.2
ETHERNET_SNAP	IBM_PCN2_SNAP
	NOVELL_RX-NET

The maximum frame size used with token-ring networks can be specified also in this section.

Novell's IPXODI.COM implements three protocols: IPX, SPX, and the Remote Diagnostics Responder. Using command-line parameters, IPXODI can be loaded without the SPX transport protocol or the Remote Diagnostics Responder. Certain network applications, such as the remote console RCONSOLE, require the services of all three protocols, however.

NetBIOS

The *Network Basic Input/Output System* (NetBIOS) is a high-level application-program interface that enables programmers to build distributed network applications. Novell provides NetBIOS support by means of a NetBIOS emulator, which accepts the NetBIOS command, encapsulates it into an IPX packet, and transmits it though the network.

Many network applications have been written using the NetBIOS interface. NetWare's support of NetBIOS enables these applications to be run on a NetWare network.

NetBIOS has a set of commands to establish communications sessions, send and receive data, and name network objects. NetBIOS provides a reliable, connection-oriented data-transfer stream as well as an unreliable, connectionless datagram service. It also includes a naming system for identifying stations on the network.

To run NetBIOS applications on a DOS workstation, the two programs NETBIOS.EXE and INT2F.EXE must be loaded. To use NetBIOS applications with OS/2 workstations, the following two lines must appear in the CONFIG.SYS file:

```
DEVICE=C:\NETWARE\NETBIOS.SYS
RUN=C:\NETWARE\NBDAEMON.EXE
```

TCP/IP

The Transmission Control Protocol (TCP), the Internet Protocol (IP), and others are the product of research funded by the United States (Defense) Advanced Research Projects Agency (ARPA, now DARPA). DARPA's goal included building extremely reliable networks to link heterogeneous computing systems. The ARPANET, an early packet-switching network, was one of the most notable results of this research.

Novell's implementation of TCP/IP consists of a set of NetWare Loadable Modules that run on a NetWare file server. The modules contain a routing capability that enables IP packets to be forwarded though an IP internet. Routing information is exchanged among NetWare servers using the Routing Information Protocol (RIP).

The TCP/IP protocol stack provides the transport services required by Novell's NetWare NFS product and the Line Printer Daemon (LPD).

NetWare TCP/IP uses four files to assist its operation. All the files are located in the SYS:ETC directory on the server and are used for the following purposes:

File	*Purpose*
HOSTS	Associates host names with IP addresses
NETWORKS	Associates network names with network addresses
PROTOCOL	Associates protocol names with IP protocol numbers
SERVICES	Associates network services with transport and port numbers

NetWare TCP/IP provides network-management support by including an NLM that implements the Simple Network Management Protocol (SNMP). SNMP enables network nodes on a TCP/IP network to be monitored and managed. A related NLM, SNMPLOG, stores incoming SNMP trap messages in a log file for future analysis and reference. An administrative program, TCPCON, is included also, to help the NetWare supervisor configure the TCP/IP protocol stack. SNMP is discussed further in Chapter 11.

IP Tunneling

The IP Tunneling service enables NetWare IPX local area networks to be linked together using an IP internetwork. To IPX, the IP internetwork looks and behaves like a standard physical network. This enables geographically separate regions to be connected to form IPX internets (see fig. 8.2).

To send an IPX packet across the IP internetwork, the IP Tunneling software encapsulates the IPX packet in a User Datagram Protocol (UDP) packet. The UDP checksum is used to ensure the integrity of the IPX packet. At the receiving end, the packet is removed and delivered to the IPX module.

The IP Tunnel module enables the administrator to configure network peers. Peers are assured of receiving broadcast messages, which frequently are used to transfer important information concerning services and routing.

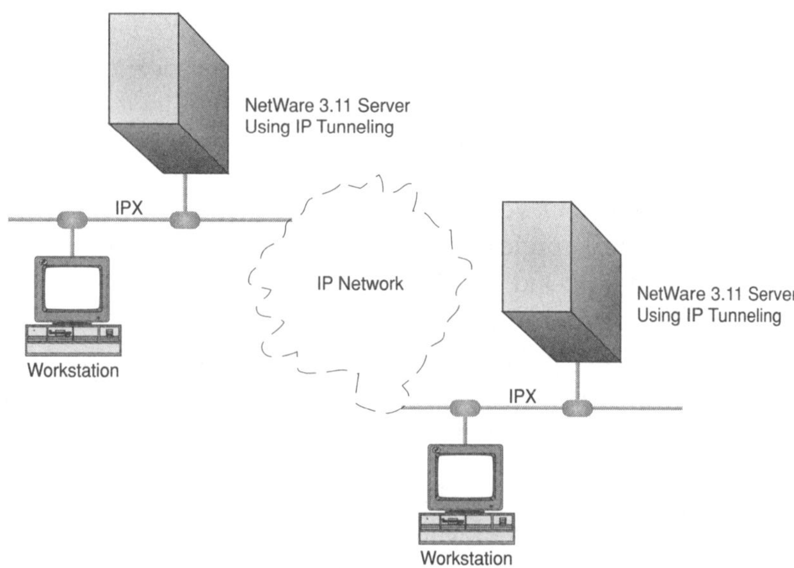

Figure 8.2:
IPX networks using IP Tunneling.

NetWare and the OSI Reference Model

The OSI Reference Model, described in Chapter 2, is a layered model that provides a framework for specifying and describing communication protocols. In the OSI model, each layer provides a set of services for the layer immediately above it and uses services provided by the layer below. An implementation of this model using a set of protocols is called a *protocol stack* (because the protocol layers are stacked on top of each other).

Conceptually, when two devices are communicating, each layer in the model communicates with the corresponding layer on the remote device by using the layer's specific protocol. This is called *peer-to-peer communication* because the two communicating layers are at the same level and are considered peers. In reality, the flow of data is down the stack of the sending device and up the stack of the remote device.

The seven layers of the OSI Reference Model are (from top to bottom) application, presentation, session, transport, network, data link, and physical. The NetWare protocol suite, like many other protocol architectures, fit rather loosely on the OSI Reference Model. Several protocols span more than one layer, so placing them in the confines of any one layer can be more misleading than useful (see fig. 8.3).

The NetWare Core Protocol (NCP), seen earlier in this chapter, controls the interaction between a workstation and a file server by establishing a connection between the workstation and the NetWare server and passing requests and responses for network services between the stations. The NCP can be placed in the application, presentation, and session layers of the Reference Model.

The session layer contains the NetBIOS application interface, implemented in NetWare by a NetBIOS emulator. The NetBIOS emulator uses the IPX protocol on a NetWare station to send data between applications on networked computers.

The transport layer contains the Sequenced Packet Exchange (SPX) protocol. A reliable, connection-oriented protocol, SPX uses IPX's datagram service to provide a sequenced data stream. SPX also provides flow control and duplicate packet suppression between network stations.

The network layer includes the Internetwork Packet Exchange (IPX) protocol and the Routing Information Protocol (RIP). IPX provides a connectionless, unreliable, datagram service and makes a best-effort attempt to deliver a packet to the destination, with no acknowledgement. The RIP is used to maintain the routing information for an internetwork. Novell's RIP was derived from the Xerox Network System's RIP.

The data link and physical layers contain the specifications for Ethernet, IEEE 802.3, IEEE 802.5 (IBM Token-Ring), ARCnet, and LocalTalk.

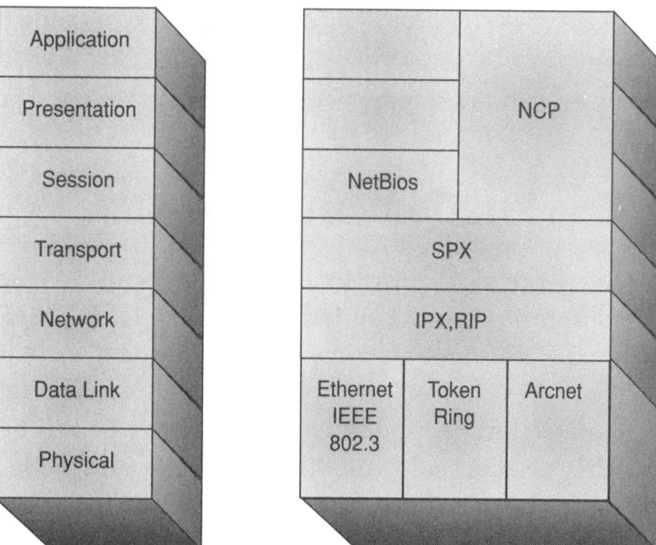

Figure 8.3:
NetWare and the OSI Reference Model.

Providing Local Area Network Support

A network operating system (NOS) must provide two levels of support for users on a network. At the lowest level, a NOS must provide extensive support for the physical media used to connect the stations on the network. At a higher level, a NOS must support the desktop operating systems and computers on which users perform their work.

NetWare provides comprehensive support at both levels. This section examines the desktop operating systems that NetWare supports. The next section covers the LAN standards that can be used to build department- and enterprise-wide networks.

Workstation Environments

NetWare v3.11 provides full client support for each of the major desktop operating systems, including DOS, OS/2, Macintosh, and UNIX workstations. Each operating system is given transparent access to NetWare, maintaining its own particular model of interaction with resources on the network. With DOS, a network drive is mapped to another drive letter and DOS users can perform the familar DOS operations on the network drive as if it were a local resource. Similarly, Macintosh users see a NetWare volume as an icon on the desktop. All the familar operations of manipulating files and folders are seamlessly extended to the network.

This section examines the major desktop operating systems (DOS, OS/2, Macintosh, and UNIX) and their support in the NetWare operating system.

DOS

The most common workstation on a NetWare LAN runs the DOS operating system. DOS was developed by Microsoft. for use with the original IBM PC computer. Despite rather serious limitations with many aspects of its resource management, DOS remains an extremely popular operating system for use with Intel-based microcomputers.

DOS workstations can be run by using the Open Data Link Interface architecture. If ODI is used, the workstation can load multiple protocol stacks and use them with a single LAN adapter card. The IPX/SPX protocol stack (IPXODI.COM), for example, can be loaded along with the TCP/IP protocol stack (TCPIP.EXE). The user at the DOS workstation can then access NetWare file servers through the NetWare Shell while simultaneously accessing a UNIX host, using the Novell LAN Workplace for DOS product.

When you use ODI, the Link Support Layer (LSL.COM) must be loaded on the workstation first, followed by the LAN adapter driver (NE2000.COM, for example). A special ODI version of the IPX/SPX protocol stack is then loaded (IPXODI.COM), followed by the NetWare Shell program (NETx.COM, NETX.COM, XMSNETX.EXE, or EMSNETX.EXE).

If the user decides not to use ODI, an IPX.COM must be generated for the workstation, using the WSGEN program. This driver must be loaded before the NetWare Shell is loaded on the workstation.

Applications programs make resource-management requests from DOS by packaging the request in a structure and invoking an interrupt (Int 21h) on the computer. The NetWare Shell on the DOS workstation works by monitoring Int 21h and deciding whether the request refers to a resource on the workstation or to one somewhere on the network. If the request can be serviced locally, the shell passes the request through to DOS, which handles it normally.

If the request is for a network resource, such as opening a file on a NetWare server, the shell packages the request in an NCP packet and sends it to the proper server. The shell accepts the response from the server and returns the result to the application as if the request were serviced locally.

In addition to using the NetWare Shell, applications programs can use either the NetBIOS or Named Pipes API for interprocess communication. NetBIOS is discussed in an earlier section. For Named Pipes, NetWare provides a terminate-and-stay resident (TSR) program that provides client support. This software can be used to create a session between the DOS client and an OS/2 Named Pipes server on the network. (To use Named Pipes, the DOS workstation must be running DOS v3.1 or higher.)

OS/2

Codeveloped by IBM and Microsoft as a powerful desktop operating system for 80286 (and higher) computers, OS/2 features a multitasking, protected-mode operation capable of directly addressing memory greater than DOS' 640K limitation.

Novell NetWare v2.15c and above (including NetWare v2.2 and v3.11) support client workstations running OS/2 Standard and Extended Editions, version 1.2 and higher. The OS/2 client is provided using the NetWare Requester for OS/2, which is implemented as a set of Dynamic Link Libraries (DLLs) installed on the OS/2 workstation. By using the NetWare Requester for OS/2, users on OS/2 workstations can have full access to NetWare servers on the network.

The NetWare Requester for OS/2 provides the OS/2 workstation with support for Named Pipes Interprocess Communication (IPC), the NetBIOS interface, network spooling and printing, and Novell's IPX and SPX protocols. The NetWare Requester for OS/2 uses the NetWare Core Protocol to request services from the file server. NCP, in turn, relies on IPX to deliver the packet from the OS/2 workstation to the NetWare file server.

Because of the OS/2 Requester, several local-area network technologies (including ARCnet, Ethernet, IBM PC Network, and token ring) can be used to attach the workstation to the network.

OS/2 workstations require their own versions of the NetWare utility programs to support OS/2 when it is running in its native protected mode. The OS/2 Requester software includes OS/2 versions of several important NetWare management utilities, including SYSCON, PCONSOLE, FILER, SALVAGE, and VOLINFO, among many others.

By using the High Performance File System (HPFS), OS/2 can support file names longer than the eight-character limit imposed by DOS. Before HPFS files can be stored on a NetWare v3.11 file server, the OS/2 name space must be added to any volumes that will contain HPFS files.

The OS/2 workstation uses two types of programs to communicate with the NetWare LAN: *device drivers* and *daemons*. These device drivers and daemons are specified in the CONFIG.SYS file and must be loaded in particular order to function correctly. The OS/2 Requester uses the NetWare Link Support Layer (LSL.SYS) to provide hardware independence for the protocol stacks running on the OS/2 workstation.

The following small section of code, taken from a CONFIG.SYS file on an OS/2 workstation, illustrates how device drivers and daemons are loaded:

```
DEVICE=C:\NETWARE\LSL.SYS
RUN=C:\NETWARE\DDAEMON.EXE
DEVICE=C:\NETWARE\TOKEN.SYS
DEVICE=C:\NETWARE\ROUTE.SYS
DEVICE=C:\NETWARE\IPX.SYS
```

Settings for the OS/2 Requester can be modified in the NET.CFG file. This ASCII file enables the user to specify parameters for the following:

- ❖ Link driver
- ❖ Link support
- ❖ IPX and SPX protocol stacks
- ❖ NetWare Requester
- ❖ NetBIOS
- ❖ IBM Token-Ring source-route driver
- ❖ NetWare spooler
- ❖ Named pipes

The maximum number of concurrently open sockets can be configured from nine to 128 for the IPX protocol. (The default number is 32.) The NetWare Requester uses nine sockets, and each connection to a NetWare file server requires three additional sockets. The amount of memory used by the IPX router can also be configured in the NET.CFG file.

Several parameters are available to govern SPX connections made using the NetWare OS/2 Requester. By default, the Requester can support 16 concurrent SPX connections; this can be changed to allow from eight to 256 SPX connections. Additionally, three timeout values used by SPX can be adjusted. Because SPX provides a reliable data stream, it relies on acknowledgments from the destination station to know that the packet was delivered. Each of the timeout parameters is measured in milliseconds (ms).

The "abort" timeout determines how long SPX will wait to receive an acknowledgment from the destination before it decides that the connection is dead and closes it. The "verify" timeout is the time waited before explicitly asking for an acknowledgment to verify that the connection is still alive. Finally, the "listen" timeout is the time SPX expects to receive a packet from the destination.

Macintosh

NetWare enables Apple Macintosh workstations to be fully integrated into the NetWare enterprise network and provides the full set of file-sharing, print, and routing services for Macintoshes that are attached to the NetWare LAN. The software that provides these services is available in an optional product from Novell, called NetWare for Macintosh v3.01. NetWare for Macintosh implements the AppleTalk protocol stack as well as the AppleTalk router on a NetWare file server. It also includes software for the client Macintosh workstation, enabling a user to perform basic NetWare functions, such as examining the NetWare print queues and setting NetWare rights for a file, directory, or volume.

NetWare for Macintosh uses the AppleTalk Filing Protocol (AFP) as the high-level service protocol for handling requests from the file server. (This is the protocol Apple uses with its AppleShare file-server product.) Because this is the native protocol used by the Macintosh, access to the NetWare file server is completely transparent to the Macintosh user. He or she uses the AppleShare Workstation software and sees the NetWare server as just another AppleShare server on the Mac desktop. They use the familiar Chooser desk accessory to select the NetWare file server from the list of available servers on the network.

NetWare for Macintosh v3.01 is fully compliant with the AppleTalk Phase I and Phase II specifications. It also implements the AppleTalk Filing Protocol v2.0. The package includes several NetWare Loadable Modules, which are used to implement the AppleTalk protocol stack, the AppleTalk Filing Protocol, the AppleTalk Print Server, and the AppleTalk administrative console utility.

The product also implements a full AppleTalk router on the NetWare file server. An AppleTalk router enables Macintosh workstations and printers located on different networks to communicate with each other. It routes AppleTalk packets from one network to another, according to the destination address in the packet.

A collection of two or more AppleTalk networks connected to each other by means of routers is known as an AppleTalk internet. When the AppleTalk router on the NetWare server is installed and configured correctly, Macintosh workstations on several attached LANs are able to access NetWare file and print services from the server (see fig. 8.4).

Because NetWare v3.11 has an internal network (in addition to the physical network to which it is attached by using LAN adapters), the AppleTalk router must be configured on the server, even if the Macintosh workstations are attached to the same LAN as the file server. Although the internal network is a completely logical network (with no physical connections), the AppleTalk router treats it as a distinct network with its own AppleTalk network number and zone name.

AppleTalk supports three major physical and data-link protocols: LocalTalk, EtherTalk (version 1.0 and 2.0), and TokenTalk. Support for LocalTalk, which is built into every Macintosh, enables Macintoshes to be networked almost directly out of the box. EtherTalk is Apple's implementation of Ethernet, and TokenTalk implements a token-ring network. NetWare for Macintosh v3.01 supports each of these protocols.

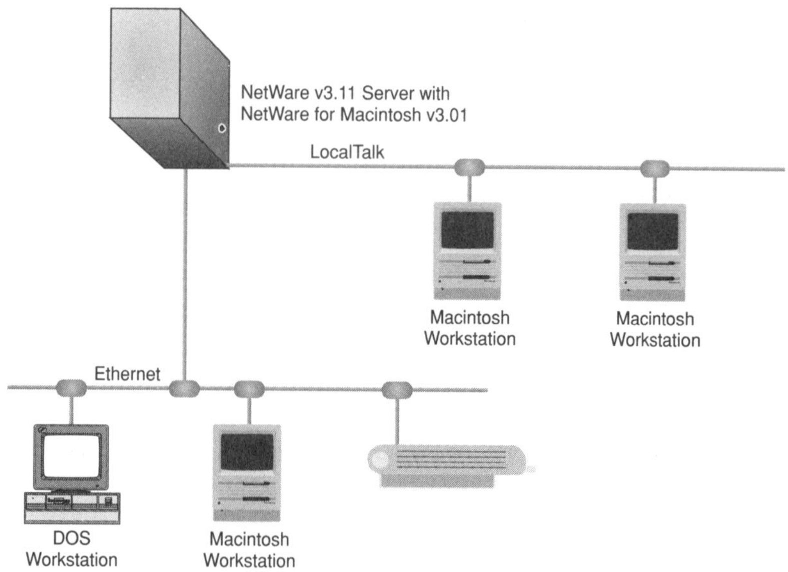

Figure 8.4:
NetWare Macintosh connectivity.

The AppleTalk Print Services (ATPS) software is used to create a NetWare print queue on the file server. Each ATPS print queue can then be configured to have the ATPS send print jobs to an Apple LaserWriter or ImageWriter printer, using the AppleTalk protocols. Both DOS and Macintosh workstations on the network can use the Apple printers.

The Macintosh file-naming system is significantly different from the one used by DOS. Macintosh file names can be as many as 32 characters long, with embedded spaces. Each file is composed of two forks (a resource fork and a data fork). To support this naming system, the Macintosh name space must be added to every volume on the NetWare server that will store Macintosh files. The software to support the Macintosh name space is included with NetWare v3.11.

UNIX

NetWare integrates UNIX workstations with the NetWare v3.11 file server, using the NetWare NFS software. NFS, the Network File System developed by Sun Microsystems, has become a standard distributed file system. By using NetWare NFS, a UNIX workstation can share files and access NetWare printers as well as DOS, OS/2, and Macintosh workstations on the network.

NetWare NFS uses the User Datagram Protocol (UDP), which is part of the TCP/IP protocol stack bundled with NetWare v3.11. NetWare NFS supports the following services:

- Network File System (NFS) version 2, which permits file sharing on the NetWare server
- External Data Representation (XDR), which implements a presentation-layer transfer syntax

- Mount Protocol, which enables a UNIX client to mount the NetWare file system (directory)
- Line Printer Daemon (LPD), which enables a UNIX client to access NetWare v3.11 print queues and printers
- File Transfer Protocol (FTP), which enables file exchange by using the FTP protocol
- LOCKD, which provides the UNIX record-locking facility

Using NetWare NFS, UNIX clients gain several additional features, including NetWare's high-performance file services, system-fault tolerance, and improved security. Because NetWare runs on industry standard microcomputers, the cost of providing a high-performance UNIX server is significantly lower when you use NetWare NFS.

NetWare NFS includes full support for the UNIX file-naming conventions through the use of a NetWare Loadable Module for the UNIX name space. This NLM is loaded on any file server that will export file systems (directories) to a UNIX client. The UNIX client uses the familar `mount` command to access the remote file system on the NetWare server.

Printing is equally straightforward. UNIX users invoke the `lpr` command to print to a NetWare printer, `lpq` to examine a NetWare printer queue, and `lprm` to remove an entry from the printer queue.

The NetWare file server controls which directories may be mounted by UNIX clients by using the EXPORTS file in the SYS:ETC directory. Only directories listed in this file may be mounted. Similarly, the list of trusted hosts allowed to mount the file system can be specified. If no hosts are explicitly listed as trusted, any host can access the file system.

NetWare NFS also enables the creation of an association between the UNIX user and a NetWare user account. This association enables NetWare to better monitor who is using which resources on the NetWare server. Similarly, UNIX groups may be associated with NetWare groups. These user and group associations are stored in the NFSUSERS and NFSGROUP files, respectively. Both of these files are located in the SYS:ETC directory.

NetWare NFS includes a C-Worthy menu-driven style NetWare Loadable Module (NLM) that is called NFSADMIN. This program enables the supervisor to administer NFS on the NetWare file server.

Examining LAN Standards

This section examines the four most popular local-area network standards used to connect network devices together to form a NetWare internetwork: Ethernet, token ring, ARCnet, and LocalTalk.

Ethernet

Ethernet is the most popular and appropriate choice for workgroup and departmental local area networks because of its relative ease of installation and maintenance and its cost-effectiveness. NetWare provides extensive support for Ethernet, which was described in detail in Chapter 4.

Novell supports Ethernet with a popular line of cards, now manufactured by Eagle Technology. The NE1000, NE2000, and NE/2 Ethernet cards are appropriate for the NetWare environment and are supported in many other software environments.

Token Ring

NetWare supports the IEEE 802.5 (IBM Token Ring) local area network system. The primary token-ring cards supported by Novell are the various token-ring adapters manufactured by IBM and others. The token ring can use IBM Type 1 and IBM Type 2 cables, which are 150-ohm shielded twisted-pair cables, and recently unshielded twisted-pair cabling. It supports two data-transmission rates; 4Mbps and 16Mbps. Type 1 and 2 cabling can support up to 260 stations, attached to a single ring.

Token ring uses a method called *source routing* to forward NetWare packets. Novell supplies the drivers ROUTE.NLM and ROUTE.COM to enable servers and workstations to use source routing on a token-ring network. ROUTE.COM is an ODI driver and must be used on ODI workstations. Non-ODI workstations can create a dedicated IPX driver using the WSGEN program.

ARCnet

ARCnet was developed by the Datapoint Corporation in 1977, and it still has a very large installed base as a cabling system for NetWare LANs. It quickly gained popularity among large IBM sites because it uses RG-62 coax cable, which is the cabling used to attach IBM 3270 terminals to IBM mainframes. The large investment that corporations made in wiring and training made ARCnet a natural choice for building local area networks.

ARCnet is marketed by Novell as RX-Net. Novell markets the Standard Microsystems Corporation PC120 and PS110 as Rx-Net II and Rx-NET/2, respectively.

ARCnet has been extended to use twisted pair and fiber optic cabling. The original speed of 2.5Mbps has also been increased to 20Mbps and 100Mbps with fiber optic cables. ARCnet uses a token bus system for media access, but this system is not the same as the one specified in the IEEE 802.4 Token Bus.

Unlike Ethernet and token ring, ARCnet station addresses must be selected by setting jumpers on the network adapter. The network is wired as a star by attaching the station to active and passive hubs on the network.

LocalTalk

LocalTalk is the network system built into every Macintosh computer. It has a relatively slow data-transfer rate of 230.4Kbps; it uses a Carrier Sense Multiple Access with Collision Avoidance system for media access. The network is physically arranged as a bus and the cabling used is shielded twisted pair.

ODI-compatible drivers are available to attach a NetWare file server to a LocalTalk network. NetWare for Macintosh v3.01 provides client and NetWare server software, enabling Apple Macintosh computers and printers on a LocalTalk LAN to be internetworked with a NetWare LAN.

Providing Asynchronous Communication Support

Novell provides a set of products to support asynchronous communications. This section examines the NetWare Asynchronous Communications Server (NACS), the NetWare Asynchronous Remote Router (NARR), and the NetWare Access Server (NAS).

The Asynchronous Communications Server enables modems to be shared among multiple workstations on the network. The Asynchronous Remote Router enables wide area networks to be created by linking NetWare LANs together using voice-grade telephone lines. The Access Server also enables remote workstations to dial into a NetWare LAN and to use the resources on the LAN as if the station were local.

NetWare Asynchronous Communications Server (NACS)

The NetWare Asynchronous Communications Server (NACS) enables modems to become shared-network resources, in much the same way that hard disks and printers can be shared by file and print servers. This enables client workstations that are attached to a NetWare LAN to have access to remote communications through modems attached to the Asynchronous Communications Server. By using the NACS, workstation clients can be given access to fast and expensive modems on a as-needed basis, while facilitating the management and maintenance of the modems because they are attached to a central server.

The client workstations and the communications server may be attached to any local area network technology and topology that NetWare itself supports, including Ethernet, token ring, ARCnet, and others. NACS require NetWare v2.0a and higher, including NetWare v2.2 and v3.11, to be running on the network. In addition, the Asynchronous Communications Server and the client workstation are both required to be running DOS 3.1 or above.

Each Asynchronous Communications Server can have up to 16 connections active at any time. In addition, multiple NACS can be installed on a single NetWare LAN, enabling any number of modems to be supported, depending on the requirements. Each asynchronous line can support speeds up to 19.2Kbps.

NACS requires an IBM PC, AT, or compatible computer to run the asynchronous communications software. The PC must be a dedicated—it must only be running the NACS software. The memory required to run the NACS software is 256K, which enables a variety of personal computers to be used as a communications server.

To support multiple simultaneous asynchronous connections, the NetWare Wide Area Network Interface Module+ (WNIM+) communications adapter can be used. These boards fit in a regular Industry Standard Architecture (ISA) slot in the server, and can have up to four ports each. A maximum of four WNIM+ adapters may be used in a NACS, enabling a maximum of 16 serial ports per communications server. The connections from the serial port to the modem can be made by using standard RS-232 cables.

The NetWare Asynchronous Communications Server is made up of two parts: one on the communications server and the other on the client workstations on the network. On the server, a program called the NACS Control Program is executed. This program performs all the duties required to manage and control the serial ports on the server and the connections being used by client workstations.

The client workstation runs the NetWare Asynchronous Interface (NASI), which provides an Application Programmer Interface (API) that enables developers to build applications that can access the ports on the communications server through the NACS Control Program. The application, by using the NASI interface, manages the communications session at the client end, generally providing an interface to a user. A typical example is a terminal-emulation program that can provide access to a remote computer.

Many popular communication applications have been written to the NASI interface and this shared modem environment.

NACS provides an additional service to clients who want to communicate by using a modem attached to a server. NACS enables the Supervisor to assign a name to each communications server and to the attached modems. Following this, a user can establish a connection by name, without regard to where the modem is physically located on the network. The system that provides this naming system is called the Distributed Asynchronous Name Service.

To manage the name service, NACS includes a menu-driven utility program that enables the Supervisor to create and maintain the Distributed Asynchronous Name Service and establish a security scheme that prevents unauthorized access to communications resources.

NetWare Asynchronous Remote Router (NARR)

The NetWare Asynchronous Remote Router enables NetWare networks to be connected together by using regular, voice-grade asynchronous lines to form a WAN. Several lines may be used to interconnect the remote networks, each using asynchronous modems at speeds up to 9600bps. The Asynchronous Remote Router works with any LAN topology that NetWare supports.

Two options exist for configuring the asynchronous router between the NetWare networks: internal and external. *Internal routers* run on the NetWare file server. For this configuration, NetWare v2.1x to v2.2 must be used as the network operating system on the server. Using an internal router has the advantage of not requiring another computer to serve the role of the router (it may be practical in a small office or workgroup environment). However, the extra work of routing packets between networks adds overhead to the server and can adversely affect other file-server operations. This is especially true if the data rate used over the asynchronous connection is greater than 1200bps.

When an internal router is used with a file server, one or two WNIM+ adapters must be used to provide the asynchronous ports that the modems will be attached to. As mentioned in the section above, each WNIM+ adapter has four asynchronous ports, so an internal router can support a maximum of eight communications lines for remote routing.

The other option is to use an *external router*. This option requires a separate PC, XT, or AT-compatible computer running DOS 3.1 or higher. Although the older XT-class computers can be used, a 286- or 386-based system is recommended for moderate to heavy traffic. External routers can run as dedicated routers or in a non-dedicated mode.

An external router can use built-in serial communications ports (COM1 or COM2), or it can use one or two installed WNIM+ adapters. The COMx ports support a maximum data rate of 2400bps; the WNIM+ adapters can operate at speeds up to 9600bps. As before, the WNIM+ boards have four communication ports each, which enable a maximum of eight lines to be attached to an external asynchronous router.

Because the NetWare Asynchronous Remote Router is simply a packet router that operates over asynchronous communication lines, multiple users can access remote network resources as if the resources were local. User and resource authorizations are provided in a consistent manner by the regular NetWare security features. The low cost of the equipment required, in combination with the familiar model for user interaction, makes the asynchronous router suitable for the occasional transfer of files and limited access to remote hosts and electronic mail.

NetWare Access Server

The NetWare Access Server v1.2 enables users to establish a communications connection to the access server and to use the resources on the NetWare LAN. The users may be *local*, meaning that they have a immediate LAN connection to the access server, or they may be *remote* (no direct connection). Remote users can connect to the NetWare Access Server by asynchronous or X.25 Public Data Network (PDN) connections.

Access server users can use an IBM PC, a Macintosh, or an ASCII terminal to log into a NetWare server and get access to the network. In each case, the access server uses the "Control Program" to create a virtual machine for the calling client. Within this virtual machine, the calling station can run DOS applications as if it were a DOS workstation directly connected to the LAN. Each access server can accommodate 16 concurrent users. The network sessions inside the virtual machines are multiplexed over the LAN adapter in the access server.

Although this service is valuable for remote stations, local stations can also take advantage of this service. For example, a Macintosh workstation that is directly connected to the access server, by means of the LAN, can use the virtual DOS machine created in the access server to run DOS programs on the network. Because the access server supports the running of expanded-memory applications with a virtual machine, a DOS PC with limited memory can use a larger virtual DOS machine to run large programs.

The NetWare Access Server v1.2 requires a 80386 or 80486 PC to function as the access server. The computer should have a base memory of 1M, with an additional 850K for each virtual machine session that the server wants to simultaneously support. If the applications that run on the server will require expanded memory, this extra requirement should be factored into the memory needs. The access server itself requires DOS 3.1 or higher to run the software; it can only be attached to networks running NetWare v2.15c or higher (including NetWare v2.2 and v3.11).

Users on the client workstations use a program called OnLAN to attach to the access server. The OnLAN/PC program is available for IBM PC computers and requires DOS 3.1 and 512K of memory to run. The program uses the familiar NetWare C-Worthy menu-driven style, and it provides support for serial (asynchronous), direct, network (IPX), and NASI connections.

Similarly, the version for the Macintosh family of computers is called OnLAN/Mac; it requires System 6.x or higher to run. OnLAN/Mac provides the user with the familiar Macintosh user interface.

The OnLAN software is included with the NetWare Access Server v1.2, and it can be duplicated, without restriction, for use with the server.

In addition to running applications on the network, the NetWare Access Server enables files to be transferred, in either direction, between the client computer and the NetWare file servers attached to the access server. Files can be printed on a network printer or on a printer attached to the local client workstation. The client workstation can also establish host access on the network by using NetWare LAN Workplace for DOS (for TCP/IP support to UNIX hosts) and NetWare 3270 LAN Workstation (for IBM mainframe host access).

Remote users have two options for connecting to the NetWare Access Server. The first is through standard voice-grade telephone lines and the second is through an X.25 PDN. The NetWare Access Server supports over 50 modems and can function at speeds up to 38.4Kbps. In order to use an X.25 packet network, the remote station and the access server must have an X.25 communications adapter and the corresponding driver software.

The NetWare Access Server v1.2 can be administered from several locations, including from the main console of the access server itself, or from any local or remote PC or Macintosh attached to the access server.

The access server enables the administrator to set up user accounts and requires the user to supply a password when connecting to the server. If extra security is required, the NetWare Access Server provides a call-back feature that calls the user back at a prearranged number. This feature greatly reduces the chance of an unauthorized connection to the access server because the call-back number restricts the location of the remote workstation.

The administrator is also able to monitor the use of the access server, along with recording and viewing an audit file of all activities on the server. The administrator is able to step in and interact with any user session on the server, in addition to resetting a port or user session if necessary.

Summary

This chapter showed you the elements of the IPX/SPX protocol stack and how the NetWare shell implements the NCP protocol that controls the interaction between the file server and a workstation. The Open DataLink Interface has also been described, which decouples the protocol stack from the LAN adapter. The NetBios and TCP/IP protocols were discussed, and the NetWare protocol stack was placed in the context of the OSI Reference Model. You also learned about local area network support, including the workstations supported, the LAN standards, and asynchronous communications.

Topics covered in this chapter:
Looking at LAN Manager 2.1
Learning LAN Manager Basics

Chapter 9

Microsoft LAN Manager

Since the introduction of the IBM Personal Computer in 1981, microcomputer technology has experienced growth that has astounded even the most visionary of computer experts. More computers are in use, a higher percentage of these computers are networked, and PCs and networks have greatly expanded their capabilities and services.

This phenomenal growth makes available to the enterprise networker resources and computing techniques that were not thought practical (or even possible) as little as three years ago. Beginning in the mid-1980s, network technology produced stable platforms for file and printer sharing. The lack of computing power made it impossible to use the file server for anything but the most basic network tasks. In recounting the development of local area networks, Chapter 1 explained that the earliest LANs were little more than devices for sharing disk space on a large, central storage device. Gradually, LAN servers evolved to provide more sophisticated file services. Servers, however, remained primarily devices for sharing files.

As the microcomputer became more powerful, it became possible to place more demands on the file server CPU. This made possible one of the fundamental concepts of the LAN Manager operating system's design—client-server computing. Workstations are the clients; the file servers are the servers. Client-server computing enables some tasks to be processed on the client and some on the server. Computing done at the workstation (client) is called *front-end computing*, and computing performed at the server is called *back-end processing*.

The advantages of client-server computing are best illustrated by first examining how things work when the primary function of the server is to provide file services to remote clients. If a workstation (client) needs to sort a remote database, every record in the database file must travel over the network cable from the file server to the workstation. Transferring large amounts of data through a network can create a bottleneck; sorting through the network is often slower than sorting files that reside on the PC's local hard drive.i

In client-server technology, the workstation gives a command to the file server to sort the file. The file server then performs the requested sort and transmits only the result back to the client workstation. Because the sort takes place on the file server, the need to pass the entire database over the slow network cable is eliminated.

The evolution of the microcomputer operating system from DOS to OS/2 plays an important role in client-server computing because it provides the preemptive multitasking environment that is necessary to handle multiple client requests on the file server.

Structured Query Language (SQL) standardizes the command interface between programs that run on a workstation and a master database that runs on a database server. SQL is the most frequently used interface for developing client-server database applications on LANs. Microsoft LAN Manager takes advantage of client-server computing as the basis for SQL computing by using the Microsoft SQL Server, which is described later in this chapter.

Another feature of LAN Manager's design is the adherence to standards. Microsoft (and IBM) designed OS/2 as the successor to the standard DOS operating system. OS/2 is not widely accepted as a desktop computer operating system. This is due primarily to the cost of hardware at its inception and the small number of users who run more than one program at a time. When OS/2 was introduced, "downsizing" from mainframes was not a commonly accepted strategy in corporate networking. Microsoft found great success with its later Windows programs, which slowly introduced the feel of OS/2 to DOS users.

Microsoft's OS/2 and LAN Manager combine to make a powerful full-featured network operating system. The next section presents some background information and describes the general nature of OS/2 LAN Manager. Later sections of this chapter describe the features most relevant to the enterprise network. (At the time of this writing, LAN Manager is designed to run with OS/2 version 1.3. If you are using the newer version 2.0, you notice some differences.)

Looking at LAN Manager 2.1

Microsoft released DOS Version 3.1 in July of 1984. This version of DOS supports a network redirector that uses the Server Message Protocol Block (SMB) and NetBIOS to access files on remote computers. These elements of the redirector formed the basis for the first IBM, 3Com, and Microsoft networks. Soon after the release of DOS 3.1, IBM released the Personal Computer Local Area Network Program or PC-LAN. Microsoft released its own version of a network operating system, Microsoft Networks (MS-NET) several months after IBM. The two systems are similar and can work together on the same network.

As hardware technology evolved with the 80286 processor chip, Microsoft initiated a project to develop an operating system that fully supports the new capabilities of the 80286. The product, developed jointly by IBM and Microsoft, became what is now known as OS/2.

Design Philosophy

The foundation of Microsoft's network operating system is OS/2. A number of features significant in a networking environment are either absent from or clumsily handled by DOS. OS/2 overcomes DOS short comings in the following areas:

- Data security
- File-sharing
- Multitasking
- Common device drivers
- File-size limits
- Limits on the total number of files
- Caching of disk data
- Virtual memory
- Memory protection

A number of new features were added to OS/2 to enhance not only network operation, but overall performance of the operating system. Foremost among these changes is a faster file system, a common set of device drivers, a graphical user interface (GUI), and utilization of the enhanced hardware instructions found only in the Intel 80286 and 80386 processor chips.

OS/2

A primary philosophy of OS/2 system operation is the premise that tasks appear to run concurrently. Remember, there is only one CPU processor chip, so the various tasks must ultimately be scheduled on the CPU one-by-one. These tasks access a common set of device drivers and operating system parameters, specified in the CONFIG.SYS file. The more significant operating system functions or parameters specified in the OS/2 CONFIG.SYS file are listed below:

- Protected-mode shell program
- Location of the OS/2 command interpreter
- Location of dynamic-link libraries
- Program-search path
- Data-search path
- Help and command reference
- Disk-cache size
- Virtual-memory parameters
- DOS parameters
- Device drivers
- Privileged instruction permission
- Multitasking parameters

The network technician must be especially aware of several features that are key to the operation of enterprise network. Network adapter card device drivers are specified with the DEVICE parameter. The card drivers in a typical LAN Manager server CONFIG.SYS file are listed below:

```
REM === LANMAN 2.1 === DO NOT MODIFY BETWEEN THESE LINES ===
DEVICE=C:\LANMAN\DRIVERS\PROTOMAN\PROTMAN.OS2 /I:C:\LANMAN
DEVICE=C:\LANMAN\DIRVERS\EHTERNET\ELNKII\ILNKII.OS2
DEVICE=C:\LANMAN\DRIVERS\PROTOCOL\NETBEUI\NETBEUI.OS2
DEVICE\C:\LANMAN\NETPROB\RDRHELP.SYS
IFS=C:\LANMAN\NETPROG\NETWKSTA.SYS /I:C:\LANMAN
REM ==== LANMAN 2.1 === DO NOT MODIFY BETWEEN THESE LINES ==
```

The device-driver specifications are defined in more detail in a later section on NDIS device drivers and in the sections on the various communication protocols supported by LAN Manager.

Microsoft created a new method of specifying different file-handling systems when the OS/2 operating system is initialized. This feature is called the Installable File System, or IFS, and it is specified in the CONFIG.SYS file. IFS enables the OS/2 computer to specify what file system(s) it is using. DOS permits the use of only one file system, the File Allocation Table (FAT) system. OS/2 can use the FAT system to maintain compatibility with DOS, or it can use other systems, such as the High Performance File System (HPFS). HPFS was designed for OS/2 and LAN Manager and provides for large files (theoretically, 7.68 gigabytes); more files on a disk than DOS; local security; fast directory searches; and fast access to the data.

Multiple file systems can run on the same computer. This capability is most convenient when linking dissimilar computer file systems—such as IBM compatible FAT and Apple Computer's Apple File Protocol (AFP) as well as network transports which install like FSDs—together on a LAN Manager file server.

Programs executed on a computer running OS/2 are called *tasks* or *processes*. Processes have their own memory and are executed by spawning *threads of execution*. Unlike DOS, in which execution begins at one point in the code and continues line-by-line, an OS/2 program can have many points in its code executing simultaneously. Processes can spawn multiple threads, threads can spawn threads, and processes can spawn other processes. Threads share the CPU and execute in a round-robin fashion, each having a time-slice in which to run. Parameters in the CONFIG.SYS file dictate the maximum number of threads that can exist at one time; control the automatic adjustment of the priority level of certain types of tasks; and set the minimum time-slice available to a thread, the maximum amount of waiting time for a task, and a maximum number of threads for all processes running on the file server.

OS/2 can create a virtual DOS machine and run programs in DOS mode. Two parameters in the CONFIG.SYS file control the enabling of the DOS mode feature and the amount of memory set aside for DOS mode. DOS mode should be disabled on all LAN Manager file servers. When you switch to DOS mode on an OS/2 computer, the processing of all tasks but the DOS task is suspended.

Learning LAN Manager Basics

Installing LAN Manager is a simple and straightforward process controlled by the SETUP program. Basic parameters are set automatically when LAN Manager is installed. LAN Manager, like OS/2, is a parameter driven program. Four files, the LANMAN.INI, PROTOCOL.INI, SETUP.INI, and SERVER.PRO contain these parameters. A brief description of these files and their contents is listed below:

SETUP.INI	Contains historical values for the parameters input into the SETUP program; used as default when the SETUP program is rerun.
PROTOCL.INI	Contains parameters necessary for the adapter card drivers and Protocol Manager; built by the SETUP program.
LANMAN.INI	Created at installation by the SETUP program; contains network operating parameters for LAN Manager.
SRVAUTO.PRO	Contains history of resources shared on the network; loaded when the SERVER Service is started. (Automatically reshares them.)

Note that, in the complex operating environment of an enterprise network, it is often necessary to modify the default parameters manually.

OS/2 must be installed on the LAN Manager server prior to the installation of LAN Manager itself. This is done automatically by the SETUP program. The 2.1 Version of LAN Manager includes a server version of OS/2.

After the OS/2 and LAN Manager programs have been installed, the various "services" of LAN Manager can be started. This usually is done automatically when the server is powered up, but can be done manually, starting the services one at a time.

Network Administration

The most common method of network administration is a pull-down menu-driven program called NET ADMIN. After initiating NET ADMIN from a command prompt, a master menu appears that displays all servers on the network and the user's own workstation. From this menu, the user can access any server on the network and administer it from this menu, as long as the user has administration rights on that server. You can hide a server from the NET ADMIN menu screen by specifying it as a hidden server at the time of server installation. NET ADMIN must be run from an OS/2 workstation or a file server.

LAN Manager 2.1's default server-administration system runs under the OS/2 Presentation Manager. There is, however, a new Windows administration tool called WINADMIN. (Because it is Windows, it does not run on the OS/2 machine. It is for remote administration from a Windows client.) The workstation's program NET.EXE is the program that contains the user interface. Notice that any commands that are available from the graphical screen are also available from the OS/2 command prompt.

LAN Manager file servers can be administered from the command line by typing certain specific commands and parameters. This method is generally used when OS/2-based computers are not available. Another method of administration permits the network administrator to enter a command mode of operation at a workstation and to control resources of the server, as if he were at the server itself.

Security

Microsoft LAN Manager has two ways to implement security on the network: share and user-level security. Under *share level security,* network users can access shared network resources, based on a password assigned to shared resources on a resource-by-resource basis. This method is seldom used because it is difficult to administer and requires the tracking of many passwords. The most common way to implement security on a LAN Manager network is through user passwords and assigned rights for individual users. This is called *user-level security.*

Security can be administered for a number of servers on an enterprise-wide network by using *domains*. A particular server is designated as a *domain controller* and provides user password information to the entire domain. Domain security is available only when user security is implemented. Network users do not log on to a particular server, they log on to the domain. A second server is designated as a backup domain controller to be used in the event that the regular domain controller malfunctions. Domain security information is shared with all servers on a domain. The LAN Manager operating system automatically distributes the security information to all the servers in a domain.

Users can be administered in groups. Rights and permissions are granted to the group and apply automatically to all members of the group.

At initial logon to the network, a series of commands from a script file can be executed automatically. Usually, this initializes drive settings and initiates menus. Users running Windows on their local workstations use the facilities of that system to log on and access network resources.

Microsoft has developed sophisticated network-installation tools for most of their products. With very little effort, Windows, Excel, and Word can be installed on a workstation from a single source on the server. This makes workstation setup simple and provides a uniform source for the programs.

NDIS Defined

Network Device Interface Specification (NDIS) is a set of standards for OS/2 and DOS programs that control network adapter cards or implement transport protocols. Jointly developed by 3Com and Microsoft, NDIS is one of the cornerstones of Microsoft's commitment to establish and utilize industry-wide standards.

The network adapter card is driven by a program called a Media Access Control (MAC) driver, which is stored in a ROM on the network card. This driver is a set of instructions that serializes the network packets and translates them into the electrical specs needed to control Ethernet, token ring, or ArcNET network adapter cards.

The NDIS standard is implemented at the data-link layer of the OSI reference model. In addition to following the NDIS rules, the MAC drivers must adhere to the IEEE 802.3 or 802.5 rules for Ethernet or token ring, respectively, or to the ArcNET conventions from Datapoint.

Protocols implemented on the LAN Manager operating system under NDIS utilize MAC drivers to communicate with the physical network adapter card. The protocols themselves are the programs or protocol drivers that implement TCP/IP, IPX, XNS, NetBEUI, or other such network protocols and must follow the rules and conventions of those protocols. Protocol drivers also operate at the Data Link level of the OSI Reference Model, but are a step above the MAC drivers. Protocol drivers conform to the IEEE 802.2 rules and conventions.

In the past, network adapter cards were typically controlled by a single program containing both the MAC and the protocol drivers. This type of program is termed a *monolithic driver.* Monolithic drivers were usually fast programs that controlled the older, slower hardware on older network adapter cards. As the networking world became more complex, demands were made on the operation of networks that monolithic drivers were unable to meet. In many situations, network designers wanted to run multiple protocols on a single network adapter card. Worse yet, different adapter card manufacturers developed their own implementations of these monolithic MAC and protocol drivers containing slight variations from one another and from standards. These slight programming differences often translated into significant differences in network operation.

NDIS brought more uniformity and flexibility to the implementation of protocol and MAC drivers. Unlike the monolithic drivers, NDIS-compliant protocol drivers are independent of MAC drivers, and enable a common protocol driver to be used on multiple MAC drivers. In practice, this enables Microsoft to use one TCP/IP protocol driver, or one NetBEUI driver with network adapter cards, from a variety of adapter card manufacturers. NDIS also led to increased standardization because Microsoft was able to write and control one protocol driver for all LAN Manager users, regardless of the network adapter card used.

Most elements of network communication are explained by comparison to the OSI Reference Model or the IEEE 802 standards. Figure 9.1 shows how NDIS MAC and protocol drivers fit into the standards of the OSI Reference Model and IEEE 802.X standards.

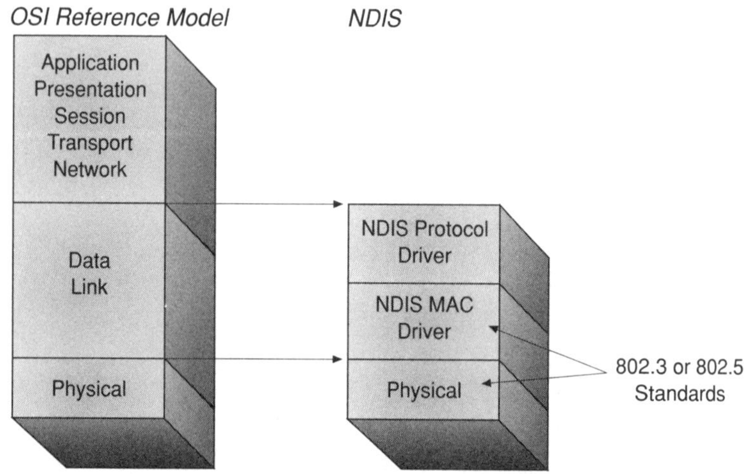

Figure 9.1:
NDIS and the OSI model.

Figure 9.2 shows the use of one NDIS MAC driver by two protocol drivers, compared to the use of two monolithic drivers. The primary benefit of this type of arrangement useing of only one memory-resident MAC driver and one network adapter card.

How NDIS Works

In the LAN Manager environment, NDIS drivers communicate with each other and the LAN Manager operating system through a common set of data parameters, communication commands, and operating commands. These commands and parameters are collectively called *NDIS Primitives*. NDIS drivers record driver status, operating requirements, and capabilities for the LAN Manager operating system and other NDIS drivers to use (by means of NDIS Primitives).

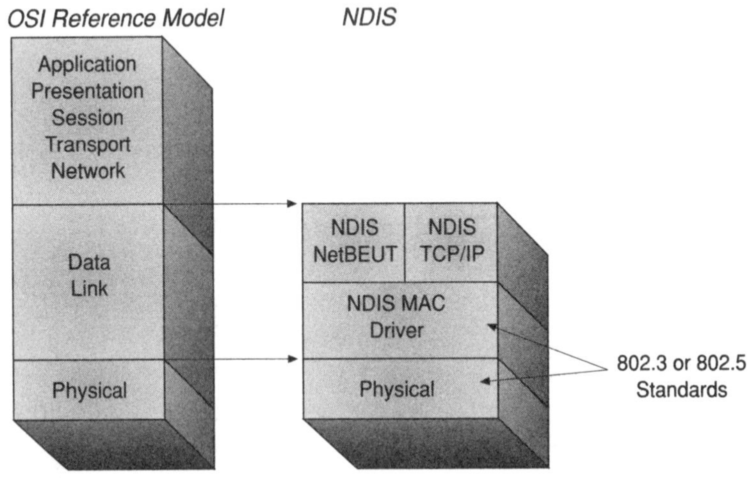

Figure 9.2:
NDIS: Single Protocol, Multiple MACs.

When the LAN Manager server or client computer is powered on or reset, the parameters in the CONFIG.SYS file initiate a program called the *Protocol Manager.* The Protocol Manager has two versions, one for DOS and one for OS/2. The Protocol Manager reads the PROTOCOL.INI file, which is an ASCII data file containing parameters that control the configuration and operation of the Protocol Manager, MAC drivers, and protocol drivers. These parameters vary, depending on the protocol and MAC being used. They are described in the Microsoft LAN Manager Installation and Configuration Guide and they accompany network adapter cards and protocol drivers purchased from third party vendors. The PROTOCOL.INI provides the following two types of information:

- Configuration parameters for individual MAC drivers/cards.

- ❖ Binding statements coupling MAC drivers to transport protocols. (Through these binding statements, LAN Manager gets multiple protocols to talk.)

The SETUP program automatically creates basic default settings for the LAN Manager's standard protocols and MACs when LAN Manager clients or servers are installed. The SETUP program also is used to add additional MAC (for additional network adapter cards) or protocol drivers after the initial installation of LAN Manager.

Parameters that must be entered manually into the PROTOCOL.INI file include simple information, such as Ethernet transceiver type or TCP/IP broadcast address, or complex items (such as the delay before retransmitting a link-level frame). You must be aware of the PROTOCOL.INI file and its contents because in the complex environment of enterprise networking, the PROTOCOL.INI file is most typically modified. Modification of the PROTOCOL.INI file can be performed to tune the network, or modifications may be necessary for the network to function at all.

The first parameter in the PROTOCOL.INI file is the name of the Protocol Manager program itself. In the present version of LAN Manager (version 2.1), the Protocol Manager program is "PROTMAN$." You do not need to specify this parameter now, but its specification might be necessary in the future. An example of a typical PROTOCOL.INI file is the following:

```
[PROTOCOL MANAGER]
   DRIVERNAME = PROTMAN$
[NETBEUI_XIF]
   DRIVERNAME = NETBEUI$
   BINDING = "ELNKII_NIF"
```

```
[ELNKII_NIF]
;protocol.ini section for the 3Com Etherlink II Adapter Card
   IOADDRESS = 0X300
   INTERRUPT = 5
   MAXTRANSMITS = 40
   DRIVERNAME = ELNKII$
   TRANSCEIVER = EXTERNAL
```

Notice that each section is given a name, enclosed in brackets, and identifies a driver by using the *DRIVERNAME* = parameter. In the preceding example, three driver sections are specified: PROTOCOL MANAGER, NETBEUI_XIF, and ELNKII_NIF. NETBEUI_XIF is the name for the section that describes the NetBEUI protocol driver and driver parameters. "XIF" indicates that the described driver is a transport (protocol) driver. The ELNKII_NIF section identifies the driver and set of parameters for the 3Com Etherlink II network adapter card. The other parameters, shown in the preceding PROTOCOL.INI file, are the Base Input/Output address, Interrupt, and transceiver type for the Ethernet adapter card in the [ELNKII_NIF] section.

The following example is a sample of the section from the CONFIG.SYS file used to configure a LAN Manager server:

```
DEVICE = C:\LANMAN\DRIVERS\PROTMAN\PROTMAN.OS2 /I:C:\LANMAN
DEVICE = C:\LANMAN\DRIVERS\ETHERNET\ELNKII\ELNKII.OS2
DEVICE = C:\LANMAN\DRIVERS\PROTOCOL\NETBEUI\NETBEUI.OS2
DEVICE = C:\LANMAN\NETPROG\RDRHELP.SYS
IFS = C:\LANMAN\NETPROG\NETWKSTA.SYS /I:C:\LANMAN
```

The *DEVICE* statements specify device drivers and their location (the same as stand-alone DOS or OS/2). The Protocol Manager is started by OS/2 from the CONFIG.SYS file. When it starts, the Protocol Manager immediately reads the parameters in the

PROTOCOL.INI file and builds a memory-resident table of the configuration.

The NDIS drivers read their portions of the PROTOCOL.INI file, extract the parameters for their operation, and initialize the network adapter cards. The MAC drivers are initialized first. Each MAC driver initializes the network adapter card it controls. A token-ring MAC, for example, initializes the adapter card and inserts into the ring. A process called *binding* connects protocol drivers to the MAC drivers. Multiple protocols are run over the same network adapter card by executing the appropriate binding command; This binds the additional protocols to the MAC driver that runs a particular network adapter card. The Protocol Manager controls multiple protocol binding by placing a program called the *Vector* between the MAC driver and the protocol drivers. The Vector then sorts out the packets received by the MAC driver and sends them to the appropriate protocol driver.

NDIS is important to the enterprise network designer and administrator because of the connectivity and control it brings to the LAN Manager network. It is important to understand the way MAC and protocol drivers communicate and how to control those drivers, so that a complex network can utilize the strengths of NDIS and LAN Manager.

NetBEUI

NetBEUI is the most commonly used protocol in LAN Manager network implementations. It supports the NetBIOS 1.0 interface standards and NetBIOS 3.0 interface standards for use on OS/2 workstations and servers. NetBIOS provides three primary communication services, local name management, virtual circuit establishment, and datagram communication.

Local names are registered with NetBIOS and provide a means to identify network resources, users, workstations, domains, computer names, or relative paths. An example of a NetBIOS name is a shared hard disk. The hard disk is given a name registered locally with NetBIOS. The local name is then used to identify that resource locally and remotely through other NetBIOS services. Each NetBIOS driver can have up to 12 names registered.

Virtual circuits are communication links between two NetBIOS names that provide for the reliable delivery of packets. This implies that the receiver must acknowledge receipt of transmitted packets. Virtual circuits are called *sessions*. When a session is established, the user's access permissions are validated for the named server resource. A typical example of this is the hard disk on the server. After NetBIOS on the workstation establishes a session connecting the workstation client to the local name on the server, the workstation can share the server's hard disk.

Datagram communications is a means to transmit packets of data from one NetBIOS name to another without a guarantee of delivery. The NetBIOS driver assumes that a datagram packet is received by the destination. If the packet is not received, it is assumed that software on a different level will recognize that a specific packet was not received and initiate a request for retransmission of the packet.

Network Control Blocks (NCBs) are the basic unit of communication for NetBIOS and are segments of memory assigned to NetBIOS tasks. NCBs are the common transfer point that enables the transfer of data and other information between, to, and from NetBIOS tasks. Microsoft's application program interface (API) contains a detailed description of NCBs and their use. Data transferred around the network is first assembled in *Server Message*

Blocks (SMBs) and then "stuffed" into NCBs for actual transmission.

The NetBIOS 3.0 protocol driver should be used when applications especially written for OS/2 are in use on the workstation. NetBIOS 3.0 is not installed automatically when SETUP is run. The CONFIG.SYS file must be edited manually to add an additional *DEVICE* = statement that specifies the NETBIOS.OS2 driver. Other parameters in the LANMAN.INI must be changed as specified in the "Microsoft LAN Manager Installation and Configuration Guide."

An aspect of NetBEUI that is important to the enterprise network designer is its lack of routing information at the protocol level. Microsoft avoids the routing problem in NetBEUI when using IBM (or compatible) Source Routing Bridges. After the call is made to NetBEUI to find a name on the network, the server returns a message that the name is recognized. If the workstation does not receive a message that the name is recognized by the server, NetBEUI retries for a specific number of times, as specified by a parameter in the PROTOCOL.INI file. When the maximum number of retries is reached, the NetBEUI protocol driver sets the most significant bit in the Source Address field of the NetBEUI packet and resends the packet. A source routing bridge recognizes the packet as being source routed, adds the ring and bridge number as routing information, and forwards the packet to the bridge ring(s).

Adjustments must be made to timing and retry parameters when using NetBEUI with communication links with speeds of 64kbps or less. The LANMAN.INI file on the server should be changed to have a value of 9 in the 15th position of the SRVHEURISTICS parameter. The SETUP program does not create a SRVHEURISTICS parameter at LAN Manager installation leaving all of the parameter values at default. To create this parameter is a tedious task because you must create all of the defaults for the preceding parameters (0 through 14).

This particular change increases the time that a server waits after breaking an "opportunistic" lock from 35 seconds to 640 seconds. Heuristics in the workstation or client LANMAN.INI file WRKHEURISTICS also must be changed. "Big Buffer" read-ahead must be turned off; position 6 must be changed from 1 to 0. The control function must be turned on for the transfer of raw data to the SMB. Position 14 value must be 1, which is the default value. Parameters of the LANMAN.INI are described in Appendix B of the "Microsoft LAN Manager Administrator's Reference."

In the PROTOCOL.INI file, you must adjust the acknowledge and retry parameters. The t1 parameter sets the delay before retransmitting a link level frame. Default for t1 is 500 milliseconds. The t2 parameter sets the delay before acknowledging a received frame when the received window limit has not been reached. Default for t2 is 200 milliseconds. You must change t1 to 5000 milliseconds and t2 to 2000 milliseconds. LAN Manager adjusts the frame window dynamically by running an "adaptive window algorithm" program. The time between executions of this program by LAN Manager needs to be increased by changing the ADAPTRATE parameter from the default of 1000 milliseconds to 2000 milliseconds.

The DLCRETRIES parameter sets the number of retries that the NETBEUI makes when the DLC layer does not respond. This parameter must be changed to a default of 5 to 20. More details about the NetBEUI PROTOCOL.INI parameters can be found in the "Microsoft LAN Manager Installation and Configuration Guide."

TCP/IP

Microsoft's LAN Manager TCP/IP implementation is an NDIS-compliant protocol driver that runs on the servers and workstations. The TCP/IP protocol driver supports all NDIS compliant device (MAC) drivers. It runs on token ring, as well as Ethernet. TCP/IP addressing conforms to the DARPA standards. If the network is going to connect to the TCP/IP Internet, a unique address must be assigned by the DDN Network Information Center.

LAN Manager IP addresses are specified in the PROTOCOL.INI file IPADDRESS0 parameter. The SETUP program requests the IP address at installation and automatically inserts it into the PROTOCOL.INI file. When the network requires broadcasts to be made to IP addresses, a second parameter, called the BCASTADDR, is specified with the broadcast address, typically 255.255.255.255.

LAN Manager automatically translates the names to IP addresses for servers at remote sites that are connected by routers to the local network. A text editor program must be used to create a LMHOSTS list used as a translation table. List the most frequently accessed remote servers first in the LMHOSTS file to optimize translation time.

Microsoft's TCP/IP Utilities are an add-on software package that enables network clients to access regular UNIX hosts through a number of utilities that include file transfer protocol (FTP), terminal emulation including VT-100, and Bridge Application Program Interface (BAPI).

The TCP/IP Utilities take advantage of high memory in the DOS workstations to free workstation memory. Installation is menu-driven through an installation program.

Client-Server Computing

The computing industry has great interest in distributed processing. IBM created interest in the concept in the 1970s, but the technology was not there to implement the concepts. Microcomputer networks appear to have grown almost spontaneously out of a desire to connect microcomputers for resource sharing and communication purposes.

The rush by computer technology firms to develop better LANs and to get market share brought about much of IBM's distributed-processing dream of the 70s. The most basic of networks brought a distribution of processing power to the desktop. But this distribution brought disadvantages as well as advantages. As network use grew, the four and ten megabit speeds which once looked so fast were suddenly painfully slow. The small company, sorting a twenty-employee payroll file, became a large company sorting a hundred-thousand-item inventory file. All of these network activities were funneled through the network "wire." Network developers—Microsoft and 3Com among them—began to realize that some computing tasks were best executed on the computer where the files were resident. This eliminated the bottleneck created by network "wires" of limited speed.

Network developers face another problem. The CPU chip of the file server has definite computing limitations. If many demands are placed on that chip, the general sharing of resources slows down appreciably. In addition, no operating system—neither DOS nor NetWare 2.X—was designed to handle the requests by remote users to execute tasks on the file server. The advent of OS/2 changed the picture completely. Not only was it much faster than DOS, but it also was capable of handling the multiple tasks requested of it on the file server.

Concurrent with the advances in hardware and software technology available to network developers, a concept called *client-server* computing was developed. In client-server computing, an application is separated into two groups: the tasks that run best on a client and the tasks that run best on a server. Tasks performed at the workstation are client, or *front-end*, tasks. Tasks executed on the server are server, or *back-end*, tasks.

This concept is not proprietary, and it is available to all network-operating system developers. Microsoft has made client-server processing a focal point of its network technology. Application of client-server technology is still in its infancy. A number of applications exist, two of which stand out as remarkable applications of client-server technology.

Microsoft's SQL Server is described later in this chapter. It is a SQL database program that runs on the OS/2 operating system. SQL Server is a server application in itself and does not require LAN Manager to make it operate.

Digital Communications Associates (DCA) and Microsoft have jointly developed a Communications Server called the Select Communications Server (SCS). It also is described later in this chapter.

These products follow Microsoft's rules for client-server relations. Under those rules, client and server computers communicate by using *named pipes* and *mailslots*—communications vehicles, available, initially, only in OS/2 and NetBios. Servers are responsible for making named pipes available. Clients generally initiate the conversation.

As client-server technology matures, more and more applications utilizing the powers of that technology will become available.

Microsoft has a list of dozens of application programs available in addition to SQL Server and Select Communications Server. Notable companies such as Oracle, Gupta, Informix, IBM, and Lotus have products available now, and with network and hardware technology growing at its present rate, no end is in sight for the power and utility of client-server applications.

Workstation Peer Services

An OS/2 workstation can be set up to run peer services under LAN Manager. This enables the workstation to perform many functions of a full LAN Manager server. Workstations running peer services must run OS/2 version 1.21 or greater and have at least five M of RAM (the Microsoft recommended amount). Multiple mailslots, named pipes, and files can be shared with others on the network, but only one printer and print queue can be shared.

A peer server can run the following LAN Manager services:

- Fault Tolerance
- Messenger
- Alerter
- Netrun
- Replicator
- UPS
- Security
- Hidden or Visible Server

A peer server cannot run the following LAN Manager services:

- HPFS386
- Local Security
- RPL
- Netlogon
- Dedicated Server
- Timeserver

OS/2 workstation peer services are important LAN Manager features that not only enable you to run the services indicated above, but also are the foundation for products like the DCA/Microsoft Communications Server and Remote Access Service.

Peer Server Installation

The first step in the installation of a peer server is the normal OS/2 workstation installation. Make sure that the EXIT command in the STARTUP.CMD file is the last statement in that file or remove it altogether. The LAN Manager SETUP program automatically inserts a DEVICE command for the RDRHELP.SYS driver in the CONFIG.SYS file. This device command must follow any COM0x.SYS device command.

Reboot the computer and the OS/2 workstation is ready to share resources as a peer server.

On the peer server, issue the following command:

```
NET SHARE LASERJET = LPT1: /COMM
```

On the file server, install the printer by using the OS/2 Printer Installer and give it the same name as the shared printer on the peer server. Choose a local (local to the file server) printer port to associate with the peer server printer, in this example, choose LPT7.

Issue the follow commands on the file server:

```
NET USE LPT7: \\PEERSERVER (peer server name)\LASERJET /COMM
NET SHARE PEERSERVER /PRINT
NET PRINT PEERPRINTER /ROUTE:LPT7
```

At the workstation that you want to print to the peer server shared printer, issue the following command:

```
NET USE LPT1 \\FILESERVER (file server name)\LASERJET
```

This command routes all printing on the workstation to the peer server printer LASERJET.

LAN Manager NetWare Connectivity Feature

This feature enables workstations to maintain simultaneous connections to LAN Manaager and NetWare servers. This feature takes advantage of the capability to load multiple protocol stacks under the NDIS standard. A workstation can support both a NetBEUI (or a TCP/IP) protocol stack for connection to a LAN Manager server and an IPX protocol stack for connection to a NetWare server. To promote efficient use of memory, the IPX protocol stack can be loaded and unloaded as needed.

LAN Manager Services for Macintosh

LAN Manager Services for Macintosh enable Macintosh users to share two important resources on the LAN Manager network disk space and printers. The services make the LAN Manager server available to Macintosh clients running System 6.0.3 or later versions of the Apple operating system. The network can be set up as an AppleTalk Phase 1 or Phase 2 network.

The LAN Manager file server runs an NDIS compliant AppleTalk protocol stack as a means of communicating to the file server. Any NDIS-supported network adapter can be used to connect the LAN Manager file server to the AppleTalk network using LocalTalk, EtherTalk, or TokenTalk.

Macintosh users log onto the network in the same manner as PC users. Passwords are not encrypted for transmission to and from Macintosh workstations because System 7 (the current Macintosh operating system) is not compatible with the LAN Manager password encryption scheme. Older versions of the Macintosh operating system did not use password encryption.

Macintosh users log on onto the LAN Manager file server by using the Chooser facility of the Macintosh operating system. Each Macintosh connection is the equivalent of a PC client connection and counts as one user toward the maximum number of users allowed for the server. LAN Manager Services for Macintosh is an OS/2 process run on the LAN Manager file server. As an OS/2 process, it is limited to a maximum of 50 threads within the OS/2 operating system. Each Macintosh user logged on to the LAN Manager file server requires a thread within that process. This means that the total number of Macintosh users is limited by two factors, an absolute maximum of 50 per LAN Manager file server and the limit placed on the number of connections to the file server by the server configuration.

Macintosh files are stored on the LAN Manager file server in *native mode* LAN Manager format. A *mapping* is created that relates

LAN Manager (PC) file names and permissions to Macintosh file names and permissions. A one-to-one correspondence does not exist between Macintosh permissions and LAN Manager permissions. Therefore, the Macintosh file is mapped to the next most restrictive LAN Manager permission. The Macintosh "see folders" permission "maps" to a "read" permission on the LAN Manager file server and enables the Macintosh user to view the parent subdirectory and the files it contains, but not the children subdirectories. On the Macintosh, the user sees the children subdirectories as folders. Macintosh file types are translated through the mapping process. An Excel file, for instance, has the extension XLS.

LAN Manager can share printers with Macintosh computers if the printers are connected to the network through AppleTalk connections or a file server serial port. At this time, LAN Manager Services for Macintosh support only Postscript printers. Network printers are selected by using the Macintosh operating system "Chooser."

LAN Manager Services for the Macintosh are installed from the Microsoft product diskette by using the LAN Manager Setup program. The product is distributed on both 3 1/2-inch and 5 1/4-inch diskettes. Default settings necessary for basic operation of LAN Manager Service for Macintosh on the LAN Manager file server are made to the LANMAN.INI file. Additional software is not required for the Macintosh client workstations.

LAN Manager for UNIX Systems

Microsoft provides access to the resources of UNIX host and PC servers via LAN Manager version 2.0 for UNIX. LAN Manager for UNIX runs on the UNIX host computer and permits DOS,

Windows, or OS/2-based workstations to access files, applications, and printers by using a common set of commands based on DOS, Windows, or OS/2 commands. This is convenient workstation users because they can use the commands they are already familiar with.

As an example of the ease of connections, Windows users—after they log on to the LAN Manager for UNIX server—can access a UNIX host drive by selecting Connect Net Drive from the disk menu in the File Manager section of the Windows workstation. Once a connection is made, the files can be copied to the UNIX host from a PC or from the UNIX host to a PC. Printers and print queue control are fully DOS-, Windows-, and OS/2-compatible.

Microsoft LAN Manager for UNIX is administered the same way as LAN Manager for PCs. This eliminates the need for additional training for network administrators. LAN Manager for UNIX servers can be included in domains.

A number of manufacturers support LAN Manager for UNIX, including Data General, Group Bull, Hewlett-Packard, NCR, Olivetti, Unisys, and Santa Cruz Operation SCO. The distributed-computing environment (DCE) from the Open Systems Foundation uses LAN Manager as its PC-connectivity solution. LAN Manager for UNIX also supports many standard UNIX connectivity protocols, including Sun (NFS), Andrew File System (AFS), and Remote File System (RFS). This broad-based support by LAN Manager for UNIX of many different platforms and standards provides a "seamless" integration to the UNIX environment.

Select Communications Server Version 1.1

The Select Communications Server—developed jointly by Digital Communications Associates and Microsoft—provides a powerful array of IBM mainframe-connectivity options to the enterprise networker. Although the SCS might be considered a third party add-on to a LAN Manager network, it plays an integral part in Microsoft's enterprise network strategy and is a prime example of the application of the client-server concept.

SCS is based on an IBM or Compaq (or compatible) 80386 or 80486 computer that runs OS/2. The SCS provides a platform from which to access mainframe host computers running CICS, MVS/TSO, or VM/CMS. Connectivity from the back-end (SCS Server) to the mainframe is provided by DFT, SDLC, X.25, or token ring (TIC) connections. SCS supports programming through IBM's APPC, Common Service Verbs, and EHLLAPI. Enterprise network designers concerned with network management have access to the NetView user and data-link alerts, link statistics, Response Time Monitor, and Common Service Verbs. Logical Unit (LU) types 1, 2, 3, and 6.2 are supported by SCS.

SCS users must be logged in to a LAN Manager 2.0 Release C or later or to an IBM LAN Server 1.3 or later file server. The server itself runs either on a LAN Manager server or an OS/2 Peer Server. The OS/2 client workstations must run OS/2 Version 1.21 or later, as provided by various microcomputer manufacturers, or IBM OS/2 SE 1.2 or later. DOS client workstations must run DOS 3.2 or later. Client workstations require a minimum of four MB of RAM under OS/2 or 512 K when running DOS.

The Select Communications Server (SCS) is one of the most advanced client-server applications available. The SCS performs tasks independent of the file server and neatly handles all the interfacing to the mainframe host environment. All client communications to the SCS Server are through named pipes and mail slots, true to Microsoft's definition of client-server computing. This enables the client workstations to freely act as PCs and to do things like task-swapping under DOSSHELL. All Physical and Logical Unit management is done on the SCS Server.

The Network Access Program (NAP) ties together all communication services components. One version of NAP runs on OS/2, and two versions run on DOS workstations (one for just 3270 emulation, the other for full APPC). The LAN Manager file server stores a master configuration file. This configuration file is used by the SCS Server and all clients using the SCS Server in the LAN Manager Domain and is similar in function to the Domain Name Server. Backup configuration servers can be specified.

A SCS Server client can access the communications through Windows 3.0 or later. The load parameter in the WIN.INI file automatically starts the client services when Windows is started.

The documentation and user interface for the DCA Select Communications Server (and clients) are excellent. Interactive setup and operation screens are similar to LAN Manager screens. Several configurations require that parameters must be edited into the LANMAN.INI and PROTOCOL.INI files. This is an inconvenience, but the documentation contains clear instruction and examples. An even more important feature of the documentation is detailed VTAM definition examples provided in the Server Administrator documentation.

The only significant shortcomings of SCS are limited token ring network adapter board support and limited (265-byte) data block size for transmissions to the mainframe host.

In its most sophisticated implementation, the SCS Servers can balance loads among servers and provide central administrations for multiple SCS Servers. The features of the DCA Select Communication Server make it the best SNA gateway available today.

SQL Server

A powerful tool in Microsoft's plan to capture the desktop computing environment is the SQL Server. The SQL Server has a number of things in common with the Select Communications Server. Microsoft has again teamed with a third party to develop a key element of its Enterprise Network technology, and that element is based on the client-server philosophy.

Microsoft—like other pioneers in the use of microcomputers for downsizing environments—realizes that the key to convincing major corporations to downsize is processing speed that is competitive with that of mainframe computers. With the client-server technology already well defined, Microsoft "partnered" with database developer Sybase to create SQL Server. This provides database processing programs at the server—or backend—of the client-server relationship. SQL Server also is compatible enough with IBM's mainframe SQL language that mainframe SQL programming expertise is "leveraged" in downsizing efforts.

SQL Server operates on a variety of computers, including those running UNIX, VMS, and OS/2 operating systems. Microsoft and Sybase have divided the market for SQL Server. Sybase supports UNIX, VMS, and other platforms; Microsoft supports the OS/2 platform. In addition to these platforms, a database gateway to mainframes is available from Micro Decisionware. Microsoft encourages others to develop gateways and a Gateway Development Kit is available.

SQL Server, as discussed here, is an OS/2-based program. It uses the multithread capabilities of the OS/2 operating system to handle the multitude of tasks necessary to provide server (backend) processing to the client workstations. Clients are attached to the SQL Server by using peer server services and named pipes. The SQL Server is compatible with LAN Manager, IBM LAN Server, Ungermann-Bass, and Novell NetWare. Novell clients must run a DOS named pipes program to connect to a SQL Server. SQL Server can run as a stand-alone server (using peer server) or on the same computer that runs LAN Manager.

Install as much RAM as possible; nine megabytes are the minimum for any significant processing.

Microsoft defines the processing necessary in a SQL Server/client-server environment as a broad spectrum that ranges from online transaction processing that is update-intensive, uses predefined queries, and runs in real-time to a "decision support" system that executes inquiries, is retrieval-intensive, and supports ad hoc reporting.

Microsoft addresses the transaction portion of this range with a system that provides guaranteed database consistency, system-wide crash and recovery, and automatic rollback or rollforward. SQL Server speeds shared (read) locks and exclusive locks by making locking programs memory resident. A "least-restrictive" locking algorithm minimizes the exclusive use of files or records. An automatic sensing program detects and resolves deadlocks.

Multiple servers can be (and frequently are) used to hold large databases. Transaction commitment logic guarantees that the data is consistent across multiple SQL Servers.

Database servers of older design place integrity checking at the client end of the processing. This can lead to variations in the integrity checking from client-to-client. SQL Server centralizes integrity checking at the server. This saves time when making changes and ensures uniformity. SQL Server has advanced integrity features for column-level integrity, default column values, and referential integrity.

SQL procedures are written in *Transact-SQL,* which enables the sharing of common logic among applications. Commonly used procedures can be compiled and even designated to be memory-cached for speedy execution.

SQL Server uses a clustered index schema; indexes are sorted and stored with the records. The performance advantage over typical non-clustered indexed databases is significant. Microsoft claims that clustered indexes require only twenty percent of the space required by ordinary indexes.

Microsoft goes to great lengths to optimize performance of the SQL Server. Unfortunately, the optimization is for File Allocation Table (FAT) based systems. A computer set up to use Microsoft's High Performance File System (HPFS) actually can run slower than a FAT-based SQL Server system. This also creates problems for those using the Compaq Computer Corporation SystemPro multiprocessor option. The second processor in a LAN Manager environment controls disk input and output (I/O) and requires the use of a special network driver. The second processor is functional only when the server uses HPFS. Despite the fact that it is optimized for a FAT system, SQL Server runs faster using HPFS on a Compaq SystemPro with multiple processors because disk I/O is much faster when using the second processor.

SQL Server provides a full range of administrative and control services. Users must be set up in a manner similar to the way they are set up in LAN Manager itself. Users are given or denied access to data based on a sophisticated permissions structure either on an individual basis or as members of a group. Additional utilities support storage management, data import and export, backup and restore, performance monitoring, and object management.

In recognition of the critical nature of many downsized applications, Microsoft has developed a number of features designed to keep the SQL Server functioning and to minimize down time. SQL Server provides for on-line backup, automatic recovery, on-line performance tuning, and on-line schema changes.

A full set of application program interface (API) calls are available to SQL Server applications developers. SQL Server provides a call-level interface, support for DOS, Windows, and OS/2. API calls for Windows and OS/2 are in the form of DLLs. A "static" library is available for DOS. The network APIs are protocol independent. Connection to UNIX and VMS is through "net libraries" for those server environments.

A broad range of three and four GL languages offer interfaces to SQL Server. On of the more popular of these languages is Advanced Revelation. Advanced Revelation and SQL Server provide powerful tools for the LAN Manager network in an enterprise network environment.

Summary

This chapter introduced you to the communication capabilities of Microsoft's LAN Manager. LAN Manager's focus is on a client-server architecture, which makes implementation of client-server applications easy to do.

LAN Manager supports large multiserver networks, using features such as domains.

There are a variety of connectivity options that are offered, including NetWare servers, Macintosh, TCP/IP, and IBM SNA hosts. Several options can be smoothly integrated because of the multitasking operation of OS/2 and the multiprotocol support offered by NDIS.

NDIS is a multivendor standard that makes LAN Manager well-suited for enterprise networking. NDIS enables workstations to support connections to a UNIX environment via TCP/IP, a NetWare server, and a LAN Manager server. This three-way connection is well supported.

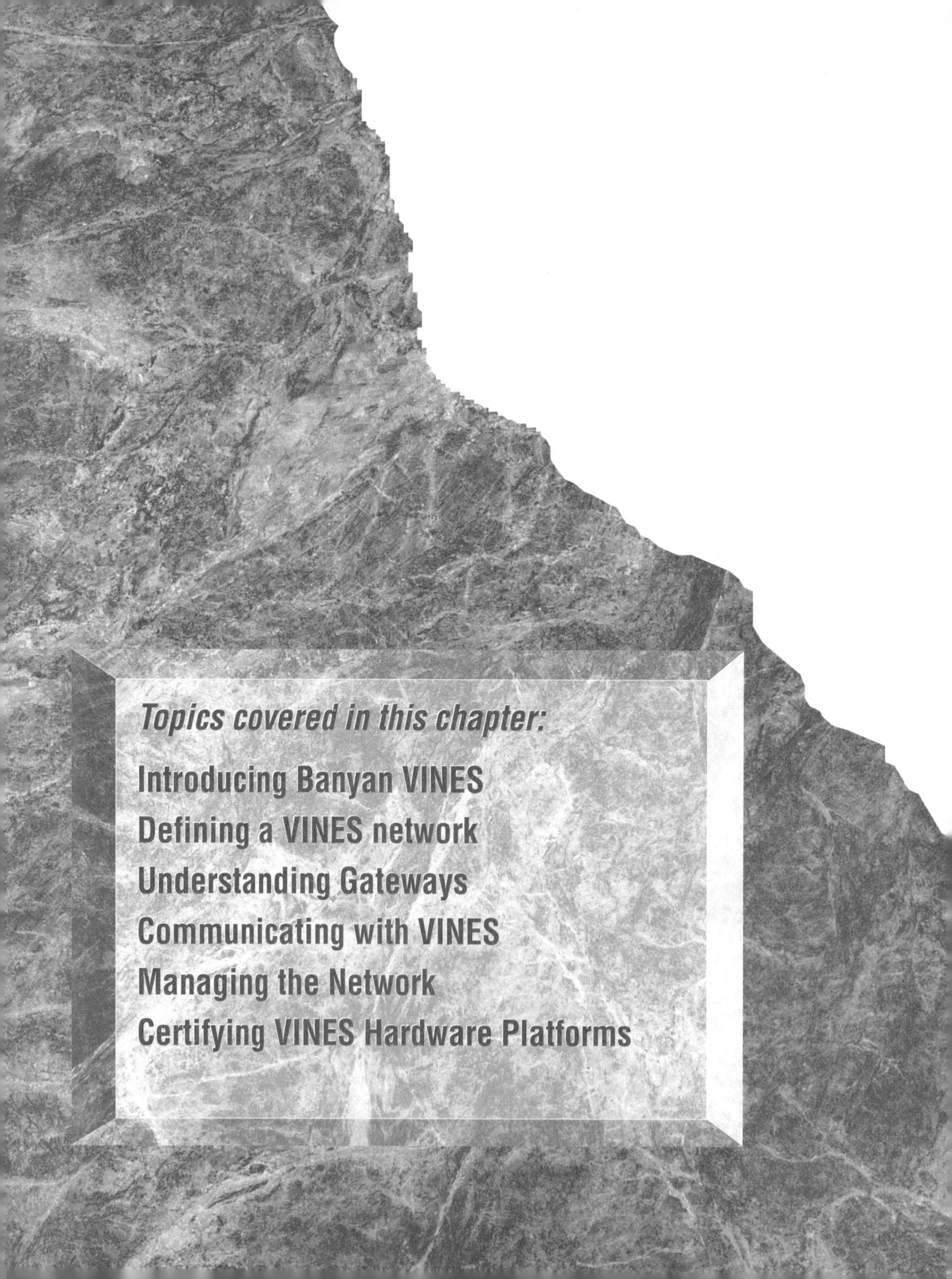

Topics covered in this chapter:
Introducing Banyan VINES
Defining a VINES network
Understanding Gateways
Communicating with VINES
Managing the Network
Certifying VINES Hardware Platforms

Chapter 10

Banyan VINES

Banyan System's VINES (*VI*rtual *NE*tworking *S*oftware) is a fully-distributed PC network operating system that exhibits the features, functionality, and level of complexity found in its base, the UNIX operating system. VINES enables organizations to interconnect an unlimited number and variety of personal computers, minicomputers, mainframes, local area networks, wide area networks, and other computer resources into a single network.

This chapter introduces you to Banyan VINES—its history, current capabilities, and directions. It outlines the functions of the server, the types and capabilities of VINES communication support, the way VINES works with other vendors' networks and protocols (interconnectivity options), and the advantages of using Banyan VINES for management, network managers, and users.

Introducing Banyan VINES

Users of the VINES NOS (Network Operating System) have the following three advantages:

- Users are provided with a single system image of the network, regardless if it is configured as a single network or a wide area network
- Users are provided with transparent access to network resources
- Users are shielded from the physical elements of the network

VINES' Multiuser Operating System

VINES itself does not limit the number of workstations it can support. This decision is usually based on the workload and required response time. Although a typical 386-based server can easily support more than 100 DOS-based workstations, each of these individual networks can be integrated seamlessly, which provides unlimited growth capability.

This "Big Network" operating system is available in licenses for networks having as few as five users. The five-to-twenty user licenses are marketed as the "VINES Team" products. (The basic license for the five-user group costs less than $1000.)

The VINES system is actually a series of applications that run on a special version of AT&T UNIX. The normal shell interface is completely hidden by VINES, and it is not available for use by other applications. A single PC that runs VINES typically performs all server functions. This concentration of functions makes the multiprocessor capabilities of VINES very important.

Future versions of VINES will also be based on (and be fully integrated with) SCO UNIX. Thus, VINES clients will be able to access applications, files, and resources in SCO UNIX systems, and SCO users with proper network security will be able to access the VINES network.

The nearest competitors in price and capability are Novell NetWare 3.x and LAN Manager. Because VINES is particularly useful for connecting widely separated file servers, it is successful in large network installations. It is also useful in smaller companies or departments that have more complex network requirements than those that are easily or economically satisfied with NetWare.

VINES servers' software capabilities are scaleable, and they run on various configurations of Intel 80386 and 80486 processors. Banyan offers a special version of VINES for the Compaq SystemPro, Everex Cube, and AT&T StarServer computers equipped with multiple processors. This version is marketed as VINES SMP (Symmetrical Multi-Processing).

VINES Provides Transparent Access to Resources

A few of the largest current users of VINES are Pacific Gas & Electric; Ericsson, LTD.; New York Telephone; the Canadian Broadcasting Corporation; the United States Marine Corps; the Norwegian Rural Police Force; and Compaq Computer Corporation.

Banyan pioneered the use of a feature called *Global Naming Services* in its naming service, StreetTalk. StreetTalk provides a location-independent way to name resources and users on various servers and nodes across the network. VINES also features StreetTalk Directory Assistance (STDA). The VINES architecture is centered around this globally-distributed directory service. Every server in a VINES network supports StreetTalk services and some portion of the StreetTalk database. Every VINES service is fully integrated with it, and it enables users to find network resources faster by dynamically posting directory and routing information across the network.

VINES is designed as a network that can cross national boundaries and still "speak the language" of the user. Every VINES server can support a mix of languages. Multilingual VINES supports native time and date formats, character and number representations, and sorting characteristics. Across the network, VINES enables users to communicate and share the same information, while working in their own native environments.

Because all service resources run in the same computer, VINES enables access, with a single password, to host gateways, e-mail, print queues, fax gateways, and other services. (This single-password access is not possible in a Novell environment.) Banyan also offered SQL server processing years before its competitors did.

Banyan works with a myriad of industry-standard network interfaces, including SMB, NetBIOS, Named Pipes, NDIS, and LAN Manager APIs. Applications written to any of these interfaces operate in the VINES environment.

The implementation of service resources running on a single processor, which can in turn be connected with other VINES or foreign gateways, provides significant opportunity for reducing external bridges, routers, and gateways. Not only are the devices themselves eliminated, but also the corresponding effort and cost of evaluating and acquiring them. From a network-management standpoint, the VINES servers provide comprehensive management capabilities for tuning, manageing, and monitoring each of its service resources.

VINES is Easy To Use

To users, the physical locale of the files on the network, anywhere in the world, is completely transparent. Instead of just using a workstation with one or two disk drives, users work with desktop systems that appear to have as many as 23 disk drives. Access to information stored on a remote server is done with the same commands that are used on the local workstation.

VINES is designed to minimize complexities in the operation and management of the network. Because network-management services are fully integrated across LAN and WAN communication boundaries, user management, system monitoring and problem resolution anywhere on the network can be done from a single location.

Version 5.0 provides the capability for remote consoles, distributed-system administration, and true/full integration for Apple Macintosh and multiple printers on a print queue. The following table lists the "firsts" for VINES.

Table 10.1
VINES "Firsts" Accomplishments

Date	*Accomplishment*
1984	Network server
1984	RPC compiler for PC LAN
1984	Global, distributed directory system
1985	Transparent multiserver network
1985	Integrated SNA and BSC host gateways
1986	Transparent X.25 gateway
1987	Internetworking version of NetBios
1988	32-bit, 80386-based NOS
1989	Oracle server for VINES
1990	True multinational network support
1990	Symmetric multiprocessing support
1990	Second-generation distributed directory system

Third-Party Products

Banyan promotes hundreds of application-software products. These products range from those that can simply run on a VINES network, to those that are fully integrated with the VINES system. Any package written to address the NetBIOS interface runs in a VINES environment. Banyan also promotes third-party packages that provide and enhance the VINES network services.

Defining a VINES Network

VINES can use a wide variety of storage, print, and backup devices, as well as communication and network cards. VINES servers can be configured as stand-alone resources, or interconnected in unlimited ways, to provide true global resource availability.

What the Server Does

A VINES network is a set of computer and other components, such as printers, plotters, serial-communication devices, and host gateways that connect to at least one VINES server. A VINES server is any Intel 80386- or 80486-based computer that runs the VIrtual NEtworking System software. This software enables computers and users to share resources. VINES is currently available for ISA, EISA, and MCA platforms. The latest release, 4.11, discontinues support for the 80286-server platform. Network licenses range from five users to a virtually unlimited number, based on internetworking. All discussion of capabilities and compatibilities in this book refers to version 4.11, unless otherwise stated.

Once VINES is installed on the fixed disk, the computer is dedicated to providing services to user PCs or other VINES servers on the network. VINES provides a single-computer solution for connecting remote servers, SNA gateways, Async services, print servers, facsimile servers, and database and mail servers.

Hardware Components

Supported hardware includes fixed disks with ST506, EDSI, and SCSI controllers, and a single tape unit. Only one controller may be used per system, with the exception of SCSI, in which two can be used. (RAID support is available for Compaq Systems.) A variety of printers can be attached to any port on the server or the workstation (a maximum of 20 with version 5.0). A full range of the most popular display adapters are supported. LAN cards are required for each computer that intends to participate in the LAN.

Single and Multiserver Networks

A VINES network can vary in size and complexity, according to the needs of the organization. It can be as simple as that shown in figure 10.1, in which server 1 connects a group of PCs in a LAN. It provides the PC users a common set of resources, such as disk space and shared printers.

The network can also be more complex, as shown in figure 10.2. This is more typical example of a network, in which multiple servers are linked via a backbone LAN, and each server also connects to a group of PCs. They can also connect to host systems or remote servers. The backbone LAN enables high-speed interconnection of servers. It is quick because only inter-server traffic passes over the cable. These examples show only two of many possible network configurations.

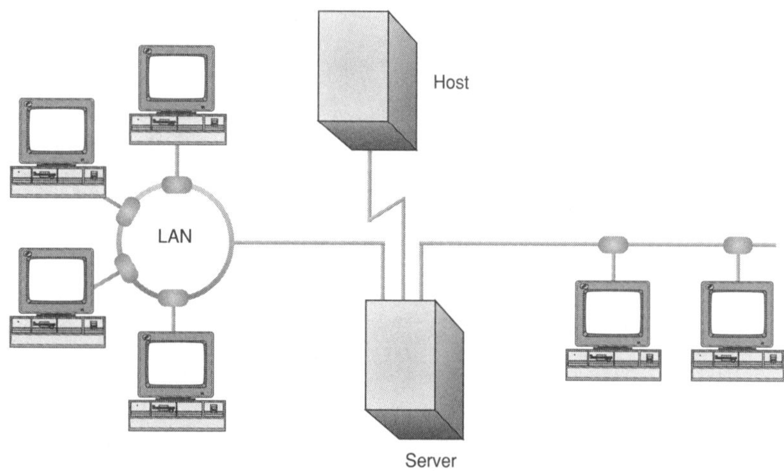

Figure 10.1:
Simple VINES network.

You determine the layout of the VINES network by the serial communications options and type of LAN options you order for the server. The network can be expanded indefinitely by adding PCs, servers, LANs, printers, plotters, and serial communications devices.

The VINES/SMP operating system is specially designed to operate on computers with multiple processors, such as the Compaq SystemPro. Unlike other operating systems that assign tasks to specific processors, VINES divides tasks evenly between processors on a "first free, first task" basis. VINES/SMP can effectively and efficiently utilize up to eight 80386 or 80486 processors in a single computer, which is a significant improvement over asymmetrical processor-assignment, which dedicates processors to specific tasks.

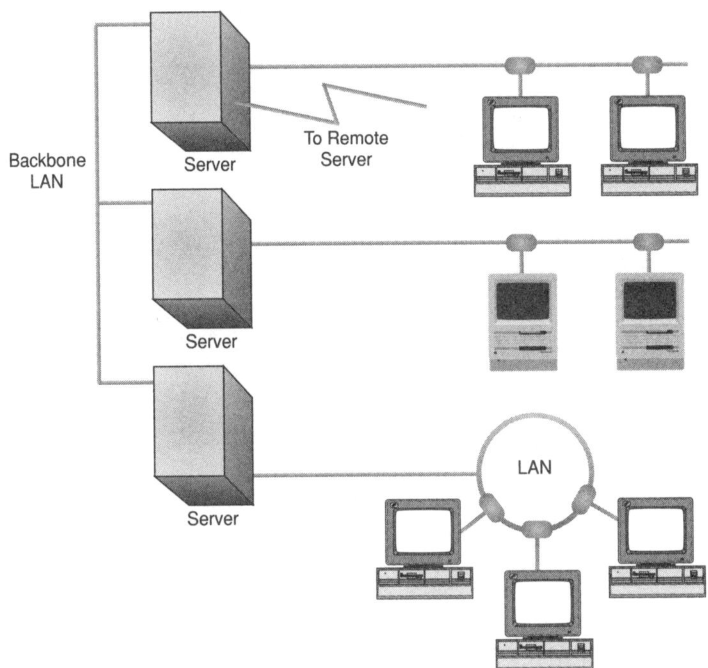

Figure 10.2:
Complex VINES network.

Internetworks

An *internetwork* is created by connecting servers through a "backbone network" or by modems and a telephone lines (a WAN connection). Internetworks enable all users on the network to communicate with each other, as well as to utilize any permissioned resources and facilities on the WAN. Although bridges and routers are attracting more attention from users of other networks in building enterprise-wide computing systems, dedicated Banyan VINES users have always had this "built-in" capability.

VINES communications are based on Banyan's low-level IP protocol, which in turn borrows conceptually from TCP/IP and Xerox's XNS protocol. The basic philosophy behind the architecture of VINES is that enterprise-wide computing is really an aggregation of its LANs. Banyan includes local routing support in all VINES servers. It also supports built-in WAN routing through optional packages. VINES supports asychronous dial-up lines, asynchronous and synchronous leased lines, HDLC, X.25, X.29, V.35, connections to several specialized routers, and the internal router option.

Network Services Linking PCs and Servers

Each PC must have a hardware (LAN card) interface to the server, and it must run VINES client software. VINES servers provide resource sharing between all networked PCs. VINES *services* running on the server provide this sharing. The services include network mail, file service, print services, and connections with host computers. Each server can contain any combination of basic and optional services that provide the resource sharing that users need. Servers can be optionally dedicated to specific tasks or for a variety of services. They provide this capability to share, based on the types of services that are running.

Understanding VINES' Naming Conventions and Services

In a large network, and especially in a WAN, the capability to provide unique, consistent names across the network (and to access resources by those names) is critical. Although most network-operating system vendors are struggling to conform to the developing X.500 standards that define this functionality, VINES users have had it in production since 1984.

Banyan StreetTalk

VINES software includes a naming service, called StreetTalk, that identifies every element (user and resource) on the network with a unique English-like name. Users access services by name and use the names to send data and network mail to other users. VINES enables you to assign each resource a name in the following form: "Item@Group@Organization." You specify the name for a resource when you add it to the system. A password can also be associated with the name. The server maintains a universal Access Rights List (ARL), containing the StreetTalk names of the resources and users allowed to access them. The administrator does this only once. This technique makes it easy to establish high levels of resource security and reduces administration headaches across the WAN.

StreetTalk provides a Global Directory Service, which enables administrators to uniquely define a user or resource name without specifying the physical location. This is analogous to a telephone system, in that the person placing the call only needs to know the number of the person he wants to speak with, without having to know or care how the physical connection is actually made.

The StreetTalk directory service is:

- ❖ Intuitive

- Adaptable to changes
- A single addressing format for all resources
- Available in LAN and WAN environments
- Based on a distributed-directory service
- A single information community

StreetTalk, a core component of VINES, has been in production for over eight years. It effectively hides the complexity of the network, and is a superset of the emerging X.500 standard.

Name Definition

In VINES, each element of the network is called an *item*. Each network user is an item, each service is an item, and each server is an item. Each item in the network belongs to, and is unique within, a group.

Groups consist of any number of items of various types, all of which have something in common. Groups are usually composed of users, services, or lists. Each group in the network belongs to, and is unique within, an organization.

Organizations consist of groups that are related in some way at the highest level of the network. Organization names are unique for a business enterprise. Like group names, organization names refer to structural areas of the business, rather than to individual pieces of it.

To define a network resource, you must specify the combination of item, group, and organization names that are unique. StreetTalk names' length limits are the following: item—31 characters, group—31 characters, and organization—15 characters.

The components of the name are separated by a @. Note that spaces are considered valid characters when they are embedded in a name component. Nicknames can also be assigned within a group organization.

StreetTalk supports multilingual naming for single-byte character sets such as Spanish, French, and Hungual. Case is ignored, as are foreign character set accent marks. StreetTalk verifies that the name is hierarchically unique. That is, organization names must be unique on the network, group names must be unique within the organization, and item names must be unique only within the group and organization.

Because each StreetTalk name is unique, access to the item is location-independent. You do not need to know the physical location of a resource on the network—VINES internally manages the correlation between physical address and StreetTalk name. This enables the administrators to move users and services around in the network with few or no changes in setup, security, or access rights.

Default Name Construction

Any time the user types the name of an item by itself, StreetTalk automatically appends the group name to it. This name is called the *default group*. As the user logs into VINES, the default group is set to the one associated with the user's logon ID. This default group enables the users to quickly access resources and other users within their own group. Similarly, the login organization name is the default organization if the user only specifies the group-name@item-name.

StreetTalk also provides a special default group facility for systems administrators. When the administrator adds or manages a group, the administrators become temporary default members of that group. The default remains in effect until they add or select another group, or log off the network.

Wild-Card Capabilities

StreetTalk has a search function that makes it easy to find network items by name. The user can display all user names in any group or organization. For services, the user displays all those of a certain type—such as file services or those maintained by a specific server. StreetTalk also provides a facility for using *pattern matching* in name specification. When this option is requested, VINES displays a special screen on which the user can type a pattern for StreetTalk to match in its search for names. The asterisk is used to specify the wild card character(s). More than one * can be used in a single pattern match.

For example, the following pattern results in VINES displaying all items in the group Marketing@South_East:

*@Marketing@South_East

The following pattern displays all items that begin with JK, in any group called Marketing, in all organizations on the network:

JK*@Marketing@*Patterned Search

VINES provides a built-in, dynamic, patterned-search capability against StreetTalk names. As names are entered, VINES qualifies the search, character-by-character.

Nicknames

StreetTalk *nicknames* are names that provide aliases for other names. These nicknames can point to users or system resources such as network printers. The nicknames facility enables users to use shortcuts for entering long names and eases the necessity to remember extensive exact spellings.

Creating Distribution Lists

StreetTalk *lists* are items that contain the StreetTalk names of other items. Lists enable the user to use one name to reference many items. This capability is useful for making distribution lists for sending network mail; administrative lists for designating administrators; and access rights for resources such as printers, data files, or connections to host computers.

Until the release of version 5.0, only an administrator could add to or modify StreetTalk lists. With version 5.0, this capability is distributable.

In multiserver networks, StreetTalk is distributed among servers on a group basis. When you add a group, you choose a server to maintain that group. This server then manages the group and coordinates access to it. Organizations, however, exist only logically, as a way of associating groups together. They are not maintained by individual servers.

Each server maintains detailed information about the items in the groups that it is responsible for. It also has a record of the groups that other servers are responsible for, including the name and location of the servers. Servers actively exchange and update StreetTalk information about groups whenever any user makes a request that involves StreetTalk. This means that routing between networks is an efficient process. Traffic is directed only to the cable segment(s) on the shortest path through which the terminating node can be reached.

This distributed approach means that there is no centralized network naming server. Duplicate checking ensures that names are unique across the network. Access to resources is consistent because the group information is maintained in only one place. Thus, a service outage only affects those resources in groups that the server maintains. Some examples of StreetTalk naming follow.

To send mail to every user in the network, address mail to:

```
*@*@*
```

To map to a file volume (service):

```
SETDRIVE F Applications@Sales@OrgName
```

To connect to a print service:

```
SETPRINT LPT1 Laserjet@MIS@OrgName
```

To connect to a host:

```
HOST IBM3090@MIS@OrgName
```

Banyan servers are set to self-synchronize the STDB files and router information at 3:00 a.m.

Understanding Banyan-Supported Protocols

Protocols are the design criteria that specify the agreements of different parts of the network on the way information is to be passed. These criteria are defined in models such as the OSI model. OSI specifies design compliance and compatibility criteria. With the basics of the model in mind, it is important to know how VINES identifies network nodes and moves data around the network.

Banyan/IP

The VINES protocol is a networking system for personal computers that was developed by Banyan; it is derived from Xerox's XNS and TCP/IP protocols. Banyan's VINES 48-bit addresses are central to the Banyan architecture. All VINES products automatically determine their addresses, and there is a guaranteed interoperability in a VINES network. The network-level address consists of two numbers, a 32-bit network number and a 16-bit number that Banyan refers to as a "subset" number (but it actually refers to a host number).

Address conflicts are impossible because VINES servers use their key serial numbers as their network numbers, and they use a subset of one. Because keys are unique, the server addresses are unique. VINES clients (end users on the network) do not have addresses—clients use a modified version of the address of the first file server found on the physical network. The clients assume the server's network number, and they are assigned a subset number by that server.

How VINES Clients Get an Address

This address-assignment scheme makes it highly probable that two clients on the same LAN will have different addresses. VINES clients boot without any knowledge of network level addresses and preferred servers.

The first thing a client does after initializing hardware interfaces is to send a broadcast message that looks for all available servers on the network. The client then waits for responses from the network. Once a message is received, it sends an address assignment request to the first server that responds to the previous message. That server computes a new, unique address based on its own network number, and then assigns the address to that client.

All of this is accomplished by sending responses directly to the MAC (Media Access Control protocol, which is data-level) address of the client, because it does not yet have a network level address. The following illustrates this sequence:

- Client => Broadcast: ?Are there any servers?
- Client <= Server2: Present
- Client <= Server1: Present
- Client => Server2: Please send me an address
- Client <= Server2: Your address is Server2:nnnn

How VINES Servers Distribute their Addresses

Every time a VINES server comes up, it broadcasts its own routing information to all other servers to which it is attached. This technique, similar to an intelligent bridge, enables all connect LANs at a single site to work as one large LAN without any human intervention.

IP Packet Contents

The typical IP packet consists of the following:

- Version number of IP in use
- Header length (the number of 32-bit words before the data field)
- Type of service indicator
- Total length of the IP packet
- 16-bit packet ID created by the originating node
- Flag that designates whether the packet may be split during transmission
- Fragmentation offset of this data in the original data (occurs only if a packet was split during the transmission process)
- Lifetime, in seconds, that a packet can exist on the network (every device that touches the packet reduces this time)
- Name of the higher-level protocol for the data portion of the packet
- Checksum of the header portion of the packet (used to ensure accuracy)
- Address assigned to the source node of the transmission
- Address assigned to the destination node of the transmission

- Free form options field used differently by various manufacturers
- Data area that holds the object of the transmission (enclosed in the envelope of a transmission control protocol such as Banyan or TCP)

TCP/IP

If you plan to integrate computers from different manufacturers that use different operating systems or different network protocols into a large-scale network, the best solution available today is TCP/IP. This standard Department of Defense transmission software consists of programs that implement two protocols: TCP (Transmission Control Protocol) and IP (Internet Protocol). TCP and IP perform primarily what the OSI model calls layer-3 (network) and layer-4 (transport) functions. TCP/IP is extensively used to communicate between different real-world computer systems because it was specifically designed and certified for this task by the DoD.

The heart of the IP portion of TCP/IP is the concept of the *internet address*, which is a 32-bit number assigned to every node on the network. It is associated with a naming convention that is very similar, externally, to the Banyan naming conventions.

Cataloging Banyan-Supported Transport Schemes

Banyan VINES supports all popular transmission media and protocols. The decision about which of these to use is influenced by several factors: media that is in place, cost, noise resistance, and speed.

Ethernet

Ethernet is a network cable and access-protocol scheme originally developed by Xerox, and now marketed primarily by Digital Equipment Corporation and 3Com. This cable scheme is used extensively in Banyan environments.

Token Ring

VINES servers and PCs can communicate through an IBM Token Ring bridge by using a protocol called *source-level routing*. An IBM Token Ring bridge connects two token ring LANs, supporting source-level communications between systems on the LAN.

Servers equipped with the token ring bridge option can emulate an IBM Token Ring bridge. This feature places the bridge inside the server and eliminates the need to dedicate PCs as Token Ring bridges. It enables VINES servers or clients to communicate across IBM Token Rring bridges to remote VINES servers. This Token Ring bridge can also be used to communicate with host processors.

A token-ring network only supports 72 workstations on the ring before the ring must be split. Ethernet does not have this limitation.

ARCnet

ARCnet is a networking architecture (marketed by Datapoint Corporation and others) that uses a token passing bus architecture, usually on coaxial cable. This scheme is quite economical, but it is best suited for applications for which speed is not the critical element.

10Base"x"

IEEE's specifications for running Ethernet over different cable types are the following:

10BaseT	Unshielded twisted pair
10Base2	Thin coaxial cable
10Base5	Thick coaxial cable

StarLAN

StarLAN is a networking system developed by AT&T that uses CSMA protocols on twisted-pair telephone wire.

Supporting Workstations with VINES

The following workstations are supported by VINES:

- **PCs**. PCs are fully supported, provided they have a supported network adapter card and run the VINES client software.
- **Apple Macintosh**. The Macintosh is supported by optional packages that are bridges to the AppleTalk protocol. (This topic is covered in more detail in the section dealing with Gateway products.)
- **OS/2**. The 4.10 and later versions of VINES provides fully-integrated support of workstations running the Microsoft or OEM versions of OS/2:

  Microsoft and all OEM Standard Edition 1.2

  IBM Standard Edition 1.2, 1.3, and 2.0

  IBM Extended Edition 1.2, 1.3, and 2.0

  Compaq Standard Edition 1.21

The optional support packages include VINES Network Mail and VINES Network Management.

OS/2 clients can access shared file services on the VINES server. DOS-compatible file names are supported. OS/2 and DOS clients can share common data files. The long-file name feature of HPFS (High Performance File System) is not supported. Files whose names do not comply with the DOS standard must be renamed for network access. Version 5.0 supports HPFS file names.

VINES also provides print redirection for OS/2 clients, so that they can share printer resources on the network (as DOS clients can).

VINES enables Microsoft Windows 3.0 and 3.1 users to access and manage network functions from within the network environment.

Expanding a VINES LAN to a WAN

A WAN is more than communication links to other servers. It also accommodates and manages different transmission protocols, and it routes transmissions quickly and efficiently.

Banyan Support

A VINES multiserver network acts like a single system with no communications boundaries. PC users have easy access to other users and to system resources, regardless of the server to which their PC is connected. Administrative control and security is consistently and comprehensively extended across the network. As each new server is added, it automatically broadcasts information about its location and communication links across the network. This information is automatically added to the dynamic routing table of other servers in the network. Banyan's internetworking capability of its IP protocol greatly facilitates WAN message delivery, and it is one of its strongest features.

The server resident dynamic routing tables enable VINES to automatically redirect interserver traffic in the event of a communications failure. When a failed link is restored, VINES automatically performs an reconnection between servers for any non-switched connection, including LAN, leased-line, X.25, and TCP/IP connections. The Server-to-Server option includes physical connections for all VINES-supported LANS via TCP/IP, X.25, SNA, Asynch, and HDLC.

One of the major advantages of Banyan is the single-vendor solution for LAN and WAN problem solving. When something goes wrong, there is a single point for support and resolution, instead of a finger-pointing battle. This can be a major advantage for ensuring the continuity of mission-critical systems.

Serial Communications Support

To utilize asynchronous dial-up, synchronous leased-line, or dial-up communications, Banyan provides an optional Intelligent Communications Adapter (ICA). For X.25 support, Banyan provides optional X.25 Server-to-Server software.

Other choices, such as ARCnet, LANSTAR, PC Net, StarLAN, VISTALAN, Ethernet, Omninet, Pronet, and token ring are covered in Banyan's WAN Server-to-Server package.

Fault Tolerance

A VINES system contains many characteristics of a fault-tolerance system. Servers "know" multiple ways to transmit data across the network. If paths are busy, blocked, or not available, VINES automatically routes the traffic through an alternate path. It can automatically choose the cheapest route for a transmission. Battery backup software is integrated into server software. The server can "sense" when normal power is interrupted, issue broadcast messages, and prepare for a controlled shutdown if normal power does not return within the specified time frame. If the server shuts itself down due to power problems, when power is restored it automatically restarts and re-establishes all dedicated communication links that were active at the time of the power failure.

The VINES/IP—TCP/IP Interface

VINES IP handles network traffic one level above the network interfaces for each network media type. Every server has a VINES IP. IP, although it is a slightly different version, is part of TCP/IP routing and TCP/IP Server-to-Server options. If a TCP/IP option is installed on a VINES server, IP traffic is automatically and cooperatively managed within that server. IP (TCP) and VINES/IP are integrated in the network level of the VINES architecture. Figure 10.3 illustrates this relationship. The TCP/IP access works, regardless of the type of LAN that the foreign system operates on.

The TCP/IP Routing option and the TCP/IP Server-to-Server option enable the server to handle IP packets, which enable TCP hosts to use VINES as a bridge. An IP packet contains data that originated from a foreign host. (*Foreign* is defined as a system that implements IP, but not the VINES IP.) These options give the server added routing functionality to handle both types of traffic. The server can route IP packets between foreign hosts—including the capability to move through several servers along the way.

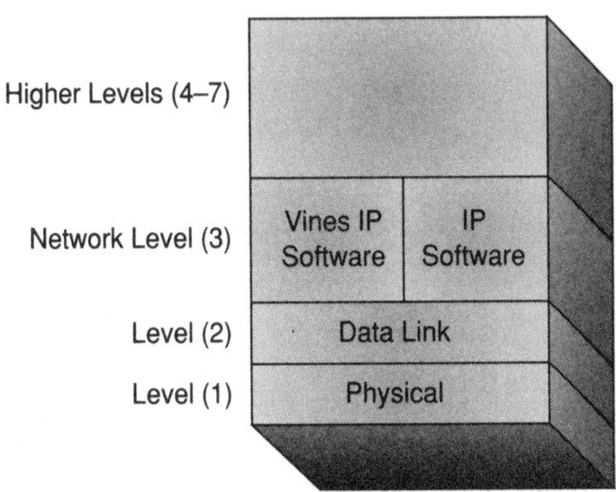

Figure 10.3:
Routing TCP/IP packets through VINES/IP.

When IP packets travel from one server to another, each server uses the VINES IP to route the IP packet. The IP packet is encapsulated in VINES IP headers. When the IP packet is routed from a VINES server to a foreign host, the VINES IP headers are removed. The TCP/IP Server-to-Server option enables a server to route VINES packets to VINES servers through foreign host gateways. A VINES packet contains data that originated on a VINES server or PC. This option enables a server to handle VINES packets that the foreign host routes to it.

When the server sends VINES packets though a foreign host gateway, VINES IP software must pass the packets to the IP software. The packets are then encapsulated in IP headers so the foreign gateway can recognize them. The reverse process happens when VINES packets are routed directly to the VINES server from a foreign host gateway.

When a server is running the TCP/IP option, sometimes VINES/IP and IP must send, receive, and route packets. Depending on the situation, VINES IP software passes packets to the IP software or reverses. When the server acts as a gateway, it decides how packets are routed. For example, if the server has to route VINES packets to a foreign host gateway, VINES IP software on the server must pass packets to IP software. The reverse process happens when VINES packets are routed to the server from a foreign host gateway, and, in turn, the server must route them to a PC or another VINES server.

Configuration and monitoring tools that are provided with the TCP/IP Routing option enable administrators to continually monitor the status of TCP/IP routes, monitor the traffic, and even read the Address Resolution Protocol (ARP) entries in the TCP/IP network.

Banyan also offers a VINES-integrated version of FTP PC/TCP. (File Transfer Protocol) PC/TCP runs on any VINES client workstation, enabling any PC on the VINES network to perform a wide range of TCP/IP applications, including the following:

- FTP file transfer
- TELENET terminal emulation
- SMTP electronic mail
- Subnetting and routing
- Berkley 4BSD UNIX "r" commands, including `flogin` and `rexec`
- IBM 3270, DEC VT100, and VT200 terminal emulations
- Printing

PC/TCP is fully integrated with VINES and requires no additional hardware. There are two versions of the product available: TCP120 and TCP121.

TCP120 operates over all VINES-supported LANs, enabling TCP/IP traffic for PC/TCP applications to travel across the VINES network and then out to a foreign host.

TCP121 operates over VINES-supported Ethernet LANs only; it is used to send TCP/IP traffic traveling directly across a TCP/IP network to a TCP/IP host, rather than traveling across a VINES network.

Understanding Gateways

A *gateway* is a device or service that provides a shared point of entry from a LAN into another (perhaps larger) information resource, such as a mainframe computer or a packet-switch network. It is a "translation point" between two different protocols. Banyan offers several optional gateways for VINES and certifies many third-party offerings.

3270 Gateway

As a communications server, the VINES system offers several ways to connect to IBM mainframes, including SNA and BSC interfaces. The 3174 emulation over token-ring connection enables VINES to communicate with the mainframe by using the SNA communications protocol.

This service enables the user to start, manage, and terminate up to four concurrent sessions on the same host. Only one of these sessions, however, can be a print session. The emulation can be resident or non-resident. The ability to "hotkey" in and out of emulation is provided for. The interface provides the capability to capture print data on disk and to customize the PC keyboard.

A 3270 file-transfer system is offered as an option. 3270/FTS works in conjunction with the time-sharing option (TSO) or the conversational monitor system (CMS) by interfacing with those editors in stand-alone mode. When used in this mode, no special software is required on the IBM mainframe computer. If an appropriate IBM host-supported file-transfer program (IND$FILE) is installed on the mainframe, however, 3270/FTS can function in host-support mode, which provides the following important advantages:

- 3270/FTS interacts with this program for extremely fast file transfers
- 3270/FTS can be executed by using the command string option, the interactive menu option, and batch command options
- 3270/FTS can transfer files between the PC and CICS (Customer Information Control System) in addition to TSO and CMS
- Record and file size restrictions imposed by TSO and CMS are eliminated

VAX/VMS Gateway

Although Banyan does not directly offer its own VAX gateway, it promotes VINES-integrated, compliance-tested products from several vendors, including: Digital Area Networks, Inc., I-Lan, Polygon, Inc., and FEL Computing.

VAX-based backup and restore features for Banyan VINES include the following:

- Provides automatic, incremental VINES logical disk backup on the VAX on-line disk storage
- Restores a lost file within 5 minutes
- Backup container files are controlled by VAX system management, and VINES logical disks to be backed up are managed by VINES Network Management
- Vax container files are dynamically allocated.

Print gateway for Banyan VINES/VAX features include the following:

- Provides bi-directional VINES-VAX print services
- Transparent printer access, without modification to VINES clients or servers
- Enables users to print by using functions with which they are already familiar
- Special features of each system's print functions are maintained
- VAX users at remove sites can use VINES wide-area servers to send print jobs from remote FAX to local VINES servers and remote print PCs

Remote-terminal capabilities for Banyan VINES/VAX features include:

- Enables the VINES user to process DEC-VAX commands and to retrieve results without terminal emulators
- VAX system commands can be requested by any VINES client user without any changes or additions to the VINES client or server
- Certain VAX commands can be executed automatically

File transfer capabilities for Banyan VINES/VAX advantages include:

- ❖ Provides bi-directional VINES-VAX file exchange
- ❖ Automatic, intelligent file transport without modifications to VINES clients or servers
- ❖ Eliminates the need for a user to know anything about the "other" system
- ❖ Special file types can be controlled or preserved during the file transfer by setting file-transfer options.

Fax routing and printing way for Banyan VINES/VAX:

- ❖ Provides for incoming and outgoing facsimile services for both VINES and VAX users
- ❖ Incoming faxes can be automatically routed to specified printers, to VAX or VINES server directories, or directly to users through VINES network mail or VAX mail
- ❖ VINES network-management feature determines which queues are available for which users
- ❖ VAX users send faxes by using the standard VMS Print command.

These products all require a dedicated gateway PC attached to the VAX.

Apple Macintosh

Banyan offers MacLAN Connect software products, which provide transparent, seamless integration of Apple Macintosh computers and Postscript printers in a Banyan VINES PC network. MacLAN serves as a gateway between VINES and AppleTalk File Protocol. It provides Macs and PCs simultaneous access to Postscript printers. Any Postscript or compatible printer connected to the VINES network can be shared by all attached workstations, Macs, or PCs.

Even non-AppleTalk printers, such as PCL printers from Hewlett-Packard, can be shared via the MacLAN connection. AFP and AppleTalk phase II-compliant software requires no software on the Macintosh side. Macs access the gateway through the chooser interface and see files stored on the VINES file server as standard Macintosh folders and icons. Printing for Macintoshes and PCs occurs in a native mode for each type of workstation. Macs use the chooser interface to select a print queue and PCs print via the VINES print-spooling mechanism.

The MacVINES Mail Gateway enables Macintosh users to exchange information across a VINES network, either with VINES client workstations or with other Macintosh computers that have access to a MacVINES Mail Gateway. The gateway works behind the scenes to convert file formats and to resolve issues between the two systems.

VINES version 5.0 encompasses Macintosh workstations within the enterprise-wide VINES environment. As a result, users can fully integrate Mac workstations with other VINES users who run DOS, OS/2, and Windows. The VINES options for Macintosh will enable AppleTalk "tunneling" through VINES. This capability makes it possible to extend the power of VINES resources to Macintosh users, and it will enable disjointed AppleTalk networks to be connected to each other over the VINES network.

AppleTalk "tunneling" is implemented through the VINES encapsulation of the AppleTalk protocol, which is similar to the VINES encapsulation of the TCP/IP protocol. Any Mac on a VINES network can access LAN and WAN resources anywhere across the enterprise. Macintosh access to VINES network services includes directory, security, management, messaging, files, and print in a transparent fashion.

To use the network resources, Mac users do not need any knowledge of network topology beyond the familiar Mac login conventions. Regardless of computing platform, VINES enables all users to run their preferred user interfaces on the same network at the same time. Version 5.0 also broadens support of VINES mail for Macintosh. The new option will seamlessly integrate Mac users into the enterprise-wide e-mail network, enabling them to create, address, read, send, and manage e-mail, along with all other VINES network mail users.

Banyan to UNIX Connectivity

Banyan VINES connectivity to UNIX-based systems is implemented through the use of the TCP/IP option. Future versions of VINES will also be based on, and be fully integrated with, SCO UNIX. This means that VINES clients will be able to access applications, files, and resources in SCO UNIX systems, and SCO users with proper network security will be able to do the same on the VINES network.

VINES provides entrance to UNIX System V on three levels (see table 10.2).

Table 10.2
VINES/UNIX Services Integration

API	*Client*	*Server*
Communications:		
IPC	Y	Y
SPP	Y	Y
NetRPC	Y	Y
Services:		
StreetTalk	Y	Y
TCP	Y	Y
X.25	Y	Y
Messaging:		
Mail		Y
Gateway		Y

Supporting Novell Internetworking

Although Banyan does not directly offer its own Novell gateway, it does promote a VINES integrated, compliance-tested product from Hughes LAN System and Trellis.

A gateway connects Novell and Banyan VINES networks in a bi-directional file bridge. There are two Banyan/Novell gateways; one handles file requests from VINES to NetWare, and the other handles file requests from NetWare to VINES. Each runs on a dedicated workstation, which remains logged into both VINES and NetWare.

The VINES-to-NetWare gateway maps drive letters to NetWare file volumes. VINES workstations then can access these logical drives. The NetWare-to-VINES gateway does the same function in the opposite direction, setting drive letters to VINES file services.

A resident program runs on each workstation that needs access to the gateway. This program intercepts cross-network file requests and routes them to the appropriate gateway.

Users who are logged into VINES can read and write data files on the NetWare server. They can also run DOS applications stored there. The NetWare file volumes look like normal DOS drives. From the NetWare side, users can read and write files on the VINES server. They can run applications that do not require VINES-integrated functions.

The Trellis gateway can bridge two physical layers, one for VINES and one for NetWare, or it can act as a go-between for both networks running on one physical layer.

Communicating with VINES

Banyan VINES supports several communications options within the network and beyond.

Serial Communications

VINES can support several serial-communications options, based on the Banyan ICA (Intelligent Communications Adapter). The ICA family consists of two serial communications cards that connect a single VINES network server to a variety of different host computers, public and private data networks, dial-in PCs, and other VINES system servers. Both cards include six high-speed communications ports.

The top of the line, ICAplus, is supported in VINES 4.11 and higher. It can communicate over fractional T1 lines at speeds in any increments from 64kps to 385kps.

The standard ICA adapter provides support for any VINES-approved platform, and it can communicate at speeds up to 64kbps. Like ICAplus, it gives users the capability to mix and match multiple protocols on a single card. It also provides serial communication ports for both ISA- and EISA-based servers. The on-board microprocessor eliminates the need to tap into system CPU power. Users can use a dedicated or a switched line, but they must tell the server which type it is when assigning the line.

The broad protocol support of the ICA family provides great flexibility in server configurations. As the network continues to evolve, this flexibility enables convenient protocol changes without having to replace the card.

For example, one ICA card can support one IBM SNA mainframe connection, one X.25 network connection, two DEC VAX connections, and two PC dial-in connections. If, at a later date, the user wants to switch from X.25 to HDLC, it is a simple matter of redefining one of the communications ports on the card. Banyan also offers a V.35 adapter, which is fully compatible with the ICA cards.

A VINES server can utilize multiple ICA and ICAplus cards, based on system configuration and licensing. The serial-communications options are discussed in the following sections.

WAN-to-WAN Server

The Wan-to-Wan server option enables users to connect two VINES servers together—either by using a block-oriented asynchronous protocol or with a synchronous protocol, such as HDLC (Hierarchical Data Link Control).

X.25/X.29

The X.25/X.29 option enables users to connect servers over an X.25/X.29 network. It supports the X.25 protocol, as defined in CCITT X.25, and uses HDLC through synchronous modems.

SDLC (3270/SNA)

The SDLC (3270/SNA) option enables users to connect a server to an IBM host that is running SNA (Systems Network Architecture). It is available in session groupings of 16, 32, 64, and 96, and it includes a file-transfer facility.

3270/BSC

The 3270/BSC option enables users to connect a server to an IBM host running BSC (Binary Synchronous Protocol). It is available in session groupings of 32 and 64, and it includes a file-transfer facility.

Asynchronous Terminal Emulation

The asynchronous terminal-emulation option enables users to connect a server to a host that uses an asynchronous character-oriented protocol.

PC Dial-in

The PC dial-in option enables users to connect a server to a host that uses a block-oriented asynchronous protocol. This optional package, called PC Dial-In, enables users to dial in over a modem to the server and log into the network.

Shared Modems and FAX

Banyan offers modem pools of up to six modems. They can range from speeds of 9600 baud through 19.2K and 56K baud. The modems are accessible via a "next available" search algorithm.

Network Management Software

The network management software is a real-time network monitor. Fully integrated with StreetTalk, it provides a comprehensive study of network-wide performance from any PC or server console. It compiles current diagnostic performance and utilization statistics. The administrator can examine the performance of all network components, including LAN/WAN connections, system configurations VINES software service, server disks, and network routing.

In addition to providing relevant statistics, the software can help the administrator improve inter-server network performance by providing a simultaneous view of activities across multiple servers to balance the loads across the network and to avoid performance bottlenecks.

Keeping the Network Secure

VINES security is fully integrated with StreetTalk. It is based conceptually on IBM's ACF (Access Control Facility). Designed to enforce a distributed security policy, it is implemented in access-rights lists, consistent across the network, and it is easy to manage.

In VINES, there is no "superuser" concept. Administration of the network is decentralized. The authorization for administration is set up by the group, as defined by the list AdminList@Group@Org. Only administrators have the capability to install and configure applications or to add new servers and organizations to the network. They also determine the administrators at the server level for each server in the list AdminList@Servername@Servers.

Administrators at the server level control the capability to add server-related functions, as well as add file services and print services.

VINES Security Features include the following:

- ❖ Password encryption with no session replay
- ❖ Unauthorized login protection and tracking
- ❖ Physical location restriction
- ❖ Password length, life, and change control
- ❖ Login time restrictions
- ❖ Limit on simultaneous workstations/user logins
- ❖ User password and profile modification restrictions
- ❖ User expiration control

- Dial-in privilege control

File-service security is provided through access-rights lists. These are applied at the directory or subdirectory level in version 4.11, and they are applicable down to the file level in version 5.0. The four levels of access control are the following:

- **Null**. No access
- **Read**. Read only
- **Modify**. Read, write, create and delete subdirectories
- **Control**. Modify access, change the ARL (access rights list)

Print-service security is provided through access-rights lists. A separate ARL is defined for each print service. It controls which users can use the printer and what levels of print-queue manipulation they have.

Logging capabilities are controlled by the server administrator. Once selected, the log files are managed automatically; they are viewable by an administrator at any workstation. Log information can be used for security, audit trails, debugging, or basic information.

VINES is the first NOS ever to apply for the C2-level security compliance from the National Security Administration.

Using Database Servers

Many database servers, such as Revelation, DataEase, Condor, dBase IV, FoxPro, Informix, Ingres, Nomad, Paradox, Focus, and Ramis, run on the VINES server. The Oracle server for VINES is specially integrated into the VINES environment.

Oracle for VINES is a relational database-management system, suited for applications development. It is a portable, distributed, and open DBMS that delivers high performance, continuous operation, and support for very large databases.

Oracle is based on the ANSI standard SQL, and it encompasses a complete set of integrated software tools for application development and decision-support systems.

The Oracle server's tight integration with VINES enables any VINES user to access and administer an Oracle database like any other VINES service. Oracle operates as a VINES server-based service, co-existing with other file, print, mail, and communications services. It is assigned a unique StreetTalk name, which enables any PC user to transparently access an Oracle database without regard for location or access path.

Oracle's file and record-locking mechanisms work with VINES' network security to ensure data integrity and to prevent unauthorized access to data resources. The Oracle server supports VINES connections over LAN and WAN configurations. It can run both VINES and TCP/IP concurrently, enabling a true integration of VINES LANS with corporate TCP/IP networks.

The Oracle server provides "fault-tolerant" data recovery, integrity, and security, as well as hot-backup capability. In addition, backup is simplified by Oracle's tight integration with VINES' backup utility. The server offers support for DOS, OS/2, UNIX, and Macintosh. The client/server architecture fully exploits all of the latest hardware, including the advanced symmetrical multiprocessors.

Managing the Network

MNET (*M*anage the *NET*work) is the VINES network performance-management tool. It provides a wide overview of the network on a semi-real-time basis. *Semi-real-time* means that some of the metrics used in network management are "snapshots" of current activity; others represent activity that takes some period of time. It can also be used as a server performance tool. MNET runs as a server-based application, which collects and distributes statistics. It provides a user interface on the console and workstation levels. Clients must register with the server service, and tell it which statistics to monitor. Some VINES internal procedures collect data continuously.

MNET selects samples once-per-second and broadcasts the information once-per-minute. The statistics are based on an exponential decaying average, that is, they are weighted toward the most recent samples collected. The four classes of available statistics include:

- Statistics collected since the server was last booted
- Statistics collected while anyone in the network is running the MNET program
- Statistics collected while users are running the MNET program
- Statistics collected while a specific MNET screen is displayed

The MNET display screen "tree" enables the system manager to selectively specify statistics for various areas of the system, as shown in Table 10.3.

Many of the MNET screens map to the OSI model, as shown in the Table 10.4.

Table 10.3

MNET Statistics and Screens

Monitored Areas	*Screen*
Service Applications	Service Statistics
Detailed Server Statistics	I/O Statistics
Node Connections	Neighbor Screen
Server Disks	Disk Usage
Cache System	File System Statistics
Comm Buffer	Communication Statistics
ICA Card	Serial Line Interface
Data Link & Physical Layer	Selected LAN Interface card
Network Layer	VINES IP Interface
TCP/IP Network	IP Interface
RS232 & X.25	Selected Communication Interface

Certifying VINES Hardware Platforms

Certification is the process that Banyan does with the PC vendor to test and verify that its platform works with VINES. The goal of this process is to help both the network procurer and Banyan understand which platforms work properly with VINES, in order to eliminate downtime and offer the best possible level of support. This process has initial testing and ongoing certification phases.

Table 10.4
MNET Statistics Screens and the OSI Model

Model Level	*Statistics Screen*
7 Application & 6 Presentation	Service Statistics & Disk Statistics
5 Session & 4 Transport	Communication Statistics
3 Network	VINES IP Detail
2 Data Link &	Summary Screen, Interface screen,
1 Physical level	Interface Details, Serial Communications, Neighbors screen

In the initial testing, the vendor tests the proposed platform for 72 continuous hours, during which the tests emulate heavy database usage. The vendor also must set up a mini-network, in which the tests emulate server-to-server communications by the use of ICA cards, as well as information from clients in both token ring and Ethernet configurations. Once these tests are completed, the tape of the results is sent to Banyan for evaluation.

Assuming that the first phase is approved, the vendor must ship the entire platform to Banyan; it is then used for ongoing support and recertification for VINES and vendor changes.

Summary

In this chapter, you learned about VINES advantages for the user. All resources appear as a single system. No matter what type of workstation you work on—DOS, OS/2, or Macintosh—or where it is physically located, access to information is as simple as your native workstation. Security of information is consistent. Network topology is completely hidden from users. You only need to know the name of the resource; VINES does the rest. VINES' access to all resources (printers, host systems, and other LANs) is simple and consistent across the network.

This chapter also discussed the VINES advantages for the administrator. VINES provides comprehensive network-management and statistical-analysis tools that can be used from any station in the network. VINES provides the flexibility to choose other tools and it also provides the administrator with complete control over all network resources.

You learned about the VINES' advantages for management, which include the fact that initial investments in hardware, software, staff, applications and tools are all protected. VINES architecture is scalable, and it can expand along with the organization. Because VINES is a standards-based product, there is longevity and continuity for the organization's investments.

VINES provides the lowest life-cycle costs for network operation and management.

Part Four: Network Management

Introduction to Network Management

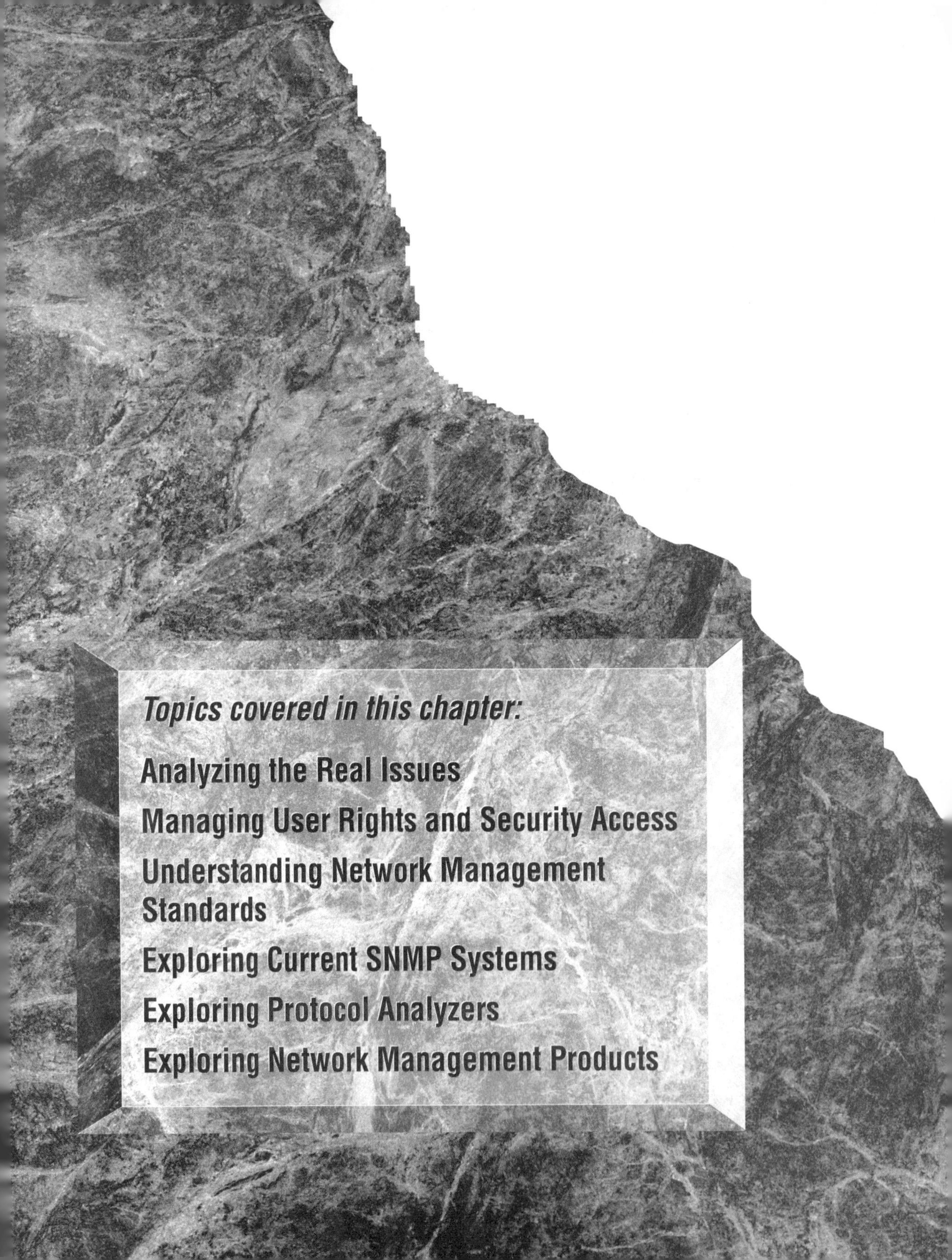
Topics covered in this chapter:
Analyzing the Real Issues
Managing User Rights and Security Access
Understanding Network Management Standards
Exploring Current SNMP Systems
Exploring Protocol Analyzers
Exploring Network Management Products

Chapter 11

Introduction to Network Management

As networks grow in size—from two and three workstation LANs to multiserver and multisegment interconnected systems with thousands of users—the task of keeping the system operating becomes more complex and difficult. The role of network management is to assist in this task and ease the growth and expansion of the network. Historically, network management has been defined by vendors in the communications industry as the configuration, control, and monitoring of the devices they provide. The subject of network management, however, has a much broader scope, particularly as users migrate from simple networks with one or two manageable devices to complex internetworks with management available for every device in the network. Recently, the focus has become enterprise-wide, integrated network management to manage all components and aspects of the network as one cooperative entity.

Network management consists of configuring, monitoring, controlling, and analyzing the resources available in the network; optimizing the use of those resources; and preventing and solving users' problems. Because of the disastrous effects of network downtime in even medium-scale networks, network management currently focuses on detecting potential faults and problems before they become critical. True network management performs the broader role of assisting network administrators in day-to-day management tasks as diverse as adding new users, manipulating printer queues, and scheduling backups.

The field of network management is rapidly evolving against a background of vague user requirements and little practical understanding by users of the tangible benefits provided. The primary function of network management is to increase the quality of the network's operation.

A network management system's effectiveness can be measured by the amount of decrease in network downtime, the efficiency with which resources are shared, and a knowledge of the assets in the network.

Analyzing the Real Issues

An early need of network users was backup. In the days of mainframe-based computing, all data was stored at a central site, which made comprehensive backup easy. But with the advent of LANs, information was spread over the network, forcing the development of more sophisticated techniques to ensure the generation of reliable backups across the network. These techniques began as simple utilities running in the background of crucial nodes and servers on the network. As networks became more complicated, additional integrated applications were required.

The backup industry, which began as a group of utilities operating independently of various network nodes, evolved into sophisticated, integrated applications that provided reliable and comprehensive network backup.

The evolution of network management products parallels the development of the backup industry. Currently, a variety of specialized utilities perform various aspects of network management, but few vendors have made attempts to integrate products that address the real and comprehensive needs of network managers.

For example, every network operating system vendor includes a group of basic tools to perform network administration. The focus of these tools, however, is on administrative tasks, such as adding and deleting users, sharing devices, and organizing print queues. In most cases, the tools display some status of workstations and servers. Very little information, if any, is provided on the efficiency of the network. And the crude presentation of the data makes it difficult or impossible to troubleshoot problems, tune the network's performance, and improve network end-user satisfaction.

This situation prompted third-party software vendors to develop utilities to address the typical administrator's needs. Utilities exist to perform tasks such as the following:

- ❖ Graphically monitor printer queues, with automatic rerouting to backup printers in the event of a failure
- ❖ View the configuration of the server in a easy-to-read format
- ❖ Perform workstation and server hardware/software inventory

- ❖ Meter server software usage for license management
- ❖ Detect viruses
- ❖ Manage server modems
- ❖ Diagnostically monitor remote workstations
- ❖ Automatically manage backup
- ❖ Manage system FAX servers

Most of these utilities are stand-alone packages, without mechanisms to work together or share data. The administrator, therefore, must be adept at switching between many separate programs to effectively manage the network. An integrated solution to this problem can improve dramatically the efficiency of network management.

The following sections discuss typical management issues that network administrators face. Real benefits come from products that provide integrated solutions across as many of the following categories as possible.

Backup

Probably the single most important network-management activity is the timely backup and archiving of network files. End users consider the network to be just another device their computer is attached to, and tend to take the integrity of data for granted. Because of the complexity involved in networks, backup can become an administrative nightmare. Most backups are made to tape, and generally occur on some sort of automated schedule. The critical issues concerning backup are listed below:

- ❖ Can the backup hardware, usually a tape drive, support the amount of server data required?

- Does the software work over the network, with the tape device located on a server different from the one from which the data is backed up?
- Can workstation data and server data be backed up? Frequently, network users want to maintain critical data files on their local hard disk, but desire automatic backup at regular intervals.
- Can the backup system store system-administration files, such as the Novell Bindery?
- Does the backup system preserve all file attributes, particularly those that apply to network files, such as sharing modes and security information.
- Can files be restored selectively from a backup?
- Can the backup be performed unattended at a prescheduled time?

There are two forms of backup that can be performed by most backup software: *incremental backups* and *full backups.* An incremental backup contains only the files that have been created or changed since the last full backup was performed. Incremental backups can be done quickly, compared to the time required to do full backups, because only data files are changed. Because each method has different advantages, most network administrators perform a combination of the two.

Because a full backup contains a complete record of all files, it should be performed initially. Typically, the network administrator performs incremental backups after a full backup. To restore data after a failure, the administrator must first restore each incremental backup, in order, up until the time of the failure. Because this process can be time-consuming, full backups should be done as often as is practical. Most network sites perform complete backups on a weekly basis and incremental backups daily.

Although backup is an important issue for network managers, the promise of backup management as a component of integrated network management appears distant. Because most backup software operates as stand-alone packages provided by network third-party vendors, integration is difficult. In the future, backup software manufacturers will be able to build in network-management capability.

Novell and Microsoft both now provide third-party developers with the capability to monitor and control their applications from a management console that uses the Simple Network Management Protocols (SNMP). Hopefully, backup software that supports these management facilities will be available in the near future.

Configuration

Proper configuration of the network servers is crucial for efficient network operation. *Configuration* includes the installation of device drivers and protocols, as well as the definition of abstract network resources such as shares, devices, queues, and services. Typically, you perform these operations by using the standard console utilities provided by the network operating system vendor. For example, when you use Microsoft LAN Manager, you perform all of these definitions by using either NET ADMIN or SETUP. Novell systems use SYSCON and FCONSOLE.

These utilities usually provide a complete description of the configuration of the server. Statistics and performance tuning also can be accomplished with these tools. Most of the data displayed by server network-management utilities can be retrieved by using the console programs. But the presentation of the data by the console programs is cryptic at best and is not designed for ease of management. Information can be difficult to interpret, even if you are very familiar with the program.

For example, server statistics for a LAN Manager server are shown in a dialog box that only can display the values for one server at a time. The only way to compare values between servers is to write down the value and flip back through the menus to select another server. Novell systems have the same problem, but there are more menus to traverse. The focus of thes system-administration utilities is the occasional reconfiguration or examination of server settings, not full-scale network management.

A number of adjustments can be made to the server configuration if performance is a problem. With Novell NetWare, the *cache-hit ratio* statistic is a strong indicator of poor server performance. This number represents the percentage of time that the server responds to a request directly from memory, without accessing the hard drive.

A server should be able to reach a cache-hit ratio of at least 90 percent, and 95-99 percent can be achieved. If you observe lower ratios, increasing the number of cache buffers solves the problem.

The real memory required is computed by multiplying the number of cache buffers by the cache-buffer size. (Usually, 50-70 percent of the total memory installed in the server should be devoted to cache buffers.

Other configuration changes that can improve server performance include installing faster disk drives and controllers, splitting cabling, and compressing the server disk-file system.

Windows Workstation, produced by Automated Design Systems, is a good example of a third-party network-configuration utility. Windows Workstation enables the network administrator to centrally control the desktops of all Microsoft Windows users on the network. In addition to extensive printer management, central definitions are provided for program location and icons. If a new program is installed on the network, the administrator can add the central database to the program; all of the workstations are updated instantly. Without this product, every Windows desktop on every workstation in the network requires manual updating.

Inventory

A rapidly emerging area of the network-management marketplace is automatic inventory software. These programs automatically determine the basic hardware, operating system, and network configuration of the workstations on the network. Their databases can provide a clear and up-to-date picture of the configuration of each workstation. Figure 11.1 shows the database description of a node using Magee's Network HQ inventory program.

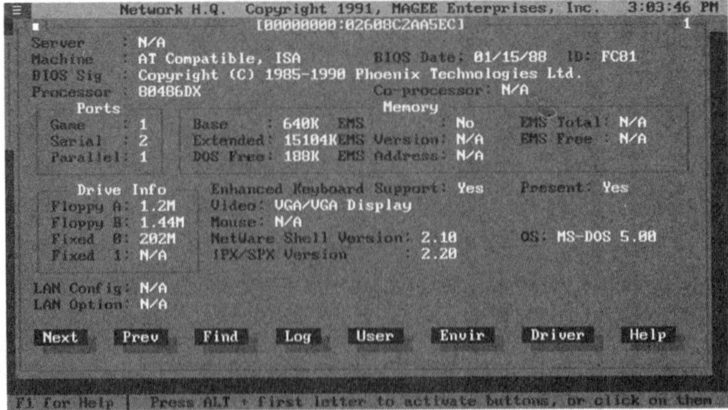

Figure 11.1:
Network HQ inventory record.

An important benefit of an accurate inventory is asset-tracking and management. Some packages enable the user to designate asset numbers for each device in the system. Reports can be generated that list all workstations containing a specified configuration, such as processor type or BIOS version number. Any change in hardware at a workstation generates an alarm, along with a log message that describes what happened. This feature is invaluable for quickly detecting the disappearance or unauthorized reconfiguration of valuable computer hardware. In some cases, it also can alert the manager of the failure of a noncritical or rarely used device, and it can enable the manager to take corrective action before the user notices the problem.

Most of the products that are available function either by login script or by an active TSR agent. Some provide data collection by diskette, but data gathered by a manager who walks around and inserts a diskette in each machine does not generate most of the benefits the manager requires. Products that use the login script have a program that is executed automatically as part of each user's login process. At that time, a program from the server is loaded on the workstation that inventories the hardware and saves the results in a database on the server. This process is usually transparent to the user, and it takes only seconds to complete. The primary advantage of this approach is that the inventory software does not disturb the user. The disadvantage is that the inventory is only as accurate as the last login to the network.

The other way to gather inventory is to place a TSR agent on each workstation. This agent is actually a program that runs in the background on the workstation at all times. The primary disadvantage of this inventory program is the amount of memory it uses; less memory is available for the user to operate regular programs. The advantages of an agent are activity-monitoring and the capability to remotely take action at the user's workstation. When a user complains about an error, the network manager can get a complete picture of the user's screen to view the message.

If necessary, the manager can take control of the user's system, reconfigure his workstation, and even reboot the machine. This saves time for the manager who no longer needs to run between machines to assist users. Most machines today are loaded to capacity with software, however, and users do not have the memory needed to devote to an active monitoring agent. Some users also may resent the ability of the manager to check up on them at any time, and thus may resist installation of the software.

Exact workstation hardware information is required to resolve certain difficult-to-catch user complaints, such as performance. For example, if a user reports that his system operates in a degraded manner under Microsoft Windows, the first place to look is at the processor, memory configuration, memory usage, and hard-disk capacity of the machine. A good inventory package provides all the information needed to get a clear picture of the workstation configuration. If the machine appears to meet the minimum requirements of Windows, then the next step is to examine the installed software and Windows setup.

Another useful feature of inventory packages is their capability to retrieve files and review the software configuration of the machine. In many situations, you must know the contents of the user's AUTOEXEC.BAT and CONFIG.SYS files. As Windows becomes popular, the WIN.INI and SYSTEM.INI files also become critical. Other software capabilities useful when the network manager is remotely debugging problems are the installed device drivers and the contents of environment variables.

As in the previous example, if a Windows program performs poorly, you may need to know that Smartdrive is specified in the

CONFIG.SYS file, but it is not listed as an active device driver. This means that it failed when loaded and was never actually activated. The capability to both retrieve files and examine what is actually loaded is important. If the network administrator has only part of the information, the actual problem may not be fully apparent, and the partial information may be misleading.

Detailed descriptions of installed network cards and the configuration of the cards also should be provided by the inventory program. Network-card configuration, network versions, and network types all can be useful for detecting equipment conflicts.

The significant questions to consider when you evaluate inventory software are the following:

- ❖ Does the product detect all of the hardware required?
- ❖ Can data fields be entered manually to designate users of workstations, their phone numbers, and asset-tracking numbers?
- ❖ Is data collected by login scripts, agents, or diskettes?
- ❖ How easily can reports be produced? Are they customizable?
- ❖ Is the product priced per node, per server, or per management console?
- ❖ Can files be retrieved and device drivers be detected?
- ❖ Can data be exported easily to other programs for statistical analysis or report generation?

Version Control and Distribution

Probably the most annoying problem for network administrators is the unmanageable number of software versions that must be supported. An administrator can spend hours working with a user to solve a problem that is caused by an out-of-date version of a application, utility, or system file. You can eliminate these problems by requiring all users on the network to use the same versions of software products. Software-distribution systems can automate this process. Automatic software distribution is an emerging area of network management because of the benefits it offers to the administrator.

These systems automatically scan for the installed versions of specified software each time a user logs on to the network. If an out-of-date program or a data file is detected, the file is updated automatically. Some of these software-distribution systems can set up a complex operating environment, such as Windows, with device-driver installation and automatic system rebooting. The only disadvantage is the length of time it takes to perform the scanning and automatic installation. Users may become annoyed by the scanning delays or installation times required.

Some systems employ an agent, which is similar to the method used for workstation inventory. The agent performs the time-consuming installation when the workstation is idle (or during after-hour periods).

Several vendors have developed, or are developing, automated software distribution systems, and many are in conjunction with groupware or similar applications. None has gained popular acceptance, but a number of products should be readily available by next year.

Software License Metering

Software license metering programs work like inventory programs. An agent monitors the number of users accessing a program simultaneously, either at the server or on the workstation. As every new user tries to access the program, a counter is checked to see if the number of users exceeds the number of licenses purchased. Some packages note that the license was exceeded and indicate that the manager needs to purchase additional copies of the desired software. Other metering systems actually prevent more than the licensed number of users from running the program; the user is told that all licenses are in use and to try later or to contact the administrator. Some packages even have the capability to graphically display the number of licenses currently in use.

A package that performs metering at the server is preferred to one that relies on agents at the client because the administration is less likely to be circumvented by network users and does not require any memory in the user's workstation. The one advantage that workstation-based monitoring provides is a count of the software in use that is actually installed on the client and not on the server.

Managing User Rights and Security Access

User or account permissions and security are controlled by the network console programs. Different network-operating systems have different degrees of flexibility in their definition of permissions. All full-featured systems provide the capability to perform the following tasks:

- ❖ Define groups of user accounts with similar permissions
- ❖ Assign rights to a user by group or individually
- ❖ Assign a logon script—a special batch file—that is executed each time a user logs into the network
- ❖ Manage access to disk directories and placing limits on the amount of space used by any account

Some network operating systems enable a supervisor to modify account information from the command line without using the console program, which is useful when a repetitive operation needs to be performed on a large number of accounts. Figure 11.2 shows an OS/2 command file that modifies each of a number of accounts to give them access to a new shared resource. This process is much quicker than using the menu systems to access every account and type in the new information.

```
net access \acctg\books /grant msmith:rwc
net access \acctg\books /grant tjones:rwc
net access \acctg\books /grant rharris:rwc
net access \acctg\books /grant droberts:rwc
net access \acctg\books /grant jdavis:rwc
net access \acctg\books /grant rpaul:rwc
```

Figure 11.2:
Command file to update accounts with access to a new shared resource.

Virus Detection

Virus-scanning programs use several techniques to detect infected programs. Some of these methods include changing file lengths, performing checksums over entire programs or regions of programs, or changing system boot and program disk areas. Data files are usually not scanned because the virus must be contained in (or activated by) a program in order to damage files or reproduce.

A combination of these methods is usually necessary to detect most viruses. Most scanning programs do not reveal which techniques they use.

Because of the proliferation of computer viruses throughout the computer industry, users have become concerned with virus prevention and detection. For example, the Michelangelo virus was so commonplace that it was distributed on factory software disks from several major software vendors. The Internet Worm spread wildly across the internet in hours. These situations clearly indicate the need for regular virus scanning and removal. Even sites that prohibit the introduction of "foreign" disks are not guaranteed to be free from the risks of viruses.

Fortunately, an entire industry for virus detection has rushed to meet this need. It is now possible to place a program in the system login script that automatically checks for viruses every time the user logs in to the network or at prescheduled times. To scan the entire hard disk on a workstation, however, can be time-consuming. Users may be annoyed by the delays caused by scanning at login. In an environment in which the risk of viruses is great, however, the benefits of virus scanning definitely outweigh the inconvenience.

As an alternative to specific virus-scanning programs, security can be gained on network drives by the careful definition of access rights. Network directories that contain executable files that are often infected by viruses can be made read-only to all users except the Supervisor. As a result, any virus attempting to infect one of the files triggers a write protection access violation. For diskless workstations this can be a particularly effective solution. Unfortunately, this method does not protect data files.

Multiprotocol Support

Most of today's network operating systems enable a single device driver to communicate with the network card in a workstation. Because of the proliferation of networks, however, many users find that they need to attach to more than one type of network server at a time. For example, suppose a company that runs NetWare with IPX acquires a new division that already has a LAN Manager network with NETBEUI. Some users need to access files in each system, using both of the protocols. This situation is particularly true for the network manager. To maintain administrative control over both networks by using two workstations or to reboot between accesses is not a good solution.

To solve this problem, multiprotocol drivers were developed. In the simplest sense, these drivers enable multiple device drivers to "share" the single network card. Only one network operating system, LAN Manager 2.1, provides these drivers by default. A number of network manufacturers and third parties, however, offer products for other network operating systems that solve the problem. This capability also is important if a network's primary protocol is a typical NOS protocol (such as IPX), and SNMP-capable bridges and routers are in the network to be managed. The management station must be able to simultaneously access the native network protocol IPX, as well as TCP/IP, to communicate with SNMP devices.

Figure 11.3 shows Windows File Manager simultaneously accessing a LAN Manager 2.1 server and a NetWare 3.11 server. The difference between the two servers and protocols is transparent to the user. Files can be copied from one to another, as if they were all on one network operating system. Activation of the appropriate support programs, such as login dialog boxes and resource connection management dialog boxes are handled automatically, according to the appropriate environment.

NetView

NetView is IBM's network-management system. NetView is based on SMA (System Management Architecture). The product depends on mainframes, and it is designed principally for the management of large-scale mainframe networks. It consists of an alarm and an event database. IBM has a variety of products that can collect LAN alarms and forward them for reporting in a NetView environment. These products include NetView/PC and IBM's System View product line. Future plans include more active management by NetView, as well as support of OSI CMIS and CMIP.

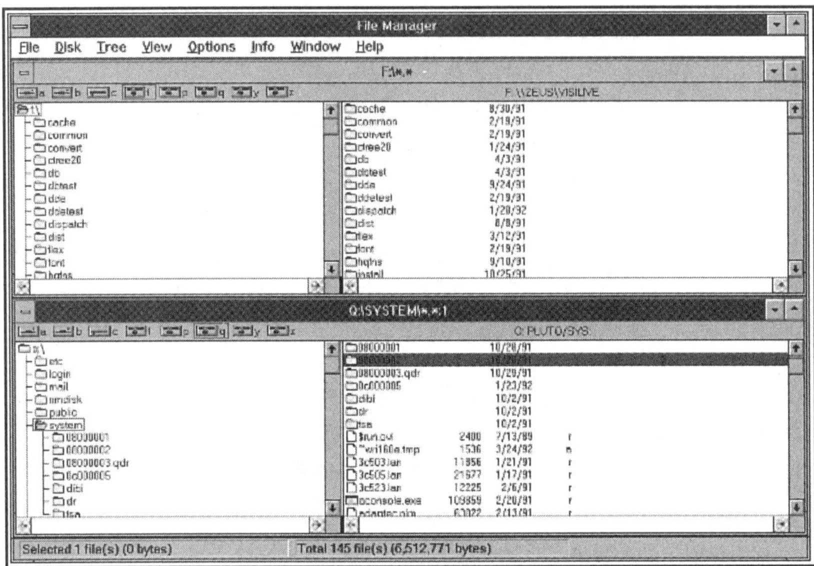

Figure 11.3:
LAN Manager and Novell NetWare connectivity in Windows File Manager.

In LAN management, references to NetView mean support of NetView connectivity or the capability to forward alarms and events to a NetView host. For example, Digital Communications Associates' Select Communications Server establishes a direct link to NetView via SNA. Alarms can then be sent to NetView, along with requests from users to the mainframe operators. Microsoft LAN Manager and Novell NetWare 3.11 offer optional packages to pass alerts to NetView. More products will provide this direct support of NetView in the near future.

Accumaster

Accumaster is AT&T's integrated, graphical network-management system. It is a component of AT&T's Unified Network Management Architecture. The product uses an X-Windows interface to associate and display logical network information with physical network data received from AT&T Element Management Systems. One of the innovations provided by Accumaster is a self-contained terminal-emulation program, in a separate window, that enables the network manager to directly connect to managed devices and to perform remote control. A goal of Accumaster is to be a "manager of managers" by tying together the multitude of individual AT&T element managers into one unified network-management system. The individual managers report to Accumaster via an AT&T-defined network management protocol, NMP. The product primarily provides alarm integration and configuration consolidation from the separate element managers.

AT&T maintains an active role in the development of OSI standards, and Accumaster is one the few network-management systems to seriously attempt to implement that complex model of management.

Understanding Network Management Standards

The goal of standards in network management is to provide simultaneous administration and management of devices from different vendors by a single console. Since it was first proposed in the mid-1980s, standardization has been more of a promise than a reality. The goal of true multivendor interoperability has only recently been realized with SNMP management systems and devices. As consumer demand for single console management grows, device manufacturers will be forced to produce standards-based products.

OSI Network Management

The creation of OSI (Open Systems Interconnection) is an attempt to define a standard mechanism for communication between computers. The standard is administered by ISO/EC, which is the International Organization for Standardization and International Electrotechnical Committee. OSI is only one of many international standards that ISO/EC manages. OSI management is the means for network management of devices within the OSI communications environment. Because of their complexity, the development and adoption of the OSI standards have been slow. All of the descriptions that follow are abstract and do not represent actual software implementations of the standards. Hopefully, this will change in the future, but you should know that management systems utilizing this model are not readily available.

A Framework for Management

The following five categories of network management are the services, components, tools, or functional areas envisioned in the OSI-management model. Note that each of these categories is a proposal for a tool that satisfies a specific need of the network manager. A network-management system is not required to provide all of the services described, or to organize the functionality according to the way the components are specified in this model.

Fault Management

According to the OSI framework, the purpose of fault management is to provide fault detection, diagnosis, correction, and administration. Fault messages are transmitted in the network data to the fault-detection component of the network manager. The OSI manager logs the fault and provides the capability to notify the user that a fault or alarm has occurred.

In practice, fault detection often results in a trouble-ticket for tracking problem resolution and response times. Fault diagnosis is intended to be an automatic system to find the cause of a fault and automatically notify the fault-correction component of the network manager. Automatic diagnosis is performed by activating diagnostic routines on which network components are remotely tested. The test results are processed by the fault-correction module, which attempts to remotely control network devices to restore the network to an operating state automatically. Fault administration provides for the definition of faults to the management system, a review of current faults, and the definitions required for the operation of the diagnosis and correction tools.

Configuration Management

The function of configuration management is to identify, configure, and control devices on the network. This function includes the capability to name, set, and modify parameters; and the capability to remotely access the device on the network.

Performance Management

Performance management provides a mechanism to evaluate the system's reliability and level of performance. This task involves the collection, storage, and reporting of performance statistics; and may include expert systems to model and suggest changes to improve performance.

Accounting Management

Accounting management provides tools to account for and to limit the resources of users in the network. Accounting management helps to determine the costs of network resources and provides the capability to inform users of the cost of resources consumed.

Security Management

Security management provides tools for the management of security and the authorization of users to access network resources.

OSI Network Management Objects

Information is transmitted between several conceptual objects within an OSI management system. Each object performs a role in the management scheme and typically consists of a separate piece of software. Figure 11.4 shows the relationships between the different types of objects. More than one software object may reside on a single node in the network.

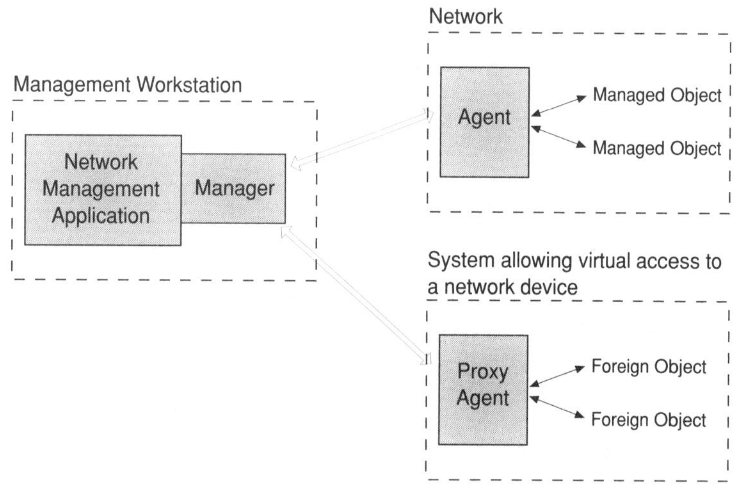

Figure 11.4:
Relationships between managed objects.

Manager

The network *manager* provides the user interface to network-management information. The manager also provides the standard management services described in the preceding sections, including any data storage and manipulation required for those services.

Managed Object

A *managed object* is any device in the network that can be monitored or controlled by using the management protocol. Managed objects run the full range of network devices: bridges, routers, servers, workstations, intelligent hubs, and software.

Agent

An *agent* is a component of the system that resides on a node and communicates to a manager by using the Common Management Information Protocol (CMIP). The agent passes control and status information between the managed object and the managers on the network.

Proxy Agent

A *proxy agent* is a special kind of agent that translates management data from foreign objects that do not support the management protocol into a form that an OSI management system understands. A proxy agent enables the management system to report on objects that reside on the network and contain important status, but which cannot directly communicate with the manager. The agent can summarize diverse information from a variety of agents for presentation to the manager.

Foreign Object

Network objects that do not understand the management protocol are called *foreign objects*. These include host systems, gateways, or even independent software residing on managed nodes.

CMIS and CMIP

Common Management Information Protocol (CMIP) is an international standard that specifies procedures for the transmission of management information between managed objects and managers. The format of the data is specified in an abstract way so that a variety of data formats can be encoded. Common Management Information Service (CMIS) is the method that network-management applications use to monitor and control network objects. CMIS requests are translated into CMIP transactions.

Current Usage

IBM, AT&T, and other large-scale network-management vendors have pledged to support the OSI standards. Few actual OSI products have been delivered to customers, however. If the market understands the advantages of OSI over other popular protocols such as SNMP, products supporting OSI protocols may become more readily available.

SNMP-Based Network Management

The Simple Network Management Protocol SNMP,, was developed to provide a common framework for network management of TCP/IP-based inter networks. The goal of SNMP is similar to that of CMIP in the OSI framework, to provide a mechanism for communication between a manager in the network and the various network objects. A clear distinction should be made between SNMP, the protocol used to manage the devices, and the management console itself. Unlike OSI, in the world of SNMP no standards are defined for the implementation of a manager and its services.

Framework Based on OSI Models

Most SNMP managers follow the OSI framework. The services SNMP provides are similar in function to the OSI model. They cover the areas of Fault Management, Configuration Management, Performance Management, Accounting Management, and Security Management. Similarly, SNMP follows the OSI model of objects and access methods as described previously under OSI.

Management Information Base

The Management Information Base (MIB) is the database of the objects to be managed. Information about a managed object is referenced by variable definitions, whose data format and meaning is defined by the MIB definition.

In common practice, the term MIB also refers to the structure of information provided by a device. For example, to monitor a Microsoft LAN Manager server from a SNMP management console, the LAN Manager MIB extensions—often referred to simply as the LAN Manager MIB—can be incorporated into the SNMP manager's standard MIB to enable it to recognize LAN Manager-specific objects.

MIB I

MIB I was the first definition of management information for SNMP and has been superseded by MIB II. It is described by RFC 1156. The first step to produce an internet standard is the publication of a Request for Comments (RFC). Most standards are referenced by an RFC number. The specification of MIB I is described by RFC 1156.

MIB II

MIB II is completely upward compatible with MIB I—incorporating all of the object definitions and adding additional object definitions. Extensions that work under MIB I also are supported by MIB II. The formal definition of a MIB is written in a subset language called ASN.1. The structure of management information, specified in RFC 1155, defines the subset of ASN representations supported. The complete definition is large and can be obtained as part of RFC 1213. The primary changes from MIB I to MIB II consist of additions to support new requirements, improved support for multiprotocol devices, and clarifications of the original RFC 1212 Concise MIB Definitions.

Manager MIB Definitions

The supported MIB may be expanded by the incorporation of MIB extensions. This capability serves three purposes. New standard objects can be defined by new versions of the Internet MIB. New MIBs can be defined and tested for standardization in the *experimental* subtree of the MIB. Private MIBs are defined within the *enterprise* subtree of the standard MIB. Private MIBs are defined for many network devices and operating systems.

Most current manager applications support MIB II. This is commonly implemented with a MIB compiler that reloads the variables' textual names that correspond to the actual object identifiers. This enables the manager to textually display the variables and their accessibility, type, and indexing to generate queries and process replies.

Networks often contain devices or systems that support proprietary MIBs. These MIBs are defined with object identifiers prefixed with the following:

ISO.ORG.DOD.INTERNET.PRIVATE.ENTERPRISES.organization
or
ISO.ORG.DOD.INTERNET.PRIVATE.ENTERPRISES.product.

For example, references to the Microsoft LAN Manager MIB object identifiers are prefixed with the following:

ISO.ORG.DOD.INTERNET.PRIVATE.ENTERPRISES.lanmanager

The hierarchy of allowable prefixes is shown in figure 11.5. This hierarchical name space enables delegated authority to define new managed objects without conflict. Experimental MIBs are defined in the same manner, but under the experimental branch of the subtree. As working groups standardize existing proprietary MIBs, or define new standard MIBs, these MIBs can move to a different portion of the namespace as they are being standardized.

SNMP Operations

In the context of SNMP, a *Get* is a request from a manager application in the network for information from a SNMP agent located at a managed object. A Get returns the contents of the variable or variables, which represents real data in the managed device. Figure 11.6 shows a Get request in a command line environment. Examples of Get variables returned by a bridge can be numbers of packets bridged or the current status of the bridge, such as PASSING or NOT-PASSING packets.

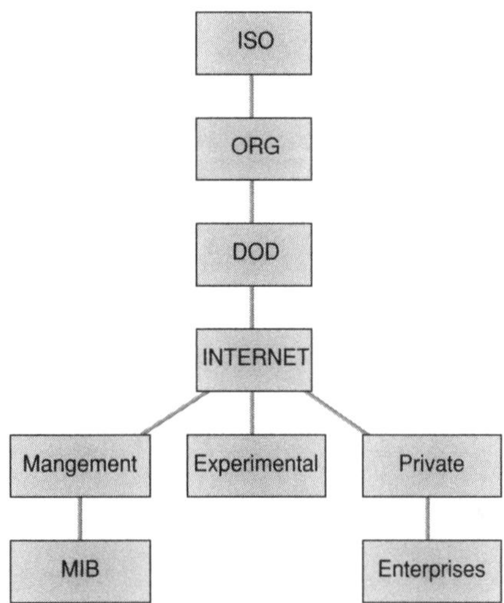

Figure 11.5:
Hierarchical name space definition.

Get-Next is a powerful extension to the Get operation. Get-Next retrieves the next defined variable following the specified variable. Get-Next provides two primary benefits: ease in accessing tables, and the capability to request variables without knowing in advance if they exist.

A Set instructs a SNMP agent to change a variable within a managed object. The variables set can be simple alarm thresholds, configuration parameters, or triggers for actions the device performs. Figure 11.7 shows a Set request in a command-line environment. The command sets a threshold for an alarm trap. Rather than provide for the definition of execute operations on a device, which would require a more complicated object definition, a Set is used to specify the time when the executed operation should take place. For example, rather than defining a reboot command for a device, this action is initiated by setting a variable that indicates the number of seconds until system reboot.

```
C:\users\cmutools\nt>
C:\users\cmutools\nt>snmpget 192.133.88.2 public
system.sysUpTime.0
Name: system.sysUpTime.0
Timeticks: (517583) 1:26:15

C:\users\cmutools\nt>snmpget 192.133.88.2 public
system.sysDescr.0
Name: system.sysDescr.0
OCTET STRING- (ascii):  NetWare 386 TCP/IP

C:\users\cmutools\nt>snmpgetn 192.133.88.2 public
system.sysDescr.0
Name: system.sysObjectID.0
OBJECT IDENTIFIER:
.iso.org.dod.internet.private.enterprises.23.1.3

C:\users\cmutools\nt>snmpgetn 192.133.88.2 public
system.sysUpTime.0
Name: interfaces.ifNumber.0
INTEGER: 2

C:\users\cmutools\nt>snmpget 192.133.88.2 public
ip.ipForwarding.0
Name: ip.ipForwarding.0
INTEGER: host(2)

C:\users\cmutools\nt>
```

Figure 11.6:
CMU SNMP command line Get request.

```
C:\users\cmutools\nt>rem The following is a private tool,
not part of cmu snmp

C:\users\cmutools\nt>snmpset 192.133.88.2 public
ip.ipForwarding.0 1
Name: ip.ipForwarding.0
INTEGER: gateway(1)

C:\users\cmutools\nt>snmpget 192.133.88.2 public
ip.ipForwarding.0
Name: ip.ipForwarding.0
INTEGER: gateway(1)

C:\users\cmutools\nt>
```

Figure 11.7:
CMU command-line Set request.

Two basic mechanisms are available to obtain information and detect faults in a network: traps and polling. A *polled* system sends requests from the management station to the device, then infers events and alarms from the result. *Traps* are asynchronous notifications from a device to a manager. Because the traps can potentially generate considerable network traffic, events that create traps must be carefully designed.

In a typical SNMP management environment, the network manager polls devices periodically to obtain status information. When a particular set of events occurs, the device automatically sends a trap to the manager, notifying it that further attention is required. The manager can then poll the device for detailed status investigation. The thresholds that define a TRAP usually may be SET by the network manager as appropriate for their network.

Comparing SNMP and CMIP

SNMP and CMIP are similar in some ways: they both have a management-information base that describes the variables to be examined and set for each network device; each MIB can contain proprietary extensions.

The most obvious difference between the two protocols is in MIB-access methods. SNMP is designed to request specific information from a device. CMIP provides for the retrieval of aggregate information with a single request. For example, if a bridge contains a routing table that consists of a source address, primary route, and route cost, a SNMP request can return the entire table as a result of a series of Get-Next requests or a single entry in the table. CMIP, however, can be presented with a request that selects a group of table entries. In this case, a request can be made for all the entries with a route cost exceeding a specified value. The difference between the two access methods in this example is the location of the query. With SNMP, the manager performs the data selection; with CMIP it is performed by the remote agent on the device.

The CMIP agent is more complex than an equivalent SNMP agent so that it can handle the additional data-management tasks. Although some network card manufacturers provide SNMP on their cards or as a TSR loaded in the background under DOS, these implementations with CMIP are difficult because of the additional complexity of the agent software. Accordingly, more CPU processing power is needed for CMIP, and the remote device requires a faster processor to support CMIP than it does to support SNMP.

Most SNMP implementations today are oriented toward polling for information instead of providing traps that result in detailed information polls. Rather than relying on polling for data, however, CMIP is designed to report changes to the manager whenever they occur. Without the overhead of polling, a CMIP manager theoretically can monitor a much larger number of devices than can an equivalent SNMP manager. In practice, the implementation efficiency of agents and managers varies so much that such differences are difficult to establish and are probably meaningless.

Exploring Current SNMP Systems

Several public-domain SNMP management tools exist today. Of these, the Carnegie-Mellon University (CMU) package is most popular. The CMU package provides a command-line interface to Get and Set SNMP MIB variables. Although these solutions are a low-cost method of accessing the SNMP data, they generally fall short of a network-management solution. Because they lack a graphical user interface, alarm and event generation, and logging capabilities, they typically are used for university research and to validate the proper interoperation of SNMP agents developed by hardware manufacturers.

VisiNet 2.0, from VisiSoft, provides a full-function SNMP network-management system that is typical of the solutions offered today. A number of the features provided by VisiNet are essential in the evaluation of an SNMP network manager. The management system provides a graphical interface. VisiNet, shown in figure 11.8, provides a user-definable hierarchy of the network in a series of views, each with a user-definable background used to display a map or floor plan. The capability to arrange custom displays and icons is particularly important for SNMP management software because they are generic and manage components from a wide variety of manufacturers.

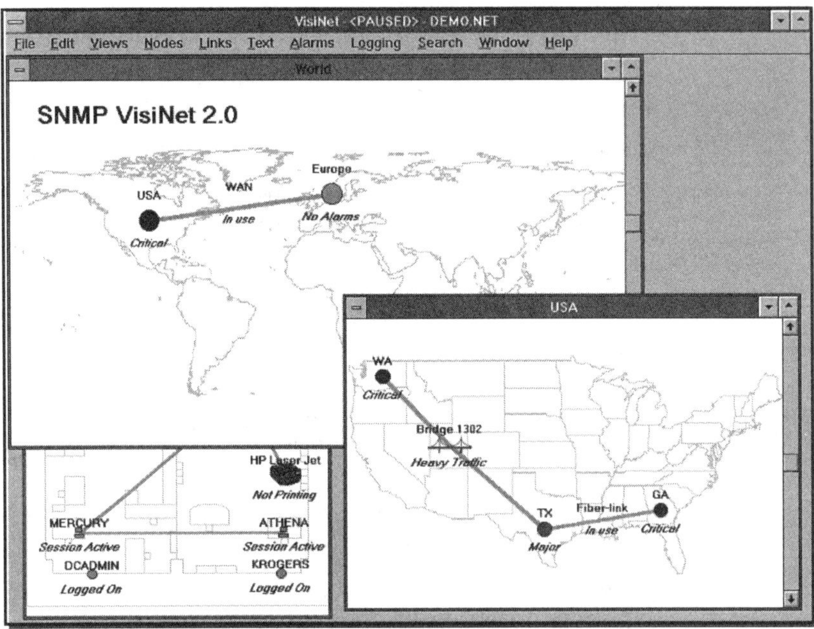

Figure 11.8:
VisiNet hierarchy of network views.

Another popular feature of SNMP managers is the capability to graphically represent the front panel of an actual hardware device. Figure 11.9 shows a graphic that mimics the front panel of a Cabletron hub. The status of the device is clearly shown by objects that represent the lights on the front of the device. The manager can reconfigure the device by clicking the mouse over the objects that represent the front panel buttons of the device.

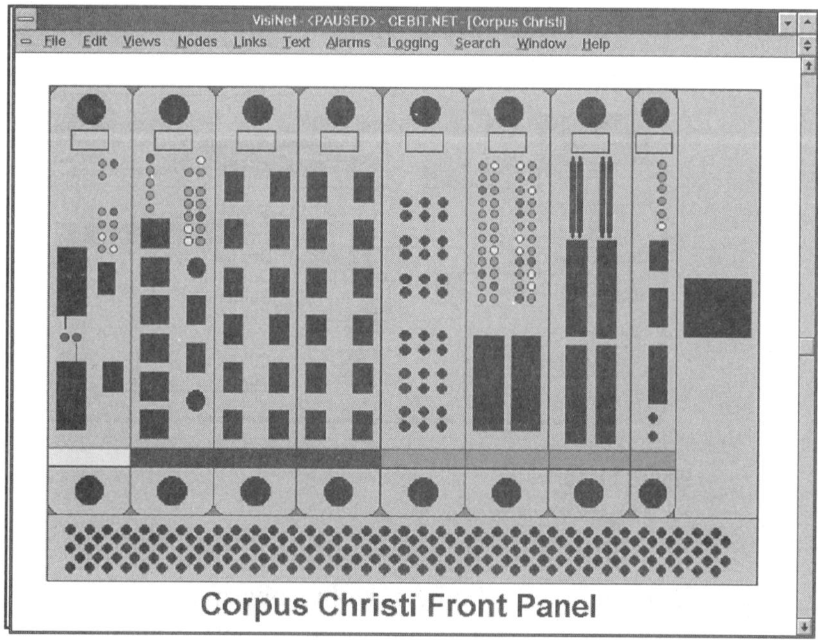

Figure 11.9:
Graphic of Cabletron hub front panel.

Just as the SNMP management software must have predefined shapes that are easy to recognize, so must administrators be able to define their own shapes. No SNMP network-management software can predefine all the possible devices currently in use or that may be designed in the future. The capability to define icons, including the portions colored based upon the state of the device, can make the system easy to use. Figure 11.10 shows a user-defined icon drawn in CorelDraw and pasted into VisiNet.

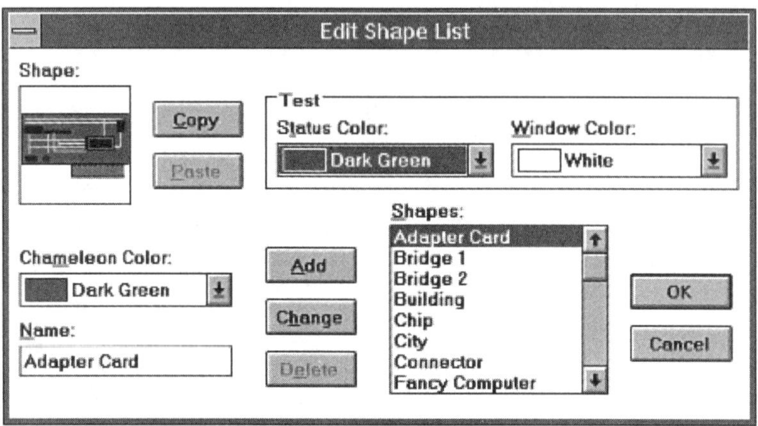

Figure 11.10:
Putting a user-defined icon into VisiNet.

In addition to defining custom icons and the portions colored based on the state of the device, an SNMP network manager must enable the administrator to customize the colors used to represent the state of the network device. Figure 11.11 shows how the states and colors for an object are defined in VisiNet.

An SNMP network manager should help the network administrator to perform management tasks that are more complex than simple Set and Get operations. The administrator must be able to combine complex information from a variety of devices to enable the software to infer network alarms, events, and actions. VisiNet gives this power to the administrator through its scripting language.

Customizable scripts perform network requests and process the data returned. A script also defines the state of an object. Figure 11.12 shows a script that defines the state of a standard bridge in VisiNet. The result of an SNMP request is compared to values

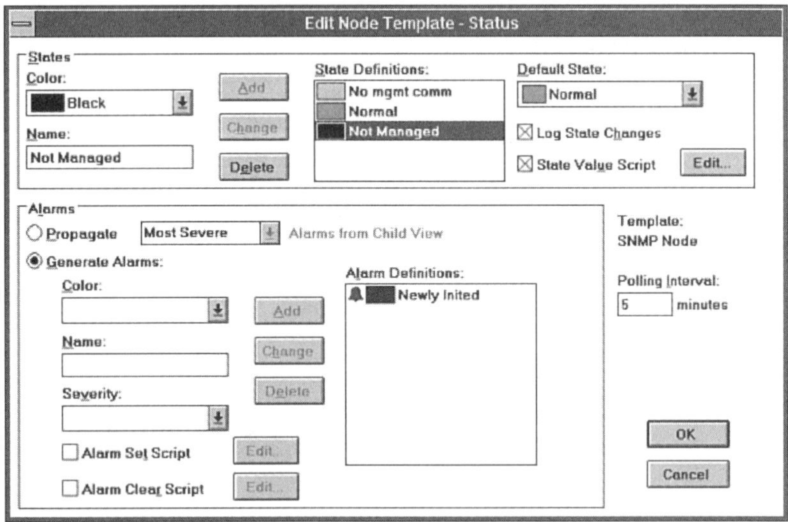

Figure 11.11:
Defining an object state in VisiNet.

predefined in the device's MIB and conversion to a textual and graphic display. Scripts are similar to macros in many computer applications. A scripting language is essential to enable intelligent processing and interpretations of the data returned by agents.

What an SNMP manager does with the information it obtains is probably its most important feature. Being able to make intelligent interpretations of network statistics is a top priority for any administrator. For example, if a bridge experiences a large number of error packets, the network manager must do more than report the number of error packets at the given bridge. The manager needs to have an alarm mechanism built in to alert the administrator about the growing potential for a network problem. VisiNet's built-in alarm capabilities interpret network conditions and alert the administrator.

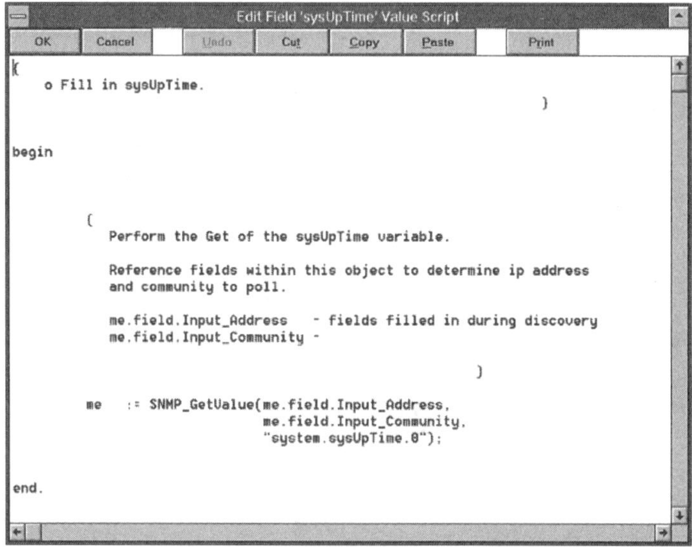

Figure 11.12:
A VisiNet script.

Figure 11.13 displays all the alarms in the network and offers the capability to clear or jump directly to any one of them. VisiNet can order the display of alarms based on the following: how severe the condition is, what time the alarm occurs, or alphabetically by the device that generated the alarm condition.

In addition to displaying current network statistics, the network-management software should provide an historical database. The capability to contrast the network's current performance with past performance gives the administrator important information about trends in the network. Historical databases should keep all relevant graphical information, as well as statistical information. If a malfunctioning bridge is drawn in red, the historical information should keep that alarm color context for easy interpretation. Figure 11.14 shows a log produced by VisiNet that keeps the color context from the mapping console.

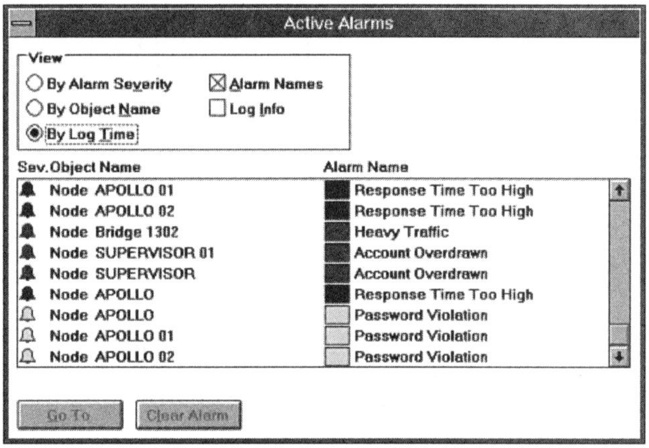

Active Alarms
View
By Alarm Severity
By Object Name
By Log Time
Alarm Names
Log Info
Sev. Object Name
Alarm Name
Node APOLLO 01 Response Time Too High
Node APOLLO 02 Response Time Too High
Node Bridge 1302 Heavy Traffic
Node SUPERVISOR 01 Account Overdrawn
Node SUPERVISOR Account Overdrawn
Node APOLLO Response Time Too High
Node APOLLO Password Violation
Node APOLLO 01 Password Violation
Node APOLLO 02 Password Violation
Go To
Clear Alarm

Figure 11.13:
List of active alarms in VisiNet.

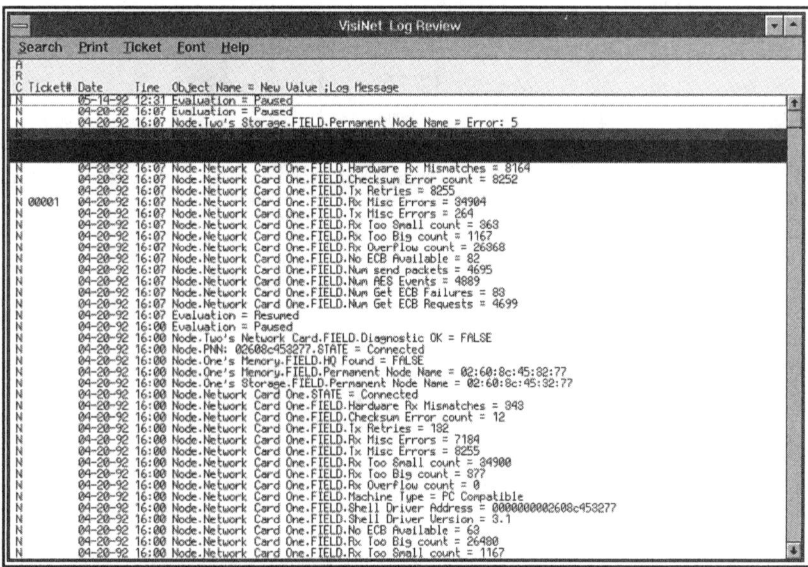

Figure 11.14:
VisiNet alarm and event log.

An SNMP network manager should provide a facility to share its data with other applications—which may provide additional value to the administrator. For example, this facility can be used by a manager to export network statistics to a spreadsheet for a complex numerical analysis that can be incorporated into a word processor for a comprehensive report on the network. One such open standard is the Dynamic Data Exchange (DDE) protocol. Figure 11.15 shows a chart in Microsoft Excel that is linked directly to the data in VisiNet. Any change in the data returned by the SNMP device immediately results in a change in the chart.

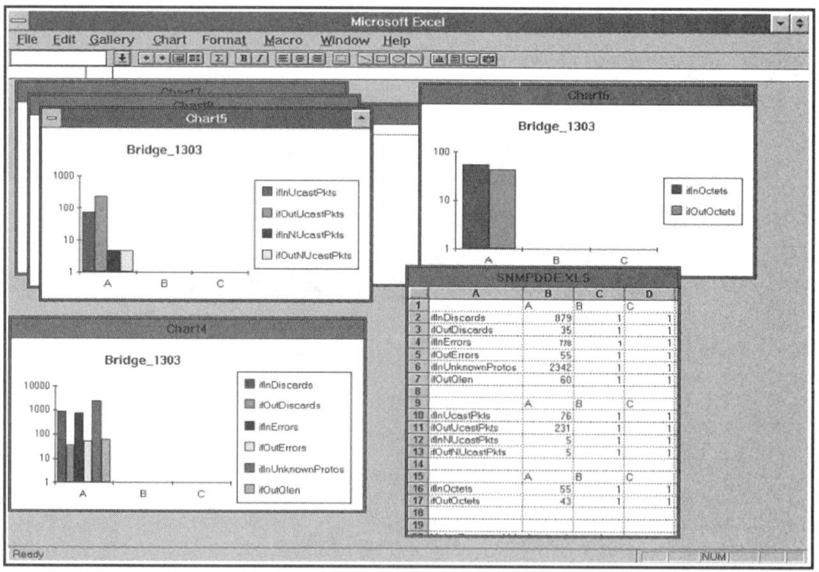

Figure 11.15:
Spreadsheet linked to VisiNet with Dynamic Data Exchange.

A new method of sharing data, which differs from exporting data to another application, is called Object Linking and Embedding

(OLE—pronounced oh-lay). OLE is a data-sharing standard that enables applications to share objects. For example, VisiNet provides the capability to embed a spreadsheet into VisiNet's window. Figure 11.16 shows a spreadsheet and chart embedded within VisiNet but drawn by Excel.

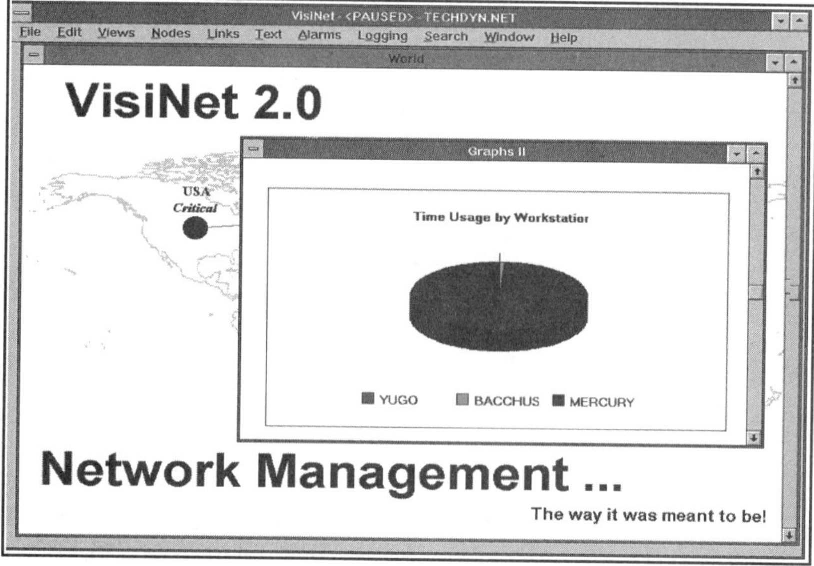

Figure 11.16:
Embedded objects within VisiNet.

The graphical aspects of network-management software are related directly to the administrator's learning curve. The administrator must be able to see a map of the logical connections and the physical connections. VisiNet provides the capability to position nodes on a floor plan drawn in AutoCAD or another popular CAD program. Figure 11.17 shows a representative office floor plan with network nodes positioned in VisiNet.

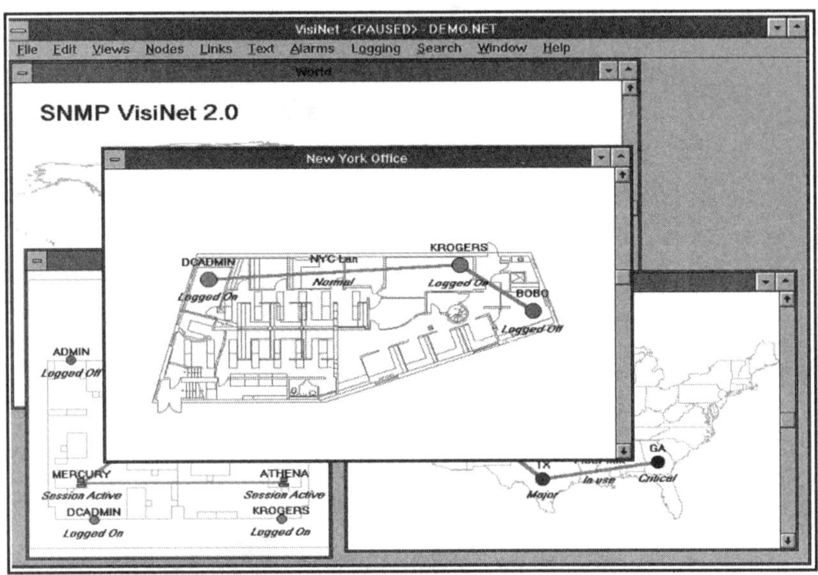

Figure 11.17:
Floor plan background file converted from AutoCAD DXF format.

Network-management software should ease the administrator's tasks at every opportunity. One such opportunity is in the creation of a database that describes the network. On a large network, an administrator should not have to input the name of each network object. One way to avoid this time-consuming task is to provide an automatic discovery system. VisiNet provides a discovery system that discovers any type of SNMP agent.

Exploring Protocol Analyzers

Computers use a layered hierarchy of protocols to communicate over a network. A *protocol analyzer* is a tool that can eavesdrop automatically on any network communication and decode the information for easy interpretation.

A protocol analyzer consists of a special network card and software for controlling the card. The card can be programmed to monitor all activity on the network instead of responding to a single preprogrammed network address. The analyzer examines all the data on the network and looks for predefined conditions to trigger data capture and analysis programs.

Features of Protocol Analyzers

To be effective, a protocol analyzer must have several features. The following sections describe some of the most important of these features.

Filters

A *filter* is a mechanism that indicates which data to monitor on the network. A filter also indicates which selection criteria to use when capturing network traffic. For example, if a particular network card is suspected of transmitting bad packets, a filter can be created to capture all packets transmitted to or from that node.

Time Domain Reflectometry

More than two-thirds of all local area network hardware problems are related to cabling. A *time domain relectometer,* (TDR) is the single most useful tool for the isolation of cable faults. The TDR tests the cable to determine if it is open, shorted, or broken; and determines the distance from the test point in the cable to the problem.

Network Operating System Support

The analyzer should automatically detect and decode all protocols used by your network environment. Normally, this includes the automatic recognition of IPX, NetBEUI, and TCP/IP protocols.

Data Collection and Logging Issues

The single most important characteristic of a protocol analyzer is performance. The device must be able to capture network data in real time and in sufficient quantity to assist in the location of network problems. The collection of data at the maximum network data rate, generally, is limited by the memory capacity of the network card.

Another important feature of protocol analyzers is their capability to precisely monitor traffic on a given cable segment. Using the traffic information, the administrator can determine how the network can be segmented into separate cable segments, bridged together to improve overall performance of the nodes and applications that use the network.

Data Transmission

Data transmission is an important feature for analysis. If the analyzer has the capability to transmit data on the network, it can perform capacity planning, load testing, and do bridge or gateway analysis. To perform true load testing, the analyzer must be capable of generating traffic at very high data rates.

Time-Stamping

The capability to time-stamp captured data can be valuable when analyzing network problems. Time of day is critical to determine peak traffic periods. The capability to calculate time between frames—or "delta time"—is important to discover race conditions. The time relative to a transmitted or received reference frame can be used to identify time-outs.

Data Export

Data export is important if the quantities of data required warrant more sophisticated analysis than can be performed by the built-in analyzer software. Captured packets can be exported to a database or to custom software for more complex reporting and analysis.

Portability

A protocol analyzer can only transmit and examine packets on a single cable at one time. Because of the high cost of analyzers, they usually are packaged within portable computers that can be manually carried from segment to segment as problems arise. If the analyzer is a card that must be placed in a workstation on the network, portability becomes a serious concern when problems exist on other cable segments. The card must be removed from one workstation and inserted in another. If this problem occurs often, the purchase of a portable computer usually can be justified.

Novell LANalyzer

The Novell LANalyzer network analyzer is designed to identify network problems and fine-tune performance by examining network protocol traffic. The LANalyzer provides automatic predefined tests for troubleshooting common network problems. An integrated help application leads the user through the troubleshooting process. The primary focus of the product is the analysis of network traffic and protocols to determine the source of network problems. It can capture network traffic selectively to assist in locating problems.

A LANalyzer is capable of monitoring traffic in increments up to eight protocol suites simultaneously. This display describes the traffic in terms of the total number of packets processed. It also displays data on a number of potential Ethernet error types. Because this Ethernet was monitored during very low traffic conditions, collisions and errors are zero. Some rate of collisions is expected during the operation of a busy Ethernet. By matching current statistics to those obtained during normal levels of network traffic, you can determine if error rates have risen to abnormal levels.

Because of the need to obtain baseline data, a protocol analyzer is not the tool to turn to when the network fails; it should be a constant factor in monitoring the network.

The LANalyzer enables users to configure application suites that perform common sets of analysis tasks. A variety of application suites are shipped, predefined with the software. The LANalyzer screen displays a variety of suites designed to manage NetWare LANs.

The primary use of this product is to locate hardware and configuration problems that may cause poor performance or application failure. It can assist the technician in locating cards or nodes that are transmitting inappropriate packets or packets with errors. The LANalyzer can be configured to collect data that show the results of dividing the cable into multiple segments, or the results of modifying the current cable-segmentation plan. This device is primarily focused on the analysis of the traffic on a single cable segment. To get a complete picture of all data traffic on a multisegment internetwork, the device must be moved from segment to segment, gathering data about each segment. Because of the time span between data acquisitions on each segment, the analysis may not be as useful as in the single-segment environment.

The LANalyzer is packaged as a specialized network card and comes with accompanying software for insertion in a single machine on the network.

Network General Sniffer

The Network General Sniffer is a family of self-contained protocol analyzers. Proprietary hardware and software is installed on portable computers delivered as a complete protocol-analysis tool. A version of the product is available for virtually every network topology and protocol.

The product presents a character-based, menu-driven interface that provides cable testing, traffic generation, filtering, capturing, and frame analysis. A fully described seven-layer decoding of each packet is available. Network traffic and statistics can be plotted with block-character histograms.

Exploring Network-Management Products

The following sections define a few network-management products that represent the many products that are currently available.

Novell NetWare Services Manager

The Novell Windows NetWare Services Manager (NSM) is a centralized server-management system for Novell networks. The Netware Services Manager provides a framework for customers and third-party developers to create applications that can interoperate with the NSM data.

NSM automatically can discover all IPX network devices. Nodes are placed on a map, which depicts the logical connections of the nodes in the network. Different cable segments are summarized by network icons linked by bridges, as shown in figure 11.18. All icons are predefined by Novell.

Zooming in on a network icon displays a single cable segment. This segment is presented as a single Ethernet cable that connects all of the nodes on the segment. The order displayed on the segment does not necessarily reflect the actual positioning of the nodes on the wire; it reflects the order in which the objects responded to a network broadcast request. Fast 486-based workstations, therefore, are located closer to the server initiating the broadcast, and slower 286-based workstations are drawn further away because they respond to requests more slowly. This network layout cannot be modified by the administrator to represent the actual layout of the nodes, even if it is known.

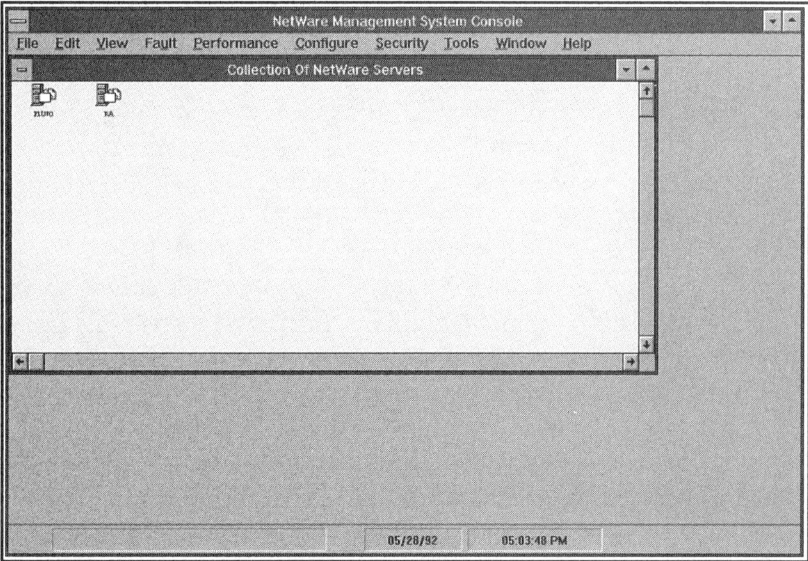

Figure 11.18:
Novell NSM logical network map.

In addition to the automatic network map, you can create a hierarchical representation—either logical or physical—of the network with background maps by using an auxiliary module (sold separately). If you use this mapping module, a graphical representation of the network hierarchy can be created manually.

Agents that reside on 3.11 servers across the network perform all data gathering. When one of the defined event thresholds is reached, a signal is sent to the management console via the network or auxiliary dialup lines. Detailed information on any server in the network is polled whenever the server's icon is double-clicked. Because the information is retrieved on demand, no information displays if the server does not respond.

Currently, the product stores all information in a Btrieve database located at the management-console computer. The database cannot be shared between multiple-management consoles. A software development kit is available to assist customers and third-party developers in creating custom applications that use information from the NSM database.

Data is retrieved from the remote server agents via SNMP, and third-party management applications can use this protocol to manage other SNMP devices.

Novell NSM is packaged as three software components: management-console applications, an autodiscovery server NLM, and a server monitoring NLM. The management console applications consist of four Microsoft Windows that provide SNMP connectivity, console, alarm management, and autodiscovery manager. The autodiscover NLM resides on a single server and constructs the logical map of the network. Every server in the network is loaded with a server monitoring NLM that detects remote alarm conditions.

VisiSoft VisiNet

VisiNet is a hardware and network topology-independent graphical network management system for LANs and WANs. VisiNet is not restricted to monitoring a specific network operating system or protocol. VisiNet can monitor Microsoft LAN Manager, Novell NetWare, IBM LAN Server, NetBIOS, and the

Banyan Vines network operating systems simultaneously (and it also supports SNMP).

The system automatically retrieves network status, attributes, and statistics for each node and link in user-definable fields, which provides a customized view of the network. The product supports the Windows and OS/2 Platforms.

VisiNet Features

All features of the SNMP version of VisiNet are included in the native network protocol versions. Automatic hardware inventory is included with all versions. Figure 11.19 shows a detailed view of some of the 38 inventory items detected by VisiNet.

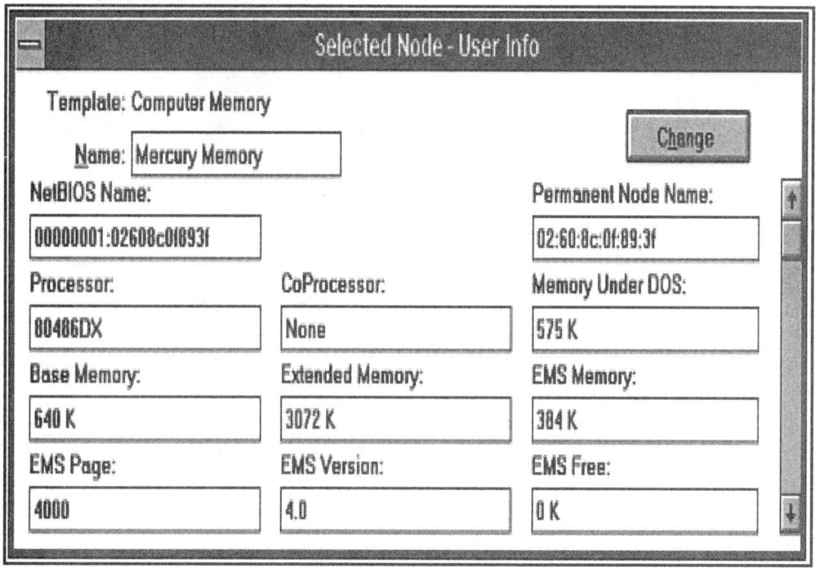

Selected Node - User Info

Template: Computer Memory

Name: Mercury Memory

Change

NetBIOS Name: 00000001:02608c0f893f

Permanent Node Name: 02:60:8c:0f:89:3f

Processor: 80486DX

CoProcessor: None

Memory Under DOS: 575 K

Base Memory: 640 K

Extended Memory: 3072 K

EMS Memory: 384 K

EMS Page: 4000

EMS Version: 4.0

EMS Free: 0 K

Figure 11.19:
Partial detail of hardware inventory.

Information displayed in a graphical format can be more quickly recognized and interpreted. Figure 11.20 shows a VisiNet view that contains a Microsoft Excel spreadsheet and graph displaying workstation idle time. The spreadsheet and graph are dynamically linked via Windows Dynamic Data Exchange (DDE) to the VisiNet database, and it will update whenever the reported information changes. This figure also illustrates Object Linking and Embedding (OLE). The spreadsheet and graph are actually embedded within a VisiNet view.

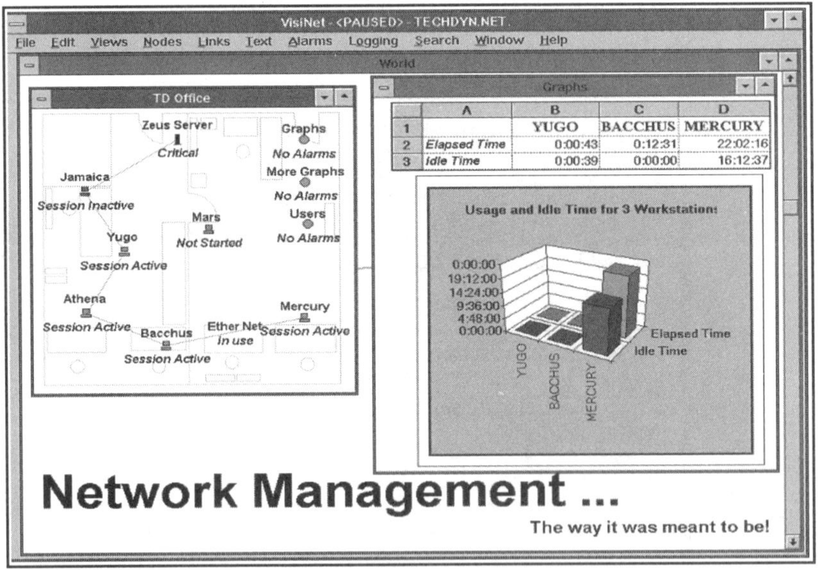

Figure 11.20:
Microsoft Excel spreadsheet and dynamic graph embedded within a VisiNet network view.

VisiNet has a built-in scripting language, which the administrator can use to customize the interpretation of network statistics.

VisiNet provides an alarm mechanism that the scripting language uses to notify the administrator of any potential or actual alarm conditions. The real power of VisiNet's scripting language is its capability to make complex interpretations of statistics, instead of comparing them to a preset value. Rarely does a single statistic provide a network manager with enough information to determine if any problems are on a node; a combination of statistics, however, provides for more intelligent processing. Figure 11.21 shows the script for an alarm condition in VisiNet.

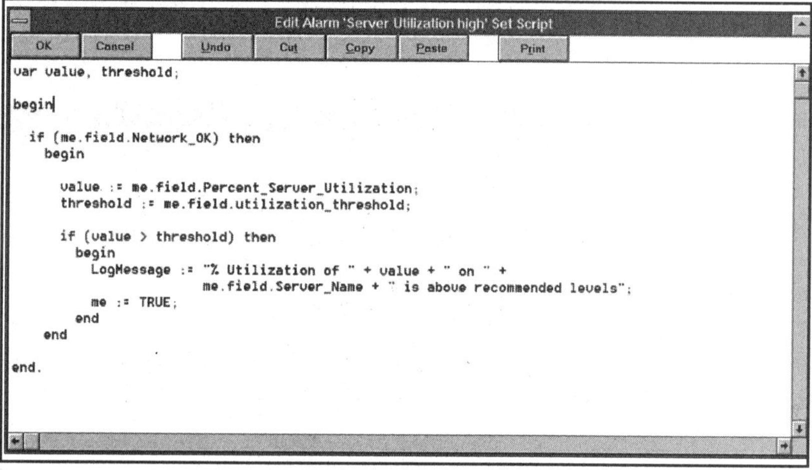

Figure 11.21:
VisiNet alarm script.

VisiNet can be configured to keep a history of network statistics and events for a few or for many objects. This historical database can be reviewed at any time and keeps the color-coded context from the mapping views. The color codes allow for quick identification of alarm conditions. Figure 11.22 shows a typical VisiNet alarm and event log.

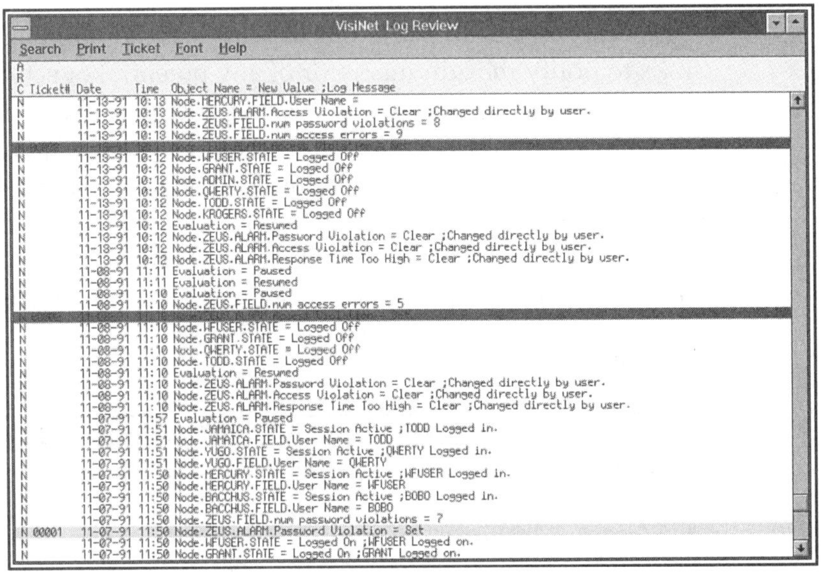

```
VisiNet Log Review
Search  Print  Ticket  Font  Help
A
R
C Ticket# Date     Time  Object Name = New Value ;Log Message
N         11-13-91 10:13 Node.MERCURY.FIELD.User Name =
N         11-13-91 10:13 Node.ZEUS.ALARM.Access Violation = Clear ;Changed directly by user.
N         11-13-91 10:13 Node.ZEUS.FIELD.num password violations = 8
N         11-13-91 10:13 Node.ZEUS.FIELD.num access errors = 9
N         11-13-91 10:12 Node.WFUSER.STATE = Logged Off
N         11-13-91 10:12 Node.GRANT.STATE = Logged Off
N         11-13-91 10:12 Node.ADMIN.STATE = Logged Off
N         11-13-91 10:12 Node.QWERTY.STATE = Logged Off
N         11-13-91 10:12 Node.TODD.STATE = Logged Off
N         11-13-91 10:12 Node.KROGERS.STATE = Logged Off
N         11-13-91 10:12 Evaluation = Resumed
N         11-13-91 10:12 Node.ZEUS.ALARM.Password Violation = Clear ;Changed directly by user.
N         11-13-91 10:12 Node.ZEUS.ALARM.Access Violation = Clear ;Changed directly by user.
N         11-13-91 10:12 Node.ZEUS.ALARM.Response Time Too High = Clear ;Changed directly by user.
N         11-08-91 11:11 Evaluation = Paused
N         11-08-91 11:11 Evaluation = Resumed
N         11-08-91 11:10 Evaluation = Paused
N         11-08-91 11:10 Node.ZEUS.FIELD.num access errors = 5
N         11-08-91 11:10 Node.WFUSER.STATE = Logged Off
N         11-08-91 11:10 Node.GRANT.STATE = Logged Off
N         11-08-91 11:10 Node.QWERTY.STATE = Logged Off
N         11-08-91 11:10 Node.TODD.STATE = Logged Off
N         11-08-91 11:10 Evaluation = Resumed
N         11-08-91 11:10 Node.ZEUS.ALARM.Password Violation = Clear ;Changed directly by user.
N         11-08-91 11:10 Node.ZEUS.ALARM.Access Violation = Clear ;Changed directly by user.
N         11-08-91 11:10 Node.ZEUS.ALARM.Response Time Too High = Clear ;Changed directly by user.
N         11-07-91 11:57 Evaluation = Paused
N         11-07-91 11:51 Node.JAMAICA.STATE = Session Active ;TODD Logged in.
N         11-07-91 11:51 Node.JAMAICA.FIELD.User Name = TODD
N         11-07-91 11:51 Node.YUGO.STATE = Session Active ;QWERTY Logged in.
N         11-07-91 11:51 Node.YUGO.FIELD.User Name = QWERTY
N         11-07-91 11:50 Node.MERCURY.STATE = Session Active ;WFUSER Logged in.
N         11-07-91 11:50 Node.MERCURY.FIELD.User Name = WFUSER
N         11-07-91 11:50 Node.BACCHUS.STATE = Session Active ;BOBO Logged in.
N         11-07-91 11:50 Node.BACCHUS.FIELD.User Name = BOBO
N         11-07-91 11:50 Node.ZEUS.FIELD.num password violations = 7
N 00001   11-07-91 11:50 Node.ZEUS.ALARM.Password Violation = Set
N         11-07-91 11:50 Node.WFUSER.STATE = Logged On ;WFUSER Logged on.
N         11-07-91 11:50 Node.GRANT.STATE = Logged On ;GRANT Logged on.
```

Figure 11.22:
VisiNet alarm and event log.

VisiNet eases the creation of the network database by providing a network discovery system. In all of VisiNet's protocol environments, the discovery system recognizes any standard network device: file servers, workstations, users, printers, modems, queues, and other shareable resources. VisiNet automatically lays out the objects in a mapping view, as shown in figure 11.23, and it enables the administrator to rearrange them.

One of the primary functions of VisiNet is to map the network, both logically and physically. To facilitate the mapping, VisiNet provides the capability to display floor plans from popular CAD packages (see fig. 11.24). The network nodes then can be positioned on the floor plans that reflect the physical layout and connections.

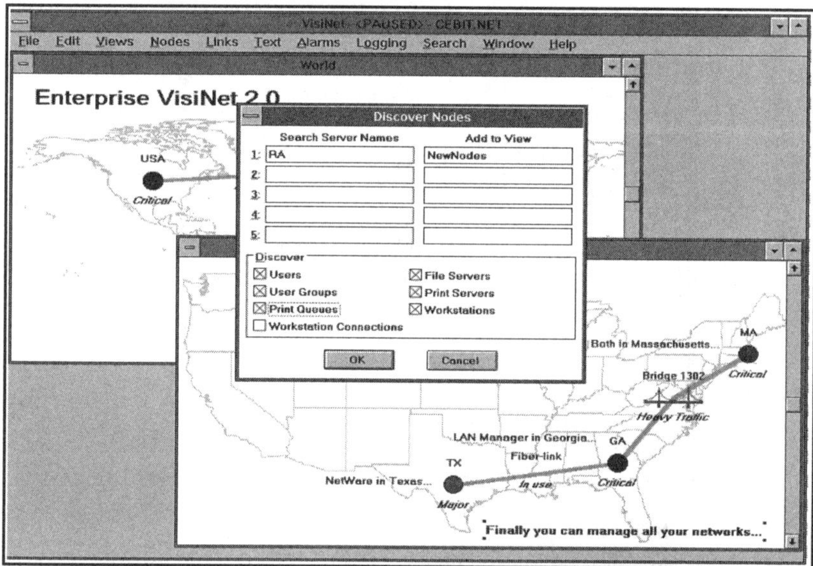

Figure 11.23:
Automatic discovery.

In addition to VisiNet's built-in reporting capabilities, VisiNet supports the Dynamic Data Exchange (DDE) protocol. The DDE protocol enables VisiNet to transmit the network data to another application for additional processing. For example, the administrator can use a spreadsheet application, such as Excel, to perform additional analysis on the network data. The benefit of DDE is that the data can be immediately transmitted to Excel when VisiNet detects a change in a network statistic. The AutoCAD of the DDE standard provides an unlimited number of ways to access the data collected by VisiNet. Figure 11.25 shows an example Excel spreadsheet with DDE links to VisiNet.

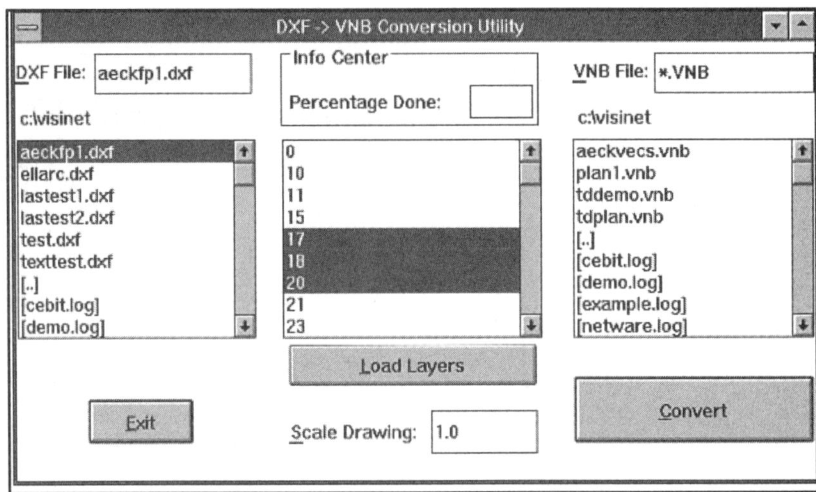

Figure 11.24:

AutoCAD DXF File conversion for background floor plans.

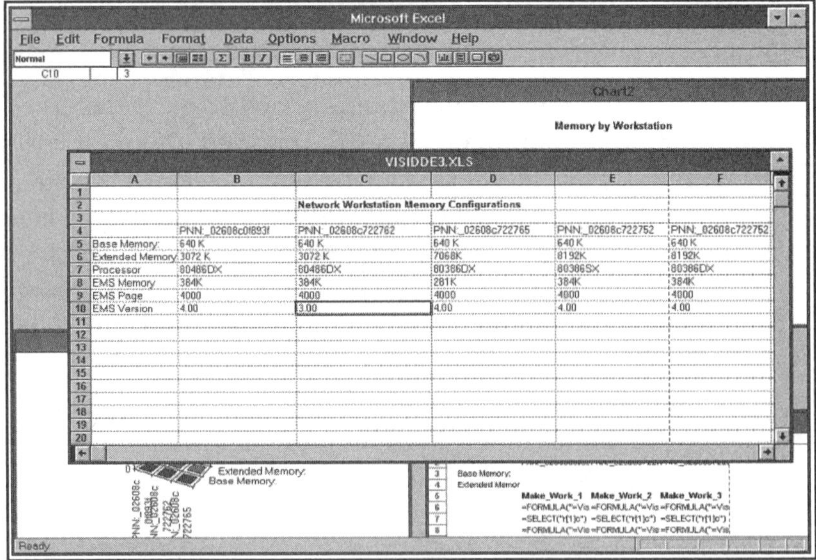

Figure 11.25:

Report generated with Excel from DDE links to VisiNet.

VisiNet can be configured to support many different network protocols. The number of available statistics differs under each protocol: Novell supports 434, Lan Manager supports 139, NetBIOS supports 31, and SNMP supports as many as are in the MIB definition. Additionally, VisiNet has 40 inventory statistics and 24 data-manipulation functions.

VisiNet is packaged and sold as a base-management console with optional packages for support of each network-operating system or SNMP. Any or all of the packages can be installed at once for simultaneous management of multiple environments from a single console.

IBM SystemView

SystemView is one of IBM's LAN network-management console products. The product represents IBM's attempt to standardize the End User Interface between a number of replaced products.

SystemView Features

SystemView is designed to be a management console for IBM SAA, SNA, and OSI environments. It is the foundation of their open systems architecture. SystemView provides a consistent structure for the development of applications and data management. When completed, the product will include inventory management, resource management, change management, performance management, event tracking, and problem analysis. SystemView is focused on the management of IBM mainframes and resources, but it is one of the products they have committed to provide compatibility with open standards such as OSI.

Summary

Network management is the most rapidly evolving segment of the network market. Selecting a product in such a marketplace is difficult. To simplify the selection process, use this chapter as an outline to prepare a checklist of your network-management needs. Using this list as a guide, you can survey the available products.

Try a demonstration disk or evaluation copy of each product. If neither is available, look at the product at your dealer. Ask how long the product has been shipping and for references.

After you decide on the product you want, try to anticipate your future requirements. Products that are designed for a single operating system face a limited marketplace with limited growth, and they may hamper your ability to expand your management system as your network grows in the future.

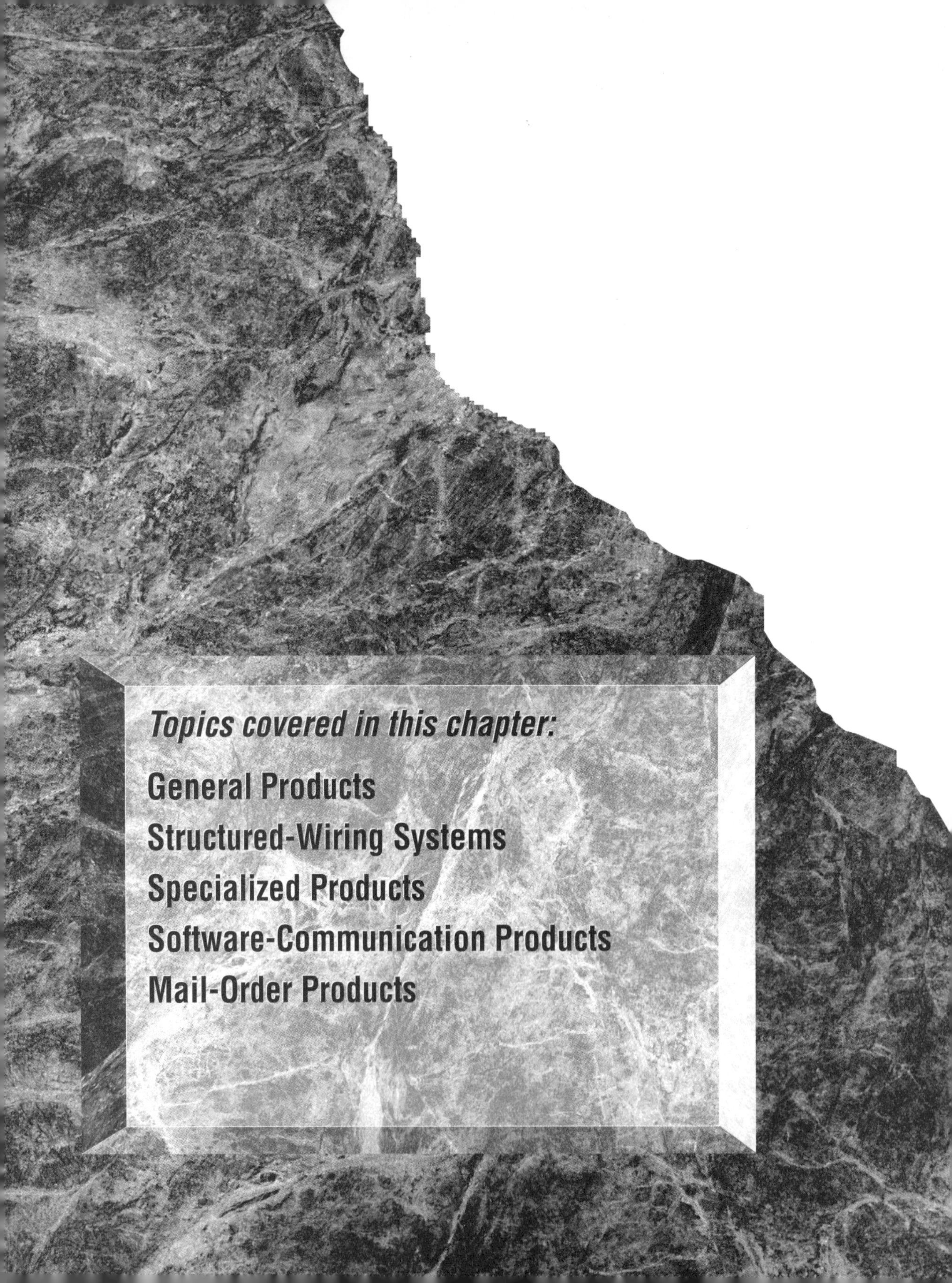
Topics covered in this chapter:
General Products
Structured-Wiring Systems
Specialized Products
Software-Communication Products
Mail-Order Products

Appendix A

Network Product Manufacturers

General Products

The product lines of the following vendors are too broad to confine into a narrow category. Some vendors provide one-stop shopping, and they can supply any network hardware or software component, either as a primary or a secondary source.

3Com Corporation
5400 Bayfront Plaza
Santa Clara, CA 95052-8145
(408)764-5000

Banyan Systems
120 Flanders Road
Westboro, MA 01581
(508)898-1000

Digital Equipment Corp.
146 Main Street
Maynard, MA 01754
(508)493-5111

Hewlett-Packard Company
3000 Hanover Street
Palo Alto, CA 94304
(800)752-0900

IBM
(800)IBM-2468

Structured-Wiring Systems

The following are vendors that provide structured-wiring systems. These vendors attempt to integrate all network connectivity functionality into a coherent system. Most can provide a completely integrated network-hardware configuration.

Cabletron Systems, Inc.
35 Industrial Way
P.O. Box 5005
Rochester, NH 03867-0505
(603)332-9400

David Systems, Inc.
701 E. Evelyn Avenue
Sunnyvale, CA 94086-3718
(408)720-8000

NetWorth, Inc.
8404 Esters Road
Irving, TX 75063
(214)929-1700

Proteon
Two Technology Drive
Westborough, MA 01581
(508)898-2800

Synoptics Communications, Inc.
4401 Great America Parkway
P.O. Box 58185
Santa Clara, CA 95052-8185
(408)988-2400

Specialized Products

The following vendors are more specialized, but are therefore more focused. Some vendors specialize in niche products, providing, for example, network cards specifically for Macintoshes or for networking portable computers. Each entry includes a category key word or phrase, indicating the focus of the company.

AMP, Inc.
P.O. Box 3608
Harrisburg, PA 17105-3608
(800)522-6752
Category: Connectors and cables

Andrew Corporation
10500 W. 153rd Street
Orland Park, IL 60462
(800)255-1479
Category: Token ring

AsantÈ Technologies, Inc.
404 Tasman Drive
Sunnyvale, CA 94089
(408)752-8388
Category: Macintosh

BICC Communications
103 Millbury Street
Auburn, MA 01501
(508)832-8650
Category: Ethernet, FDDI, Management

Cheyenne Software, Inc.
55 Bryant Avenue
Roslyn, NY 11576
(516)484-5100
Category: Server-management software

Cisco Systems, Inc.
1522 O'Brien Drive
Menlo Park, CA 94025
(415)326-1941
Category: Internetworking

Codenoll Technology, Inc.
1086 North Broadway
Yonkers, NY 10701
(914)965-6300
Category: Optical fiber, Network management

Eagle Technology
1160 Ridder Park Drive
San Jose, CA 95131
(408)441-7453
Category: Network interface cards

Farallon Computing, Inc.
2000 Powell Street, Suite 600
Emeryville, CA 94608
(510)596-9000
Category: Macintosh

FiberNet Research, Inc.
1 Tara Boulevard
Nashua, NH 03062
(603)891-2600
Category: FDDI

Fibronics International, Inc.
1 Communications Way
Hyannis, MA 02601
(508)778-0700
Category: FDDI

Frye Computer Systems, Inc.
19 Temple Place
Boston, MA 02111
(617)451-6364
Category: Server-management software

Gateway Communications, Inc.
2941 Alton Avenue
Irvine, CA 92714
(714)553-1555
Category: Ethernet, Remote communications

IMC Networks Corporation
16931 Milliken Avenue
Irvine, CA 92714
(714)724-1070
Category: Ethernet connectivity

Instant Information
7618 SW Mohawk Street
Tualtin, OR 97062
(503)692-9711
Category: Communications software

Integrated Workstations, Inc.
1648 Mabury Road
San Jose, CA 95133
(408)923-0301
Category: Application servers

Intel Corp.
5200 N.E. Elam Young Parkway
Hillsboro, OR 97124-6497
(800)538-3373
Category: Connectivity and management

Megahertz Corporation
4505 South Wasatch Boulevard
Salt Lake City, UT 84124
(801)272-6000
Category: Ethernet, Token ring

Microdyne Corporation
207 S. Peyton Stgreet
Alexandria, VA 22314
(703)739-0500
Category: Connectivity

Microsoft Corp.
One Microsoft Way
Redmond, WA 98052-9399
(206)882-8080
Category: Operating systems, Connectivity-software systems

Mod-Tap
P.O. Box 706
Harvard, MA 01451
(508)772-5630
Category: Connectors and cables

Motorola, Inc.
Altair Products Operations
3209 N. Wilke Road
Arlington Heights, IL 60004
(708)632-4723
Category: Wireless LANs

Network General Corporation
4200 Bohannon Drive
Menlo Park, CA 94025
(415)688-2700
Category: Protocol analyzers

Novell, Inc.
122 East 1700
South Provo, UT 84606
(801)429-7000
Category: Operating systems, Connectivity-software systems

Olicom USA, Inc.
1002 North Central Expressway
Suite 239
Richardson, TX 75080
(214)680-8131
Category: Connectivity hardware

Persoft, Inc.
565 Science Drive
Madison, WI 53711
(608)273-6000
Category: Connectivity software

PlusNet Corporation
3751 Pacific Avenue
Ogden, UT 84405
(800)468-9032
Category: FDDI

ProTools, Inc.
14976 NW Greenbriar Parkway
Beaverton, OR 97006
(503)645-5400
Category: Network management

Racal-Datacom
1601 North Harrison Parkway
Sunrise, FL 33323-2899
(800)722-2555
Category: Connectivity hardware

Racore Computer Products, Inc.
170 Knowless Drive
Suite 204
Los Gatos, CA 95030
(800)635-1274
Category: Token ring

Saber Software Corp.
P.O. Box 9088
Dallas, TX 75209-9088
(800)338-8754
Category: Server-management software

Shiva Corporation
One Cambridge Center
Cambridge, MA 02142
(617)252-6300
Category: Network modems

Spider Systems, Inc.
12 New England Executive Park
Burlington, MA 01803
(800)447-7807
Category: Protocol analyzers

Star-Tek, Inc.
71 Lyman Street
Northboro, MA 01532
(508)393-9393
Category: Intelligent hubs, Network-management software

Synernetics Inc.
85 Rangeway Road
North Billerica, MA 01862
(508)670-9009
Category: Intelligent hubs

Telebit Corporation
1315 Chesapeake Terrace
Sunnyvale, CA 94089
(408)734-4333
Category: Dial-up connectivity

Tiara Computer Systems
1091 Shoreline Drive
Mountain View, CA 94065
(415)965-1700
Category: Connectivity hardware

Visisoft
430 Tenth Street
Suite S-008
Atlanta, GA 30318
(404)874-0428
Category: Network-management software

Wellfleet Communications, Inc.
15 Crosby Drive
Bedford, MA 01730
(617)275-2400
Category: Internetworking

Xircom
26025 Mureau Road
Calabasas, CA 91302
(818)878-7600
Category: Laptop connectivity

Software-Communication Products

The following section lists vendors that specialize in software-communication products.

DataStorm Technologies
3212 Lemone Industrial Blvd.
Columbia, MO 65201
(314)443-3282

Digital Communications Associates, Inc. (DCA)
1000 Alderman Dr.
Alpharetta, GA 30202-4199
(800)348-3221

FutureSoft, Inc.
1001 S. Dairy Ashford, #101
Houston, TX 77077
(713)496-9400

Hayes Microcomputer Products, Inc.
P.O. Box 105203
Atlanta, GA 30348
(404)840-9200

Microcom, Inc.
55 Federal Road
Danbury, CT 06810
(203)798-3830

Symantec Corporation
10201 Torre Avenue
Cupertino, CA 95014-4694
(408)253-9600

Triton Technologies
200 Middlesex Turnpike
Iselin, NJ 08830
(908)855-9440

US Robotics
8100 N. McCormick Blvd.
Skokie, IL 60076
(800)342-5877

Mail-Order Products

The following are some sources that provide mail-order support for network components or for specialty tools that are often unavailable through retail outlets. Copies of their catalogs should certainly be on your bookshelf.

Black Box Corporation
P.O. Box 12800
Pittsburgh, PA 15241
(800)552-6816

Jensen Tools, Inc.
7815 S. 46th Street
Phoenix, AZ 85044
(602)968-6241

Topics covered in this chapter:
Glossary

Appendix B

Glossary

A

3270. The standard terminal type of the IBM SNA environment. Although officially an "intelligent" terminal, 3270 terminals are dependent on the host computer for application processing. In part, the intelligence relates to the terminal's capability to perform rudimentary data entry, one screen at a time, without transmitting each keystroke in real time to the host.

ACK character. An ASCII control character (ASCII 6), signaling an Acknowledgment. This character is used in ACK frames under the ARCnet protocol.

alternating current. An electrical current that periodically reverses the direction of current flow. *See also* direct current.

analog. Describes an energy form or mechanical device that is characterized by a continuously varying physical property. Sound is one example of analog energy, as are the electrical signals used to transmit sound information through telephone lines.

AppleTalk. A protocol, defined by Apple, that is associated with Macintosh network communication on a LocalTalk network.

application layer. The seventh layer of the OSI network model. The application layer is responsible for presenting a consistent network interface to applications.

architecture. In computer engineering, the structure of a complete system that includes all hardware and software components required for proper operation.

ASCII character set. Acronym for American Standard Code for Information Interchange character set. The most common system for encoding character data on microcomputers and minicomputers. The standard ASCII character set uses seven bits and can represent 128 characters. Characters 0 through 31 are control characters and are used in various protocols to control data communication, screen display, and other functions. Characters 32 through 127 represent displayable characters. An informal extended ASCII character set uses eight bits to represent 256 characters. Characters 128 through 255 are used to represent additional printable characters for graphics, foreign languages, mathematics, and other functions.

asynchronous transmission. Any serial communication that is not controlled by a master timer. Asynchronous transmissions start with a specific data pattern to indicate the beginning of a message, but they then depend on the transmitting device to send data at the same rate that is expected by the receiving device. Because sender and receiver are likely to drift apart slightly, asynchronous transmissions are limited to short messages, usually one character at a time. Modems to support asynchronous transmissions are inexpensive, but they make inefficient use of the available communication bandwidth.

attenuation. Describes the loss of signal strength that results when a signal is transmitted through a medium. Because of attenuation, all data networks have a maximum operating range. If the signal has not been degraded by other factors, such as noise or distortion, the operating range of a data network can be extended through the use of repeaters, which amplify the weakened signal.

AUI. Abbreviation for Attachment Unit Interface. Found on many Ethernet devices, the AUI is a multi-pin connector used to interface devices to transceivers.

B

backbone. A high-performance network ordinarily used for transmitting data between several more conventional networks. An organization that chooses to connect user workstations with 16Mbit token rings, for example, can internetwork the various token-ring segments through an FDDI backbone.

bandwidth. The range of frequencies that can be transmitted through a medium. All media have a practical upper limit of frequencies that may be transmitted. A typical voice telephone system has a bandwidth of 3000Hz, and it can accommodate frequencies ranging from 300Hz to 3000Hz.

Baseband. A data-transmission technique that operates at the basic frequency of the signal. A telephone is an example of a baseband device; the frequencies of the electrical waves in the telephone circuitry correspond to the frequencies of the original sound waves. Most LANs operate as baseband networks, including Ethernet and token ring.

baud. A measure of the number of signal changes that can be accommodated by a transmission medium. A voice-grade telephone line can support a maximum baud rate of 2400. Baud is frequently misconstrued to represent the bit rate that can be transmitted by a given modem. The proper measure, however, is bits-per-second (bps). For data rates exceeding 2400bps, multiple bits are encoded for each signal change by combining modulation techniques; a 9600bps modem encodes four bits for each signal change by utilizing a combination of amplitude modulation and phase modulation.

bit. The smallest unit of computer data, a bit can have only two states, usually defined as 1 or 0, or as ON or OFF.

BNC connector. A standard connector used with coaxial cable. BNC connectors lock together with a 90-degree bayonet attachment.

bridge. An internetworking device used at the data-link layer. Bridges consist of media interfaces, buffers, address tables, and one or more processors. Bridges receive packets, store them in a buffer, look up the packet's address in the bridge's address table, and either discard the packets or forward them to another LAN segment, depending on whether the source and destination nodes are on the same side of the bridge.

Broadband. A data-transmission technique in which signals are modulated in some way to take advantage of a communication medium that has high bandwidth. *See also* multiplexing.

bus. An electrical circuit configured so that all components on the circuit receive all available signals. The expansion bus in an IBM-compatible microcomputer is one example of a bus that consists of multiple lines for the transmission of electrical power, computer data, and control signals. A control system is usually incorporated into the bus design so that specific components react to specific sets of signals on the bus.

bus network. A network configured as an electrical bus. Ethernet, IEEE 802.3, and ARCnet are common examples of bus networks. Each node on a network segment receives and processes each message on a bus network. A unique address is assigned to each node on the segment, so that data transmissions intended for that node can be identified.

byte. A unit of computer data, consisting of eight bits. A byte is capable of representing 256 possible values.

C

cable. A configuration of wires in a common jacket. Examples are shielded and unshielded twisted-pair, coaxial, and optical fiber.

CCITT. Abbreviation for the Comité Consultatif International de Télégraphie et Téléphonie, which is an organization of the United Nations that is responsible for a variety of international communication recommendations.

CCITT V series. A series of CCITT recommendations regarding modem communications. Common examples are V.22bis, which defines 2400bps modems used with dial-up and leased lines, and V.32, which defines 9600bps modems.

CCITT X series. A series of CCITT recommendations relating to computer networks. X.25 documents a packet-switching network. The X.200 series documents the Open Systems Interconnect (OSI) network-protocol model.

client-server architecture. Originally (and most properly), this term was used to define a network application architecture, in which an application was split into two or more parts that executed on separate processors. The *client* processor is a user workstation that is responsible for accepting user input and displaying data. The *server* processor is a database or other network server that receives a processing request from the client, performs a processing task, and transmits the result to the client. This division of labor between clients and servers is intended to reduce the amount of data that needs to be transmitted through the network. A database server accepts a request for a report from a client, performs all report processing, and returns only the completed report to the client. Recently, the network industry has begun to refer to all workstations as clients, and to all LANs as having a client-server architecture. However, this usage does not imply that applications on the network are necessarily designed with a client-server application architecture.

coaxial cable. A cable design in which a central conductor is surrounded by a concentric shield. The conductor and shield are separated by an insulating layer called a *dielectric*. This shield may be constructed of braided wire or of metal foil, and it serves to isolate the conductor from the influences of external electromagnetic interference.

communication protocol. A formal set of rules that defines the way data is transmitted between devices. Common examples are the Open System Interconnect standards, CSMA/CD, IPX, and RS-232C.

communication server. A station on a LAN that shares communication facilities with other nodes. Communication servers may be used to share modems and to provide access to minicomputer and microcomputer systems.

concentrator. A device that serves as a common housing for a variety of communication devices in a structured wiring system. Concentrators provide power, and they support a bus structure used to interface the installed devices. Concentrators can also serve as focal points for network management. Increasingly, concentrators are being used to house routers, bridges, and special-purpose network servers.

connectionless protocol. A protocol that does not establish a formal connection between communicating nodes. Under this approach, also known as a *datagram approach*, packets are treated independently. It is the responsibility of applications in the nodes to sequence multiple packets. Connectionless protocols involve less overhead than do connection-oriented protocols. They are often suitable for use on LANs that offer highly reliable data transmission.

The NetWare IPX protocol is a common example of a connectionless protocol.

contention. In networks, the process in which stations compete for transmitting time on the network medium. A station is allowed to transmit a packet whenever it is unable to detect existing network traffic. If two stations transmit simultaneously, their transmissions interfere; an error condition then exists, which requires both stations to cease transmitting and to try again after a random interval. Despite theoretical drawbacks, this is a simple and efficient control mechanism, provided the ratio of network bandwidth to traffic remains moderately high. Because an Ethernet has a bandwidth of 10Mbps, and an Ethernet packet cannot exceed 1518 bytes in length, many packets are required to significantly fill the available bandwidth.

control character. In the ASCII character set, the first 32 characters (numbers 0 through 31) are used to control data-communication functions. The XON (Transmit On, ASCII 19, also designated as DC3) and XOFF (Transmit Off, ASCII 17, also designated as DC1) are frequently transmitted to initiate and halt text transmissions. In many terminal sessions, transmission can be paused by pressing Ctrl-Q, which transmits an XOFF character to the transmitting station.

CRC. Abbreviation for Cyclical Redundancy Check, which consists of a calculation that generates a number, based on the data being transmitted. A CRC is calculated by the transmitting station and attached to the data packet. The receiving station extracts the data, recalculates the CRC, and compares the original CRC value to the value that was calculated from the received data. If the CRC values match, a high probability exists that the transmission was accomplished without error.

CSMA/CD. Abbreviation for Carrier Sense Multiple Access/Collision Detection. The network access-control mechanism utilized by Ethernet and IEEE 802.3. This is a contention-based protocol, in which any station on the network can access the network and transmit information after determining that the network is idle (a carrier is sensed). If multiple transmissions occur simultaneously, a collision-detection mechanism goes into effect; the stations generate a jamming pulse to notify the network that a collision has occurred. Stations then wait a random amount of time before attempting again to transmit. Collisions are normal control mechanisms of CSMA/CD networks, and they do not become a problem except under high traffic levels.

D

D connector. A connector that has a D-shaped lip surrounding the pins. A 25-pin D connector is commonly used to implement RS-232C serial connections, although a nine-pin connector can be used in simple situations.

data. In data processing, data describes symbolic information that is to be transmitted, stored, or processed.

data frame. A block of data that is transmitted on a network. The data-frame format is defined by the standards and protocols applicable to the specific network. Frames always carry network control information. Data may be encapsulated in the frame between the control information sections.

data-link layer. Layer 2 of the OSI network mode; it is responsible for packaging and addressing data frames. The data-link layer is the lowest layer that is concerned with data at the frame level.

data network. A communication network that specializes in the transmission of computer data.

datagram. *See* connectionless protocol.

DCE. Abbreviation for Data Communication Equipment. *See* RS-232C.

demodulation. The process of extracting original data from the modulating signal. *See also* Modulation.

demultiplex. The process of extracting a single signal from a multiplexed signal. *See also* Multiplex.

dielectric. The insulating layer that separates conductors in a coaxial cable.

digital. In data processing, the technique of representing data symbolically in numeric format.

direct current. An electrical current that flows in one direction only. *See also* alternating current.

document imaging. The technology of recording a digital image of a physical document, as opposed to recording the text of the document only. Document imaging is performed by capturing a bit-by-bit scan of the document. Because this can result in large amounts of data (a one-inch square at a resolution of 300 dots-per-inch requires 11,250 bytes for storage), data-compression techniques are commonly implemented to reduce storage requirements. Even with effective data compression, however, imaging data can be voluminous, and document-imaging systems can make intensive use of networks.

DTE. Abbreviation for Data Terminal Equipment. *See* RS-232C.

E

ESC character. An ASCII control character (ASCII 27) used in some communication protocols.

Ethernet. A network standard, developed by Xerox in 1976, from which the IEEE 802.3 standard was derived. Ethernet uses a bus architecture and the CSMA/CD protocol to control media access. Ethernet supports a data rate of 10Mbps. Although the term *Ethernet* is often used generically to describe CSMA/CD networks, the Ethernet and IEEE 802.3 standards are distinct and incompatible.

F

FDDI. Abbreviation for Fiber Distributed Data Interface. A standard, developed by ANSI, which specifies a fiber optic network operating at a data rate of 100Mbps. The network design is derived from token-ring technologies, but FDDI can be cabled as a physical ring or as a star.

frame. A sequence of network data identified by a specific beginning and ending sequence. Each physical layer protocol defines how frames are to be formatted for the network.

Prior to transmitting data, the data are encapsulated into a frame by adding beginning and ending frame delimiters.

frequency-division multiplexing. The technique of transmitting multiple signals on the same medium by modulating the individual signals with different frequency carriers. This is the technique used to transmit multiple television signals through a common cable. Each channel signal is modulated onto a specific radio frequency. The tuner in the receiving television can be set to each frequency and can retrieve an individual modulated signal, from which the original program can be recovered.

front-end processor. On mainframe computers, the front-end processor (FEP) serves as a processing interface between the central processing unit and other devices. The most common use for front-end processors is to manage the receipt and transmission of data on the network. FEPs reduce the processing load on the central processor.

full-duplex transmission. Communication in which information can travel both ways simultaneously. Full-duplex transmission can be implemented by providing multiple media paths, or through techniques such as *frequency-division multiplexing*. Also designated as *duplex*.

G

gateway. A device used to interconnect two technologically different networks. For example, gateways are frequently used to connect network workstations with IBM SNA networks or with X.25 packet-switching networks. In an unrelated use of the term, host-based routers on the internet are called gateways.

H

half-duplex transmission/full-duplex transmission. Two-way communication in which data can travel in only a single direction at a given time. Nodes engaged in half-duplex communication must notify each other that they are finished transmitting, so that the corresponding node has an opportunity to transmit.

Hayes-compatible. A vendor-defined standard, defining a command set that controls functions of asynchronous modems. This command set is also known as the *AT command set* because all control sequences begin with the characters "AT". The majority of modern commercial modems support the Hayes AT command set.

hertz. The standard measure of the frequency of a wave form in cycles-per-second. Abbreviated as Hz. Ordinary house current has a frequency of 60Hz.

hub. A module serving as a central connecting point for a star-wired network. Hubs are used in 10BASE-T, token ring, and ARCnet networks. Hubs may be installed in concentrators to interface them with different network topologies.

Hz. *See* hertz.

I

IEEE. Abbreviation for the Institute of Electrical and Electronics Engineers. The IEEE is a professional organization that develops a wide variety of standards, including the 802 group of standards relating to local area networks.

IEEE 802.3. The IEEE standard that defines CSMA/CD networks derived from Ethernet. Although similar, 802.3 networks differ in several respects from Ethernet networks. The 802.3 standard defines standards for broadband and baseband networks utilizing coaxial cable and unshielded twisted-pair cable.

IEEE 802.5. The IEEE standard defining networks derived from IBM's token-ring technology.

impedance. The sum of opposition to the flow of alternating current in a conductor. The impedance of a cable summarizes a variety of factors, including the resistance of the conductors (also frequency, reactance, and capacitance). The impedance of a cable must match the impedance required by the attached electronic devices if the circuit is to function optimally.

input/output controller. *See* front-end controller.

internet. Abbreviation for *internetwork*. A collection of networks, often having different technologies, that are interconnected by using bridges, routers, and gateways. When capitalized, Internet refers to the ARPANET, a network of over 50,000 computers originally established by the U.S. Department of Defense to facilitate the exchange of research information.

ISDN. Abbreviation for Integrated Services Digital Network, an international data-communication network. ISDN seeks to replace conventional telephone systems with a worldwide digital network.

ISO. Abbreviation for the International Organization for Standardization, an international organization that develops standards for communication and information interchange. The ISO is best known in data processing as the developer of the seven-layer OSI network model. *See also* OSI model.

K

kilo-. Except in data processing, a prefix designating "thousand", as in kilometer, which is abbreviated km. In data processing, kilo ordinarily designates the quantity 1024 (2^{10}), which conforms more closely with computer data because powers of two are the most common measurements of computer memory capacity and other quantities. To distinguish the two usages, it is common to use lower-case k to designate 1000 and upper-case K to designate 1024. Thus, 1024 bytes of memory is conventionally designated as 1KB.

L

laser. A device that emits *coherent light*, which is light that is of a single frequency and phase. That is, all of the individual waves in the light beam have the same color and their peaks and valleys are synchronized. The inherent purity of laser light makes it especially well-suited for transmitting digital data. When generated by a laser tube, laser light may be *collimated*, meaning that all waves travel in parallel. Collimated laser light diverges only slightly as it travels, and it can transmit computer data in line-of-sight wireless networks.

laser diode. A semiconductor device that is similar to a light-emitting diode (LED), which emits coherent light in response to an electrical current. Laser diodes are frequently used as signal sources in optical fibers.

layer zero. The informal layer that resides below layer 1, the physical layer of the OSI network model. The OSI physical-layer standards do not define the characteristics of the underlying medium. Layer zero describes the cables, connectors, hubs, and other devices that form the physical basis of the network.

light-emitting diode. A semiconductor device that emits light in response to an electrical current. Abbreviated as LED.

logical topology. Describes the way data travels through a network. In a logical ring, such as token ring, data is transmitted from station to station—each station receives data from the previous station and retransmits the data to the next station in the ring. At any given time, only one station in the ring will be able to interact with the data. In a logical bus, signals are broadcast into the network and they propagate throughout the network so that all stations on the network receive each data transmission more or less simultaneously.

M

mainframe computer. The largest class of computer, designed for the most demanding computing tasks. Mainframe computers are designed to support extremely large applications or to provide large numbers of users with access to a single data repository. Mainframe computers are usually organized into specialized subsystems that handle processing, disk storage, communication, and other functions.

MAU. Abbreviation for Medium Attachment Unit. In Ethernet, the device used to connect a device to the Ethernet coaxial cable. An Ethernet MAU can consist of a separate device that attaches to the transceiver port of a networked device. Alternatively, MAU functionality may be built into the network interface card, as is frequently done with thin Ethernet; in this case, the coaxial cable attaches directly to the network card with a T connector. The MAU is also known as an Ethernet transceiver. In token ring, a multistation access unit, serves as the hub for the token ring star wiring topology.

mega-. Except in data processing, a prefix designating "one million" (10^6). In data processing, mega ordinarily designates the quantity 1,024,576, which corresponds to 2^{20}. The abbreviation used in data processing is ordinarily a capital letter M. For example, MB conventionally represents megabytes.

microcomputer. Traditionally, a computer that incorporates a microprocessor as its central processing unit. As microprocessors have become more powerful, they have been incorporated into the designs of mini- and mainframe computers, so a sharp distinction no longer exists between the categories.

microprocessor. An integrated circuit that incorporates the functionality of a complete central processing unit.

minicomputer. A computer that is intermediate in capacity between a microcomputer and a mainframe. Minicomputers are ordinarily configured to support several users through terminal interfaces. Minicomputers are often configured as front-end processors for mainframe computers.

modem. A contraction of the terms *mod*ulate/*dem*odulate. A device that modulates digital data into analog form, enabling the data to be transmitted through non-digital telephone lines. At the receiving end, the modem demodulates the signal to recover the digital data.

modulate. The practice of varying one or more characteristics of a signal. Techniques include amplitude modulation, frequency modulation, and phase modulation.

modulation. The process of changing the characteristics of a basic signal so that the variations correspond to the information in another signal. The basic signal is called the *carrier.* A modem varies the frequency (or other characteristic) of an audio signal to reflect the ones and zeros of the binary data to be translated.

MSAU. Abbreviation for the token ring Multistation Access Unit, used to distinguish it from the Ethernet Medium Attachment Unit.

multimode optical fiber. Light that is introduced to a multimode optical fiber enters at a variety of angles. At some angles, the light escapes the fiber and is absorbed by the cladding. At other angles, the light is continuously reflected down the length of the fiber. The reflections in step-index fibers are slightly imperfect, and spurious reflections limit the bandwidth that the fiber can support. Multimode fiber has the lowest bandwidth of all optical fiber types.

multitasking. Describes the process in which a computer executes several tasks simultaneously. In some computers, multitasking is accomplished by incorporating more than one central processing unit. In many cases, however, multitasking is a matter of sharing the central processing unit among several tasks, each of which takes a turn. This sharing process takes place rapidly enough so that it is normally invisible to the end user.

N

NAK character. An ASCII control character (ASCII 21) that signals a Negative Acknowledgment. This character is used in NAK frames under the ARCnet protocol.

NetBEUI. The network protocol that is most commonly used with Microsoft LAN Manager. NetBEUI is compatible with the NetBIOS interface standards.

NetBIOS. An application program interface that provides a consistent set of commands for requesting network services.

network interface card. A card installed in a PC or other computer that is used to connect the computer to a local area network.

network layer. Layer 3 of the OSI network model. This layer routes network packets from source to destination. Network routers function at this level.

network operating system. A software product that manages a local area network server, as well as data communications on the LAN. Commonly abbreviated as NOS, the network operating system is responsible for a wide variety of functions, including file services, security, internetwork routing, and network communications. Add-in modules can expand the server's roles, adding services such as database management and asynchronous modem communication.

node. In computer networks, any component on a network that is addressable as a unique entity. Workstations, file servers, and routers are examples of network nodes. Repeaters are not network nodes because they are not associated with network addresses.

noise. Any interferance that degrades the integrity or clarity of a transmitted signal. Noise can be generated by natural or man-made sources. Designers of data networks take elaborate precautions to prevent noise from introducing errors into data.

NOS. Acronym for network operating system. *See* network operating system.

OEM. Acronym for Original Equipment Manufacturer, the manufacturer of a piece of equipment. Occasionally used as a verb, meaning "manufacture."

ohm. The standard unit of resistance to the flow of an electrical current. This unit is frequently used to indicate the impedance of coaxial cable. *See also* impedance.

optical fiber. A data-transmission medium, consisting of a fine plastic or glass fiber core, surrounded by a protective jacket. The glass fiber core is generally constructed of highly refined silicon, and can transmit light signals for considerable distances. The most desirable characteristic of optical fibers is their high bandwidth. Data rates of 100Mbps are commonplace, and signal rates in the gigahertz range are frequently used.

OSI model. The seven-layer network model defined by the International Organization for Standardization (ISO). This model serves as a conceptual model for understanding the relationships of various network standards and protocols. OSI also consists of a set of standards that will eventually result in more standard network products.

P

pad character. A character added to a data packet to meet a certain size requirement. For example, Ethernet data frames must contain a minimum of 64 bytes. If fewer bytes are required, pad characters are added.

parity. A simple data-integrity check that indicates if any bits in a data transmission have been altered. If parity calculations at the transmitting and receiving end produce identical results, the data can be assumed to have arrived unaltered. *See also* parity bit.

parity bit. A bit appended to the data at the time of transmission. This bit represents the result of a calculation that is performed on the data bits. Under even parity, the parity bit is set to one if the number of ones in the data is even; otherwise, the parity bit is set to zero. Under odd parity, the parity bit is one if an odd number of ones are transmitted, and to zero for an even number of ones. Other parity types are *space parity,* in which the parity bit is always set to zero; *mark parity,* in which the parity bit is always set to one; and *no parity,* in which the parity bit is ignored.

phase. Describes the relative timing of the peaks and valleys of two wave forms such as electrical signals. If the peaks and valleys of the signals occur at the same time, the signals are *in phase.* If the peaks and valleys of the signals occur at different times, the signals are *out of phase.*

phase modulation. A modulation technique that varies the phase of the carrier to reflect the data to be transmitted.

phone connector. The familiar, standard, snap-in telephone connector used for connecting a variety of data networks cabled with unshielded twisted-pair wiring.

physical layer. The layer of the OSI model responsible for controlling the transmission of data on the network medium. The physical layer specification describes the control processes, but it does not address the medium itself.

physical topology. Describes the mechanical layout of a data network. Examples of physical topologies are the star, the bus, and the ring. The physical configuration of the wiring does not necessarily reflect the logic that is used to manage the data transmissions on the network; that is the function of the network logical topology.

presentation layer. Layer 6 of the OSI model. Performs any conversions that may be required prior to sending data to the application layer. Translations of data formats may be performed at this layer—translation between the ASCII and EBCDIC encoding schemes, for example. Data encryption and compression may also be presentation-layer functions. The function of this layer is frequently misunderstood as presenting data to the user. In reality, it is a network communication layer. This level is not fully defined yet, or widely used.

R

radio frequency. A band of electromagnetic energy, ranging in frequency between 10 kilohertz and 3000 gigahertz.

RF. Abbreviation for radio frequency. *See also* radio frequency.

ring network. A network topology that functions by passing data from one network node to the next. The most common examples are token ring and FDDI. Although these network standards have a ring logical topology, they are normally cabled with star physical topologies.

RJ-11. A phone connector that has six conductors.

RJ-45. A phone connector that has eight conductors. This is the most popular connector for networks cabled with unshielded twisted pair wiring.

router. An internetworking device used at the network layer, which is the layer that manages information for routing data-packets through the network. Routers are transparent to the data-link layer. This means that, as long as a router has interfaces to more than one LAN type, it can connect dissimilar LANs. Using routers remains the simplest way of connecting token ring and Ethernet. The basic function of a router is to forward packets between networks. Because networks usually have more than one path between them, routers must find the best path along which to send the packets. The best path is determined by routing algorithms.

RS-232C. An industry standard that describes serial-communication connections and protocols. This is the standard that is adhered to by most serial devices such as modems. Originally intended only to interface terminals (data terminal equipment, or DTEs) with modems (data communication equipment, or DCEs), the standard has been stretched by manufacturers for interfacing many other device types, including printers, plotters, and mice.

S

serial communication. Data communication that transmits data one bit at a time. Serial communication can be done with as few as two wires (actually, with one wire and a ground).

session. A logical connection between two nodes on a network. A session enables two devices to behave as though they were directly connected. Session protocols manage transmissions between the nodes, perform message-sequencing, and do error-checking. The process of establishing and managing a session introduces processing overhead into the communication process—this processing overhead can often be dispensed with. Most LAN network operating sessions maintain communication between nodes through processes that execute in the nodes themselves, rather than in the network interface layers.

session layer. Layer 5 of the OSI model. Responsible for maintaining sessions between communicating computers. LAN operating systems frequently do not incorporate protocols at the session layer, they leave this function to the operating system or to the application.

shield. A wire or conductive foil jacket that surrounds the conductors of a shielded cable. The shield protects signals on the conductors from interference and prevents the radiation of signals into the environment.

sine wave. The smooth, pure wave form generated by certain objects vibrating at a single frequency. The equations that describe the curve of this wave form involve the trigonometric sin function.

single-mode optical fiber. In this cable type, the diameter of the glass fiber is reduced so that only one coherent light signal is transmitted. This coherency eliminates the light reflections and bending that occur in multi-mode cables, and dramatically increases bandwidth. Single-mode fiber has high bandwidth of up to 50 GHz/km.

SNA. Abbreviation for System Network Architecture. *See* System Network Architecture.

SOH character. An ASCII control character (ASCII 6), signaling Start of Header. This character is used in PAC frames under the ARCnet protocol.

star network. A network physical topology, in which each computer is networked by an individual cable connected to a central wiring hub. Token ring and ARCnet are examples of networks that have a star physical topology.

start bit. A bit used to signal the beginning of a character in asynchronous communication.

statistical multiplexing. A form of time-division multiplexing that assigns network bandwidth, based on the current needs of each channel, rather than by dividing the bandwidth into fixed time slots. Using this technique, a 100Mbit network can service more than ten 10Mbit Ethernets because it is statistically unlikely that all Ethernet segments will require a full 10Mbits of bandwidth at the same time.

stop bit. A bit that signals the end of a character in asynchronous communications. A character may be followed by 1, 1.5, or 2 stop bits; the sender and receiver must agree on the number of stop bits to be used.

structured wiring system. A network wiring system that organizes cabling around central points that consist of hubs or concentrators. Structured wiring systematizes network cabling and supports the interconnection of networks of various topologies and protocols.

synchronization. The matching of timing between two devices. A wide variety of data-communication processes depend on synchronization between the communicating devices. In some cases, a master clock may send synchronizing signals to the various devices. In others, devices may exchange a series of signals that enable them to agree on a common data rate and timing.

System Network Architecture. IBM's master plan for computer networking. Like OSI, SNA is a layered set of standards, although the layers do not correspond between the two models.

T

T connector. A connector that joins three segments of coaxial cable. The main segment is connected to the crossbar of the T; the branching segment is connected to the base of the T.

TCP/IP. Abbreviation for Transport Control Protocol/Internet Protocol. A suite of protocols originally developed for the Internet. The emphasis of the Internet protocols is the efficient and reliable internetworking of dissimilar computer systems. IP is a datagram-oriented service that is used by higher-level protocols; TCP provides reliable, connection-oriented service.

terminal emulation. The use of a PC or other computer to imitate the functions of a specific type of computer terminal. By executing different terminal-emulation software, a PC can communicate as an IBM 3270 or 3101 terminal; as a DEC VT52, VT102, or VT220; or as other types of terminals. In enterprise networks, terminal emulation is often used with communication servers and gateways to enable workstations to act as terminals on attached mainframes and minicomputers.

thick Ethernet. Ethernet based on a cable having a diameter of approximately .4 inch. The equivalent IEEE 802.3 standard is 10BASE5, which describes a CSMA/CD network, operating in baseband mode, at data rate of 10 megabits-per-second. The 5 designates a maximum segment length of approximately 500 meters. It is also referred to as *standard* Ethernet or *thicknet*. Because of its cost and the difficulty of working with the cable, thick Ethernet cable is used primarily for installations that must span more than 185 meters. *See also* thin Ethernet.

thin Ethernet. Ethernet that is based on coaxial cable with a small diameter. The equivalent IEEE 802.3 standard is 10BASE2, which describes a CSMA/CD network that operates in baseband mode at a data rate of 10 megabits-per-second. The 2 designates the maximum segment length of approximately 200 meters (actually, 185 meters). Also referred to as *thinnet* or *cheapernet*. *See also* thick Ethernet.

time-division multiplexing. The technique of transmitting multiple signals on the same medium by dividing the available time into segments, each of which carries an individual signal. For example, a 100Mbit network can support communication for ten 10Mbit Ethernets by dividing the available time into ten equal slots and transmitting data for each of the Ethernets in turn. The drawback of such a simple time division is that each Ethernet has a claim on a full 10Mbits of bandwidth, even when it is idle. *See also* statistical multiplexing.

time-sharing. The technique of sharing the computing resources of a powerful computer among several users. The computer performs multitasking to service each user in turn. This is the traditional model of interactive computing used in mainframe and minicomputer environments, in which the processing power is concentrated in a central computer.

token passing. A media access control technology, in which a station must have a token before it can transmit data to the network. The *token* is a specific type of packet that is defined by the network protocol in use. Because only one station can have the token at any time, contention cannot exist on a token-passing network. Also, because the token is passed from station to station, according to a predetermined method, each station is guaranteed a regular opportunity to transmit. Token-passing networks are preferred in applications, such as manufacturing-process control, in which it is essential to guarantee all stations access to the network, regardless of the level of network traffic. Token ring, FDDI, and ARCnet use token passing to arbitrate network access.

token ring. A network standard developed by IBM that uses token passing to manage network access. Token rings have a ring logical topology and a star physical topology. Each station is cabled to a central concentrator, designated as n MAU or a MSAU, which consists of relays or electronic switches that connect or disconnect the station from the network ring. Two wire pairs connect each station with the MAU: one to receive data and one to transmit data. Packets are passed from station to station on the ring; each station receives the packet, reamplifies it, and then transmits the packet to the next station. When referring to IBM-specific products, the term is frequently capitalized: Token Ring.

token-bus network. A network that has a bus topology but uses token passing to arbitrate network access. ARCnet is the most common example of a token-bus network.

transceiver. Another name for an Ethernet Medium Attachment Unit (MAU). *See* MAU.

transceiver cable. The cable used to interface Ethernet cables by using the transceiver or AUI connectors.

transport layer. Layer four of the OSI model. Responsible for providing reliable network service. This is the highest level that moves data between network devices.

U

UNIX. A multi-user, multitasking operating system developed by AT&T and now widely used on minicomputers and engineering workstations.

X

X.25. A CCITT-recommended standard that describes packet-switching networks.

XOFF character. An ASCII control character (ASCII 17) that means "transmit off." XOFF is transmitted under the XON/XOFF protocol to indicate that a device is unable to receive data. Also designated as DC1. *See also* XON character.

XON character. An ASCII control character (ASCII 19) that means "transmit on." XON is transmitted under the XON/XOFF protocol to indicate that a device is prepared to receive data. Also designated as DC3. *See also* XOFF character.

XON/XOFF. A protocol used to control asynchronous transmissions. The receiving station transmits an XON control character to indicate that it is prepared to receive data or it transmits an XOFF character to indicate that it cannot accept additional data transmissions.

Index

Symbols

A

B

C

D

E

F

G

H

I

L

M

N

P

R

S

T

U

V

X

Add to Your New Riders Library Today with the Best Books for the Best Software

Yes, please send me the productivity-boosting material I have checked below. Make check payable to New Riders Publishing.

❑ **Check enclosed.**

Charge to my credit card:

❑ **VISA** ❑ **MasterCard**

Card # ______________________

Expiration date: ______________________

Signature: ______________________

Name: ______________________

Company: ______________________

Address: ______________________

City: ______________________

State: ______________ ZIP: ______________

Phone: ______________________

The easiest way to order is to pick up the phone and call 1-800-541-6789 between 9:00 a.m. and 5:00 p.m., EST. Please have your credit card available, and your order can be placed in a snap!

Quantity	Description of Item	Unit Cost	Total Cost
	Inside CorelDRAW!, 2nd Edition	$29.95	
	AutoCAD 3D Design & Presentation*	$29.95	
	Maximizing Windows 3 (Book-and-Disk set)	$39.95	
	Inside AutoCAD, Special Edition (for Releases 10 and 11)*	$34.95	
	Maximizing AutoCAD: Volume I (Book-and-Disk set) Customizing AutoCAD with Macros and Menus	$34.95	
	AutoCAD for Beginners	$19.95	
	Inside Autodesk Animator*	$29.95	
	Maximizing AutoCAD: Volume II (Book-and-Disk set) Inside AutoLISP	$34.95	
	Inside AutoSketch, 2nd Edition*	$24.95	
	AutoCAD Reference Guide, 2nd Edition	$14.95	
	AutoCAD Reference Guide on Disk, 2nd Edition	$14.95	
	Inside CompuServe (Book-and-Disk set)	$29.95	
	Managing and Networking AutoCAD*	$29.95	
	Inside AutoCAD, Release 11, Metric Ed. (Book-and-Disk set)	$34.95	
	Maximizing MS-DOS 5 (Book-and-Disk set)	$34.95	
	Inside Generic CADD*	$29.95	
	Inside Windows	$29.95	
	AutoCAD Bible	$39.95	
	*Companion Disk available for these books	$14.95 ea.	
	Shipping and Handling: See information below.		
	TOTAL		

❑ **3½″ disk**

❑ **5¼″ disk**

Shipping and Handling: $4.00 for the first book and $1.75 for each additional book. Floppy disk: add $1.75 for shipping and handling. If you need to have it NOW, we can ship product to you in 24 to 48 hours for an additional charge, and you will receive your item overnight or in two days. Add $20.00 per book and $8.00 for up to three disks overseas. Prices subject to change. Call for availability and pricing information on latest editions.

New Riders Publishing • 11711 N. College Avenue • P.O. Box 90 • Carmel, Indiana 46032

1-800-541-6789 **1-800-448-3804**

Orders/Customer Service **FAX**

To order: Fill in the reverse side, fold, and mail

NO POSTAGE NECESSARY IF MAILED IN THE UNITED STATES

BUSINESS REPLY MAIL

FIRST CLASS PERMIT NO. 6008 INDIANAPOLIS, IN

POSTAGE WILL BE PAID BY ADDRESSEE

NEW RIDERS PUBLISHING
P.O. Box 90
Carmel, Indiana 46032